BLUE RIBBONS BITTER BREAD

BLUE RIBBONS BITTER BREAD

'An outstanding book about a great woman.'
                    (Jena Woodhouse, *International Herald Tribune*)

'It is a tribute to de Vries's writing that Loch's character seems to flower continuously, making her an increasingly admirable and compelling personality.'
                    (Mary Rose Liverani, *The Weekend Australian*)

SUSANNA DE VRIES is an art historian and lectures at the Continuing Education Department of the University of Queensland. She was born in London and attended the Sorbonne in Paris and the University of Madrid. She came to Australia in 1975, has been the recipient of a Churchill Fellowship and has written extensively on art history, both here and abroad. She was made a member of the Order of Australia in 1996 'for services to Australian and European art'.

In addition to writing *Blue Ribbons Bitter Bread*, which has won several awards, Susanna is the author of the following books: *Historic Brisbane and its Early Artists; Historic Sydney—the Founding of Australia; Pioneer Women, Pioneer Land; The Impressionists Revealed; Conrad Martens on the 'Beagle' and in Australia; Ethel Carrick Fox—Travels and Triumphs of a Post-Impressionist; Strength of Spirit—Pioneering Women of Achievement from First Fleet to Federation* and *Strength of Purpose—Australian Women of Achievement;* part-author of *Parenting Girls* with Dr Janet Irwin. For HarperCollins she has written a four-volume paperback series on *Great Australia Women*. Volumes One and Two have now been reissued as a double volume titled *Great Australian Women, 36 Women who Changed Australia,* and Volume Three *Heroic Australian Women in War* [HarperCollins, 2004]. Volume Four is titled *Great Women of the Outback* [HarperCollins 2005]. Together with her husband, *Jake de Vries* she has written the illustrated book *Historic Brisbane—Convict Settlement to River City* [published by Pandanus Press and distributed by Tower Books] and *To Hell and Back, the banned account of Gallipoli.*

BLUE RIBBONS BITTER BREAD

THE LIFE OF
JOICE NANKIVELL LOCH

Susanna de Vries

PIRGOS PRESS

© Susanna de Vries, 2000

This book is copyright. Apart from any fair dealing for the purposes of study, research, criticism, review, or as otherwise permitted under the Copyright Act, no part may be reproduced by any process without written permission. Inquiries should be made to the publisher.

First published in 2000. Reprinted in 2001
Revised and reprinted in 2004
Updated and reprinted in 2007
Fifth edition updated and reprinted in 2009
Sixth edition as a print on demand book, republished 2012 (without index).
Seventh updated edition including 'Smyrna 1922' author prologue, published 2016

This edition published by Pirgos Press
Brisbane — Australia
Phone 07 3378 0150
Fax   07 3378 2744

Distributed by Dennis Jones & Associates Pty Ltd
1/10 Melrich Rd Bayswater Victoria 3153
Phone 61 3 9762 9100
Fax   61 3 9762 9200
E: dennis@dennisjones.com.au

National Library of Australia
Cataloguing in Publication entry:
De Vries, Susanna.
BLUE RIBBONS BITTER BREAD
JOICE LOCH — Australia's most heroic woman.

Bibliography.

ISBN: 9781925281781 (pbk)
ISBN: 9781925281798 (ebook)

1. Loch, Joice NanKivell.. 1887-1982. 2. Women journalists Australia - Biography.
3. Women authors - Australia - Biography. 4. World War, 1939-1945 - Jews - Rescue.
5. Women philanthropists - Australia - Biography. 6. Political refugees - Greece.
7. Political refugees Poland. 8. Political refugees - Soviet Union. 9. Greece Foreign relations - Turkey. I. Title.

361.74092

CONTENTS

	Author's Preface	i
	Dedication and Preface	6
	Introduction	7
1	Child of the Cyclone	9
2	Parrot Pie and Pigweed Salad	23
3	Rural Poverty at Boolara	30
4	The Wild Colonial Girl	39
5	'The Cobweb Ladder'	51
6	A Hero of Gallipoli	60
7	Ireland	75
8	Ireland's Bitter War of Independence	84
9	'Ireland in Travail'-The Final Chapters	93
10	Off on a Mission	111
11	A Palace in Warsaw	119
12	Wolves in the Blizzard	129
13	'The Fourteen Thumbs of St Peter'	137
14	Ribbons of Blue that Bind Forever	149
15	Greece-The Dream and the Reality	159
16	'The Art of Being Kind'	170
17	In the Shadow of the Holy Mountain	180
18	Wild Herbs and Bitter Bread	188
19	The Tower by the Sea	198
20	Rug Weaving Saves a Village	209
21	Earthquake	217
22	The Rape of Poland	232
23	A Medal from King Carol	245
24	Escape from the Iron Guard	257
25	Operation Pied Piper	275
26	The Camp of a Thousand Orphans	290
27	Return to Greece: Civil War	303
28	'Kyria Loch'-The Lady in the Tower	314
29	The End of the Road	327
	The Eleven Medals of Joice Loch	339
	Epilogue	340
	Bibliography	343
	Endnotes	346

AUTHOR'S PREFACE
TO 'SMYRNA 1922' EDITION

Joice Nankivell Loch was awarded medals by Greece, Poland, Romania, Serbia and Britain and is regarded as one of the great humanitarians of the twentieth century. Since the publication of *Blue Ribbons Bitter Bread* in 2000, she has been recognised as Australia's most decorated woman.

In the early 1920s Joice and her husband Sydney Loch cared for starving children in Poland and Russia. In World War Two in a daring rescue they saved some 2,000 Poles and Jews from Nazi death camps. However Joice's work assisting Greek refugees in the aftermath of the Greco-Turkish war of 1919–1922 began her passionate love of Greece, the country she eventually made her home.

Joice first heard in 1922 about what was happening to Greeks residing in Turkey, while working as a volunteer in the medical centre of a Quaker-run refugee camp in Poland. As a result of the Greco-Turkish war, penniless refugees were pouring into Greece, a country virtually bankrupt after four years of fighting. The Quakers had funding for a large camp at Thessaloniki and desperately need volunteers with medical or nursing experience. Joice was so moved by hearing about the thousands of Greeks fleeing from Turkish violence that she volunteered to work at the new refugee camp in northern Greece.

Some of the refugees Joice cared for at Thessaloniki had been rescued from Smyrna, a prosperous tobacco exporting port on the Aegean coast of Turkey. Smyrna had been a cosmopolitan city, home to Greeks, Turks, Armenians and Jews with fine hotels, cafés, excellent shops, several yacht clubs and an opera house. However, after the victorious Turkish army arrived there in 1922 and the defeated Greek army departed for Athens magnificent Smyrna was burned to the ground. Today the rebuilt port is known by its Turkish name, Izmir.

Back in 1922 my father was a British naval lieutenant on the British battleship HMS *King George V* during the fire that destroyed Smyrna and took part in the daring whaleboat rescue of 2,000 Greek refugees from the burning city.

When a family friend of the NanKivells asked me to write the biography of Joice Loch as the saviour of a Greek refugee village, the fact that my father had rescued hundreds of Greek refugees and I was familiar with his photos of refugees in the burning city then called Smyrna made

i

me want to pursue the story. I became determined to go to Greece in search of this amazing story. Joice Loch had died in 1982 in her tower home in Ouranoupolis but when I went there with my late husband in 1999 I was able to interview Martha Handschin, Joice's assistant and Fani Mitroupolou before they died and learn the hidden story of Joice Loch and the refugee village she saved from starvation.

THE TREATY OF SÈVRES & ITS CONSEQUENCES

The seeds of Smyrna's destruction by fire were sown in the aftermath of the First World War. The Treaty of Sèvres was intended to exact war reparations from the defeated Ottoman Empire. The treaty was signed in 1920 by Britain, France, Italy and endorsed by Turkey's ruler, the Ottoman Sultan Mehmed VI. The Turks never forgave Sultan Mehmed for the humiliation this treaty inflicted on them, opening the way for Mustafa Kemal (later known as Ataturk), the victor at Gallipoli and a national hero, to become their leader.

Ottoman Turks had once ruled over a mighty empire stretching from Venice in the west to Syria and Palestine in the east. Under the Treaty of Sèvres Turkey was to surrender huge swathes of territory including Palestine (given to Britain under a mandate), Armenia, and several Aegean islands, including Rhodes. As an ally of Britain and France during the First World War, Greece was given a mandate over the wealthy and strategically important port of Smyrna. However, as the ownership of Smyrna was disputed, it was agreed that a plebiscite should be held in five years' time under the auspices of the League of Nations to decide if Smyrna belonged to Turkey or to Greece.

Some years earlier, Britain's Prime Minister Lloyd George had encouraged Greek President Venizelos in his *Megali Idea* (Grand Concept) of recapturing Constantinople and re-establishing a Greek empire on Turkish soil. President Venizelos wanted to protect the many thousands of Greeks in the Ottoman Empire who were being harassed and murdered by Turks, as were many Armenians. Muslim Turks regarded Christian Greeks and Armenians as infidels, and referred to Smyrna disparagingly as 'infidel Izmir'.

Venizelos's *Megali Idea* took hold among aggressive Greek generals, confident that Britain would support them against the Turks. In May 1919 a large Greek army invaded Smyrna and placed the city under Greek control, albeit with a Turkish governor. The invading army was led by Prince Andrew of Greece (father of Prince Philip, the Duke of Edinburgh) who would later write a book describing the Greco-Turkish war as a disaster. Prince Andrew claimed Greece should never have pursued the Turks into Anatolia but his advice had been ignored by belligerent Greek generals.

On their arrival in Smyrna in 1919 the Greek Army was given a rousing welcome by the Greek community, and as fellow Christians some, but not all, Armenians joined in.[1] The Patriarch of the Greek Orthodox church blessed the incoming army in a public ceremony. Greek troops took up residence in the former Turkish barracks. To the Turks the Patriarch's blessing of Turkey's enemies represented an act of treachery, and in the resulting war Greek residents of Smyrna were regarded as traitors.

However the Greeks, had not reckoned with the growing importance of oil in international politics. Turkey still had oil—and plenty of it—in Turkish Mesopotamia (although they had lost oil-rich Mosul to the Kurds). Mesopotamia was alleged to have the same geological characteristics as Texas. The newly formed Soviet Union stepped forward and offered Turkey gold and guns to fight against the Greeks in return for concessions for Russian companies to prospect for oil in the area of Mesopotamia still controlled by the new Turkish leader, Mustafa Kemal and the Turkish nationalist government.

The governments of Britain, France, Italy and America also needed oil to power their warships, tanks and motor vehicles. Consequently the British Government had to be on better terms with Mustafa Kemal, if they wanted valuable oil concessions. With this in mind Britain refused to assist the Greek army to invade Anatolia and capture Kemal's stronghold of Ankara.

By 1922, after almost four years of desert warfare, Prince Andrew's army was exhausted and short of food. Thousands of young men on both sides had died, but Kemal's troops were in far better condition, thanks to the supplies from the Soviet Union. The Greek army fought bravely but was finally defeated at the Battle of Dunlupinar in the summer of 1922. Shabby and hungry, the Greek soldiers fled across the plains of Anatolia to Greek-controlled Smyrna, with the Turkish army in hot pursuit.

The League of Nations and others feared trouble at Smyrna as the armies of two bitter enemies converged on the magnificent harbour city. Eleven British warships, headed by Admiral Osmond de Brock aboard

---

[1] Prince Andrew would face a court martial for the defeat of the Greek Army and flee to Paris with his wife and children. In 1930 Joice Loch's publisher, John Murray published Prince Andrew's account of the war, *Towards Disaster, the Greek Army in Asia Minor* but the Prince was a broken man. He left his family in Paris and fled to Monte Carlo and became a playboy haunting the gambling tables.

the flagship HMS *Iron Duke* and the battleship HMS *King George V*, were sent to Smyrna with orders to protect British passport holders and the British Consulate. According to my father, the British fleet was anchored in front of the British Consulate behind which was the Greek quarter.[2] HMS *King George V* was one of the largest battleships in the British Navy with a crew of 850 men and a detachment of armed marines on board.

HMS *King George V* with her gun turrets fixed on the British Consulate was anchored off Smyrna as an official observer when the defeated Greek army returned there on 7 September 1922. They were pursued by the victorious Turkish army intent on repossessing the port they considered as part of Turkey, © Pirgos Press

The British warships were joined by two American destroyers and a hospital ship under the command of Admiral Mark Bristol, the U.S. Commissioner in Constantinople. The bluff Admiral and his social-climbing wife were cultivating the friendship of Mustafa Kemal in order to obtain an oil concession for their friends the Rockefellers, owners of the Standard Oil Company. The American Admiral distrusted Britain's aristocratic Admiral of the Fleet Osmund de Brock, and de Brock reciprocated the feeling.

---

[2] My father, Lieutenant James Guthrie Adamson was 21, had a degree in engineering from King's College Cambridge and had served at the Battle of Jutland. Like all her crew he was proud of the *King George V's* war record and he would receive a commendation for saving hundreds of Greek refugees at Smyrna.

Also anchored off Smyrna, to the north of the city's Greek Quarter facing the Armenian Quarter, were a further six warships: five French and one Italian.[3] Like the Russians and the British, the French and Italians did not want to offend the now powerful Mustafa Kemal, now a leading political figure as well as a successful military commander in the war with Greece.

OLD SCORES SETTLED IN SMYRNA (THE FUTURE IZMIR)

After the Battle of Dunlupinar, defeated Greek soldiers shared crowded cattle wagons with peasant families also fleeing Turkish vengeance in Anatolia. Feelings were running high: not only had Turkish families lost sons in the conflict, but during the campaign Greek soldiers had set fire to Anatolian villages in a scorched earth policy as they retreated to Smyrna.

The victorious Turkish army also arrived in harbour city of Smyrna and took up residence in the barracks in the Turkish Quarter. They were followed by a troop of wild Balkan brigands known as *chettes*. Mounted on horses and mules and equipped with ancient hunting rifles (or more modern weapons stolen from the dead on the battlefield), the *chettes* were Muslim fanatics who hated Christians as they had lost their farms to the Greeks in the Balkan wars as well as the city of Salonika (later renamed Thessaloniki) and were thirsting for revenge.

Wounded Greek soldiers from Prince Andrew's army return to Smyrna in goods wagons; others were so terrified of Turkish vengeance they were prepared to travel on the roofs of rail carriages in order to return to mainland Greece in Greek warships sent from Athens. © Pirgos Press

---

[3] The placement of British ships in front of the Greek quarter explains why the British saved Greeks from the Quayside, as the Armenian Quarter was further to the north of where the British were anchored. Today Izmir is known as a port for people smugglers as it is only 65 nautical miles from the Greek island of Lesbos. To date over 1,000 Syrian and Afghan refugees have been killed at sea in overcrowded boats owned by people smugglers.

On Friday 8 September Captain Thesiger of the *King George V* sent a detachment of marines ashore to guard the British Consulate and British-owned enterprises like the British Telegraph Company and the British Gas Company, which provided lighting for the entire city.

My father went ashore and walked through the Armenian Quarter to Cassaba Station. There he photographed soldiers from the defeated Greek army balancing precariously on the wooden roofs of cattle wagons where wounded soldiers lay on straw mattresses. The Greek cavalry arrived in Smyrna with wounded men slung across the saddles of their horses.

Emaciated horses bring back to Smyrna exhausted defeated Greek soldiers seeking to escape to Greece, © Pirgos Press.

The Greek refugees that my father photographed camping in the streets around the harbour hoped to find a Greek warship that would take them to Athens. Their meagre belongings were stuffed into pillowcases or rolled inside rugs. Some refugees were from central Turkey and had worked as rug weavers. Photos show they brought with them rugs that were samples of their work; Turkey being famous for hand-woven rugs. (This discovery made in 1925 inspired Joice Loch to found a refugee women's carpet weaving co-operative to bring money to 'her' refugee village).

The roads to the harbour were now jammed with bullock carts loaded with refugees and families trudging through the summer heat, all intent on finding a ship that would take them away from the persecution endured during the bitter war between Greece and Turkey. Most refugees were widows and children or grandparents; young men of fighting age had been killed or taken prisoner by the Turks.

These Greek refugees had lived in Turkey for generations; many had worked their small farms since the days of the Greek-speaking Byzantine empire, conquered by Ottoman Turks in the fifteenth century. Although they were Christians, the women dressed in the Turkish style with scarves round their heads and some of them could not even speak Greek. At the Quayside they were dismayed to find there was no room for them on the Greek warships, which were already overflowing with soldiers and Greek members of the Smyrna police force. Fearing violence from Turkish soldiers, wealthy Greek merchants loaded up their vessels ready to depart. Others decided to remain in Smyrna, believing the presence of British warships anchored nearby would protect them.

Greek refugees from Turkey camp in the streets of Smyrna and along the Quayside, © Pirgos Press

The wide two-mile long boulevard called The Quayside that was a feature of Smyrna still exists in present-day Izmir. It borders the harbour and much of it has a high sea wall separating the quay from the water. In 1922 many refugees who could not afford to pay for accommodation camped here. Thousands more joined them, hoping to find a ship to take them to Greece, the homeland they had never seen. Refugees from the interior of Greece ejected from their homes by Turkish soldiers arrived with very little food and water, unaware that they would be spending up to two harrowing weeks on the Quayside. Lack of water would be responsible for the deaths of many of them, particularly children and the elderly.[4]

---

[4] For a fuller description of the massacre and the fire at Smyrna from eye witnesses see Giles Milton, *Paradise Lost, Smyrna 1922, The Destruction of Islam's City of Tolerance*, Sceptre, London,

Henry Morgenthau, America's former ambassador to Constantinople, who had a great love for Greece warned the American government in Washington of the dangers to Greek refugees arriving in a city filled with Turkish soldiers seeking revenge for Turkish villages burned by the retreating Greek army. He predicted Mustafa Kemal's victory could end in a massacre of Greek and Armenian residents of Smyrna and Greek refugees from the interior.[5]

On Saturday 9 September 1922, my father and other young officers put on their freshly laundered white dress uniforms and went ashore with Captain Thesiger, who feared that the sight of the triumphant Turkish cavalry riding through the city might cause trouble from Greeks or Armenian residents. The British naval officers waited on the Quayside as the Turkish cavalry rode towards them on magnificent black horses with the blades of their naked sabres glinting in the sun.

Keen to keep the peace, Captain Thesiger walked onto the wide boulevard and raised one hand. My father feared his commanding officer might be trampled underfoot and was relieved when the leading horseman checked his horse and the column halted.

In schoolboy French Captain Thesiger politely requested the Turkish major leading the column to ask his troops to sheathe their sabres. The Greek and Armenian populations were fearful of what might happen and it was vital the city remained calm. The major took Captain Thesiger to be the admiral of the fleet in his white tropical uniform and medals, and agreed they would enter the city with their sabres sheathed.

Satisfied, Captain Thesiger and his lieutenants including my father returned to the *King George V* and awaited developments. That night there were scuffles in the streets between Greek and Turkish soldiers. Without a police force to keep order, warehouses facing the Quayside were broken into and looted by *chettes* and young civilians. The following day the new Turkish governor, General Noureddin, placed the city under martial law.

Kemal Ataturk, future President of Turkey, arrived by car but kept a low profile intent on courting his future bride. He was worried by what might happen but left the administration of Smyrna to the new governor. General Noureddin was a battle-hardened soldier and a fierce enemy of Patriarch Chrysostomos, whom he regarded as a traitor for blessing the Greek army that had killed so many of his soldiers. Noureddin had the Patriarch arrested, but rather than hanging him as a traitor, the new

---

2009, pages 226-228 and Lou Ureneck, *Smyrna September 1922, The American Mission to Rescue Victims of the 20th Century's First Genocide.* HarperCollins, New York, 2015 which details the despicable behaviour of Admiral Mark Bristol.

[5] Henry Morgenthau, *Ambassador Morgenthau's Story, A Personal Account of the Armenian Genocide.* New York, Cosimo, 2008 and *I was sent to Athens*, Doubleday, New York, 1929.

governor handed him to a mob of Balkan *chettes* and Turkish soldiers and civilians who hated the Patriarch as much as he did. The result of this action was that the leader of the Greek Orthodox Church had his eyes gouged out and was stabbed to death.

On 10 September 1922 a worried Mustafa Kemal sent a telegram to the League of Nations in Geneva warning them that the Turkish population was so worked up 'that the Ankara Government refuses to be held responsible for any massacres'.[6]

Balkan *chettes* ('irregulars') with ancient rifles arrest Greek soldiers wearing army caps. Greek soldiers who did not find a place on Greek warships taking them to Athens were shot as prisoners of war or used as slave labour. © Pirgos Press

On 13 September, the fourth day after the Turkish army arrived fire broke out in the Armenian quarter and soon spread to the adjacent Greek quarter. Reliable witnesses such as doctors, lawyers and Miss Minnie Mills, head of an American mission whose eye-witness account of the blazing city was printed in the *New York Times*, saw Turkish soldiers using rags soaked with petrol or poured from cans to accelerate the fire.[7]

---

[6] Telegram to the League of Nations reported by Edwin L. James in a *New York Times* article dated 11 September, 1922 titled *Kemal won't insure against massacres*. By the time the paper reached Smyrna it was too late as one of the great crimes of the twentieth century had already occurred.

[7] In 1924, two years after fire, in a London court the American Tobacco Company tried to collect on the losses of its warehouse in an insurance claim brought against the Guardian Assurance Company. Called as witnesses were two sergeants from the Smyrna fire brigade.

Firemen from the Smyrna fire service would later testify under oath in an insurance claim heard in a London court they had witnessed Turkish soldiers lighting fires using rags soaked in petrol and that the soldiers when questioned had replied they were 'doing this under orders'.[8]

US Admiral Mark Bristol in Constantinople was cabled by his Naval Intelligence Officer in Smyrna, Lieutenant A.S. Merrell, telling him in no uncertain terms that 'the Turks had burned Smyrna; as part of a plan to get the Allies to evacuate all Christians from the city'. As part of his plan to keep on good terms with Mustafa Kemal (future President of Turkey) and gain oil concessions for Americans, Admiral Bristol deliberately ignored this cable. He claimed that the Greeks and Armenians had set fire to their own quarters, a claim repeated by successive Turkish governments. It has been alleged the fires were lit to cover up an orgy of looting, rape and murder in the Armenian and Greek Quarters—the bodies of the victims would be consumed by the flames, along with Greek and Armenian churches where many had sought sanctuary.

The exact death toll of Smyrna's Greek and Armenian residents during the fire is hard to assess accurately but it is generally agreed numbered hundreds of thousands. No death certificates were issued, since the police and magistrates had departed, and Turkish soldiers soon joined the *chettes* in the looting and killing that took place.

The fires joined into one vast blaze two miles long which spread to the warehouses, offices and consulates that lined the Quayside. From the deck of his ship my father took a series of photographs with his Leica camera documenting the progress of the fire.

Conditions for the refugees on the Quayside were horrific. The stench of burning flesh filled the air, there was no sanitation, and frightened refugees and those whose homes had been destroyed huddled together. The Turks saw the refugees on the Quay as prisoners of war who were forbidden to leave the city on the orders of Governor Nourreddin. He ordered Turkish soldiers to place machine guns at every exit from the Quayside. The walls of the buildings and even the paving stones heated up and there was only polluted water to drink. Numbers of refugees became feverish and many of the elderly and children died.

They testified under oath they saw Turkish soldiers and civilians using rags soaked in petrol to ignite fires who claimed they were merely 'acting under orders'

[8] This court case is cited by Professor Marjorie Housepian Dobkin, *Smyrna 1922, the Destruction of a City*, Faber and Faber, London 1972. Her account is principally concerned with deaths in the Armenian Quarter but fails to mention the burning of Turkish villages by Armenian and Greek troops was a factor in Turkish revenge.

Smyrna burning.
The fire lit by Turkish soldiers spread from the Armenian Quarter into the Greek Quarter, totally destroying them and reaching the seafront The fire began when the wind changed and did not burn the Turkish Quarter on far right of photo, which was undamaged, © Pirgos Press.

Men swam out to the British ships, begging to be taken aboard, but the crews had to ignore them; they knew that if they took out row boats to help the refugees they would face a court martial for disobeying orders.

My father and other officers watched through binoculars and saw Turkish soldiers robbing elderly refugees, arresting young men, and dragging young girls into alleyways, presumably to rape them. The water around the ships was dense with the swollen corpses of Greeks and Armenians who had been murdered, their bodies thrown into the water. Urchins swam around the corpses cutting off their fingers to get the rings and removing necklaces from female corpses.

On two occasions my father and other young officers, horrified by what they were seeing, requested permission from Captain Thesiger to take the heavy whaleboats and row ashore to rescue refugees. Each time they were told the Admiralty in Whitehall refused permission for this. Captain Thesiger and Admiral Osmond de Brock on HMS *Iron Duke* had been telegraphing details of the terrible events taking place on the Quayside to Whitehall. But the British Admiralty refused to allow a rescue for political reasons. British ships must be seen to be neutral and could not intervene.

Lieutenant James Guthrie Adamson aged 21 from the HMS *King George V* watched Greek soldiers killed by the Turks and asked to be allowed to take a rescue party ashore to rescue Greek refugees but was forbidden to do so. Later my father was allowed to command a rescue party, © Pirgos Press

To drown out the screams and prayers of the refugees coming across the water and into the wardroom of HMS *Iron Duke* at dinner, Admiral Osmond de Brock told the orchestra to play louder.

For commercial reasons Admiral Mark Butler chose to blame the Greeks for starting the fire, and initially refused to let any American ships rescue refugees. The American Admiral gave false reports to journalists who interviewed him, playing down the numbers who had died at Smyrna. (His warped version of events has been repeated down the years by enemies of Greece).

Aboard HMS *Iron Duke* and HMS *King George V* plans were made to mount rescue operations for British passport holders only, with a motor launch towing whaleboats to bring in *bona fide* British subjects including the consul Sir Harry Lamb and his staff at the British Consulate. This rescue was carried out by the crew and the British Consul and his staff accommodated on the *Iron Duke*. Meanwhile the crew and officers of both warships were becoming more and more concerned at the desperate plight of the women and children on the Quayside, and increasingly angry that they were not allowed to help them, as Captain Thesiger was made aware and also wanted to intervene.

After several telegraphed requests from Captain Thesiger to Whitehall, finally at 2.40 a.m. on Friday 15 September senior officials at Whitehall relented and telegraphed permission for rescue parties to collect as many refugees as the warships would hold. Another cable added that the refugees were to be fed and given all necessary medical assistance.[9]

'BOATS AWAY!'

My father and his fellow officers were prepared for action and had changed out of their white mess kits into dark blue shirts and trousers. On hearing the command 'Boats away!' over the loud speaker system, rescue boats were winched down into the water. My father was placed in command of a whaleboat crewed by burly sailors and an armed escort of marines, as it was feared Turkish soldiers would open fire on the rescuers. He felt relief that at long last they were doing something to help.

Captain Thesiger headed the rescue commanding the *King George V*'s motor launch, which towed a line of men sitting in small row boats. The larger heavy whaleboats from the *Iron Duke* and *King George V* were rowed towards the high sea wall on which refugees were standing. Several women had committed suicide by jumping from the wall into the sea, and children had fallen over the edge and drowned. As a result the water was full of floating corpses.

When the crew of my father's whaleboat went ashore, they were confronted by frantic refugees pushing and shoving to secure places on the rescue boats. *Chettes* armed with clubs stood menacingly at the rear of the Quayside. My father feared that the refugees might stampede into his boat, capsizing it, as happened to another whaleboat. He ordered the armed marines to cut out a manageable group of women and children, link arms and form a cordon around those selected to provide safe access to the whaleboat. The rest of the marines were to train their pistols on the crowd, many of whom were crazed with fear and thirst, desperate to reach the boats and escape the advancing flames.

The night air was dense with smoke and flaming cinders. The stench of burning flesh was something my father would never forget. Many of these unfortunate refugees had not eaten for days and were desperately

---

[9] Records of telegraphed messages from HMS *King George V* and HMS *Iron Duke* are in British Naval Records, The British National Archives, Kew, London.

thirsty. Turkish soldiers or *chettes* had robbed most of them of any valuables they still possessed.

The once beautiful city of Smyrna reduced to rubble and ashes and only the framework of some buildings remains.

Space on the *King George V* was now at a premium, but so harrowing had been the refugees' experiences that the final boatload made no complaint when the decks were full and they had to be accommodated in the heat of the engine and boiler rooms. So grateful were the women to arrive on board a British ship that some of them knelt and kissed the deck while others kissed the hands of crew members in gratitude. Feeding vast numbers was a problem for the *King George V*'s cooks, as was finding enough plates and bowls for 2,000 people. Officers and crew lent a hand to bring meals to the refugees and erected a canvas awning on the upper deck to shield the refugees from the summer sun.

The ship's sick bay soon filled with patients. Some were in need of treatment for third-degree burns as their bundles had been set on fire by flying sparks, but they had stubbornly clung to their few remaining possessions. Some had been clubbed by the *chettes* and had broken bones, or had deep cuts from being slashed by Turkish sabres. Others had drunk polluted water, and several would die of typhoid fever.[10]

---

[10] *Blue Ribbons,* page 162 details Joice Loch seeing piles of corpses beside the road as she drove out to the Quaker camp at Thessaloniki. She was told by her driver they were Greek refugees who had died of typhoid contracted at Smyrna.

Equally pitiable were the young Greek girls who had been gang raped or had metal objects inserted into their vaginas and could scarcely walk. Some of these girls died on board from severe internal injuries. Others would give birth as a result when they arrived at the camp at Thessaloniki where Joice Loch worked. With the aid of an interpreter, the ship's medical officer heard horrific stories of what these girls had endured.

The Greek refugees were fed and housed on the *King George V* for two days before being transferred to mercantile vessels owned by the Levantine Mercantile Company, which came from the port of Mitilene on the Greek island of Lesbos, some 65 nautical miles away. These chartered ships took the refugees to Thessaloniki and a Quaker-run refugee camp. Eventually 110,000 refugees were housed in the spacious grounds of the American Farm School in large army tents and in a disused barracks. Refugees virtually doubled the population of the now Greek city of Thesssaloniki which under Balkan rule had been known as Salonika.

The transport of these 4,000 Greek refugees from Smyrna to Thessaloniki was arranged through the British Consul, Sir Harry Lamb, and the charter fee of their ships was paid by the British Government which, had it acted earlier, could have saved many more lives at Smyrna.[11]

For the rest of 1922 and 1923 Greek refugees continued to leave Turkey from every available port, so dangerous had Turkey become for them and their families.[12]

THE AFTERMATH OF THE BURNING OF SMYRNA

Negotiations for the League of Nations Exchange of Populations programme were not completed until July 1923: the governments of. Greece and Turkey agreed to an exchange of populations whereby all

---

[11] A much larger rescue operation was later mounted by Asa Jennings, a Baptist minister from upstate New York working in Smyrna and Lt Commander Halsey Powell, who defied the orders of Admiral Mark Butler who had refused to let American naval vessels provide help to Greek refugees. However Asa Jennings and Halsey organized the escape of many thousands of Smyrna victims (related by Leo Ureneck in *Smyrna September 1922, The American mission to rescue victims of the 20th century's first genocide*') Most Greeks refer to events that took place at Smyrna in September 1922 as 'The Great Catastrophe.'

[12] Statistics from Matthew J. Gibney, *Immigration and Asylum from 1900 to the Present*, Randall Hansen, Volume 3, 2005. It has been estimated that 'a total of 1.2 million Orthodox Christian Greeks fled to Greece from Turkey *before* the signing of the Exchange of Populations ratified this arrangement.' Other sources claim 1,500,000 Greeks fled to Greece but in the general chaos few headcounts were made. After the Exchange of Populations programme began in July 1923 a further 189,916 Orthodox Christian Greeks were given assistance to come to Greece.

Christians had to leave Turkey and all Moslems had to leave Greece. Under a second treaty known as the Treaty of Lausanne, which revoked the Treaty of Sevres, Turkey's boundaries were redefined. Greeks leaving Turkey were protected by police but had to list all goods they were taking with them, as well as those they were made to leave behind, and give the list to the Turkish police.

Smyrna would eventually be rebuilt and renamed Izmir. It is now a stylish Turkish city of four million people, its wide Quayside elegant with café tables and striped umbrellas where once refugees huddled in fear of their lives against the backdrop of the burning city.

On my last visit to Izmir in 2006 en route to the Roman ruins of Ephesus, I saw no memorial to the many thousands of Greek refugees who died on the Quayside and in the Greek and Armenian Quarters of Smyrna.

During the Syrian war which began in 2012 Izmir became the main point of departure for people smugglers who took hundreds of thousands of Syrian and Afghan refugees across the sea to the nearest Greek islands on their journey to the Greek mainland and northern Europe. Current EU measures to outlaw people smugglers by offering money to the Turkish government have resulted in a substantial decrease in the numbers of flimsy boats overcrowded with fee-paying refugees leaving Izmir for the islands of Lesbos and Chios where many refugees who drowned when their boats sank are buried. Today prices charged by those who chose to remain in the illegal people smuggling business have increased but those who continue this nefarious trade claim they need to pay large bribes to police and customs officials in order to continue in business.

My father died two decades ago but never forgot his experiences at Smyrna. Relating the events of the night of the rescue in his old age, he was still visibly moved by his memories of the burning of Smyrna. His photos and his account of events related to me have made this Smyrna edition possible. This prologue links my father's rescue of Greek refugees at Smyrna with the subsequent work of Joice Loch in saving refugees from Smyrna and other parts of Greece and providing them with medicines and nursing care at Thessaloniki and in the refugee village of Ouranoupolis. My father's story and the cables from the Admiralty to several Admirals at Smyrna telling them to proceed with the (belated) rescue operation and ordering vessels to be chartered to take the refugees to Thessaloniki, stored in the British National Archives at Kew, refute allegations that the British did nothing to help the Greeks.

****

Today refugees from many countries are cared for by Doctors without Borders (Médecins sans Frontières), an inspiring charitable organisation in which doctors, surgeons, mental health professionals and nurses volunteer to work in refugee camps and on hospital ships owned by the organisation in areas where medical help is not available.

A percentage of royalties from the Smyrna edition of *Blue Ribbons* will be donated to Doctors without Borders to help their devoted and skilful work in what has become the great problem of our times and I have added a bequest to them in my will.

I would ask anyone moved by the story of Joice's work with refugees to make a donation in her memory to Doctors without Borders (which can be done online at msf.org.au). As her literary executor I continue to protect her memory and give powerpoint talks about Joice and her work.

Since her tower home containing many of her personal effects is preserved in Ouranoupolis, an attractive unspoiled Greek village I hope that eventually funds will be found to make a documentary film about her life and work in Greece. I am glad that in 1999 I was able to interview Joice's friends and helpers, Fani Mitroupoulou and Martha Handchin who died a few years later and learn from them the importance of Joice's work in saving Ouranoupolis from starvation. Her motto, 'Kindness to others is what matters' is equally relevant today when some 100,000 refugees are held in camps all over Greece, as I saw on my recent visit.

Some readers have written to tell me that they visited Ouranoupolis which has avoided developers and their tower blocks and has pleasant small hotels and apartments for rental. They described seeing the tower by the sea where Joice lived, visiting her grave and scattering gum leaves on it in her memory. In my old age it makes me happy to think my book has inspired them to do this and that Australians are honouring Joice's work and visiting her grave.

SUSANNA DE VRIES, OAM.

DEDICATION

In memory of my late husband, Jake de Vries, who designed the cover of this book and of our friend, the late Alex Freeleagus, former Greek Consul for Queensland who tried to have a film made about Joice in Greece but died before this aim could be realised

PREFACE

I would like to thank all those who read one of the previous editions of *Blue Ribbons Bitter Bread* and told me how the story of this extraordinary Australian woman has touched their hearts. After reading the book an American lady of Greek extraction donated funds towards the restoration of Joice's former home, the ancient tower of Prosforion at Ouranoupolis. On 6 July 2006 a small museum, honouring the work of Joice and Sydney Loch, was opened in the Lochs former home. Visitors to the village, which is a two-hour journey from Thessaloniki, can now see a vast improvement to the exterior of the ancient tower and visit the museum.

I am often asked what the title of the book means. The significance of 'Blue Ribbons' is explained below while 'Bitter Bread' is the bread of famine which was given out to refugees in camps in Greece and Poland. This bread was made of dough to which roasted ground-up acorns were added to increase its volume.

SUSANNA DE VRIES, AM, 2007

'...they shall make fringes in the borders of their garments ... and put on the fringes of blue ribbons, as a sign they will remember the commandments of the Lord and follow them.'

Book of Numbers: Chapter 15

This passage from the Old Testament was quoted to Joice NanKivell Loch in 1923 when she received a medal from the Polish President. She was wearing a silk stole fringed with blue ribbons. Roget's *Thesaurus* gives blue ribbons as a synonym for medals and honours.

INTRODUCTION
JOICE NANKIVELL LOCH—
born Ingham, Queensland, 1887—died Ouranoupolis, Greece, 1982

Fani Mitropoulou, Joice Loch's widowed housekeeper and Martha Handschin, Joice's former assistant, led us along the steep path from the village through silver-leaved olive-trees to reach her grave. Wild thyme perfumed the air and the humming of cicadas rang in our ears. Away to the right, the snow-covered peak of Athos, the Holy Mountain, glinted in the sun. Far below, silhouetted against the peacock-blue Aegean, lay the mediaeval stone tower where Joice lived while she wrote seven books, ran Pirgos Rugs, delivered babies, and, in her words, 'patched up the wounds of monks and villagers'.

Fani and Martha explained that, following the Greek Orthodox custom, after four years the remains of the dead are exhumed and the bones stored in the village bone-house so that graves, hacked out of unyielding granite, can be re-used. But Joice Loch was so loved and honoured in the village of Ouranoupolis that she and her husband are permitted to remain in their quiet grave in the shadow of the Holy Mountain.

This story of a resourceful Australian young woman who wanted to see the world shows the triumph of hope, courage and determination over difficulties. At times Joice's life resembled a gripping drama or movie. Her rescue of hundreds of earthquake victims, the role she played in the release of a Jewish scientist from an enemy prison in World War 2, and her leadership of a party of a thousand women and children escaping from the Nazis are three examples.

Joice had the compassion and charisma of her contemporary Katharine Susannah Prichard allied to the courage of Nancy Wake, 'the White Mouse'. It seems a remarkable omission that Joice Loch's achievements and her many international honours are not recorded in the *Australian Dictionary of National Biography*. However, under the name NanKivell, many of her books are recorded in *The Oxford Companion* to English Literature as well as in Debra Adelaide's *Bibliography of Australian Women's Literature*.

The beautifully written timeless stories of the Greek village where Joice lived, *Tales of Christophilos*, was an Honor Book of the Year in New York and became an American best-seller. It was typical that Joice should use the proceeds from this book about 'her' village to bring a supply of pure water to Ouranoupolis and repair some of the ravages of the Greek Civil War that took place in the aftermath of the Second World War. Extraordinary compassion for the homeless, the sick and the dying were what prevented her from using her talent for words to write more books. Had she done so, she might have earned more money to give to poor and starving Greek villagers, and she would certainly have gained greater literary fame.

Through decades of hard work in refugee camps in Poland and Greece, and by organising Operation Pied Piper for Polish and Jewish women and children to escape Nazi persecution, Joice Loch saved thousands of lives. In addition her rescue work in an earthquake and her successful anti-malaria program explain why she received eleven medals from Kings, Queens and Presidents of Greece, Poland, Rumania and Britain. Joice Loch may well be the world's most highly decorated woman for humanitarian work. She is certainly Australia's most decorated woman.

All her life Joice insisted she was Australian and worked with a miniature Australian flag on her desk. However, in spite of this, a computerised list of her works held in America's Library of Congress catalogues her as an 'English' rather than 'Australian' author. It is even more unfortunate that, living in such a remote part of Greece, her inspiring story has almost vanished through the cracks of history. At her funeral Timothy Kallistos Ware, the Greek Orthodox Bishop of Oxford, named Joice NanKivell Loch as 'one of the greatest women of the twentieth century'.

1 CHILD OF THE CYCLONE

January is the cruellest month in tropical Queensland—a time when cyclones tear buildings apart and bring death and injury in their wake.

In January 1887 a cyclone sweeping in without warning across the ink-blue waters of the Pacific marked Joice NanKivell's dramatic entry into the world. Joice's mother, seventeen-year-old Edith NanKivell, found to her horror that the river steamer on which she had booked her passage to Brisbane for the birth of her baby had been cancelled. She was trapped in the homestead at Farnham, her husband's isolated sugar plantation, facing the birth of her first child without the assistance of a doctor or midwife. The previous year someone on a neighbouring cane plantation had died in childbirth under similar circumstances; perhaps Edith remembered that unfortunate woman as she went into premature labour.

George NanKivell, Edith's husband, was equally apprehensive that the Herbert River would rise and flood the plantation. He refused to have anything to do with the birth of his child, protesting that his sole experience of midwifery consisted of dragging calves out of cows with a rope. Only Daisy, a young housemaid, one of the Kanaka servants employed at Farnham, kept calm. She instructed Wang, the Chinese cook, to boil plenty of hot water.

Outside the wind howled and roared, uprooting huge poinciana and casuarina trees and tossing them around like reeds. It seemed as though the wind was about to tear the iron roof off the homestead. Daisy sat quietly beside her frightened young mistress, insisting she squeeze her hand at the height of each contraction. 'Push, missee, push,' Daisy whispered over and over again during that long night of terror, as Edith struggled to give birth.

The howling of the wind was replaced by an eerie silence as the eye of the cyclone passed overhead. Some of the Pacific Islanders who worked in the canfields took advantage of the brief respite to flee to the Big House. They sheltered between the huge wooden stumps which raised the homestead above the ground to prevent the entry of snakes and rats.

As the wind began to howl again, Daisy prayed desperately that Edith would not die. At the height of her labour pains her mistress lost consciousness, and when she came to, Daisy told her the baby's head had appeared. Finally, in a rush, the infant emerged.

'It's a girl,' Daisy announced. But the premature baby lay still and silent. Fearful that it might be still-born, she slapped the tiny creature. Miraculously the baby began to breathe. Daisy cut the cord, washed the child and wrapped her in a shawl.

George was summoned to view his first child. When he learned it was a girl and not the hoped-for male heir, he gazed down at the baby and said: 'We'll call her Joice, a good Cornish name like NanKivell.'

Edith's mother, Emily, had been divorced and created a family scandal so using her name was out of the question. Instead Edith had hoped to call the little girl Isabella Mary, after her English grandmother, but she was too exhausted to object. 'Mary' became Joice's second name.

Meanwhile the storm had abated, and the Kanaka labourers emerged from their shelter beneath the homestead to enquire whether the white Missus had had her 'bubba'. George picked up his little daughter, carried her onto the veranda and held her aloft above the iron-lace railing. His labourers cried out in delight when they saw the fair-skinned baby.

But George NanKivell's immediate concern was for his horses, his prize cattle and the young green cane on which his fortunes depended. He set off on horseback for a tour of inspection. He found the topmost leaves of the cane were shredded to ribbons, but the lower leaves and the all-important cane stalks had escaped damage. The crop was saved, but as he rode around the huge plantation he noted that the storage sheds, private jetty and the mill would all need repairing.

Of all the wealthy young planters in the Ingham district, most of whose fathers hailed from Melbourne, young George NanKivell had been considered the most eligible. His father, the shipping and pastoral tycoon Thomas NanKivell, was known as Australia's richest man. He boasted of his descent from a Cornish family which had once owned land around Truro, which it later lost through gambling debts. One NanKivell had turned pirate, preying on shipping around the Breton and Cornish coasts.[1] Thomas, left penniless as a young man, had migrated to Australia, lived rough in a bark hut, borrowed money, invested (or gambled) in cattle and sheep at the right time, and now enjoyed all the trappings of a gentleman: a Toorak mansion in Melbourne, a large yacht and a stable of racehorses. 'From bandits to tycoons in three generations' was his proud boast.

Thomas NanKivell had nine sons and daughters and wanted all his children to 'marry well'. Like many self-made, wealthy men, he was avaricious, and felt disappointed that George's bride was not bringing money to the family; never one to shy away from expressing his feelings, he regretted that his son was 'marrying a sickly girl without a penny to her name'. His wedding gift to George and Edith was scarcely generous for 'Australia's richest man': a silver teapot engraved with the NanKivell family crest—a subtle message designed to show Edith's family that his forbears were as good as hers.[2]

Edith was the daughter of a Colonel Alexander Lawson, who had divorced his flighty young wife, Emily, after she ran away with another man many years younger than herself whom she later married, causing even more scandal. The Lawsons had two daughters, Edith and her older sister, Lily, but Emily did not want to have anything to do with them, fearing that her second husband would guess her real age if he met the two teenage girls.[3]

In 1878, in an attempt to escape from the scandal of the divorce, their father brought Lily and Edith to Australia. Edith was sent to an expensive boarding school in Sydney's eastern suburbs. On her fourteenth birthday she was called into the headmistress's office to be told that Colonel Lawson had died of a heart attack. The headmistress explained that she was awaiting word from the Colonel's lawyers to know whether they would pay Edith's school fees, which were long overdue. If they did not, Edith would have to leave school or else stay on and work as a pupil teacher.

Edith recalled another girl reduced to this lowly status after her father died—she had become an overworked Cinderella. But where would she live and what could she do if she left school? Soon afterwards, Edith and Lily learned that they would not receive a single penny from their father's estate: the lawyers told them it had been drained by 'unwise investments'. Lily found work as a poorly paid governess, then made a convenient marriage to elderly Harry Hodgson, who managed a bank at Ingham, in north Queensland. The only solution was that Edith should live with Lily and her miserly husband. After Colonel Lawson's death, John Turner, her mother's brother, who had also settled in Australia, became her guardian. Turner was a member of the Queensland parliament. Both he and his wife, Ada, felt a loving concern for their niece.[4]

Lily and Harry Hodgson saw a good marriage for Edith as the only solution. Lily cleverly manipulated the situation by holding candlelit dinner parties for her pretty younger sister, inviting the local bachelor cane planters. One of these was George NanKivell, an agreeable but fairly unremarkable fair-haired young man in his early twenties. He had been sent to boarding school, and afterwards worked as a jackaroo on an outback property. His father then put him in charge of a sheep and cattle property at Tambo, in central Queensland, before he was sent to manage Farnham plantation near Ingham.

Lily invited George to the Hodgsons' musical evenings. Inexperienced where women were concerned, George was entranced by Edith's blonde curls and hourglass figure. Edith, in her white lace tea-gown, played the piano, and as George turned the pages of her music, he felt as though he was falling in love with this beautiful, talented girl. He asked Harry Hodgson's permission to propose to Edith; the bank manager was delighted at the thought of being relieved of the expense of sheltering his young sister-in-law. He had checked with his counterparts in Melbourne and was told that although Thomas NanKivell was considered Australia's wealthiest man he had huge bank loans. However, this did not deter him from giving George permission to propose.

Edith herself was still undecided but Lily told her sister she should not forgo the chance of such a wonderful match. Knowing little of the world or of George, but excited by the prospect of her own home and escape from her dependant situation, Edith, urged on by Lily, accepted George's stammered proposal and his sapphire and diamond ring.

John Turner, as Edith's guardian, went to see Thomas NanKivell. Turner and his wife were worried about their niece's future financial security; they were convinced the Queensland sugar industry would not be able to survive if the Queensland Government decided to ban the importation of Pacific Islanders, or Kanakas, the indentured labourers who worked on the plantations. The unfortunate Islanders were kidnapped or lured aboard the ships by unscrupulous sea captains who promised them gold from foreign lands, then chained them and kept them below deck. This practice was known as 'blackbirding'. On arrival in north Queensland they were inspected like horseflesh before being sold into three years of indentured labour. Without passports or immigration papers, the Kanakas had no option but to work for low wages. At the end of their three years they could stay on for a further period of indenture or be returned to any island in the Pacific group that suited the blackbirders. Some were returned to islands inhabited by tribal enemies, where they faced certain death.

Dirt-cheap labour was the foundation of cane plantations worldwide. African slaves had been responsible for building the wealth of Thomas NanKivell's partners, the Fanning family, on sugar plantations in Cuba and the West Indies.[5] But now searching questions about blackbirding were being asked in the British parliament as well as in several Australian State parliaments. It seemed that all importation of Kanaka labour might soon be banned. Then, without cheap labour, all four of the cane plantations owned by Fanning NanKivell would become unworkable and their values would crash.

John Turner hoped that as Chairman of the company Fanning NanKivell, Thomas would agree to place the title deeds to Farnham plantation in George and Edith's name. But Thomas NanKivell insisted that Farnham was a company asset, and as such it must remain the property of Fanning NanKivell. (He was careful not to reveal that Farnham and the three other Queensland plantations owned by the company were eighty per cent mortgaged either to banks or to their previous owners.) The two powerful men argued hotly. Thomas refused to sign anything over to his son, declaring that 'Queensland sugar could not fail'. Turner declared with equal conviction that within five years the Queensland Government would ban Kanaka labour and then the bottom would fall out of sugar prices. As a result, financial ruin could face Edith and George. The two men almost came to blows and had to be dragged apart by the butler and the cook.

After their Brisbane wedding on 1st April 1886 (All Fool's Day, scarcely a good omen) George and Edith spent their honeymoon on a boat steaming north from Brisbane to the Herbert River. Edith loved Farnham from the first moment she arrived there. The plantation covered almost five thousand acres, though a large part of the land had still to be reclaimed from rainforest jungle. The homestead stood high above the Herbert River, set amidst red-flowering coral and poinciana trees and gigantic palms. Steamers from Cardwell and others specially chartered by Fanning NanKivell docked at their private jetty and were the planters' only contact with the outside world.

After almost three years of dependency on her sister and brother-in-law, Edith enjoyed having her own home and servants, with a horse and canopied buggy at her disposal when she went visiting her sisters-in-law at their Herbert River plantations—Gairloch, Macknade and Hamleigh.

At dinner parties, where Edith wore elegant gowns and perfume imported from France in Fanning NanKivell's own ships, George took pleasure in showing off his beautiful wife to his family and friends. Long French windows, kept open to catch the breeze, led from the dining room and drawing-room on to the veranda. The gentlemen wore white jackets and trousers, and the bare shoulders of the ladies were enhanced by the gleam of pearls or the glitter of diamonds. After dinner, Edith would play the grand piano, and the ladies' silk or satin skirts would rustle across the polished floors as they waltzed with their partners.

But once the novelty of marriage had worn off, Edith was dismayed to discover how little she and her husband had in common. George NanKivell's consuming interests were shooting, fishing, and horse racing, all of which bored Edith. He soon dropped any pretensions to the enjoyment of classical music or literature, the two passions of Edith's life. In spite of her luxurious lifestyle, nothing could disguise the fact that Edith and George NanKivell were an ill-matched couple.

Seven weeks after Joice's birth, George took the steamer to Ingham to register the arrival of his daughter. The Registrar of the Cardwell Shire, Colony of Queensland, recorded the birth of Joice Mary NanKivell thus: 24 January, 1887 at Farnham Plantation, Herbert River district, to Edith Ada NanKivell (nee Lawson), born Jersey, Channel Islands and George Griffiths NanKivell, born in Brighton, Victoria.[6]

Edith had tried to be a good wife and was determined to be a good mother. But she found it distressingly difficult to breast-feed her baby. A Pacific Islander woman whose own baby had recently died was employed as a wet nurse. Queensland's steamy summer humidity made Edith tired and depressed. She loved Farnham in the winter but dreaded the tropical wet season, which she endured wearing tight corsets and long petticoats under her gowns, according to the customs of her time. After Joice was weaned she thrived on a diet of goat's milk (considered much better for her than cow's milk), mashed banana and fresh orange juice. Her cot was placed on the wide veranda, shaded by a huge mango tree and a scarlet-flowering poinciana. Daisy proved a patient, loving and responsible nursemaid and companion for the little girl; it is possible that Joice's lifelong sympathy and concern for the dispossessed was sparked by the experience of growing up among the Kanakas her father employed, who had been torn from their homes and families and everything they loved.

Daisy was one of the few Kanaka women who had attended mission school and learned to read and write. As a house-servant she was relatively privileged. Other Kanaka women on Fanning Nan-Kivell's vast plantations had to work under white overseers, planting cane shoots and hoeing weeds from the rows of young plants.[7] In later life, when Joice NanKivell wrote about her early days on a huge

Queensland plantation, she showed herself sympathetic to the plight of the Kanakas.

But she claimed her father's employees were well-treated, unlike those of many other planters, who simply ignored Government regulations of the period. The tyranny of distance meant that regulations were often hard to enforce.

When Joice was old enough, her mother would read fairy stories to her on the wide veranda. In later life, Joice remembered scarlet-and green lorikeets swooping and chattering amid the canopy of trees, the distant drumming of the cicadas and the harsh calls of kookaburras before tropical storms.

Joice's sunny nature, wide smile and fair curly hair won her the love of the Kanaka and Chinese house staff. It was prophesied that the 'child of the cyclone' would lead a charmed life. Was she not the granddaughter of Australia's wealthiest man? One white overseer told his wife that Joice NanKivell was 'born with a silver spoon in her mouth'.

Shortly after Joice's second birthday, Edith's guardian, Uncle John Turner, arrived by river steamer from Cardwell. As a senior member of the Liberal party in Queensland he brought grim news from Brisbane's Parliament House. Importation of Kanaka labourers to replace those departing at the end of their three-year indentures was soon to be scaled down. Samuel Griffith's Liberal Government, urged on by Queensland's strong trade unions, was committed to ending the blackbirding system. John Turner felt he should warn George NanKivell that it was only a matter of time before the Queensland Parliament passed a bill outlawing the importation of all Kanakas. He repeated the warning he had given to George's father: Fanning NanKivell's heavily mortgaged plantations would become unworkable and unsaleable. No white man would work in them for fear of Weil's disease or leptospirosis, a fatal disease spread by rats that lived amongst the cane. Lacking the income from their sugar crops, Turner feared that Messrs Fanning, NanKivell and Sons would not be able to pay the huge mortgages on their bank loans.

George NanKivell refused to believe this grim prediction. He clung to his father's assurances that growing sugar cane in Queensland was the way to get rich, defending his father's promises that his sons would eventually become millionaires once the mortgages on the plantations had been paid off. He repeated Thomas NanKivell's assurances that the Griffith Government in Queensland would never 'cut off its nose to spite its face' and ban all Kanaka labour.

All the same, George took the trouble to write to his father as well as conferring with his brothers at Gairloch, Macknade and Hamleigh. But Thomas NanKivell refused to come north and view the situation for himself. He stayed in his Toorak mansion and wrote to his sons assuring them yet again that they would become millionaires one day.

By the time Joice's blue eyes had darkened to hazel, Edith was pregnant again. Fearing another difficult birth on the isolated property she departed on the steamer for Brisbane, leaving Joice in Daisy's care. Three months later she returned with George's son and heir, to be christened Charles Gordon Lincoln NanKivell, after the British General Gordon, hero of Khartoum, and America's President Abraham Lincoln (who, ironically enough, secured for America the abolition of slavery). The infant's birth was duly registered at Cardwell; he was twenty-one months younger than Joice. In spite of his heroic names, he was always known to family and friends as 'Geoff'.

Joice adored her little brother from the first time she saw him. Geoff grew into a handsome little boy with a wonderful smile and a happy-go-lucky nature. But he often showed distressing symptoms of a condition that would eventually be diagnosed as asthma, and this caused Edith much anguish. He was Joice's adoring slave. Daisy helped to look after the new baby as she had cared for Joice.

Joice's first memories of her childhood provide valuable insights into the early days of what was largely a Melbourne-funded sugar industry in tropical Queensland. With compassion for the Kanakas she records plantation homesteads filled with black and Chinese house servants, and reckless high living based on virtual slave labour in the canfields.

Farnham, with its five thousand acres, resembled a feudal village with the 'Big House' or homestead as its centre and the crushing mill as its power house. Near the homestead were stables for George's Arab horses, a blacksmith's forge and a tin-roofed store containing supplies for the Kanakas: beef slaughtered on the property, flour, jam, tea as well as clothing—trousers, jackets and straw hats, one-size calico dresses and kerchiefs. The married Kanakas had their own huts where they cooked their meals; the single men lived in a barracks where an evil-tempered Chinese cook was employed.

One night this temperamental Chinese cook ran amok in the kitchen of the Kanaka barracks, brandishing a huge meat cleaver and threatening to kill a South Sea Islander whom he held hostage. As there was no policeman to summon in this frontier society, George was called out by the manager to deal with the situation. Vainly he attempted to calm the raging Chinaman who had his cleaver poised above the unfortunate Kanaka crouched beside him. Keeping calm and collected, George reached for the huge pan of curry bubbling away on the stove and flung the entire contents into the cook's face, saving the Kanaka's life.[8]

When George returned to the homestead he found that Edith, fearing a riot in the barracks, had bolted the door and taken Joice and Geoff into her bed. Joice remembered that it took some time for George to persuade her mother that it really was him at the front door. On Sundays, Daisy dressed Joice in a white broderie anglaise frock with a ribbon sash and she and Geoff would accompany their parents to croquet and tennis parties. Ladies in high-necked blouses and long skirts played a gentle game of tennis against gentlemen in long white trousers and straw boaters. Wealthiest of all the planters were the Swallows of Hambledon, with their huge library and a ballroom lit by Waterford crystal chandeliers. When Joice and Geoff visited Hambledon to play with the Swallow children, they would be led around on a pony by a little Kanaka boy in uniform. It was evident that Joice loved riding. For her third birthday, her father gave her a Shetland pony of her own.

John Turner had foretold events correctly: the importation of Kanaka labour was scaled down, whereupon Joice's father and uncles petitioned the British Government for political independence for North Queensland as well as permission to retain their Kanaka labour. Their efforts were unsuccessful. In desperation, Thomas NanKivell and his partners attempted to import Indian labour, something which the previous Queensland Government of Sir Thomas McIlwraith had favoured, but the new Liberal Government of Sir Samuel Griffith would not allow it. What was even worse for the over-committed and over-mortgaged firm of Fanning NanKivell was that Queensland sugar prices were falling sharply, affected by competition on world markets from Javanese cane and cheap sugar beet grown in Germany and Holland. Proceeds from the sugar crops of their Queensland plantations could no longer cover the vast sums Fanning NanKivell needed to pay off their loans and mortgages. The company still owed the Neame brothers, the former owners of two of their plantations, almost half their purchase price, and there were huge bank loans outstanding on the other two.[9] Then, in the summer of 1890, much of the growing cane was destroyed by a cyclone, and the following year it was attacked by red rust, a fungus that ruined much of the harvest.

Joice was still far too young to understand that things were not going well at Farnham. When she was five, her Aunt Ellis Rowan (nee Ryan) came to stay at the homestead: her advent was the event of major importance in Joice's young life at this time. There was a complex network of inter-marriages: two NanKivell girls had married Ryan men. One had married Herbert Ryan, and George's sister Denise was married to Harry Ryan.

Ellis Rowan was a remarkable woman, a professional artist at a time when it was considered unbecoming for ladies to earn money from painting. Aunt Ellis painted the flame trees in the garden, the blue water lilies on the lagoon, and made drawings of the orchids which grew in the trees fringing the Herbert River. She was a strong-minded woman who defied convention by travelling around the world alone, leaving her husband behind in Melbourne. Ellis had no interest in domesticity. Her burning ambition was to paint all the tropical wildflowers of Australia and send specimens of them to her father's old friend, the distinguished botanist Baron von Mueller.

Aunt Ellis believed women could do whatever they set their minds to; in later years she was to become a role model for Joice. Ellis Rowan had spent part of her girlhood in England; she urged Edith NanKivell that when Joice turned seventeen, she too should travel to London and be presented at court. Ellis' sister Ada had married Lord Charles Montagu-Douglas-Scott, fourth son of the Duke of Buccleuch and Queensberry. She promised that Ada would introduce Joice to London society and arrange a debutante ball for her; hopefully Joice would make a 'good' marriage there.

During this visit, Edith arranged boat trips for Ellis. They made stops at private jetties, where servants spread a luncheon cloth on the grass, and afterwards Edith, Joice and Ellis would search for wild orchids. In the evenings, after Joice had been put to bed, Ellis would change into a white, lace-embroidered gown and entertain the guests in Farnham's drawing room with tales of her adventures in search of wild flowers. Soon, Ellis would plead that she must start 'her work'. She would retire to her bedroom and write up her notes, then get out her water-colours and paint the orchids and water-lilies she had collected that day, intent on capturing the flowers' freshness and colour before they faded.

Joice was fascinated by Aunt Ellis' exuberance, her passion for travel and her creative talent. And Ellis adored her lively little niece.

Hearing Joice read aloud, Ellis realised she had a talent for words. Over the years her aunt gave her gifts of books and played an important role in encouraging Joice to become a writer.

Apart from a talent for story-telling, from an early age Joice enjoyed brewing up 'medicines', imagining that she might become a doctor, still a strictly male profession in the early 1890s. Geoff, her faithful shadow, would be assigned the role of wounded patient and bandaged from head to toe.

Aborigines often visited Farnham, but always refused to work in the cane fields. In periods of prolonged drought, Aboriginal women going walkabout into the rainforest would sometimes leave babies or small children they could no longer keep on the steps of homesteads where they had been treated kindly. This is what happened to one infant at Farnham. He was named Tinker, but cruelly dubbed 'Stinker' by the Kanakas, who envied the Aborigines their freedom to come and go as they pleased.

Joice and Geoff befriended Tinker. Sometimes at meals they would wrap scraps of food in their table napkins, which they smuggled out to him. Tinker used to visit the native encampments, but he never found his mother, so he always returned 'home' to Farnham. When the weather turned wet he would make himself a bed on a pile of old sacks in the huge sugar-crushing mill, which was worked by Chinese labour, as the Kanakas would not allow him to sleep in their barracks. Among the vast storage vats, which smelt of warm sweet molasses and cats' urine, the three children would catch huge cockroaches to use as bait on their fishing expeditions.

The vats themselves, filled with sticky brown molasses, had a horrific fascination for the NanKivell children. The Chinese labourers toiled away in the blazing heat, crusted with sugar from head to toe until they resembled life-sized cake ornaments. Joice would watch, fascinated, as they trampled the sugar cane, sweat pouring down their bare legs as they shovelled it into the centrifuges. She knew that a Chinese had once fallen into one of the vats and drowned in the treacly liquid. The corpse lay in the vat for five days: the molasses caused the body to swell but also preserved it. Finally, like a huge candied sugar plum, the body was fished out by the man's workmates. 'I don't suppose an ounce of the precious liquid molasses was thrown away . . . Nothing more was ever said about the incident,' Joice wrote later, disgusted by the rough, tough life on the canfields.

Joice and Geoff admired Tinker's knowledge of native birds and animals; he taught them how to track wildlife and climb coconut palms, and showed them how to fish with a spear in the shallow lagoons. Later, Joice wrote that this knowledge was more valuable than anything she learned in the schoolroom.

One day George NanKivell invited some of his neighbours to shoot wild duck on the lagoon; he arranged for two Kanakas to bring along a plentiful supply of liquor and a picnic lunch. Both Joice, now six, and Geoff were allowed to join the shooting party in return for carrying their father's game bags, and Tinker came with them. After a long, boozy lunch, the planters amused themselves by employing Tinker as a gun dog, calling on him to swim out into the lagoon and fetch dead game, even though there was the danger of a crocodile lurking below the surface. The small boy gallantly retrieved duck after duck, but finally he refused to dive in again. Several planters brandished their whips and insisted he should return to the dark waters of the lagoon on pain of a thrashing. Tinker was terrified. He shook his head, his eyes piteous as those of a dog who knows he has done wrong.

'*Mulloka dardu* there,' he whispered. '*Kurreah*, he catchem little fella quick.'

Despite his pleas, the planters, including George NanKivell, ordered the little boy to swim into the middle of the lagoon where the dead ducks were floating. Joice and Geoff knew that Tinker was always right about anything concerning native creatures, but no one listened to their entreaties on his behalf. A drunken planter prodded the boy with his gun and at last, with great reluctance, Tinker entered the water once again.

Joice and Geoff burst into tears. They watched in horror as their playmate dived into the lagoon and swam towards the ducks, his head bobbing through the huge blue and white water lilies. He had almost reached the ducks when suddenly something that looked like a submerged log reared up beside him and flailed the water with its huge tail.

A despairing wail resounded across the lagoon. Joice and Geoff looked on, powerless, as the crocodile tossed poor Tinker in mid-air, then caught his body in its gaping jaws. Another scream from Tinker echoed across the lagoon before the crocodile, holding its prey, plunged and rolled, leaving blood-streaked foam smeared across the water. Then came total silence.

The planters looked at each other grimly, knowing they were guilty of sending a child to his death. Not a word was said as they gathered up their guns and their game. Joice and Geoff were racked with sobs. For Joice, horrified at the cruelty of these adults, including her father, it was the end of innocence. She refused to be comforted or to speak to him. An embarrassed George NanKivell ordered one of the Kanakas to take his sobbing children back to the homestead.

For months after that Joice slept badly, remembering Tinker's horrific and pointless death. From now on she would have scant respect for her father, and was racked with remorse that she had lacked the courage to stand up to him and protect poor little Tinker. For years she wondered whether the planters would have taken notice if her entreaties had been more forceful. She vowed that when she grew up she would help those who could not defend themselves. She and Geoff did not forget their friend. 'The horror of Tinker's death remained seared on our memories for years,' Joice wrote.[10]

Gradually the 1885 Act of Samuel Griffith's Liberal Queensland Government took effect: after 31 December 1890, no Kanaka whose three-year indenture had expired could be replaced by another South Sea Islander. By the early 1890s planters were desperate to keep their existing Kanaka workforce and offered them much better working conditions, in spite of falling sugar prices and poor harvests. The overall result was that the planters or their holding companies could neither sell leased land nor pay the interest on their mortgages. Joice was now old enough to know that the planters' toast around the dinner tables, 'D.S.G.!' was a cryptic message—'Damn Sam Griffith for ruining us!'

George and his brothers appealed to their father, but Thomas Nan-Kivell refused to sell out. He told his sons that they must trust him as chairman of the company. He did not believe the Queensland Government would be so stupid as to ruin its sugar industry. He advised George that he and Edith must economise for a few more seasons and 'everything would come right'. A huge bounty was charged for any Kanakas the blackbirders managed to slip through. Messrs Fanning NanKivell tried to import Chinese coolies instead of Kanakas, but their applications for import permits were turned down. Late nineteenth century Queensland was extremely racist, as some gross cartoons in *The Queenslander* featuring pigtailed Chinese workers reveal. Samuel Griffith's Government had given power to the trade unions, who were fearful of the long hours and low wages Chinese workers would accept.

The planters of north Queensland were in despair, their resources dwindling. They petitioned the Government to rescind the Abolition of Islander Labour Act. Finally, in 1892, the government acceded to their request. However, the conditions under which they could employ Kanaka labour in the future were stringently regulated.[11]

For Joice's parents, the rescinding of the Act came too late. In the boom years of the 1880s Thomas NanKivell, dubbed 'Australia's richest man', had been worth many millions . . . on paper. But he had inherited the gambling instincts of his Cornish ancestors as well as something of their piratical instincts. Mindful of the fact that his forbears had lost their land in Cornwall, he now took the precaution of putting his Toorak mansion and his personal assets in his wife's name. Unforgivably, he failed to inform his sons that his investment in huge mortgages on sugar cane plantations was by far the riskiest step he had ever taken in his life, and that very soon they and their young families would be bankrupt.

2   PARROT PIE AND PIGWEED SALAD

On the verge of ruin, with hundreds of acres of cane uncut, George and his brothers tackled the job themselves, aided by the handful of Pacific Islanders who still remained and two of the white overseers, who agreed to work without pay. They found the temperature among the rows of cane was several degrees higher than elsewhere. The Europeans, unaccustomed to sustained physical work, suffered from prolonged mosquito bites and scrub-ticks; huge welts arose on their skin and one overseer almost died from tick-born paralysis. Their valiant attempts at self-sufficiency failed when the second overseer was bitten by one of the rats that lived among the cane and developed leptospirosis. Edith nursed the unfortunate man, but his limbs turned black and he died in agony. The horror of leptospirosis so terrified Australian workers that they flatly refused to come north to cut cane, however high the wages advertised by Fanning NanKivell.

Edith made drastic economies. Parrot pie and stewed kangaroo or wallaby shot by George now featured on the menu instead of pedigree beef from their own herd, which had been sold off. '

We must eat vegetables or we'll catch scurvy,' Edith insisted. She placed sun-hats on Joice and Geoff's heads, lined with a layer of damp straw to ward off the fierce tropical sun. Assisting their mother they staggered under heavy buckets of water, carrying them to water the vegetables in the kitchen garden. Pigweed salad now featured on the menu.

Their glittering drawing-room chandelier was taken down and sent to Melbourne for sale along with choice items of furniture to provide some working capital. Thomas NanKivell never complied with his son's request to come north and letters asking for his instructions remained unanswered. Lawyers called the Fannings and NanKivells involved with the company to a meeting in Melbourne. It seemed that even after selling off company assets, Fanning NanKivell & Sons still could not settle all the mortgages on its sugar properties. 'The banks have foreclosed: Fanning NanKivell is bankrupt' George and his brothers were told. Their plantations, their homes and furniture, all acquired with company funds, must be sold to pay off the company's creditors. Lacking cheap labour and with sugar prices still low,   there were no takers for their huge Herbert River plantations: all the interest paid out on loans and mortgages over the years would be lost.[1]

Eventually the lawyers and accountants worked out a compromise. Macknade was handed back to its previous owners, the Neame brothers, who came out of retirement in England to settle the whole sad affair. Gairloch, the largest of the plantations, would be subdivided and small blocks offered for sale at a loss. Hamleigh was owned jointly by Fanning NanKivell and its original founder, who now took over the property again; he had not been fully paid out. Farnham and its large homestead, Edith's pride and joy, would be offered at auction along with the subdivisions of Gairloch. But confidence had faded. Queensland sugar no longer seemed to hold such a bright future. Not a single hand was raised at auction. Both Farnham and Gairloch remained unsold as the banks awaited an upturn in the economy.

Financial disaster aggravated the strained relationship between Joice's parents. Edith blamed Lily and her husband for pressuring her into marrying George, and George for failing to stand up to his father and not listening to her guardian's warnings about the risk inherent in a sugar industry dependant on Kanaka labour.

Bailiffs arrived at Farnham and argued over what was company property. They demanded Edith's pearls and everything in her jewel box other than her engagement and wedding rings. Joice saw her mother sitting on the bed sobbing and tried to comfort her. She was bewildered to see their dining-room table and chairs and the huge mirrors from the drawing room crated up and put on the river steamer to be auctioned in Sydney. And she burst into tears when her beloved Shetland pony was led off to be sold.

Daisy was so fond of the children that she wanted to remain with the NanKivells, but as they lacked money to pay her wages, she decided to return to her former home in the New Hebrides. Wang, their Chinese cook, went south to work. Everything around the NanKivells crumbled.

For the rest of her life Joice would love warm climates and remember the lush tropical beauty of northern Queensland, the sound of summer rainfall on the iron roof of their home, the deep red of the soil, the scarlet flowers of the coral trees and poincianas and the scent of creamy frangipani.[2]

George decided to seek his fortune on the gold-fields of Western Australia, while Edith, with Joice and Geoff, took the steamer south from Cardwell to Brisbane. From there they went second-class by steam train to Melbourne. To Joice and Geoff, travelling by train was a big adventure. In Melbourne they stayed in the huge, square-turreted stone mansion on Toorak Road where Thomas NanKivell and his wife lived. Reluctantly, Thomas had agreed to shelter them for the time being.

The loss of his Queensland 'investments' had been a huge shock to Thomas NanKivell, who had fondly imagined himself growing richer and richer on the labours of his sons. He took his frustrations out on Edith and his grandchildren, seeming to enjoy a macabre delight in making them feel poverty-stricken and unwelcome. For Joice's seventh birthday there was not one present from her grandparents. Thomas NanKivell had become a domestic tyrant and a miser. All his assets were held in his wife's name, effectively hidden away from Fanning NanKivell's creditors. In her memoirs Joice recorded how mean and sanctimonious her grandfather was. Family prayers with the servants were held night and morning. After prayers each Saturday night, Thomas would dole out eight matches to each member of staff, one for every day of the week and one 'in case of accidents'. Everything was monitored, from the food Edith and the children consumed to the coal the maids took upstairs to heat chilly bedrooms in winter.

Joice's grandmother, Elizabeth Murray NanKivell, claimed to love her grandchildren but never demonstrated it. She remained cold and distant towards Edith and ordered her around like a servant. One evening, Joice was sent to bed early for some trifling infraction of house rules. Unable to sleep, the little girl wandered around the upper floor of the huge mansion, peeking into her grandmother's bedroom. She watched in amazement as her grandmother removed what Joice thought was her hair, revealing a skull bare as a billiard ball. Her grandmother must surely have some sort of magic power to be able to take off her hair completely! The next day at lunch, Joice piped up in front of some visitors about her grandmother's magic power to remove her hair at will.[3] Her grandmother was furious: now everyone would know she wore a wig. Joice was punished by being locked in her room.

The atmosphere became so hostile in Toorak that Edith ate humble pie and wrote to Lily asking if she and the children could stay with her and her husband. The answer came back in the affirmative. So Edith took the children by train to Brisbane, where Lily lived in a house owned by the bank for which her husband worked as manager. A few weeks later, however, Harry was transferred to Ipswich, a quiet pastoral town upriver from Brisbane.

Joice hated staying with Aunt Lily, who had a passion for attending church at least twice each Sunday. She gave Geoff and Joice a penny a week if they were good but expected them to put it in the church collection plate. This experience largely helped to put Joice off churchgoing for life.

Meanwhile, letters arrived from George, who was still vainly trying to find gold at Kalgoorlie, in Western Australia.

Fanning NanKivell's properties were offered by the receivers at auction once more, but even at a vastly reduced price no one wanted them. Finally they were sold for a fraction of what the company had paid for them. Farnham was left to slowly decay: the verandas crumbled away, the iron roofs rusted, and lantana and native vegetation gradually overran the gardens. After standing empty for years, the homestead was eventually pulled down and the land subdivided into relatively small blocks.[4]

Edith, Geoff and Joice, the poor relations, endured hospitality from Lily and her husband for a year before they were told they had outstayed their welcome. Lily's relationship with Edith was ambivalent; she would continue to be highly critical of the way Edith reared her children, and for decades she criticised everything Joice did or wanted to do.

The effect of the bankruptcy on George's brothers and fellow plantation managers had been equally devastating. One brother left for the West Indies to work in the sugar industry as an under-manager, and horrified his parents when he wrote to tell them he had married a half-caste girl.[5] Another brother, Jack NanKivell, went from being the manager of a huge property to becoming a travelling 'odd job man' fixing fences and leaking taps around Brisbane, unable to find a proper job in the depression years of the 1890s. He had forged a cheque in his father's name and Thomas NanKivell threatened to prosecute him.

George turned down John Turner's offer of an office job, probably because he feared he lacked the ability to cope with office life. He had attended Wesley College at Prahran, but had not done well academically. He now thought private education was a waste of money. Because one of his uncles had become rich at Kalgoorlie, George thought he could follow in his golden footsteps. But although he worked hard with pick and shovel, the specks of gold that remained after panning were not enough to meet the high costs of fresh food, dried provisions and drinking water on the gold-fields. Slowly George's optimism was worn down by disappointment. Finally he was forced to return to his wife and children empty-handed; once again his judgement had been wrong.

To lessen Edith's anxieties, George accepted a job on a sheep property in Gippsland. His uncle Hugh NanKivell, a lawyer, had become the owner of an isolated sheep farm at Boolara, in settlement of a bad debt. He offered George the position of farm manager on a minute salary, provided George invested in the property by paying off the rest of the mortgage. George was able to do this out of a small legacy which Edith had recently received from an aunt in England. In those days, before the passing of the Married Women's Property Act, all money in a marriage was regarded as the property of the husband. Edith was not even consulted about her legacy.

It was agreed George would go to the property first and prepare the house there for them. Edith fondly imagined they had been offered a pleasant home surrounded by gardens and a fruit orchard. She thought this would be better for Joice and Geoff than staying as unwanted guests with unwilling relatives, although a reunion with George was not something she really wanted. However, having experienced the repercussions of her mother's divorce, she felt she had no other option. While Thomas NanKivell had been careful to protect his own assets during the company's bankruptcy, he had completely omitted to make any financial provision for his children and grandchildren. After some more tense months with Lily and her husband, Edith decided it was time to travel south to Boolara. Jessie, the sixteen-year-old daughter of a carpenter, accompanied them. She said she would be happy to help look after the NanKivell children in return for bed and board.

Edith had refused an invitation to stay overnight in Toorak with her grumpy in-laws.[8] Seeing them living in luxury brought back only too vividly all that she had lost. She was convinced that her father-in-law's lack of foresight had bankrupted her husband. Repeatedly she would ask, 'Having ruined us, how could he be so unconcerned? Joice and Geoff are his grandchildren, his own flesh and blood.'

Once more Edith and her children took the steam train from Brisbane to Melbourne. Edith was elegant in her dark travelling suit topped by a straw boater with a veil that lent her face an air of mystery. They sat in a grimy third-class carriage on slatted wooden benches. Joice and Geoff did not care about specks of soot from the engine or sitting on hard seats—travelling south again was a big adventure, as long as they did not have to go to their grandparents' gloomy mansion in Toorak Road. Instead, they stayed at a small hotel in Collins Street. Joice was excited by the bustling thoroughfare, the trams, the horse-drawn cabs, the exclusive shops and, as a special treat, a visit to one of the new moving-picture houses.

The next morning they took the train south-east to Morwell, the nearest station to their new farm, where George met them with a buggy and loaded up the crates containing the few possessions spared them by the bailiffs, including Edith's precious books. Before they set off for their new home they bought provisions to take with them. It was so isolated that the travelling grocer with his provision cart called there only once every two months. The buggy had a large canvas canopy called a 'tilt' to keep off the rain. The road soon petered out into a bush track, winding its way through huge gum trees.

It started to rain. Edith had no idea that Gippsland could be so cold and wet in winter . . . or, as she would learn, so hot and dry in summer. While she sat silent and despairing in the pouring rain, George told his children: 'It's a big adventure—you'll love the farm.'

The buggy jolted and rattled over deeply rutted bush tracks. For hours, without seeing a single soul, they drove through acres of dark Gippsland forest. Enormous gums with strips of peeling bark hanging from their branches towered above them, tall as the masts of sailing ships. Joice's fertile imagination saw witches and hobgoblins lurking among the huge trees, but she did not want to tell Geoff of her fears. Instead she tried to cheer him up. 'At Boolara, we'll be like early Australian explorers, make our own maps and name places after ourselves,' she told him as cheerfully as she could.

Their journey continued until early afternoon. Ascending a steep hill, they arrived in a clearing surrounded by a stockade that sloped down to a creek at the rear. All around them were more gigantic gums and miles of silent forest. Behind the paling stockade, built to keep out the livestock, they saw a small wooden shack with dirt-encrusted windows. Two slab sheds—the kitchen and toilet—sagged against the wooden walls of the shack.

'This is our new home,' George said, smiling nervously. As though trapped in a nightmare Edith looked around. The rough bush shack was so different from the pretty farmhouse surrounded by gardens and fruit trees in blossom she had imagined from memories of her English childhood and Uncle Hugh NanKivell's description that it took her breath away. Not wanting to upset her children she stayed silent, but she was on the verge of tears as she clambered down from the buggy.

Taking a child in either hand she walked through the sagging front door and entered her new home. It consisted of three small dark rooms, lined with stained newspapers and hessian sugar bags to block out the biting wind which whistled through the weatherboards. The sitting room reeked of rat droppings and the dirt floor was covered with empty beer bottles. Obviously it had not been cleaned for decades. Edith opened the cupboard in the main bedroom. Something moved. A gigantic carpet snake uncoiled from the corner and shot out through the door.

While George unharnessed the mare from the buggy and Joice and Geoff listened to mice squeaking behind the hessian-covered walls, Edith and Jessie went outside to inspect the cooking facilities. The kitchen was an ancient shed without any water supply. It had a dirt floor, one small cupboard, a wobbly pine table and half an upended kerosene tin to serve as a sink.

The realisation that there was no water tank drew a wail of dismay from Jessie. Manfully George tried to demonstrate how they could obtain water using a bucket on a wire, like a flying fox, that ran down to the creek, many metres below the house.

'Water for washing or laundry has to be heated on the wood stove,' George explained. Jessie shot George a sulky look, signifying there was no way she would be staying here for long. Edith realised with horror that her husband had invested her aunt's legacy in this shack that was to be their home. She vowed she would never forgive him. Uncle John Turner had been right: marrying a farmer who lacked foresight meant complete disaster. But memories of her own mother, whose scandalous divorce had been responsible for their emigration, meant that she would not risk her children's future at a time when the divorce laws would place them in their father's care.

3 RURAL POVERTY AT BOOLARA

*E*dith was only in her early twenties but she realised that the survival and education of her children rested on her.¹ George talked of big schemes but he was weak and a dreamer. Edith, the family 'beauty', who had married in haste due to pressure from her elder sister, now repented bitterly.

Joice's privileged early childhood had fallen from her like a snake sloughing its skin. She learned at an early age that to survive she must take her share of responsibility and hard work. Adversity would keep mother and daughter close.

Rain continued falling for the next month—so did Edith's spirits. Braving the rain, George built a chicken run. He traded a calf with a neighbour for some fluffy ducklings which the children loved. But within a few weeks foxes had eaten the chicks and ducklings that Edith valiantly attempted to raise.²

Edith struggled on bravely, doing all the cooking and washing. Her blonde curls were now a lank mess, her hands hardened and blistered, her clothes and shoes ruined by carrying buckets of water through the mud. The contrast between Queensland's tropical heat in a luxurious homestead and stark rural poverty in a bush hut in chilly damp Gippsland could not have been greater. Edith realised with horror that Boolara had become her prison. Loneliness, deprivation of the lifestyle she was used to, bouts of migraine and the constant rain that dripped from the surrounding trees finally wore her down. She burst into floods of tears and implored her husband to let them leave the property. She realised that Boolara was totally unsuitable for Geoff, whose asthma attacks made her desperate with worry that he might die without medical attention. The nearest doctor was a day's ride away on horseback. There was no form of communication with the outside world.

George kept up a brave face. 'Don't worry, old girl. Things will get better, I promise.'

'They could hardly get worse,' said Edith grimly. She knew her children depended on her remaining healthy enough to run the house and teach them their lessons.

'All Mother's forces went into the battle for our survival,' Joice wrote afterwards.

Finally the rain stopped. Joice and Geoff made excursions into the surrounding forest. Huge gums, fantastic tree ferns and flowering tea trees surrounded them. Joice adapted to the change in her life by creating a world of her own. To amuse Geoff she made up stories about two children called Robin and Cynthia, alter-egos of Geoff and herself.

Joice adored her little brother. Unlike most siblings, she and Geoff rarely argued—isolation and hardship drew them even closer together than before. In winter she would sit up with him night after night as he wheezed and coughed; at times it seemed as though he might stop breathing altogether. She heated water and brought him steaming bowls of Friar's Balsam to inhale, to ease the tightness in his chest. She had the born instincts of a nurse or doctor, consulting her mother's medical encyclopaedia in an attempt to help her brother.

George's brother-in-law Uncle Harry Mitchell, a Melbourne doctor, had given Edith some old medical books and a nursing manual he thought might be useful in the bush. Joice pored over these and set about disinfecting and bandaging the wounds of any Aboriginal children who came to the property. If the vet arrived to doctor a sick horse or cow she would watch him eagerly and ask questions. She watched her father deliver calves and helped him to treat wounds when sheep or cows cut themselves on wire fences, using iodine or powdered alum, an old bush remedy. In return he taught her to become an excellent rider so she could help round up the stock. Her father taught her to conquer fear by placing her on a wild horse who threw her off, and insisting she got back up again and again until she could master it.

Joice loved 'going bush' with Geoff. They took with them a tent, a billy-can of water, matches and potatoes to roast over a campfire. One day they tried to obtain honey from wild bees, as the Aborigines did, but were badly stung in the attempt.

When not roaming the bush with Geoff, helping her mother with cooking and housework or bottle-feeding sickly lambs and calves, Joice enjoyed nothing more than immersing herself in a book. 'Reading, always reading some damned book or other,' her father would complain testily.

Summer brought sweltering heat. Gradually the grass withered and died. The drought continued for two months and the stock suffered badly. The cattle and sheep began to die of hunger. Thousands of blowflies swarmed around the dead animals. The remaining calves and cows gathered around the shack lowing piteously. At night Joice covered her ears to avoid hearing their pathetic moans. When the drought finally broke half their stock had died. It was terrible for the children, who had to help their father to burn corpses of calves and lambs crawling with maggots.

Then George's elder brother Jack came to live with them at Boolara. Jack NanKivell, declared bankrupt at the same time as George, was still in trouble with his father over the matter of the forged cheque. He had been unable to find another job in these depression years of the 1890s, and in return for board and lodging had agreed to help George clear more land on Boolara. Sharing the overcrowded dirt-floored shack with Jack meant even more work for Edith and Joice, as well as Jessie, who was by now thoroughly discontented and planning to return home.

Edith was now convinced that living deep in Gippsland's forests placed Geoff's life at risk. She wanted to live somewhere that could offer the children the chance of a good education and the services of a doctor. How could she achieve this? She had no money of her own and no chances of earning any. As a married woman she had no legal rights. If she left George without his consent, the children were legally his and he had the right to keep them.

Jack NanKivell worried more about Edith's health and the conditions she was living in than her husband. Jack urged her to have a break with the children, to stay either with Thomas NanKivell in Melbourne or with Lily in Queensland. Edith obviously preferred to go to Queensland. She was only too happy to let George remain on the property with his brother. They seemed content enough, farming, riding and shooting being the only things they truly cared for. A long holiday away from Boolara was something she desperately needed and finally George agreed to pay their fares to Queensland.

Edith and the children spent the next ten months with Aunt Lily in Ipswich. After winters spent at chilly Boolara, Edith described Queensland as heaven. The sub-tropical climate suited her and Geoff and she dreamed of having enough money to rent a house in Brisbane and send Joice to a private school like Somerville House and Geoff to Brisbane Grammar School.

Lily had virtually 'pushed' Edith into becoming a teenage bride and marrying George, to get her off her hands. However, once Edith was married, Lily had felt twinges of jealousy of her more attractive younger sister playing the elegant hostess on a large plantation homestead, while she and her children lived in a variety of rented homes owned by the bank. Now their roles were reversed. Edith was once more penniless and homeless. She had dreamed of being a teacher but she lacked qualifications for paid work outside the home. Though she did not admit it to herself, Lily gained a sense of satisfaction from her younger sister's humiliation. Through no fault of their own, Edith and her children found themselves cast in the role of poor relations. Joice never had anything new and wore her cousins' cast-off clothes, often patched and mended. She made the best of it and refused to show that she minded. In fact she did not care much about clothes. Life in the bush had turned her into quite a tomboy, loathing the housework she was forced to do.

After ten months, repeated hints from Lily's husband forced Edith and the children to return home. She borrowed the money for her rail fare from her sister and returned to Boolara. She found the farm in even worse condition than before she left. After her stay in Lily's comfortable house it was extremely difficult for her to adapt once more to the primitive conditions at Boolara.

One day, George's uncle, Hugh NanKivell, arrived unannounced to inspect 'his' property and his stock. Edith, at the end of her tether, was faced with mounds of washing and ironing. With Geoff in the throes of an asthma attack she lost her normal self-control and told Hugh NanKivell exactly where he could put his poorly-paid job as farm manager *and* his 'pretty little farmhouse'.

The result of Edith's pent-up burst of rage was that soon afterwards, she and her children once again went to Queensland. This time she vowed that she would never return to Boolara. Realising that Edith was serious, Uncle Hugh took over George's share in the property and finally sold it to another unsuspecting victim.[3]

Once again George went off to the gold-fields at Kalgoorlie, but his luck was worse than ever. He nearly died there in a tented hospital after getting typhoid fever.

Uncle Hugh, feeling guilty, had written to Edith that he could buy another farm for them at Myaree, about 100 km from Wangaratta. Lily persuaded Edith to go back to Victoria and accept Uncle Hugh's offer. Although most apprehensive, Edith reluctantly agreed to a reconciliation with George and to give farming another try.

In many respects the farm at Myaree turned out to be worse than the one at Boolara. Once again they lived in a three-room shack with a dirt floor.[4] This time it was in rough, dry country infested with rabbits.

When Edith and the children arrived there the area was drought-stricken.

On the property the children found a gaunt old black horse with broken knees and a thin body scarred with years of misuse. She managed to survive the drought because Joice and Geoff took her water and fed her with apple cores and stale bread. That tired old horse they named Fan and she became their pride and joy. The locals whispered that Fan had once belonged to Ned Kelly. The children rode her bareback, using an old sack as a saddle. She could only amble along very slowly and after trotting she would have to rest for at least ten minutes. Fan accompanied them when, in search of pocket money from the Government's rabbit bounty, they went out to collect the carcasses of poisoned rabbits, often fly-blown and crawling with maggots. They carried the carcasses home in a bag slung round the horse's neck. Forty rabbit corpses delivered to their father meant a penny for each child.[5]

The heat was searing and bushfires a constant danger. One day the children were out collecting rabbits with Fan. She was having one of her enforced rests when they heard the sound of a horse galloping. Their father appeared and yelled 'Home immediately! *Fire!* ' Joice looked behind her and saw the sky dark with smoke.

'Leave that wretched horse. Cut along, quick smart,' their father ordered.

'We can't leave Fan. She won't move.'

'Go now! I'll look after her!'

The children ran home, stumbling over fallen branches. Fan stood where they had left her, head lowered in exhaustion, swishing away the flies with her tail. Joice thought the old horse would break into a trot once she saw the flames, follow her father's horse and be home before them.

As always Joice's first thoughts were not to alarm Geoff for fear of triggering an asthma attack. 'Fan must have come through lots of fires,' she said reassuringly. 'Dad'll see she gets home.'

Arriving exhausted at the clearing by their house they found Edith on the verge of tears, exhausted from calling them. Tongues of fire crackled around the fence that enclosed the vegetable garden and the rows of beehives. Neighbours tried to thrash out the licking flames with wet sacks. They saw frightened animals fleeing before the roaring fire deep in the bush. Their father arrived but there was no sign of poor Fan.

Joice announced she was going back to save her pet horse, but her father said it was impossible to risk one's life for an animal who, according to the Anglican church, lacked a soul. Furious, Joice started walking, insisting she was going back to save Fan. George rushed after Joice, picked her up, opened the door of the shack and locked her inside. Edith screamed at George to let her out, as the fire was now closing in on their house.

Once released, Joice helped her parents and the neighbours beat out the flames that threatened their wooden shack. The men wore damp sacks over their heads to prevent them from inhaling the smoke. Geoff burst into tears, imagining poor old Fan burning to death. His anxiety over Fan and the smoke which hovered over them brought on a bad attack of asthma. Joice held Geoff tight, terrified that he might die.

Once the flames had died away they found themselves in a blackened smoking world of charred tree stumps. A dozen exhausted men lounged in the shade of an iron shed. Only a few hundred yards of bush around the house had escaped. Two cows had burned to death as had countless wombats, koalas and other small animals. A couple of horses, the dogs, the pigs and even the poultry had survived. But Fan? Joice did not dare ask her father for fear of setting off Geoff's asthma again.

By unspoken agreement neither child mentioned dear old Fan's name again. From then on both NanKivell children avoided the place where their father had forced them to abandon her. George's broken promise and the horse's death in the bushfire revived Joice's hostility towards her father over Tinker's death.

The bushfire at Myaree was yet another nail in the coffin of the NanKivells' already rocky marriage. Edith could never forgive her husband that her children might have died in the bushfire. For the rest of her life she would maintain that if George had not arrived in the nick of time Joice and Geoff would have refused to leave Fan and burned to death.

Recriminations between husband and wife meant that the marriage went from bad to worse. George, with his eternal optimism, swore no bushfires would occur again. Edith no longer had any faith in him. Their marriage became a battleground, but divorce was still impossible. George started to drink and pretended that his bankruptcy had never happened. Joice took her mother's side, despising her father for being insensitive and impractical, breaking her mother's heart and her spirit. She continued to help her father with farm work during the day but communication was strained between them. At night by the light of an oil lamp she would read. She decided she would study hard and become a doctor.

In contrast Geoff never opened a book and was determined to work on the land. He had no interest in anything else. But Edith wanted Joice to get an education, some qualifications and, if possible, go to work in England and marry someone with money who could give her a decent life. She feared that if Joice stayed on the farm, she might fall in love with a bushman and marry him, never escaping from the backbreaking work and rural poverty that she saw among their poorer neighbours in the bush.

George laughed at Edith's ambitions. He said that his father had paid for 'a good education' for all the NanKivell boys, but education had done him and his brothers no good at all—most of them were bankrupt. Farming was quite good enough for his son and his daughter. Joice would marry a farmer and settle down.

Thanks to Edith and Joice's gardening skills and frugality, the family managed to live cheaply off their own vegetables, rabbits George trapped or shot and their own mutton and corned beef which Joice and Edith salted down. Joice kept bees which provided them with honey and in summer they collected wild pigweed to add to salads. The grocer with his horse and cart arrived every second month with dry goods, but some neighbours had a distressing way of arriving just before the grocer's visits when food supplies were low.

One evening, as the NanKivells were sitting down to a dinner of stewed rabbit, home-grown carrots and roast potatoes, the McGregors arrived in a wagonette drawn by thoroughbred horses. The McGregors were prosperous neighbours with pretensions to gentility. They were wearing their Sunday best while the NanKivells were in their patched and faded working clothes. George had sat down to dinner in a shirt with a frayed collar and an old tweed jacket with holes in the elbows. He was no longer the well-dressed young planter. He wore his old clothes day in and day out, shaved rarely and with a growth of stubble hated meeting his more prosperous neighbours, aware that they gossiped about his bankruptcy and his disastrous attempt at cane farming. He knew only too well that the McGregors would gossip about finding Mr and Mrs George NanKivell, once so rich, in old clothes without a crumb in the larder for visitors.

'The McGregors!' George's tone showed his anxiety at being caught dressed like a tramp. 'Good God! They'll think us as poor as we really are'. He disappeared into the bedroom. After a frenzied hunt through the wardrobe he emerged in what had once been his best coat, now green with mould around the shoulders, and a white shirt with a stiff collar.

Their larder was bare of anything suitable for guests. All Edith could offer the McGregors was the food she had served out onto the children's plates. She tipped her children's rabbit and potatoes back onto the serving dishes, then gently pushed Joice and Geoff outside and told them to wait in the kitchen. She had no time to change. She patted her hair, took off her long white apron and followed George outside as he greeted their guests.

'My dear Mrs McGregor! Such a pleasure. You'll stay to dinner? The children? Oh, they had theirs long ago. They get hungry early, you know.'

Meanwhile Joice and Geoff were ravenous. In the kitchen they raided the meat safe covered in sacking and helped themselves to slices of bread and dripping, followed by a dessert of bread and treacle and drank black tea which had been stewing on the hob for hours. In the dining room with its dirt floor Mr and Mrs McGregor dined off the children's portions of rabbit stew and drank some of Edith's homemade elderberry wine in crystal glasses which had once adorned her beautiful dining table at Farnham.[6]

Joice was given a fox terrier puppy for her birthday. It almost broke her heart when Foxy went missing and she discovered he had eaten poisoned rabbit bait. Despite her frantic efforts to save little Foxy, he died writhing in convulsions. She sobbed her heart out and buried him under a gum tree close to the house. After that she only had cats as pets; her love for them would stay with her all her life.

Whenever Joice or Geoff needed a dentist or a doctor they had to go with their mother to Melbourne. They took the tram to visit their favourite uncle, Dr Harry Mitchell, married to George's sister Lena. To Aunt Lena's despair, Dr Harry was so kind-hearted he would not charge his patients if he thought they could not afford to pay him. Uncle Harry would examine Geoff's wheezing chest through his stethoscope, shake his head and then proffer wise counsel that Geoff was over the worst.

Edith had her own health problems to cope with. One day she and Joice visited the consulting rooms of an uncle by marriage, the famous Sir Charles Ryan, who felt sorry for Edith's changed circumstances and did not charge her a consultation fee. They were invited to a meal at the Ryans' Toorak mansion, where Joice was given cast-off clothes and shoes from Sir Charles Ryan's daughter, Maie. Instead of being friendly,

Cousin Maie, who was not as pretty as Joice, was both competitive and snobbish, only too aware of the difference in their social positions.

Subtly Maie made Joice feel that she and her parents were only entertaining their 'poor relations' out of Christian charity. Small wonder that Joice heartily disliked Cousin Maie and her cold-hearted snobbish mother. Maie, urged on by her mother, would take her cousin up to her bedroom to show off her wardrobe of new clothes and sort out some old ones that might fit Joice.

The girls were approaching puberty. Both showed great promise and would make their mark on the world: Maie as a diplomat's wife and outstanding hostess as well as a painter and an author—Joice as a author and humanitarian worker. However, in spite of their childhood association they would never be friends. Maie's mother boasted to Edith that when Maie turned seventeen, her husband would pay to rent a house in Mayfair for the London season so that her daughter could have a grand coming-out ball. She would be presented at Court by her Great Aunt Ada, who had married into the British aristocracy. Maie's future was glittering.[7] Unable to reply, Edith, 'the poor relation' stayed silent.

Joice did not enjoy the role of Cinderella in which Sir Charles and Lady Ryan and their spoiled daughter had cast her. She vowed to herself that instead of aiming to marry for money and social position, like Cousin Mae, she would somehow or other gain entry to Melbourne University and become either a doctor or a writer.

4 THE WILD COLONIAL GIRL

It became evident that Edith's grandiose plans of university for Geoff and a 'coming out' season in London for Joice were totally unrealistic. As an undischarged bankrupt George could not even borrow money for boarding and school fees for his children, let alone the cost of sending his daughter overseas. Yet Edith kept warning her son and daughter over and over again about the hazards of farming in Australia. She was so worried about Joice's future that she supervised her daughter's education herself. Obviously it was haphazard, consisting mainly of reading books they had salvaged from the library at Farnham. Fortunately, a positive influence on Joice's future came from Aunt Ellis Rowan. Unlike some of George and Edith's relatives, Aunt Ellis did not ignore the NanKivells in their rural poverty. She was sympathetic. Her own life had changed drastically after her husband died and her parents lost most of their money in the 1890s bank crash. In her quest for new wildflowers to paint, she came to stay with Edith and George several times, putting up with all the discomforts of bush life at Myaree.

Ellis was proud of her two intelligent nieces, Maie Ryan and Joice NanKivell, but was particularly fond of Joice. She saw in this hardworking, talented girl something of herself when young, and she invited Joice for a lengthy stay with her and her unmarried sister Blanche at Derriweit Heights, high on the slopes of Mount Macedon. The house was surrounded by landscaped grounds filled with rare plants imported from many different countries by their father, Harry Ryan.

Joice had always admired Aunt Ellis, who was now in her sixties. She found her appearance unusual, describing her brilliant red hair as 'raddled with henna'. Ellis Rowan had had a face-lift during one of her trips around America, carried out in the early days of plastic surgery and it had given her beautiful elfin face a mask-like quality, emphasised by her liberal use of *poudre de riz*. In spite of her reduced finances, Aunt Ellis was always immaculately dressed, usually in white, her tiny waist circled with a coloured sash.

Joice described Aunt Ellis as 'positive and energetic'. She wrote: 'She could tell a good story better than most, and, while she has been accused of exaggeration, I am convinced that Aunt Ellis firmly believed everything she said. She was a thin wisp of a woman; neck and waist about the same size, red hair swept back from a startlingly dead-white face; penetrating eyes pricked into it. There was wit and power in that face.'[1]

Ellis saw literary promise in both Joice NanKivell and Maie Ryan and encouraged both girls in their ambition to become writers. She suggested that when Joice was old enough she might write her biography.

Surviving genteel poverty and keeping up appearances formed another bond between Aunt Ellis and Joice and her family. And Ellis frankly confided to Joice that her marriage to Captain Frederick Ryan had often been 'boring' and that one way of escaping from what she called her 'matrimonial duties', had been to tour Australia and paint wildflowers. Ellis took Joice seriously and treated her like an adult. She inspired in her favourite niece a desire to travel in foreign lands and earn her living by writing about them. Joice loved staying at the cottage at Derriweit Heights. Aunt Blanche cooked her special meals and made a great fuss of her, while Aunt Ellis raised Joice's self-esteem, giving her the impression that a woman, if she set her mind to it, could do what she wanted in life.

In addition to her skills as a painter, Ellis had published two books, one about her travels around Queensland in search of wildflowers, the second a children's book about Bill Bailey, her pet bandicoot. Joice learned a vital lesson from Aunt Ellis about story-telling: that a simple recitation of everyday doings is not enough to hold the attention of the reader. For a story to be successful, the minutiae of real life must be condensed and the point of the story made vivid. It was a lesson she never forgot.

Joice would eventually become just as good a raconteur as her aunt. Like Ellis Rowan, in later life Joice never worried about embroidering an adventure in order to make a good story better. By sheer force of personality both had the ability to create excitement around them. The happy times Joice spent at Derriweit made a huge contrast to the situation at Myaree, where she was witness to bitter arguments and recriminations between her parents. At other times George and Edith did not speak to each other for days on end. Joice's father hoped to redeem himself by succeeding on the land through hard work. His sole topics of conversation were sheep, cattle and crops. Edith hated bush life. She also deplored the way George regarded his children as cheap labour, using Joice to collect poisoned rabbits, move stock and mend fences.

After one particularly severe dust storm in which the family huddled inside the old wooden shack, which rattled and strained under the onslaught, letting in clouds of dirt through the cracks, Edith made up her mind to leave George again. She had received some money from sympathetic Aunt Ethel Lawson, who was also worried about the children's education. And Uncle John Turner, fearing his niece and nephew would grow up to be a 'savages', sent money as well. This meant that Edith was able to take Joice and Geoff to Melbourne, and at last send both of them to private schools.

They found pleasant lodgings at Brighton Beach, where Joice attended a small private school for girls.[2] She loved Brighton, the beach and pier and the excitement of living where there were shops and libraries. Joice, now in her early teens, was a pretty girl with a peaches-and-cream complexion, dark gold ringlets and hazel eyes, still happiest of all with her nose in a book. At school she wore a straw boater, a white muslin dress and black stockings. She excelled in English literature and composition. Like most adolescent girls, she soon acquired a best friend with whom she shared confidences. Estelle Simson lived at *Trawalla*, close to Thomas NanKivell's Toorak mansion. The two girls would remain friends for the rest of their lives.

Lacking Joice's application and intelligence, Geoff did not do well at his school and experienced reading difficulties. Edith and Joice had to give him special coaching in the evenings.

After school both children returned home through the grounds of Bolton Hall, former home of the Australian poet Adam Lindsay Gordon. At twilight, returning from the beach where the poet had committed suicide in a fit of depression, along an avenue of gigantic pines Geoff would tease Joice by pretending he could see his ghost. 'Don't you see him, there, over there! The gun's about to go off!' Joice would catch her breath in horror, then run as fast as she could until she reached their boarding house, with Geoff hard on her heels.

Grandfather NanKivell sometimes brought his yacht to Brighton and took his grandchildren sailing. He cannot have failed to realise just how little money Edith had to live on and educate the children but offered no financial help at all. However, he promised that his grandchildren would be 'looked after' when he died—a false promise, as it turned out. Thomas NanKivell died when Joice was in her twenties, leaving very little money to any of his nine children or numerous grandchildren and passing on his remaining money to his wife, who in turn left most of it to her relatives, the Murrays.

Joice and Geoff were occasionally invited to play with their cousin Maie Ryan, but relations between Joice and Maie did not improve on further acquaintance.

Edith's departure from the isolation of Myaree finally made George NanKivell consider his priorities. He released the extent to which loneliness and overwork had sapped Edith's strength and how she hated living away from civilisation. Desperately lonely without his family, he decided he must consider the children's education and Edith's failing health and swallow his pride. He knew he must leave Myaree in order to save his marriage. He had heard that a suitable property was for sale near Drouin, much closer to Melbourne than Myaree. There was a large cherry orchard on the property, and the house had running water and an indoor toilet. George borrowed money from Edith's uncle for a deposit, so that he could purchase the farm on a mortgage. He begged Edith to return with the children. Finally, her money running out and with the promise of a school nearby—the property was some seven kilometres from the small town of Drouin, which had a school, a doctor, a church and a few shops—Edith relented, and the family resettled itself yet again.

In winter, their boots heavy with mud, Joice and Geoff walked to the township each day in wind and rain. At the back of the schoolroom a sulky fire spluttered feebly. The children's fingers turned purple with cold and their breath hung like mist on the chill air. In summer, the classroom became so hot that some children fainted.[3]

Most of the pupils came to school on horseback. These farm children left school when they were twelve to work on the land. Joice, aged fourteen, was the oldest pupil. In return for acting as a school monitor or unpaid teacher's aid her school fees were waived. She was responsible for filling the inkwells, keeping order and helping teach the younger children to read and write. The overworked teacher found Joice 'the best pupil she had ever taught'. But Joice found no replacement for Estelle, her best friend. Instead, she and Geoff remained tightly bonded together, existing in their own world to survive the harshness of rural life at Drouin.

Edith worried that during the bleak Victorian winter a journey of twenty kilometres twice a day over muddy tracks was too much for them. She was distressed when Geoff developed chilblains, cold sores and a constant hacking cough.

Geoff told his mother that he hated school and wanted to leave. In desperation Edith sent a letter to Uncle John Turner, who once more saved the day by sending enough money for Geoff to attend a boarding school in Brisbane, where he and his wife, Aunt Ada, could keep an eye on him.

Edith did not want Joice to walk to school every day by herself, even though she was now fifteen. She arranged for Joice to join in classes given by the governess who taught the daughters of the Campbells, a family of wealthy graziers. This was far less expensive than sending her to a private girls' school and ensured she received intensive tuition from an excellent teacher—a niece of Vida Goldstein, the celebrated feminist. The governess always stressed that women's brains were as good as those of any man (contrary to the theories of Dr Henry Maudsley, the founder of a famous London psychiatric hospital).

Joice missed her brother desperately. She found she had very little in common with the Campbell girls, who talked only of attending balls and meeting eligible young men. This meant that Joice was given virtually one-to-one tuition by that rarity in this era, a woman graduate, who was able to educate Joice to the standard required for matriculation, a necessary qualification for entry to university. But George refused, or did not have the means, to pay university fees for Joice—and at a period when university places for females were very limited, there were no scholarships available.

Mr North, their nearest neighbour, recognised Joice's love of words and talent for writing. He himself loved books and gave Joice the run of his library. She devoured everything: Thackeray, Dickens, histories, biographies . . . She wrote that 'his library provided me with hours of pleasure. He made me see human relations with new eyes'. Mr North had a soft spot for Edith and warned Joice: 'Leave Drouin. If you don't, the tremendous sacrifice your mother has made for you will be wasted.'

Alexander Cameron Macdonald, the famous surveyor and geographer, was living in retirement on a property close to Drouin. A Fellow of the Royal Geographical Society, he was head of its Victorian branch. He was a recognised authority on Australian place-names and customs, and spoke several Aboriginal dialects. Joice loved to listen to his fund of stories. Mr Macdonald also urged Joice to leave Drouin; if she could not go to university, he advised her to take a typing course and try to obtain work on a newspaper so she could escape from her burden of farm work. She now rose each morning at six, fed the hens, tended the beehives and worked in the vegetable garden before helping Edith with household chores. Then she would mount her horse and go off to help her father.

Geoff came home from Brisbane for most of his school holidays. Together they would clean out the watering troughs, maintain windmills, round up flocks and trim and dress fly-infected sheep. They would move the sheep from one paddock to another on horseback. Joice, as a first-rate horsewoman, could handle many of the tasks normally given to a stockman. Whenever Edith was well enough she would help Joice cook dinner on the wood-fired stove. Their only means of refrigeration was a Coolgardie safe, a box covered in hessian which dripped with water. After dinner, if any of the livestock were sick or having trouble calving, Joice and George would take oil lamps and go out to attend to them.

There was no electricity on the property. Joice trimmed the wicks of oil lamps and made slush lamps that reeked of mutton fat. Each Monday she and her mother heated water in buckets on top of the wood-fired stove for the weekly wash, boiling the sheets and white garments in the copper and scrubbing coloureds by hand. If the weather was fine everything was hung outside to dry. On Tuesday they did the ironing, using flat-irons heated on top of the stove. Wednesday and Thursday were for roasting meat and baking, mainly scones and pound cakes. The following day they made meat pies from left-overs. There were no shops close by if they ran out of essentials. Joice collected honey in the comb from her beehives and eggs from the fowls, and she and her mother made all their own bread and churned butter.

There was rarely money available to pay a vet. With the aid of an old veterinary manual Joice helped her father to doctor sick animals, splint broken limbs and help cows or ewes having difficulty in labour.

Both she and Geoff had been taught to be self-reliant. Joice hated so much of nature's cruelty that surrounded them: the slow, horrific deaths of their cows and sheep in times of drought; in spring, finding sick lambs with their eyes picked out by crows, which caused her to weep over them. Her life revolved around the land; her only escape was reading. With Geoff beside her, the back-breaking work had often seemed like an adventure. Left alone with her short-tempered father, who issued orders like a general, it was sheer drudgery.

Their horses, Nugget, Miner and Peggy, were not as fast as they had been. If they had to go for the doctor it was a half-day's ride there and back. There was no chance of connection to a telephone line, even if they could have afforded it. They had no radio either—they were still very isolated.

Joice, who longed to return to Melbourne to work or study, could not leave her mother with all the work and escape from Drouin as Mr North and Mr Macdonald urged her to do. The years wore on. In 1910 Joice was twenty-three and feared her youth was slipping away. She was still helping her parents run the house and doing the farm chores, receiving no money for all her hard work. She was desperate to escape from Drouin. Shortly after Geoff left his Brisbane boarding school, he went to work as a jackeroo on a large cattle property in central Queensland which belonged to Edith's wealthy relations, the Stuarts.

Inspired by the financial success of Aunt Ellis Rowan's book about her pet bandicoot, Joice planned to write a children's book herself and make enough money to leave home and pay someone else to live in and help her parents. Aunt Ellis told her that many Australian children's books sold well in Britain as well as Australia.

Illustrated fantasy books such as those of the talented sisters Ida Rentoul Outhwaite and Annie Rentoul (an outstanding graduate of the University of Melbourne) were very popular. In those early years of the twentieth century, middle-class parents lived in a relatively secure world; they were charmed by these large-format illustrated books containing stories about elves, fairies and well-behaved children. To fit the pattern, Joice plotted a story about two children who climb a cobweb ladder and find a fantasy world. Her only free time for writing was at night. Whenever she was not too tired she would sit up in bed working on this book, which she wrote out in longhand on blocks of cheap writing paper.

Fortunately George was preoccupied with making money from grandiose but impractical farming schemes; he still dreamed that one day a combination of good ideas and hard work would make them rich again. Unfortunately, his schemes failed one after another, largely due to floods, bushfires, drought and other disasters. Stone fruit was the only thing that seemed to make money for them at Drouin. Cherries made money, provided George did not have to employ paid labourers to pick them. Instead he depended on free labour from his family. Cherry picking season after season and packing the boxes to send to the city was exhausting work for Joice and Edith. Every year George prayed for a good harvest, but Joice hoped it would be meagre: the back-breaking work took a heavy toll on her and her mother.

During the summer, Dr Harry Mitchell, Aunt Lena's long-suffering husband, would spend part of his annual holidays on the NanKivells' farm. He had been the Government's Chief Medical Officer in New Guinea and was used to operating and improvising under difficult circumstances. He admired his niece for the calm way in which she treated sick animals and coped with her mother's migraines and bouts of depression. He taught Joice the basic principles of medicine and human anatomy and gave her a manual of home surgery. He and Joice were the best of friends, but Uncle Harry had little time for George.

NanKivell, regarding him as a hopeless failure. Whenever he stayed with them he would volunteer his services as a surgeon to local people free of charge, with Joice acting as his medical orderly. She assisted her uncle for the first time when he performed an emergency operation without anaesthetic on a screaming baby whose fingers had been jammed in a door; they had turned black with gangrene. Joice covered the dining table with a sheet and hung more sheets over the door, all soaked in disinfectant. Calmly she helped Uncle Harry sterilise his instruments and passed them to him one by one as he amputated the child's fingers, watching his skilful work with interest.

Under his tuition she stitched up cows wounded on barbed wire and helped him set broken legs. 'My young medical orderly,' Uncle Harry would call her with pride. Unlike her mother and Aunt Lena, who fainted at the sight of blood, operating techniques fascinated Joice. She enjoyed learning how the human body worked and still cherished the hope that one day she too might become a doctor. But Uncle Harry warned her that even if she could find the money to enter the Medical Faculty of the University of Melbourne, she, like other female graduates, would come up against a wall of prejudice against women doctors.

Due to a combination of monotonous diet, overwork and worry about the future, Joice became seriously run-down. When Uncle Harry arrived for his annual holiday in the bush, he took one look at her and told her she badly needed a holiday, and warned George that Joice had taken on far too much responsibility for a girl of her age. He prescribed a break away from farm work, saying 'It would do Joice good to see another side of life'.

George NanKivell's sister, Aunt Lena Mitchell, had rented a house in Launceston for the summer, hoping her rather homely teenage daughters would have a chance to meet eligible young men there. At that time Tasmania was one of the richest states in Australia. At her husband's instigation she wrote to Edith, inviting Joice for three months and offering to pay her boat and rail fare to Tasmania. Faced with Dr Harry's diagnosis, George did not object to his daughter having a cost-free holiday with Aunt Lena and her cousins.

Joice was now twenty-four, with dark-blonde hair, large expressive eyes and an attractive figure. However, both Aunt Lena and Aunt Lily thought that it would not be long before Joice was past marriageable age and 'on the shelf'. Joice herself was well aware that her meddlesome aunts hoped to find her a 'suitable' husband . . . just as Aunt Lily had found one for her mother. But Joice was older and wiser than Edith had been—she was determined to marry for love or else remain single.

Joice took the steamer to Launceston, where she was met by Aunt Lena. Her aunt took one horrified look at her niece, seeing a 'wild colonial girl', clad in unfashionable clothes. As Joice had nothing suitable to wear to the round of dances and tea-parties to which her cousins were invited, Aunt Lena gave her a lecture on the importance of wearing 'good' clothes. Not wanting her niece to disgrace her cousins at debutante functions, she bought Joice a smart jacket and matching ankle-length skirt for daytime events, an afternoon frock in pale rose silk for tea-parties and a white net ball gown, long white kid gloves and a silk evening bag for debutante balls.

In Tasmania's restricted and snobbish old-money society, Joice saw a totally different way of life. At that time Australia still lived off the sheep's back, and some of the snobbish Tasmanian squattocracy possessed considerable fortunes. Convinced the good times would last forever, they enjoyed spending their money among their own kind.

At dances and parties to which Joice accompanied her debutante cousins, Dorothy and Eleanor Mitchell, she realised that this was the kind of life she would have had if the NanKivell fortunes had not been lost. But beneath her elegant clothes and new hair-style, Joice remained at heart a bush girl—one dedicated to writing and acquiring an education. Dorothy and Eleanor never opened a book. They talked only of the ball gowns they would wear and who their dancing partners would be. Clothes meant little to Joice; she had never had either the time or the money to fuss about her own appearance. Despite her awareness of the facts of life from medical books and the animals she had tended, Joice was very innocent about men. Most of the young men she had known had been itinerant labourers who came begging for work on their farm. Now she found herself exposed to what was in effect a marriage market, where at dances and parties carefully selected young girls from 'good' families met wealthy young men. Most mothers hoped their daughters would be engaged to an eligible man by the end of the summer season.

To Joice's surprise, she discovered that in her white ball gown, with her hair expertly styled by Cousin Dorothy, men found her attractive. However, the 'eligibles' who marked her dance card and whirled her round the floor soon discovered that in spite of her ready repartee, Joice was more serious than the debutantes they normally mixed with.

Joice was invited to balls and tea-parties at some of Tasmania's most beautiful Georgian homesteads. At the tea-parties mothers discussed arrangements for the dinners that took place before the formal dances. As tea was poured from silver teapots and cucumber sandwiches handed round, Joice realised that most of these wealthy young girls dreamed only of being the belle of the ball, finding a 'suitable' husband and bearing and raising children. She found the Tasmanian squattocracy snobbish, preoccupied with status symbols, sheep, family bloodlines and inheritances. Aunt Lena and her daughters were accepted in this close-knit society because Uncle Harry's family, the Mitchells, were important pastoralists in New South Wales.

Aunt Lena warned Joice not to discuss books she had read or show the young men who flocked round her that she had ideas of her own. 'Men prefer women who are good listeners,' Aunt Lena insisted. It was whispered among the mothers that poor Joice NanKivell's father had gone bankrupt and Thomas NanKivell had so many children there was scant chance Joice would inherit what remained of his fortune. It was conceded that Miss NanKivell's looks and bubbly personality might find her a husband of sorts, but not a really good 'catch'.

These same mothers were taken aback when the supremely eligible Percy B, son and heir of one of Tasmania's oldest landowning families, fell head over heels in love with Joice. Initially Joice believed Percy, whom she considered excessively boring, was pursuing her cousin Dorothy as his visits to Aunt Lena's house increased. The Mitchell girls were not allowed to be left unchaperoned with a young man. Together with Joice, they had to sit in the elegant drawing room of the colonial home Aunt Lena had rented, making strained conversation. It took some time for Joice to realise that she was in fact the subject of Percy's interest.[4]

His feelings were definitely not reciprocated by Joice. He and his circle enjoyed racing, rugger and rowing. They annoyed Joice with their loud, braying laughs and their talk of shooting which she had loathed ever since the tragic duck shoot at Farnham, when Tinker, the little Aboriginal boy, had died so tragically.

Whenever they met at debutante functions, Percy's mother, who was 'bringing out' her own daughter that season, was markedly cold to

Aunt Lena and Joice. Mrs B (this is how Joice referred to the Tasmanian family in her memoirs, preferring not to disclose their full name), was greatly miffed by the discovery that little Miss Nobody from Nowhere had enslaved her son, one of Tasmania's most eligible bachelors. She regarded Joice as a fortune hunter.

For her part, Joice was not at all impressed by the fact that Percy's family was one of the oldest in Tasmania with broad acres and a very large fortune. Like Mr Darcy in *Pride and Prejudice*, Percy refused to believe that Joice could not appreciate how lucky she was that he had shown interest in her, someone with no money and no social position.

At the ball held at the Bs' convict-built Georgian house for Percy's sister, Aunt Lena insisted that Joice should accept Percy's invitation to have the last waltz with him. He promptly waltzed Joice into the flower-filled conservatory and proposed marriage. She was too kind-hearted to say she found him physically repellent. Percy, heir to vast wealth, whose every wish had always been granted, refused to take 'no' for an answer and continued to declare his love. Finally Joice had had enough. She told Percy she did not love him and would only marry for love. When Percy attempted to blackmail her into marriage by swearing he would throw himself into the sea at the Blow Hole, a famous cliff top landmark, if she did not marry him, she did not take him seriously. The next moment Percy rushed out of the conservatory and disappeared into the night.

His flight inspired a stampede amongst Tasmania's bright young things to the Blow Hole, which Joice described as 'the perfect place to end your life in a spectacular manner. Perched on the brink of the gigantic hole through which waves pounded, thrown up from the depths below, there on the brink neatly placed side by side were Percy's black patent dancing pumps. Aunt Lena was aghast. The moonlit setting was like something out of a Romantic painting. Gigantic waves pounded through the hole in the rock. The youth and beauty of Launceston shuddered at what might have happened to poor Percy'. Public feeling was against Joice. Hissed comments surrounded her. Aunt Lena burst into tears as the police arrived and collected the dancing shoes. Then Joice caught sight of Cedric, Percy B's small brother, roaring with laughter. She pointed him out and two of Percy's rowing friends pounced on him. Cedric's giggles turned to tears as the truth was shaken out of him. Percy had told him to place the shoes there while he went home to bed. Public opinion swung to Joice's side. 'What a shabby trick,' someone said.

But the next day Aunt Lena was furious. She pointed out that Joice was reaching an age when very few men would want to marry her because she would soon be past the age doctors considered it 'safe' to have her first child. Her aunt rhapsodised about the pleasant life her niece would have if she married Percy, living in a beautiful colonial mansion with thoroughbred horses to ride, tours overseas, servants, beautiful clothes and jewels—all the good things in life. She urged Joice to give Percy a second chance. 'Do you really want to finish up an old maid?' Aunt Lena demanded.

'Percy's face reminds me of that foetus in a bottle Uncle Harry keeps in his surgery,' her niece retorted. 'Besides, he can't be a nice person if he pulls a stunt like that one. I've absolutely no intention of selling myself for money, if that's what you're getting at. If I can't become a doctor, then I'll support myself by writing.'

Joice refused to attend any more dances and spent her time reading every book she could lay hands on.

Aunt Lena worked herself into a fury of rage and frustration. She came into the library, wrenching the book Joice was reading out of her hand. 'If ever there's a girl going nowhere it's you, Joice NanKivell,' she told her niece through gritted teeth. 'Think of your poor mother. Do you want to spend the rest of your life in poverty?' 'Rather an old maid in a hovel than a loveless marriage,' Joice replied with conviction, remembering the story of how Aunt Lily had virtually forced her mother into a 'brilliant' marriage.

By now Joice's refusal of Tasmania's most eligible bachelor was the chief subject of gossip amongst the debutantes' mothers. Aunt Lena feared that Joice's 'modern' ideas about female independence and her notoriety following events at the Blow Hole might jeopardise Dorothy and Eleanor's marriage prospects. It was high time her niece returned to Drouin.

'You'll go to the dogs if you carry on like this,' was her aunt's parting shot. She dumped Joice and her suitcase beside the gangplank of the Melbourne ferry and instructed the hansom cab to drive away again without bothering to bid her niece goodbye.

5   'THE COBWEB LADDER'

On her return to Drouin, Joice was delighted to find Geoff sitting at the kitchen table having a cup of tea with Edith and Aunt Lily, who was there on a visit.

George, who imagined that Geoff had returned to help on the property, came in, pulled off his muddy boots and joined them. He exploded with rage when he learned his son and heir was planning to spend only two weeks at home before returning to central Queensland, where he was enjoying his work as a jackeroo. The fact that Uncle Herbert Stuart's vast cattle property was doing so well, while George's small farm paid badly, made his father even angrier. He told Geoff he should stay and help build up Drouin, which he would eventually inherit. To lure him back, George made Geoff an offer of a half-share in the property right away.

'Thanks, Dad, but I prefer working for Uncle Herbert,' Geoff told him. 'Besides, the Queensland climate suits me better.'

A heated argument ensued about the duties of an only son to his family. It ended with Geoff telling his father he refused to spend the rest of his life on 'a struggling farm in the middle of bloody nowhere'. George stormed out of the room, banging the door.

Joice remembered how, as children, she and Geoff used to plan how they could get away from the drudgery of working for their father. George, locked in his failed dreams, had become increasingly demanding. Nothing his family did seemed to please him.

Geoff confided to Joice and Edith that once he had finished jackerooing for Uncle Herbert and saved some money, he would train as a wool classer in Queensland. Wool classing was a well-paid job with no academic requirements and offered a lifestyle he was sure he would enjoy. Joice and Edith were pleased that he now had a chance to make some sort of life for himself, but sad that Geoff saw his future in Queensland rather than Victoria. Geoff told them that the Stuart cousins employed two Aboriginal maids, a Chinese cook and a butler in their large homestead. After work the family always changed into evening dress for dinner, served by the uniformed maids.[1] Joice made up her mind that as soon as she had money she would buy Geoff some good shirts to replace the ones she and Edith had made for him out of striped mattress ticking.

Life at Drouin was certainly different to Geoff's descriptions of life on the cattle station. At Drouin meals were usually taken in the kitchen. George rarely grunted a word to either Joice or Edith, who had acquired the habit of eating with books open in front of them. Edith wished it were possible for Joice to escape their rural drudgery. But with shearers and harvesters to feed in the season, this was clearly impossible. Edith longed for George to abandon his dream of establishing a large mixed farm. A small place in the country with a few cattle and chickens was all she dreamed of now.

Joice had worked for her father for more than ten years without receiving pay or even pocket-money. It was regarded as the duty of an eldest daughter to stay home and help her parents. Not until the upheaval and carnage of World War I had ended did women obtain a measure of independence.

Farm work had always been hard. At Drouin, without Geoff doing his share, it became overwhelming. Fortunately, Joice was strong and active. She rose before sunrise to milk cows, feed hens and tend sick lambs. She was still working by ten at night, kneading dough for bread and churning butter. The only paid help her father could afford were gangs of itinerant men, some of them petty criminals, who travelled the country looking for work at harvest time. Joice had to brew beer for harvesters and shearers; in the dirt-floored larder, four barrels of beer were always kept cool beneath damp sacks. Harvest and shearing time meant heavy additions to the normal workload.

Joice described with despair how 'only lion-hearted women could exist on an Australian farm in those days. Bitter toil for women like us who fed itinerant farm labourers.[2] They expected a meat and vegetable breakfast at daylight; a mid-morning "smoko" of scones and butter, tea and cakes, a three course lunch, (which they called dinner) of roast home-grown mutton, gravy and roast potatoes from the garden. Then came afternoon tea with more scones, sandwiches, cakes and huge cups of tea. The harvesters (and shearers when they were necessary) would work till dark when we were expected to supply a supper of cold roast meat or meat pies, vegetables, boiled eggs followed by suet pudding and treacle and vast quantities of bread, butter, jam and cheese. To wash it all down the men had home-made hop beer and huge jugs of oatmeal water, flavoured with lemon'.[3] After serving the food, clearing away and washing up, Joice and Edith would fall into bed exhausted.

Joice's only relaxation was to escape into her own private world by writing. By this time she had finished her children's book, which she called *The Cobweb Ladder* and had sent the manuscript to the Lothian Book Publishing Company in Melbourne without telling her father; he had always jeered at her poems, and she knew he would mock her ambition to become a published writer. When she wasn't too exhausted she would still settle down to write short stories or poems, or read herself to sleep by the light of an oil lamp. Her mother encouraged her but her father continually sneered at her poems, describing them as 'jingles'. Defiantly Joice adopted her father's disparaging term and made it her own, filling notebooks with 'jingles'. They, together with her short stories and projected book, were the only things that kept her going through the monotony of farm and domestic chores. She used to recite poetry to herself as she worked.

Gradually Joice took on most of her mother's workload as well as nursing her. Edith's migraines were becoming more and more frequent; she often spent days at a time in a darkened bedroom. Joice consulted Uncle Harry's battered two volume-copy of *The Complete and Concise Companion to Medicine*, but there seemed little she could do to help restore her mother's fading health. Knowing George could not afford to send Edith away to convalesce, John Turner paid for his niece and great-niece to holiday at a small boarding house at Lakes Entrance, and Aunt Lily volunteered to come and keep house for George, though she would never contemplate tackling Joice's workload.

Joice was delighted by Lakes Entrance and the Pacific surf that thundered ashore onto white sand. She was as fearless in the water as she was everywhere else. Although it was not considered 'nice' for girls to surf, Joice managed to persuade some of the local boys to teach her at Ninety Mile Beach. This was a holiday that made Joice wish that someday she might live beside the sea.

Together mother and daughter visited an Aboriginal Mission on Lake Tyres. Remembering Tinker, her childhood playmate, Joice observed with sadness how the mission Aborigines had become alienated from their own culture. Many were part-Aboriginal 'stolen children' taken away from their mothers by force, re-christened and taught to read and write basic English, clean houses and sing hymns. She learned that every few months the Aborigines would refuse to eat the Mission food. They would slip away into the bush and live on what they gathered, just as their forefathers had done. Throwing off their clothes they hunted for birds' eggs in woven canoes, fished, stripped the bark from the trees in search of witchety grubs, and roasted snakes and goannas over their campfires.

At Lakes Entrance Edith gradually became stronger and recovered her spirits. But finally John Turner's money ran out and they had to return to Drouin. In Joice's absence George had been forced to employ a man to do her share of work on the farm. The whole experience had taught him a lesson and he now decided that a smaller farm might eventually be a good idea.

Joice was overjoyed to find a letter from the Lothian Publishing Company awaiting her at home, accepting the manuscript she had sent them. The editor explained that they had sent away her manuscript to two assessors. Both had found the subject matter and the writing delightful and were sure *The Cobweb Ladder* would be a great success for the Christmas children's market. Lothian would find a suitable illustrator and publish the story in a large format with full-page black-and-white illustrations. As illustrator they suggested Edith Alsop, a talented artist who had held several exhibitions and had illustrated Angus and Robertson's big success *The Children's Song Book*, a rival to the Rentoul sisters' equally popular *Bush Songs of Australia for Young and Old*.[4]

Edith was thrilled by her daughter's chance of success. But when Aunt Lily was told that Joice was to have her first book published, she sniffed and said acidly that no good ever came from women writing. It would be better for Joice to concentrate on finding a wealthy husband who could do something for Edith, rather than making all this fuss over a book. But her aunt's narrow-mindedness could not hurt Joice, who was thrilled to receive a contract and a handsome cheque as an advance against royalties. It was the first money she had ever earned. How wonderful was independence. She wrote the good news to Aunt Ellis, who replied that she was delighted there would now be *two* authors in the family.

First came the editor's corrections. Then long slips of paper called galley proofs arrived for Joice to make more corrections. At last her dream of authorship and financial independence was coming true. Eventually Edith Alsop's pictures arrived along with the page proofs. The illustrations were delicate yet lively and blended well with Joice's text. Advance reactions and orders from bookstores were good. Lothian were convinced the book would be a big seller in both Australia and Britain.

Believing her publisher's forecast of good sales and in anticipation of receiving a large cheque six months after the book appeared, generously Joice spent her whole advance payment on employing tradesmen to modernise the kitchen at Drouin. This would make things easier for her mother if she left home. Pipes now brought water from the tank into the kitchen, saving them the back-breaking job of drawing water in buckets. A metal sink replaced the old stained porcelain one. Lacking gas or electricity, the two women still had to heat the water on top of the stove to wash dishes and to fill the chipped enamelled bath in the lean-to shed they called a bathroom.

Joice sent Geoff money to get a good suit made as well as some decent shirts. For herself she purchased an Underwood portable typewriter in a carrying case, some stationery for her next book and an afternoon dress suitable for going to Melbourne.

With the prospect of earning money, she hit on the idea of setting up a trout hatchery at Lilydale—a very new concept at that period. She thought this would be a good way of earning extra income and getting herself and her mother away from drudgery on the farm. At that time women could not borrow money from banks. Instead, Joice asked her Great Uncle Hugh NanKivell, who had by now sold their old property at Boolara for a profit (mainly due to her parents' hard work) if she could borrow money against future book royalties. Great Uncle Hugh was not impressed by the thought of lending money to a woman to run a business. Sternly he told Joice: 'You're still a girl. Don't even think about borrowing money or opening up a business. These are things only *men* can do.'

Joice found her uncle's rejection insulting. She may have been 'just a girl' in Hugh NanKivell's eyes, but he seemed to have forgotten that for years she had been carrying an adult workload. Admittedly, she looked far younger than her real age with her long dark-blonde hair worn up on her head or in a plait, her large candid eyes and her fresh, unlined complexion.

It became obvious that the trout hatchery must remain a dream. If she could neither go to university, nor start her own business, Joice's one remaining wish was to become a writer and travel to Europe. But with Geoff in Queensland, she realised that she would be stuck at home with her parents for a long time yet. The only other alternative for a bush woman was to marry a local farmer, work even harder and rear children.

Her spirit lifted when she learned that one of her poems had been accepted by *Contrast*, a Melbourne literary magazine. She was told her poem had been read aloud and given a favourable critique at a meeting of the Victorian Literary Society. How she wished she could have been there! She loved writing poetry but realised that it did not pay; she must stick to books or take up journalism if she wanted to leave home and become independent.

George finally realised that without Geoff and with Edith so often prostrate with ill health, running Drouin had become far too much work for Joice and himself. He sold the farm and freed up some money by moving to a smaller property called Neerim, an isolated fruit farm near Lilydale, high in the mountains north-west of Drouin.

The property, which George bought at a very good price, had a shabby house on it. The owner had been ill for some time and the farm had run down. George had now received a little money from his mother's will so was able to put down a substantial deposit on the property.

Joice and Edith packed up their furniture, clothes and books. Geoff came south from Queensland to help them load their boxes onto farm carts. Joice was not sorry to leave. 'Maybe at long last Dad will be able to make farming pay,' she said to Geoff, who pulled a face and shrugged.

Neerim was far more beautiful than Drouin, Myaree or Boolara. The house even had water supply, an inside water closet and a separate dining-room panelled in cedar. From the veranda they looked down on Westernport Bay, though many kilometres of scrub and forest separated them from the sea. The land was suitable for grazing cattle and fattening lambs. The fields were planted with wheat and barley, there were orchards of plums and apples and a good vegetable garden. George insisted that as heir to the property, Geoff must help them establish Neerim as a going concern before he could train as a wool classer. (At that time sons always inherited the farm). It would eventually belong to him, no matter how much unpaid work Joice put into it. That was the way things were in a man's world.

Joice spent two years helping to establish Neerim as a viable farm. It was a heavy task, but working alongside Geoff was a delight. Looking back, she saw this as a pleasant period of her life. And at Neerim her mother seemed happier and her health improved, so that she and Joice were able to create together a large, beautiful garden.

At the beginning of 1914 life seemed to be improving for the NanKivells. But there was disturbing news from overseas: Europe was threatened by war. Germany, under Kaiser Wilhelm, was preparing to invade Belgium.

By now *The Cobweb Ladder* was ready to go to the printer. The publishers were confident it would be 'the big Christmas book' that year. Joice and Edith hoped it would sell as well as Ellis Rowan's *Bill Baillie, his Life and Adventures*, so that Joice could leave Neerim with a clear conscience and provide money for someone else to take over her domestic and farm duties.

Uncle John Turner arrived to visit Neerim and was appalled to see Joice working as hard as any farm labourer. She was getting run-down again, so at the beginning of August he paid for her to have a weekend in Melbourne, bought her an evening gown and took her to see her first opera. Joice was enthralled by the performance of *Tosca*. However, right in the middle of the second act, the huge red velvet curtain descended. The house manager appeared through the curtain. 'Ladies and gentlemen, we are officially at war with Germany,' he announced. The audience gasped. The orchestra burst into the first bars of 'God save the King'. Everyone rose to their feet and joined in the anthem. Women wept as they realised their husbands and sons might go to join the fighting. The young men in the audience looked either grim or excited, according to their temperaments and responsibilities. With horror Joice realised that Geoff, in a rush of patriotism, might volunteer for the Army and put his life at risk.

As she feared, Geoff was amongst the first of the volunteers. He received a commission and was issued with a khaki uniform and slouch hat. At the beginning of this horrific war, to the young men of Geoff's generation enlisting in the Army and being sent overseas seemed like a huge 'Boy's Own' adventure. Patriotic fervour swept the country. In the streets of many Australian cities and towns girls handed white feathers to young men who remained in civilian clothes, as a sign of cowardice.

The war of 1914–18 was to become known as 'The War to End all Wars'. Initially Australians had little idea how deeply the conflict with Germany would affect them: of the 416,809 who entered the services, 331,781 saw active service. Of these, 59,342 were killed, 152,171 were wounded.

After a brief training course and an even briefer period of home leave, Geoff was sent off on a troopship. The long voyage seemed like a holiday; they eventually landed in Europe and were dispatched into the carnage of Gallipoli. His brief letters from the front were eagerly read and re-read at Neerim. For those at home it was agonising to read the huge toll of deaths in France and the Dardanelles. Joice and Edith knitted garments for the soldiers and took part in fund-raising for the International Red Cross.

World War I changed life for many middle-class women. Before the war, worthwhile paid work outside the home was denied them. Apart from low-paid nursing and teaching, only domestic work was available. Now there were office vacancies in Melbourne and Sydney with employers desperate for women to fill them. Professions normally denied to women reluctantly admitted females to do jobs previously reserved for men.

Joice longed to work in Melbourne, but with Geoff away in the Army it seemed impossible to leave Neerim. She missed Geoff terribly and worried about him constantly.

The onset of war brought paper rationing, and publication of Joice's potential best-seller had to be postponed. *The Cobweb Ladder* would not now be published until September 1916. In the end it was printed in Britain instead of Australia.[5] 2,000 copies were sold in Britain, America and Canada, and a further 2,000 (half the original intended print run) were shipped to Australia in time for the Christmas market. The thrill of unwrapping copies of her first book gave Joice a sense of joy and achievement. All she wanted now was to be a full-time author.

Unfortunately, Australia was in the midst of wartime austerity and recession. Sales of *The Cobweb Ladder* suffered from a reduced book-buying public as well as fierce competition from another book published that same year, also by Lothian, written by Annie Rentoul and illustrated by her sister, Ida Rentoul Outhwaite—*Elves and Fairies*. Worried that the combination of Joice's text and Edith Alsop's beautiful black-and-white illustrations would steal their thunder, Ida's husband, Grenbry Outhwaite, paid for superb full-colour illustrations for *Elves and Fairies*, and Lothian pushed the marketing and display of this heavily subsidised book at the expense of *The Cobweb Ladder*. Joice NanKivell was a new, unknown author; Annie Rentoul and her sister were already well established.[6] All proceeds from *Elves and Fairies* were donated to the Red Cross. Nothing like Ida's coloured illustrations had ever been seen in Australia, and Lothian suggested in advertisements that the plates could be extracted from the book and framed. Ludicrously, the publishers also suggested in an advertisement in the Melbourne *Argus*: 'Just think what a delight it will be to a man in the trenches to receive such a beautiful Australian book . . . that will give him many a laugh and quiet hour's enjoyment.' The beautiful book was thirty-eight centimetres long and weighed almost two kilograms. Apart from this, its contents could hardly have been more inappropriate for anyone suffering trench warfare. An exhibition of the original paintings was held to coincide with the publication of *Elves and Fairies*, opened by the Governor General, it was a great success. However, the wartime depression also had an effect on the sales of *Elves and Fairies*. A year after publication a substantial number of copies remained unsold, and Grenbry Outhwaite wrote to Lothians, pointing out that the book would not make any profit until the edition was exhausted.

Joice received a much smaller royalty cheque than she had hoped, but in spite of this setback she was determined to continue writing—it was the only thing that gave meaning to her life. *The Cobweb Ladder* received some excellent reviews and many people considered Joice NanKivell (the name she would continue to use as an author) a far better writer than Annie Rentoul. But it was clear that in wartime the Australian children's market simply could not support both teams of writers and illustrators in large-format gift books. Joice realised her next children's book would have to be smaller in format, with fewer pages and without illustrations (she had to split royalties with the illustrator).

'I told you, there's no money in writing,' Joice's father observed with satisfaction. 'Why not make plum jam and sell it in Lilydale, instead of indulging in all this arty nonsense?' Joice ignored him.

Aunt Lena and Aunt Lily had now succeeded in marrying off all their daughters. In their frequent letters to Edith, they were quick to point out that Joice was not getting any younger. She was nearing thirty and *still* single. Aunt Lena added her usual comment: 'Joice *must* remember, men don't like clever women. Men like women who listen to *them*.' Determined that her aunts should not upset Edith in her fragile emotional state and bring on more migraines or other illness, Joice reassured her mother that if she finally managed to find work in Melbourne, she would have a far better chance of meeting someone compatible there.

6   A HERO OF GALLIPOLI

Before Geoff sailed off on his troopship, there had been another heated argument with his father about his ambition to become a wool classer in Queensland. Brooding on Geoff's refusal to help him run the farm when he returned, George told the family: 'I'm not going to kill myself slaving away for Geoff to inherit the farm when he doesn't give a damn about the place. So I've decided to sell all the livestock and not grow any more wheat. That means there'll be no men to feed at harvest time. Joice can go and work in the city. I can run the orchards on my own.'

Joice was clearly thrilled to hear this, which infuriated her father even more. Banging his clenched fist on the table he added: 'On one condition—Joice, you must take your annual holidays during the fruit-picking season.' Hastily she agreed. At long last she could leave home with a clear conscience.

Aunt Lily sent Edith dire warnings about the perils awaiting unmarried girls who left home to earn their living. She prophesied Joice would come to a bad end in the city. How *could* Edith think of letting her go there alone? Reading her sister's gloomy predictions, Edith burst into tears. Joice reassured her mother that her sole intention was to get a good job in Melbourne and to earn enough money to go overseas, once the war was over.

First she had to acquire more work skills. She sent away for a book on touch-typing and once she felt her typing speed was good enough, she applied for a job advertised in the Melbourne *Herald* that sounded interesting. Trinity College at Melbourne University was advertising a part-time job as secretary to Dr Alexander Leeper, Warden of the College, who was also the Head of the Classics Department. A good command of the English language was required. Joice typed a letter of application including the fact that she was a published author, and was summoned to an interview. The famous Dr Leeper turned out to be not nearly as terrifying as Joice had feared. He seemed impressed that Joice was an author and talked at some length about his own publications.

'What I need is a responsible person to act as my editorial assistant, liaise with publishers, correct the spelling and punctuation in   journal articles and books. Typing speed isn't so important, accuracy and a flair for language are.'

Joice showed Dr Leeper several articles she had written and a copy of her book. Without bothering to interview anyone else, he gave her the job.

She was excited by the thought of working in the University. Even though she was only a part-time staff member, Dr Leeper said she could attend lectures in his department free of charge and use the library facilities.

Joice insisted on taking her beehives as well as her books to Melbourne. With the help of Estelle Simson, Joice found inexpensive lodgings in East Melbourne in a boarding house with a large garden, where she was allowed to keep her precious bees. However, complaints ensued among other lodgers and Estelle and her father had to come round and move Joice to new lodgings. This happened more than once. Joice had brought her beehives to Melbourne with the intention of raising extra income by selling honey. She had colonies of rare bees called Golden Italian, and soon found out that far more money could be made by breeding and selling her queen bees to breeders.[1]

Joice enjoyed working for Dr Leeper and got on well with his daughter Molly, who acted as her father's secretary. He appreciated Joice's strong sense of loyalty and her boundless capacity for hard work.[2] In her memoirs Joice describes her job with the distinguished historian as a 'learning and earning experience'. Dr Leeper had a passion for literature; he was also an ardent advocate of university education for women. This job with its flexible hours gave Joice plenty of opportunity to attend lectures that interested her.

Her early education had been wide-ranging but somewhat haphazard. At last she had the time and the opportunity to acquire a solid foundation in ancient history and English literature. From typing up Dr Leeper's lecture notes and manuscripts, together with her wide reading in the University Library, she learned a great deal about ancient Greece: its civilisation, language, literature and architecture. Access to the library was a great privilege. She learned research techniques from the librarians and intellectual rigour from Dr Leeper, and came into close contact with other members of the Classics Department, who inspired in her a passion for Greece, a passion that would never leave her. Her warm, friendly nature made her popular—she talked to everyone and made friends easily.

Joice also became a member of the prestigious Lyceum Club. She may have been proposed for membership by her illustrator, Edith Alsop. Membership was reserved for women in the arts, the professions and sciences. Joice attended a book circle at the Lyceum and met leading professional women of her day.

Her activities spread beyond the University. So many male journalists had enlisted in the Army that newspaper positions previously reserved for men were now open to women of talent. Miss Joice NanKivell was invited to review books by the Melbourne *Evening Herald*, which also published some of her poems. The paper's literary editor, a Scotsman named Guy Innes, was so impressed by Joice's work that he commissioned her to write a weekly book review column, 'Under the Clock'. Although reviewing paid a pittance, it meant Joice got her own by-line and received free review copies. Her private library steadily increased in size. She and Guy Innes, who was eventually promoted to editor of the paper, became good friends. He recommended Joice for some more part-time work, doing publicity for the productions of a Melbourne theatrical company. This meant that Joice often had to work in the evenings. At the end of a theatrical performance, she would walk back alone to her lodgings through the Fitzroy Gardens.

Joice's aunts were horrified to learn that their niece was working in something as disreputable as the theatre and dared to walk home in the dark, unchaperoned. They regarded actors and actresses as 'immoral' and sent reproachful letters to Edith. As usual Aunt Lily prophesied disaster, which distressed Edith enormously, and to give her mother peace of mind, Joice had to stop working for the theatre company. She could not bear to see her mother upset. She knew that Edith was also deeply worried that Geoff might be killed or wounded in action, like so many other young Australians. Joice was convinced that a good deal of her mother's 'nerves' and migraines were attributable to the constant nagging of Aunt Lily and Aunt Lena.

Gradually Joice's financial position improved. She was determined to save enough money for her passage to London as soon as the war was over. And she hoped that one day she would be able to go to Greece, the country she now yearned to visit.

Geoff had miraculously come through the carnage of Gallipoli, one of only seven members of his battalion who survived. Shortage of manpower meant that although he was desperately battle-weary, he missed out on home leave. Instead, he and the few survivors from his regiment were shipped immediately to northern France where a burnt-out landscape and muddy trenches awaited them. The carnage of trench warfare in northern France was, in its own way, as bad as Gallipoli—yet Geoff never complained and saw his heroism at the front as normal.

At long last, however, he wrote that he would be allowed home leave after a few more months. Joice, thrilled at the thought of being with her brother again, applied to the University for extended leave to coincide with his visit to Neerim. Excitedly she planned things they would do together and places they would visit. The thought of seeing Geoff again made the weeks fly past. In her memoirs Joice relates the following incredible story: 'One night . . . the door of my room opened, and there, to my amazement, stood Geoff! He had a telegram in his hand. He said nothing, but held the telegram up for me to read:

Go to Lilydale. Hemphill will meet you with horses. Urgent.'

When she awoke, Joice wondered whether it really had been just a dream, although the telegram certainly made sense—Geoff was expected home any day now. In those days there was no telephone line to Neerim. It was difficult to get there by road and the small steam train only ran there twice a week. Lilydale lay on the far side of the mountain from Neerim, through kilometres of forest. Joice thought that seeing Geoff holding the telegram was proof of the strong telepathy that existed between them. How wonderful it would be to see him again!

Next morning she ran downstairs and asked the landlady whether she had received a telegram.—'No, there's no telegram for you, Miss NanKivell,' she was told. She then decided to follow the advice in the telegram she had seen in her dream. She thought Geoff must have arrived home already. So she caught the next train to Lilydale. Sure enough, Mr Hemphill, a neighbour who had often fetched Joice from the tiny Lilydale station, was there, sitting on the box of his horse-drawn wagon looking sad and drawn. 'Sorry ter be the one ter tell you. Yer brother's been killed in France,' he blurted out. Like most bushmen he struggled for words when dealing with anything emotional. He blew his nose in embarrassment and looked down at his horse. 'Yer Mum's in a terrible state. Best get you home as soon as we can.'

Joice felt as though she had been hit in the stomach. In her agony, she wanted to scream out that what Mr Hemphill had told her was not, could not be true. Geoff, her closest friend and companion, could not be dead! God would not allow it. Instead she said nothing and remained silent for the whole journey, wrapped in grief. When they drew up at the farm, Joice still wanted to believe that there had been some mistake . . . but she was terrified that Mr Hemphill had told the truth.

She hugged a white-faced Edith, who had not slept since she heard the dreadful news. Racked with sobs, Edith explained how, three days before Geoff was due to go on leave, his regimental colonel had called for volunteers to take ammunition to the trenches. Although desperately tired, Geoff had volunteered along with six other Australians. They traversed the maze of trenches bearing crates of ammunition. A shell fired by the Germans had blown all of them to pieces. Geoff's remains had not been found.

Strangely enough, Edith had also, as in a dream, seen Geoff in full military uniform. But her dream differed from Joice's experience. Geoff had told her: 'Not to worry Mum, I'm fine and coming home soon.' As a result when the telegram arrived with the news of her son's death, she flatly refused to believe it. Joice then discovered that her father *had* composed the telegram telling her that Mr Hemphill would meet her at Lilydale, but her mother had prevented him from sending it, convinced by her vivid dream that Geoff must still be alive. The following day Joice made inquiries and discovered that Judy, the Neerim postmistress, had, after some delay, sent George's telegram, although Joice's landlady flatly denied that it had ever arrived. The whole affair remained something of a mystery.

Several weeks later George and Edith received a personal letter from Geoff's colonel, praising their son's courage. He wrote that a cross would be erected in Geoff's memory in northern France. It was all they had to console themselves with.

Geoff's death had a terrible effect on Edith. Sometimes she became hysterical, at other times she would insist he was still alive—she would laugh and sing and make up the bed for his homecoming and set a place for him at the table. Then, when he failed to arrive her mood would change and she would begin to sob, knowing he was dead.

Joice was also in shock. Her grief was as deep as her mother's, but she knew that if Edith was to recover, she herself must remain calm and stable. Joice would comfort and soothe her mother—she was the only person Edith would allow near her. She sat alone in her room for days, refusing to eat and unable to sleep. Her once-beautiful face had become mask-like with sorrow. She lost a great deal of weight and her hair started to turn white. When Uncle Harry was consulted he expressed his fear that Edith might have to be committed to an asylum. George was of little help, dismissing his wife's grief as 'hysterical'. He tried to escape from his own grief by drinking rather than showing his emotions. All he could say was 'Geoff was the best son a man could have'. For weeks George scarcely spoke, but each night he drank himself insensible.

One of the hardest things for the whole family to come to terms with was the fact that without a corpse there could be no funeral. Instead, they held a short memorial service. Geoff had no grave, only a wooden cross beside a road in northern France.

After a few weeks, Joice's holiday leave was up. She had to return to Melbourne if she wanted to keep her job. But Dr Leeper was extremely sympathetic when she explained what had happened, and she was granted leave of absence on compassionate grounds. She also persuaded Guy Innes to arrange for someone else to do her book review column until she finally returned to Melbourne. She spent the next four months at Neerim, lending emotional support to her mother and taking the burden of housekeeping off her hands.

At the outbreak of the war Joice had poured out her feelings in blank verse, in a poem about killing lambs. The poem had won her an award in a competition organised by Melbourne's Literary Society:

The young crying of lambs about to be slaughtered,
The endless bleating of ewes bereft of their young,
The tender young, so soon to come to their dying,
How can I sing of the spring with small lambs crying?

Joice read and re-read this poem, seeing it now as a metaphor for the slaughter of young men fighting a senseless war.

It was during this bleak time that she wrote her second book. Writing it was a form of catharsis that helped her cope with the shock of Geoff's death. The Solitary Pedestrian: A Book of Sketches is the most Australian of all Joice's published writings. It took six months to write in longhand on lined blocks of paper. It was published in paperback in Melbourne at the end of 1918, just as the Armistice was declared. The book, dedicated to Geoff, celebrates his brief life. At the beginning Joice wrote 'A Few Words of Explanation': with pride and love she refers to the wooden cross erected in her brother's memory, which bore the inscription 'Served in Gallipoli and France'. In the form of twenty-one short stories about Joice and Geoff's childhood experiences in Queensland and Victoria, she describes bush life seen through the eyes of children. In *The Solitary Pedestrian* Joice is forming her own narrative style, using strong verbs and vividly recreating characters and places. Geoff is called 'Robin', and Joice 'Cynthia'. The narrative is not sad; it is a collection of happy memories.[3] Joice relates how she and Geoff observed the eccentric characters of people living in an isolated world. She also describes their aunts, forever fussing over them, telling them they will 'come to no good' and dragging them off to church. The title conveys Joice's feeling that without Geoff, her life was bound to be a solitary one. The front cover shows a young woman walking fearlessly along a lonely road. Joice, who is normally extremely reticent about her emotional life, writes in *The Solitary Pedestrian* about her love for her brother and her sorrow at his death. She describes how their family has to go on with life, saying at the beginning that Robin (Geoff) would not have wanted them to grieve: 'Robin was a joyous boy who journeyed through life with a light in his hands. That light did not go out because he died. As the tragedy was ours alone, there will be no hint of sorrow in this book.'

By now Joice had returned to Melbourne and her job at the University. When *The Solitary Pedestrian* appeared, one reviewer mentioned that Joice NanKivell worked for the famous Dr Leeper and said: 'Her new book is a series of clever sketches which record impressions since her extreme youth in Banana land. An earlier dip in the NanKivell inkwell resulted in *The Cobweb Ladder*, a children's book which has been very well received in Australia, the United States and Canada.'[4]

In the final year of the war Edith's mental and physical health improved. She came to terms with Geoff's death. The workload on the farm was now relatively light, so she was able to visit Joice in Melbourne. Edith urged her daughter to find work in London as soon as the war was over. Friends in the Victorian Literary Society and in the University Classics Department gave the same advice. Joice *must* go to London—the centre of the publishing world—if she wanted a serious career in writing, something she certainly had the talent and the determination to achieve.

The death of Joice's handsome, happy-go-lucky brother left an aching vacuum in her life. Uncle Harry Mitchell advised her that the best way to recover from grief was to keep busy. In addition to her work and lectures at the University, she began writing her book review column again. Each week she went to the Melbourne *Herald* offices, where she and Guy Innes would discuss which books she would review.

One book Guy Innes asked Joice to review was *Straits Impregnable* by Sydney de Loghe. Innes considered it an important work about the

Gallipoli campaign. The author's real name was Sydney Loch, a Scotsman now living in Australia.[5] As Geoff had fought at Gallipoli the book immediately aroused Joice's interest. She gave it an excellent review, describing it as the best book she had read on Gallipoli. In fact she was so intrigued by *Straits Impregnable* that she arranged to meet the author. During their very first conversation she discovered that she and Sydney Loch had a great deal in common: his love of books and words was as strong as her own.

Sydney had fought at Gallipoli, where he had been wounded. When Joice met him he still walked with a limp. His book, which centred around aspects of the Dardanelles warfare, had made him something of a hero. Talking to Sydney about the war helped Joice to understand what Geoff had gone through; with Sydney Loch she could freely express her grief about her brother's death.

Sydney told Joice that he had been born in London but raised in Scotland. He was a man of action as well as words. Not wanting a desk job, he had sailed to Australia in 1905, aged seventeen, with only twenty pounds in his pocket. His great-uncle, Sir Henry Brougham Loch, was a popular Governor of Victoria from 1884-89; he was now Baron Loch of Drylaw. One of Sydney's aunts was married to the son of the Duke of Richmond and Gordon. His father referred to himself as a 'gentleman by profession'; he owned land but little money. Sydney had to make his own way in the world.

Sydney had stayed with some kind and supportive family friends in Melbourne, then gone as a jackeroo on a large sheep property in Victoria's western districts. He was good with horses and loved the open-air life. However, wanting to see more of Australia, he moved north to manage a vast cattle station in Queensland. After some time he knew he wanted to be a writer: with some money in his pocket he travelled around the far north of Australia and worked on pearling luggers off Darwin and Thursday Island to provide material for a novel published under the title *Pelican Pool*. Sydney had fallen in love with Australia and its climate and planned to remain in the Antipodes. When war was declared he volunteered to join the AIF rather than the British Army.

He was tall, broad-shouldered and distinguished-looking. He was a good listener, while Joice was a brilliant raconteur. They discovered an affinity for each other that gradually deepened into love. Sydney's presence in Joice's life helped to fill the vacuum left by Geoff's death.

It took a long time for their relationship to develop: after witnessing her parents' bitter arguments, their loveless marriage and her mother's inability to escape from it, Joice was wary about the bonds of matrimony. However, by holding back on a romantic relationship, Sydney slowly captured Joice's critical heart. Those who knew Sydney described him as a man truly worthy of Joice's exceptional qualities.[6]

Sydney Loch, a bachelor with an impeccable background, was highly eligible in spite of his lack of fortune. Several wealthy squatters' daughters had tried to snare him as a husband for his good looks and aristocratic connections. But it was his strength of character and passion for writing which drew Joice to him.[7]

Taunted by her father about her 'arty literary friends' in Melbourne, Joice made no mention of Sydney at home. And she feared that her aunts would meddle if they sensed romance in the air with someone who had no money. Worry could easily upset her mother's fragile equilibrium again.

Like Joice, Sydney had reached a turning point in his life. After he was wounded at Gallipoli he had been shipped to the British military hospital at Alexandria and was invalided out of the AIF on a small pension. He had then signed on as crew on a schooner which sailed to Australia via Cape Horn. In chilly evenings in his cramped cabin he had written the first draft of a novel about the voyage, *Three Predatory Women*. He was determined to be a professional author even though he realised it was an extremely hazardous way to earn a living.

Sydney Loch was totally unlike any man Joice had ever met. He had immense reserves of courage but never boasted about his exploits. Although he seldom raised his voice it became apparent to Joice that he had a will as strong as her own. He was an excellent all-rounder: a superb athlete, a good swimmer, sailor and horseman, a deep thinker, a man of integrity with an incisive mind, an excellent administrator and organiser. His rational and analytical nature complemented Joice's vivacious and amusing personality.

Joice was now in her early thirties. At that time most women were married by twenty-one and bore their children young. Although Sydney was two years younger than herself, she realised that he was the man with whom she wanted to share the rest of her life. He was the lover, friend and colleague she had waited for all these years. She realised that so far as her father and aunts were concerned, his only drawback as a husband was his lack of income and his reliance on the hazardous profession of writing. The damaged knee he had suffered at Gallipoli prevented him from going on the land—this was a relief for Joice, who had experienced quite enough of what she termed 'the rigours and eccentricities of bush life'.

By now Joice had saved up enough money to go to London. She and Sydney planned to get married and then travel overseas together.

Aunt Lena had never forgiven her niece for turning down a marriage proposal from Percy B, the wealthy Tasmanian. When she heard that Joice had saved up enough money to go to England, she wrote to Edith recommending that Joice should abandon her plans and give her mother the money instead. 'That girl will go to the dogs if you let her live alone in London', Aunt Lena wrote, not knowing that Joice was engaged.

Joice kept quiet about Sydney for as long as possible. She could imagine what Aunt Lena and Aunt Lily would say if they learned she had fallen in love with a man younger than herself, with a wounded knee, without a job or any regular source of income. She may have told her mother about her relationship with Sydney, but certainly not her father. She had never been close to him and had no faith in his judgement. She despised his macho view of the world and the way he sneered at everything she considered beautiful and important. Through her writing Joice had escaped from the narrow rigidity of George NanKivell's world. She did not intend to take her father's advice on anything, least of all the suitability of a marriage partner.

She remembered the disapproval she had encountered from Percy B's family, and feared a similar reaction from the Loch family as well. She was well aware that 'establishment' families liked their sons to marry girls who would inherit money. In the eyes of Sydney's relatives Joice was a 'colonial', without family money and (even worse in the eyes of future in-laws), *older* than Sydney.

Being two years older than Sydney may have embarrassed Joice. Her bubbling vivacity, her high cheekbones, delicate chiselled profile and fresh complexion made her seem younger. It seems that at this stage of her life she only admitted to being twenty-six instead of thirty-two. At that time the main responsibility of a wife was to bear her husband a male heir. If Joice had revealed her real age she may have feared Sydney's family would try to discourage him from marrying her by saying she was past childbearing age. She must surely have felt sensitive about her limited chances of childbearing.

Sydney Loch and Joice NanKivell were married at The Manse, Royal Parade, Melbourne on 22 February, 1919 at a quiet ceremony. On her marriage certificate Joice's age is given as twenty-six, Sydney's as thirty. It was ironic that her maternal grandmother had also lowered her age when she divorced and remarried.

Joice and Sydney made plans for a delayed honeymoon in Europe. Joice had given notice to Melbourne University and was trying hard to get a passage to England, not an easy task immediately following the Armistice. Guy Innes helped by guaranteeing her work as a freelance correspondent for the *Herald*'s London office. This would provide some income until she and Sydney secured a book contract, which they were determined to do. She was given a cramped 'economy' berth on the *Orcha*, a troopship bound for London. Sydney was not able to find a passage until later.[8]

Although Joice did not realise it at the time, it would be decades before she saw her mother again. Edith would miss her daughter, but she was relieved to think Joice had finally escaped from 'the ups and downs of bush life'. Edith spent what little money she had managed to save on a ticket to Adelaide to see Joice's ship depart. Joice boarded the *Orcha* excited at the prospect of seeing more of the world at long last. Of course she wished Sydney could have accompanied her, but it would not be long before she saw him again. Steadfastly Edith held back her tears as she embraced her daughter and kissed her goodbye. Her mother's parting gift was a miniature Australian flag on a stand—'to remind you of home and us', she told Joice. From the deck the passengers threw down coiled paper streamers which unfurled into rainbows of colour. Edith held onto the one thrown by her daughter. As the ship pulled away from the dock and the streamer broke in two, Joice realised she was severing contact with the country she had known all her life.

In London I imagine Joice exploring avidly, choosing different walking routes each day. She was entranced by names she had read in books: Baker Street, where Sherlock Holmes and Dr Watson resided; Dickens' Old Curiosity Shop, and dark courtyards off Fleet Street where she imagined Fagin and the Artful Dodger plying their pick-pocketing trade.

As an overseas member Joice was able to live relatively inexpensively at the Lyceum Club at 138 Piccadilly which had a spacious library, well-furnished public rooms and attentive staff. Cousin Maie Ryan also belonged to the Lyceum, but it was unlikely that she would have helped Joice to settle into London life. Now that the war was over Maie was leaving for Germany, where she would act as official hostess for her brother Rupert, the newly appointed Deputy Head of the Rhineland Inter-Allied High Commission.[9] Maie intended to use her brother's position to make her own social contacts and, eventually, a brilliant marriage. Her long-term suitor and future husband, Dick Casey, was working as liaison officer in London for Australia's Prime Minister, Stanley Bruce.

In May 1919, Joice watched the Victory Day celebrations from the casement windows of the Lyceum Club. Survivors from many famous regiments marched that day. Some regiments had only twenty survivors, others as few as six. Joice described the procession as 'the ghastly empty ranks of the decimated regiments, the armaments, the flags'. And she wrote of 'Sorrowful, lonely men and a vast crowd waiting to honour them'. Amongst the survivors were Australians wearing their slouch hats. Inevitably the procession brought back memories of Geoff's death. That night, some Australians dragged the pews from the church of St Martin's in the Fields, piled them high around Nelson's column and lit a bonfire around which they danced.

There was a joyful reunion when Sydney arrived a few months later. They spent a honeymoon in Europe and then rented an apartment which Joice described as 'close to Hyde Park'.[10] At heart Sydney and Joice were both country lovers; they did not intend to remain in London for long. What they sought was the chance to travel and write books together. They were in their early thirties, talented and in love. The future seemed theirs for the taking.

Strong narrative journalism was Joice's forte. Guy Innes kept his word. He asked her for stories about literary and other events in London and travel pieces. At this time it was more usual for women to write about fashions, cookery and high society.[11]

Joice's marriage made her extremely happy from the start. Sydney fulfilled her idea of the perfect partner, both mentally and physically. He was as quiet as she was talkative, but when Sydney did talk others listened. He had a dry sense of humour which specially appealed to Joice. Each valued the other's skills; they bounced ideas off each other and worked on joint writing projects.

By now Joice had written short stories and poems about Australia for British literary magazines, including *The Edinburgh Review* and *Blackwood's Magazine*. Soon after Sydney's arrival, she received a telegram from Guy Innes, saying he had taken a job as an editor for the newspaper proprietor Lord Northcliffe, and would be arriving in London the following month. He told her that the Melbourne *Herald* would continue to use her as their London correspondent. When Guy Innes took up his new appointment in London he gave Joice and Sydney a few commissions for articles, although few of them appeared under their by-lines. They were not earning much money but they were extremely happy.

Sydney's relatives, all except his favourite aunt, the artistic Lady Margaret Loch, viewed his marriage with disapproval. They had hoped Sydney would become wealthy by farming in Australia. Now here he was back again, having 'thrown himself away' on an obscure colonial girl with no prospect of an inheritance. Why on earth, if Sydney wanted to follow a precarious career as a writer, hadn't he married some wealthy daughter of the squattocracy, rather than the daughter of a colonial sugar planter who had gone bankrupt?

Now that the novelty of being in London had worn off, Joice was finding this capital of the Empire crowded, grimy and uncomfortable. Sydney agreed with her; they both missed the wide open spaces and clean air of Australia.

One warm August evening Joice came home exhausted, having spent the whole day chasing a story for an editor. She prepared dinner but Sydney was late returning to their rented apartment. When he did arrive he told Joice he had met an old school friend who was now an officer in British Military Intelligence. They had adjourned to a pub for a few drinks and a yarn.

'Does Military Intelligence mean your friend's a spy?' Joice asked.

'I suppose so,' Sydney admitted.

His old school chum had previously been serving as an undercover agent in Turkey and the Balkans. Now he and sixteen other officers had been hand-picked from British Intelligence by Winston Churchill, Home Secretary in Lloyd George's Coalition Government, to serve as undercover agents in Dublin and find the man who was fomenting rebellion against British rule. That man was no woolly-minded visionary but a well-organised leader. All they knew about him was his name—Michael Collins. No one knew what he looked like. Mr Collins and his Irish Republican gunmen were said to be shooting British undercover agents in the streets of Dublin, yet no one had been able to capture the murderers, who had the knack of merging into the crowd and disappearing. Collins planned actions with military precision; his men, known as the Sinn Fein, had captured British guns from remote country barracks and were using them against British-paid informers to deadly effect.

Sydney thought his friend's assignment and the hunt for the mysterious Michael Collins would be a fascinating topic for a book. Ireland was in turmoil; it seemed that the country was sliding into a guerrilla war with Britain. As a Scotsman whose own country had also suffered from centuries of British rule, Sydney was convinced that such a book would need to be totally unbiased. Joice agreed with him. Eagerly they began to discuss the project over the dinner which Joice retrieved from the oven. They should interview both Catholics and Protestants. The question of whether the whole of Ireland or only the south should be granted Home Rule was a hot topic. A book on Ireland would have a huge readership.

The idea of going to Ireland to write their book really appealed to Joice. It was also a way to escape from their cramped and expensive rented apartment and London's murky fogs. At the same time she could look at the possibility for setting up an adoption scheme under which infertile English and Australian mothers could adopt orphaned Irish babies. She would love to bear Sydney's child, but she feared she might be too old to conceive. Perhaps she might be able to persuade Sydney to adopt a baby. But she kept these thoughts to herself.

Sydney's relatives and Joice's cousins were not so enthusiastic. 'You're mad,' they said. 'The Sinn Fein are a violent lot. You'll both be found down some dark alley riddled with bullets.'

The Lochs refused to listen.

The publishers John Murray & Sons had had their offices in Albermarle Street, Mayfair, since 1812. They had published many of the most renowned writers of their day, from Lord Byron and William Makepiece Thackeray to William Butler Yeats, the renowned Irish poet whom Joice hoped to meet. It was Sir John Murray who had edited Sydney's work on the Dardanelles campaign. Sir John knew that the Irish republican question was highly topical, arousing strong passions in Britain and America besides Ireland itself.[12] Many British people were beginning to think it was time to sever ties with Ireland; there was widespread speculation about an Irish Free State or even an independent Irish Republic in the south. It cost Britain a great deal to keep a garrison in Dublin—money that might be better spent.

Sir John wondered whether they would be able to interview the elusive Michael Collins. 'A difficult assignment,' was Sydney's response. He told the publisher that his friend in Intelligence (in the Lochs' narrative always referred to as 'Major X' to protect his identity from the IRA) had said there was a price of ten thousand pounds on Collins' head. 'Collins wants to remain unknown. He's always guarded by armed men. We're keen to do this book but not to get shot,' he added laconically.

Because the Sinn Fein movement had a literary background, Sydney thought that if they went to Dublin armed with letters of introduction to important Irish writers they might be able to interview some of its other members. Sinn Fein (meaning 'we ourselves' in Gaelic) had actually originated from the movement to revive the Gaelic language in Ireland.

Sir John Murray assured Sydney that letters of introduction to Yeats and other Irish writers would be provided. Interviews with these authors would add a literary flavour to their proposed book, which had been given the working title *Ireland in Travail*. Following their discussion, a contract was drawn up and signed by both authors. Each would write alternate chapters and they would split the royalty payments between them.

The contract provided an advance against living expenses. The next day, after cashing the cheque, Joice used some of the advance to buy household items and clothes for her mother at Harrods. These would be shipped to Melbourne. For her new career of professional author she bought herself a pair of comfortable walking shoes, two lambs wool sweaters, an ankle-length tweed skirt, a navy coat and skirt and a white silk shirt.

Joice had already written to Edith about their plans. Now a telegram arrived from her mother, imploring her not to go to Ireland—it was far too risky. Aunt Lily sent a much stronger letter, *forbidding* Joice to go there. Joice threw it in the wastepaper basket. She wrote back to her mother, explaining that their joint book was to be published by one of the most prestigious British publishers, and that it was an excellent project for both their careers. She mentioned the clothes and household goods that Harrods were shipping out to Edith. She promised to write every week and told her mother she must not worry—she and Sydney would be fine.

Apart from books, the Lochs had not accumulated many possessions in London. Joice managed to fit her clothes into one large suitcase. She placed their few bits of furniture and most of their books in storage, cleaned the apartment and handed over the key to the managing agent. The die was cast. No matter how dangerous their Irish assignment, there was no turning back.

7   IRELAND

'Any firearms in that parcel, Paddy?' demanded the British soldier guarding the gangplank to the Dublin ferry from Holyhead. The cloth-capped Irishman reluctantly unwrapped his package, whose contents turned out to be nothing more lethal than a fishing rod.

Joice Loch had reached the head of the queue. Behind her were more soldiers carrying rifles and kitbags, waiting to board the ferry. She hefted her suitcase in one hand and a portable typewriter in the other.

The soldier on guard asked her to open her suitcase, looked at its contents, examined her passport and saw her birthplace was Queensland, Australia. Puzzled that she was off to a known trouble spot rather than sightseeing in Europe, he demanded suspiciously, 'What's a nice lady like you doing setting off alone to a dangerous place like Ireland?' Joice explained that she was not alone. Somewhere between the boat train and the ferry, she had lost her husband. They would be spending between six months and a year in Dublin, writing a book about 'the Troubles' in Ireland. The soldier looked suspicious, but fortunately another soldier hailed him at this crucial moment. Brusquely he told Joice to board the ferry.

Eventually she found Sydney leaning over the rail, trying to spot her in the crowd below. He had gone on ahead to reserve a cabin, but it seemed that this very week the British Government were transporting hundreds of newly enlisted forces to Ireland in a desperate attempt to stop civil war breaking out.

'All cabins are reserved for officers. The soldiers have bagged all the lounge chairs. If we want a seat we'll have to go to one of the bars,' he told her.

Joice longed to sink into a soft bed; however, brought up in a hard school, she rarely complained about anything. The crowded saloon bar stank of beer. A young soldier shared their bench. He wore a motley uniform consisting of a black policeman's tunic, high brown leather boots over cream breeches and a large black beret topped by a tan-coloured pom-pom. 'Aha! A Black and Tan,' thought Joice. She always made a point of talking to as many people as possible when she was working on a story. 'Why did you volunteer to serve in Ireland if it's as dangerous as they say?' she asked the young man.

'Couldn't get any work after I came home from the war in France, lady.' It transpired that 'home' was two rooms in a tenement in London's East End, where he lived with his widowed Mum, an unmarried sister, his young wife and their newborn baby.

'Me Army pension scarcely bought our food, a packet of fags and a beer on Saturday, let alone keep the whole bleedin' family. So me and me mates re-enlisted in the Black and Tans. The pay's good. Our orders are to reinforce the Royal Irish Constabulary and make life 'ell for them Shinners.'

'Shinners?'

'What we call the Sinn Fein. Them as keeps shootin' police constables and civilians.'[1]

It seemed the Black and Tans were English, Scottish and Northern Irish soldiers, all nominally Protestant. Most were recruited from the ranks of the unemployed—there were plenty of those in 1920. Joice dozed off, her head on Sydney's shoulder, to be woken by the announcement over the loud hailer that the ferry was about to dock. They collected their luggage, went down the gangplank, had their passports inspected, and informed the authorities they were journalists and authors.

They took a horse-drawn cab to the centre of Dublin, found a room in an inexpensive hotel, then went for a walk around the city. It was evident that this was a city of strife. In Merrion Square they saw once elegant Georgian terrace houses with broken windows. Halfway down O'Connell Street the huge portico of the General Post Office was pockmarked by bullets. It had been stormed during the 1916 Easter Rising against British rule because all Irish Republicans saw it as a symbol of hated authority. O'Connell Street was swarming with Black and Tans as well as soldiers of the regular British Army. The pavements were filled with men who wore black armbands in mourning for Irishmen killed in the Easter Rising.[2]

The Lochs bought a newspaper. 'Murderin' bastards, the lot o'them,' said the news vendor, glancing across at an open lorry transport of Black and Tans, seated back-to-back and holding loaded rifles pointing outwards. 'We call them lorries chicken coops,' he added, pointing to a metal frame covered with chicken wire on the back of the lorry. 'The wire frame's to protect 'em from petrol bombs the IRA throw down from upstairs windows.' The Lochs learned later that some lorries were fitted with hitching posts, so that the Tans could tie suspects to them as hostages, knowing the IRA would not lob down any bombs on fellow Republicans.

They spent a week finding their bearings. In pubs and cafes they were told tales of ancestors who had died in the great potato famine and relatives who had emigrated to America and Australia. One of their letters of introduction from Sir John Murray was to the writer Jack White and his beautiful Spanish wife, who had a large house in Ely Place and welcomed Joice and Sydney to their Bohemian circle. Jack White took them to a smoke-filled pub called *The Sod of Turf* where they found foreign journalists, 'Shinners' and British intelligence agents all rubbing shoulders at the bar.[3] Jack White was well-known round the pubs. The landlord's wife at Devlin's in Parnell Square made a great fuss of Jack and Sydney. After a few rounds of Guiness, she dropped her voice and confided: 'Michael Collins, the Big Fella himself, knows Irish revolts in the past have been betrayed by British spies. The Big Fella says his "Twelve Apostles" will shoot all paid informers.'

'Would I be able to interview Michael Collins?' Sydney asked her. Mrs Devlin looked shocked, fearful she had revealed too much. 'It's more than my life's worth to tell you more,' she replied, glancing at her husband further down the bar.

Sydney decided to get the other side of the story from his old school friend Major X, the British Intelligence agent, who was staying with his wife at the luxurious Gresham Hotel. That evening the Lochs walked into the foyer of the Gresham and asked for Major X under another of his aliases, 'Sandy O'Donnell'.[4] They found him in the Gresham's cosy bar, drinking pink gins with his tall blonde English wife. The four of them settled in a secluded alcove and talked. It seemed that in spite of their efforts in sending over a new batch of agents, British Intelligence had not been able to trace Michael Collins or even identify him.

'Collins is clever and well-organised. He uses guns and ammunition captured from British police and Army barracks to shoot our men. His "Twelve Apostles" have already killed ten British informers,' the Major told them.

Apparently British Intelligence files in Dublin Castle, their headquarters, *still* lacked any photograph from which to identify Michael Collins; a spy within the Castle, centre of the British Administration, had removed the only ID photo. The only information they had was that Collins was athletic in build and spoke with a strong Cork accent.[5] It seemed that Michael Collins had a series of 'safe houses' and to avoid detection his 'boys' would spend each night in a different one. During the day he and the rest of the IRA went about their normal business as butchers, bakers and candlestick makers. 'The Twelve Apostles' followed Collins' orders. After murdering British informers or secret agents they would simply melt away into the safety of the crowd. The following week Joice and Sydney visited the Cairo Cafe, where Major X and his colleagues in cloth caps and shabby suits were trying to mingle with the locals unnoticed; Joice reckoned they stuck out like sore thumbs. Major X bought them a drink and they sat in a dark corner. Joice hoped this wouldn't put them on Collins' black list. Major X leant across the table and whispered the sad news that two more British agents had been murdered. No matter how much money the British offered Irish civilians, no one would inform on Michael Collins. The Major looked depressed and told them he feared he was being followed.

The next day Joice received a telegram from London. Estelle Simson, in Europe from Melbourne, would be arriving in Dublin in two days time. She intended to rent a car. Would the Lochs join her in touring the Irish countryside? Joice was thrilled by the thought of seeing her closest friend.

Estelle arrived with a letter from Joice's mother. Having lost her son, Edith was terrified her only daughter might be killed in what seemed to be developing into an Irish civil war. The Irish in Melbourne and Sydney were raising funds to buy arms for the IRA: Cardinal Mannix had caused a scandal in Melbourne when he announced from the pulpit that it was no sin for a convinced Republican to kill British soldiers. Estelle hired a small black Morris and the three of them set off to the West Coast. They found trenches dug at the meeting of roads, trees felled, walls torn down to cause obstructions. They knew that at any hour, at some strategic spot IRA forces could materialise: round a corner, over the shoulder of a hill or from some wooded height above the road. When they spotted the enemy, a volley of shots would pour down. Invariably the gunmen would escape—they knew every inch of ground. Out in the country, the nerves of the police and the Black and Tans were stretched to breaking point. Hate was breeding in them like maggots in meat.[6]

Cork was too dangerous—several people had been shot there—so they drove through Athlone to Galway, once an Anglo-Norman stronghold. The Irish Catholics, stripped of their lands by Cromwell's ruthless army, had fled to this remote area for safety. Joice found people who spoke of the horrors of Cromwell's reign of terror as though it had happened yesterday.

The bracken browns, soft blues and violet shadows of Connemara enchanted them. Its unspoiled sandy beaches made Joice and Estelle homesick for Australia. They saw green mountains sweeping down to blue sea, lanes fringed by hedges of purple fuchsia, ancient dry-stone walls and Celtic ringed stone crosses, covered in lichens. At the small fishing hamlet of Cushindrum they stayed with an aunt of their Dublin friend Jack White. In the evenings old Mrs White read poetry to them. Sydney fished, while Joice and Estelle went for long walks and talked ceaselessly; their mouths got more exercise than their bodies, Sydney teased them. On clear nights they watched barrels of fiery poteen rolled down the slopes into the surf, to be loaded into small boats that carried them to ships waiting out at sea. It was prohibition time in America, and that was where the ships were headed. 'Coastguards patrolled the shores, but, somehow or other, they always turned up too late to catch anyone,' Joice observed.[7]

Mrs White provided background material, telling them that the diet of an average Irish family consisted of boiled potatoes washed down with strong tea. Few working people could afford meat; in Connemara they gathered seaweed or kelp and sold it to earn a few pence to help feed their children.

Slowly they made their way back to Dublin, staying each night in a different pub. In every bar they heard dramatic accounts of Michael Collins' Republican army attacking courthouses. In revenge the Black and Tans had sacked and burned the small town of Balbriggan and bayoneted to death two men they believed were members of Sinn Fein, though the locals insisted they were not. Joice's Australian accent encouraged the Irish, many of whom had relatives in Australia, to talk freely. Many told her they hoped to emigrate to Australia. They talked of Irish patriots tortured in Dublin Castle, of Irishwomen dragged from their beds at night by Black and Tans in their search for arms and ammunition and how men who were ordinary tradesmen by day became armed guerrillas by night, raiding police stations and capturing guns.

The Black and Tans' motto was 'two Irish deaths for every murder of a British subject'. They had been on a drunken, murderous rampage through Limerick. Joice remembered the Cockney soldier on the boat with the wife, child and his mother and sister all living in two rooms in London. Was he behaving like that? On the way back to Dublin they were delayed because a bridge had been blown up by Collins' men. When they reached the city it was time for Estelle to leave for Europe. She and Joice embraced, wondering when they would meet again.

By now the advance paid to the Lochs by their London publisher was dwindling. A rented apartment would be cheaper than a hotel. Unfortunately, apartments with hot water, heating and space for Joice to type up her notes were scarce as hen's teeth. Major X told them why so little inexpensive accommodation was available. The IRA, using funds which the Irish leader Eamon de Valera had raised in America, had rented entire lodging houses whose owners were sympathetic to the Republican cause, to store their stolen guns and ammunition.

The Lochs spent the next three days inspecting slatternly boarding houses. As soon as the landladies heard Sydney's English accent they would say the apartment was taken. Then the Whites found them a relatively cheap first-floor apartment in the street where they lived, Ely Place. It seemed ideal. There was a sitting-room which Joice could also use as an office, a bedroom, and a bathroom with an iron bath on claw feet and a gas geyser. Wallpaper was peeling from the walls, but the mahogany doors retained their handsome brass furniture and there were marble mantelpieces. The windows overlooking the street were covered by grubby lace curtains, and one of the windowpanes was broken. Joice noticed, too, that a pane of glass was missing from the beautiful Georgian fanlight above the front door—which strangely enough in such a dangerous city, could not be locked. The landlady, a widow called Mrs Slaney, promised faithfully that the window and the broken front-door lock would be fixed. The apartment was let serviced: the price included a cooked breakfast, a two-course dinner and cleaning and laundry. The Lochs moved in the following day.

Ely Place was very close to the city centre and to St Stephen's Green with its superb gardens. Joice liked the idea of an afternoon walk there after spending the morning researching in the Irish National Library.[8] Mrs Slaney was a staunch Irish Republican with a loathing for the British and their Monarchy. She only agreed to rent them the apartment because Joice was Australian. Mrs Slaney believed Australia had also suffered grievously from British imperialism. When she heard Sydney's English accent she shot him a withering look but said no more.

Her liking for Joice proved something of a liability. In search of 'a good craick' she would descend from her own rooms on the third floor and talk endlessly, smoking packet after packet of Joice's cigarettes. She told Joice that her husband and eldest son had both been killed in the Easter Rebellion, while her younger son was away in England, an officer in the British Army. This seemed strange to Joice, but Mrs Slaney explained that because of the high rate of unemployment, a large number of patriotic Irish had enlisted in the British Army as career soldiers.

Mrs Slaney liked the fact that the Lochs were writers, believing they lent a touch of class to her boarding house. In return for smoking their cigarettes and drinking their whiskey, the Lochs hoped Mrs Slaney would provide them with local colour for their book. In the event, their landlady proved to be mean, devious and manipulative, forever asking Joice to buy food and other household items for which she never paid her back. Eventually they discovered the only way to recoup the money was to deduct it from their weekly account for board and lodging. The weeks went by, but the promised repairs to their leaking window and the broken front-door lock were never made.

After several sessions of chat with Mrs Slaney, it became apparent that many of her closest friends were involved with the IRA. Joice hoped devoutly that if they were indeed living in a house with strong Irish Republican links, Sinn Fein would not catch sight of Sydney talking to Major X in a pub, take him for a spy and shoot him. In the evenings, after dining on one of Mrs Slaney's gristly stews accompanied by boiled potatoes, the Lochs would go out to visit the pubs with Jack White and his circle of writers. As authors and lovers of poetry they found themselves warmly accepted in a country which, unlike Australia, honoured writers and poets above sportsmen. Sir John Murray's letter of introduction to the poet William Butler Yeats was not needed. One evening, sheltering from crossfire between the Tans and the Sinn Fein in a doorway, they met Yeats' friend, the poet and writer George Russell, better known under his pen-name of 'Æ'.[9] When he heard they were writing a book for Sir John Murray, he promptly invited them to a party at his home.

At George Russell's house alcohol flowed freely as Irish patriots, writers and politicians mingled. The first person the Lochs met there was the elderly politician, Arthur Griffith, who had founded the Celtic Literary Society. Griffith, as elected member for Cavan in the Westminster Parliament, had come up with the idea that none of the elected Irish MPs should take up their seats in Westminster; instead, they should form their own Irish National Assembly, or Dail. Several Irish MPs with strong Republican leanings had followed his suggestion.

It was Griffith who finally introduced them to William Butler Yeats, whose poetry Joice loved so much. But Yeats was surrounded by a crowd of admirers and they did not get much chance to talk with him.

More approachable was the equally famous, striking-looking Constance Markiewicz. Daughter of Sir Henry Gore-Booth and a member of the Irish Protestant Ascendancy, as a young girl she had been sent to study in Paris, where, discarding other lovers, she had married the Polish-born Count Casimir Markiewicz. Eventually, however, her conscience as an Irish patriot had made her return to Ireland and abandon her unfaithful husband. Her brilliance as a speaker won her a seat at the Westminster Parliament—the first woman ever to be elected there—but she had followed Arthur Griffith's advice: she renounced the honour of being the first woman in Westminster in favour of a seat in the Dail. She had served as second-in-command during the 1916 Easter Uprising, was caught, sentenced to life imprisonment and finally reprieved after a public outcry. Now in her fifties, Constance Gore-Booth, as she preferred to be known, was Minister for Labour in the Dail. Joice was fascinated by Constance, impressed that a woman could achieve so much.

The Lochs became regular guests at George Russell's Sunday parties. They met Professor Douglas Hyde, the famous expert on Irish literature, who explained to the Lochs how the potato famine had 'knocked the heart out of the Irish language', because Gaelic became identified with poverty and peasanthood. After the famine the Irish middle-classes joined the British in forcing Irish children to abandon the Gaelic tongue and learning to speak and write in English. At school, any child who spoke Irish was given a penalty: as a result, the Irish language was dying out.

This lively group of talented writers and politicians was inspired by the belief that Irish art, folk dancing and literature must be rediscovered and promoted. Most of them were anti-violence; they had joined Sinn Fein because they feared they might be the last generation to read and speak Gaelic. They saw it as a tragedy that the Irish, the most literate people on earth, were being denied their own heritage. Most of them did not support the violence of Collins and his henchmen. They wanted to achieve their aims by political means . . . although a few of Arthur Griffith's guests confided to the Lochs their hope that Michael Collins' strong-arm tactics would force the British Prime Minister Lloyd George and his Government into negotiations over a Republic.

Summer was waning, the leaves were falling. At Mrs Slaney's lodging house, elderly Mrs O'Grady mopped and dusted the rooms each morning. She had spent weeks silently watching Joice typing up notes, until she was convinced the Lochs really were journalists rather than British spies. One morning Mrs O'Grady confided to Joice that the reason Mrs Slaney always kept the front door open was because she sometimes sheltered Irish Republic Army members overnight. Mrs O'Grady made it plain that she did not approve of Mrs Slaney's Sinn Fein connections, but would never broach the subject to her employer. Mrs O'Grady had a sick husband to support, and having been evicted from their previous home, they needed the basement apartment which Mrs Slaney provided free of charge. Mrs O'Grady also helped Polly, a pert, pretty girl of sixteen, to serve breakfast and the evening meal, or 'high tea', as well as doing the tenants' washing and ironing.

'All I wish is that herself would stop bringing Collins' men here. We could be shot in our beds,' she told Joice.

The apartment directly below the Lochs, on the ground floor, was let to a young woman with golden-brown curly hair, a sweet smile and a small baby. 'She's a writer like youse,' Mrs O'Grady told them. 'Her husband visits occasionally but only at night. They say he is on the run from the Tans.'

When Sydney interviewed the Irish around the pubs, he was careful not to talk to one side about the fears and aims of the other; he had no wish to get shot. He learned that Michael Collins' hidden supporters included typists, station-masters and porters, farm labourers, waiters and barmen, all of whom passed information onto Collins and his Apostles about British movements. One day he bumped into Major X again at the *Sod of Turf*. The Major was disguised as a working-class Irishman. 'My wife's terrified the IRA are onto us. Something terrible's going to happen soon,' he whispered to Sydney.

Sydney was amazed that the IRA had not noticed Major X and his friends earlier. They seemed far more concerned about their expense accounts than their disguises, and the stagey Irish accents they adopted must make them the laughing stock of Collins and his men. Major X seemed to know less about Collins and his men than Joice had learned simply from studying the Irish newspapers each morning. She suggested to Sydney that perhaps British Intelligence should have saved their money and subscribed to a newspaper-cutting agency instead of sending Major X and his colleagues to live in Dublin's most expensive hotel. The Lochs concluded that by now Collins could not fail to know the whereabouts of Major X and his Intelligence colleagues, and be planning the right moment to shoot them all. The situation was a powder keg awaiting a spark to ignite it.

8   IRELAND'S BITTER WAR OF INDEPENDENCE

The adoption scheme Joice had wanted to pursue, under which English and Australian mothers might adopt orphaned Irish babies, was still in her mind. In search of orphaned children she visited Dublin slums where fathers and breadwinners had been murdered or were in jail. She gave food and toys to neglected, starving and abused children, and was horrified by their living conditions. In many cases a single cold tap in a backyard provided washing and drinking water for thirty or forty people. On several occasions she found rats had gnawed the arms and legs of babies she hoped might be given up for adoption. But whenever she tried to persuade these families living under such terrible conditions to release a baby for adoption, as Catholics they insisted that they must first talk to the priest. The priests invariably counselled the families: 'Better a dead child than one brought up in England among heathen Protestants.'

The story was the same with Irish Protestants, who also refused to surrender orphaned nephews, nieces or cousins to the wicked English. Confronted by such hostility, Joice's adoption scheme withered away.

She realised she would do better to concentrate her efforts on writing. By now she was feeling the strain of being surrounded by guerrilla warfare. After dark she often saw lights shining out from Mrs Slaney's top floor.[1] One night she heard screams and gunfire in Ely Place, and on her way to the Library next morning, she saw a pool of blood on the front steps, with bloody footprints receding down Ely Place. Were there IRA members living in Mrs Slaney's house? By the time she got home the bloodstains had vanished and Mrs Slaney denied any knowledge of them.

Meanwhile, Major X was growing ever more nervous because Michael Collins and his boys, having eliminated most of the Irish informers, were now honing in on Winston Churchill's hand-picked British spies. Three had been murdered in the streets. Major X and his colleagues had to report each week to Dublin Castle. Were they being betrayed by a double agent? Joice felt sorry for Major X's wife and went round to the Gresham Hotel to see her. She found that the Xs were no longer there, and had left no forwarding address. Sydney managed to discover that they had moved to a rented apartment under the name of Mr and Mrs Dermot O'Reilly.

On Sunday, 21 November 1920, Joice and Sydney rose early, planning a day off. They caught the tram to the small fishing town of Howth, north of Dublin, walked to Howth Head to see the view over Dublin bay, and took a boat ride out to the rocky islet known as Ireland's Eye, home to a colony of puffins. They thoroughly enjoyed their day; tired but happy, they caught the tram back to Dublin . . . and as they neared the city they were stunned to see a blaze on the far side of the water, as if a ship were on fire.

As they descended from the bus, a British Army lorry roared past. Poking out from the canvas they saw what appeared to be the legs of a dead soldier. More lorries roared by, full of Black and Tans with rifles at the ready, disappearing over O'Connell Bridge in the direction of Dublin Castle.

On a street corner a newsboy cried out: 'British spies murdered! Read all about it.'

Sydney bought an evening paper. The front-page headline leapt out at them: 'Fourteen British Officers Involved in Intelligence Work Murdered'. It seemed that Michael Collins' men had murdered the fourteen officers as they lay in their beds, in the presence of their wives. Was Major X one of these victims? They read how the wife of one of the officers had flung herself across her husband's body to save him, but the gunmen had dragged her off before despatching him.

The newsboy told them the very latest events, not yet in the paper. It seemed the Black and Tans, insisting that they were searching for IRA gunmen in the Sunday football crowd, had driven two of their armoured cars onto the turf at Croke Park Stadium during the All-Ireland football match. Without warning they opened fire, killing a footballer. Amid general hysteria, they fired into the crowd, killing a dozen Irishmen, a British soldier and a small boy and wounding hundreds more. The names of the dead and wounded would be published in the next day's paper.

It was not yet curfew time. In the streets Army patrols, fearing a mass riot, were firing off blank cartridges as a warning to everyone to stay indoors. It wasn't safe to go to Major X's rented apartment as yet, so the Lochs returned to Mrs Slaney's lodging house. They leaned out of their window watching the scene in the street below. A passing officer, seeing them silhouetted against the light from the room, yelled, 'Keep your bloody heads inside!'

Mrs Slaney bustled in, her eyes blazing with triumph. 'British spies, every one of them!' she declared. 'Military justice from our Republican Army!'

It was too much. Joice thought of Major X's wife. She turned on Mrs Slaney. 'Those men were shot as they lay in bed, in front of their wives. Their murderers were not in uniform. What sort of military justice is that?'

The next morning, leaving Joice to read the Irish papers and write up an account of 'Bloody Sunday', Sydney went round to Major X's apartment. He found him alive but badly shaken by the deaths of his colleagues. He told Sydney how his colonel, a bachelor who lived in the Gresham, had opened his door to the girl who cleaned his room. A gunman had stepped out from behind her and shot him dead.

Major X's wife was on the verge of hysteria, complaining that none of the undercover agents had been issued with guns. Their friends had been shot while sleeping, bathing or shaving. 'Collins and his men have been watching us for weeks,' Major X said, white-faced. His wife was packing her suitcase and tearfully insisted he must buy a gun or get one from the Army and sleep with it beside him.

The Major told Sydney that one quick-witted wife had saved her husband when the IRA called by saying that he had just gone out. With a long list of intended victims, the two gunmen departed and went to shoot the next man on the list instead.

Another British Intelligence wife was not so lucky: her husband was badly wounded, and she rushed into the street looking for a doctor. Wild-eyed, she approached a pleasant-looking Irishman.

'My husband has just been shot,' she gasped, 'but he's alive. Please could you get a doctor?'

'Still alive! My God, I'll finish the bastard off!' The man ran into the house, pulling out his gun. He shot the wounded man in the head and killed him.

The following afternoon Sydney and Joice watched the funeral of the fourteen British Intelligence officers murdered by the IRA. All Dublin seemed to have turned out to see the fourteen coffins pass by, each draped in the Union Jack. Shops were closed and the Black and Tans threw any young Irishmen who seemed disrespectful into the Liffey.[2]

Each day the guerrilla war intensified and the armoured cars of the Black and Tans conducted more and more house-to-house searches.

'Open up in the King's name! Open up or we break down the door!' Women and children, barefoot and half-dressed, were turned into the street as the houses were searched for hidden arms and secret documents, and the breadwinner dragged off for interrogation to Dublin Castle. By now Ireland's prisons were overflowing. The Tans in their chicken-coop lorries and armoured cars patrolled the streets day and night hunting for elusive enemies who were everywhere and nowhere. Terrible tales were whispered in those final weeks of 1920 of men hunted by bloodhounds, police slaughtered and their bodies hacked to pieces with axes, burnt-out shops and farms, and blindfolded prisoners taken to lonely places by night and made to dig their own graves, but promised the gift of life if they would reveal which of their neighbours belonged to Sinn Fein.[3]

By now the Sinn Fein were hard-pressed. Many of their leaders had been imprisoned.[4]

One night Mrs Slaney proudly announced to the Lochs that the mysterious tenant with the baby on the ground floor was none other than Mrs Fitzgerald, wife of Desmond Fitzgerald, the Minister for Information and Propaganda in the Dail who was wanted by the Black and Tans. 'I did it for Ireland,' Mrs Slaney told them proudly. 'No one else would take Mrs Fitzgerald in. They're too afraid of being raided. Her husband only comes here occasionally, poor soul. A most cultured man, another writer like yourselves.'[5] Mrs O'Grady told Joice that Mabel Fitzgerald was an educated lady, a former Protestant from Belfast who had converted to Catholicism for love of her husband. Desmond Fitzgerald was another Irish politician who had been elected to the British Parliament, but had not taken up his seat. The British had a price on his head.

When Mrs O'Grady came in to clean the Loch's apartment next day, she took a different view and confided: 'if you ask me it's downright wicked of Mrs Slaney to have rented rooms to that Mrs Fitzgerald, whose husband's a wanted man. And now you know why the front door is always left open at night. This house could be searched at any moment—Jaysus, Mary and Joseph protect us!'

Joice always listened to Mrs O'Grady with a slightly sceptical ear. However, next time Mrs Slaney came down for the 'loan' of a cigarette she asked her once again why she left the front door unlocked at night when so many burglars and murderers were about.

'Sure to goodness, Mrs Loch, I'm only after letting the rooms to a poor young woman with a baby. What is it to you if her husband chooses to visit his wife during the night? Mr Fitzgerald's a fine Irish patriot—he'll be a member of the Cabinet once Ireland's a Republic. We should be just as proud of him as we are of Michael Collins.' When Mrs Slaney saw the look on Joice's face at the mention of Michael Collins' name, she clammed up and refused to answer any more questions.

That afternoon Joice watched Mrs Fitzgerald in her long green cape wheel out a pram containing a chubby blond baby. She told Mrs Fitzgerald how handsome her baby boy was. Mrs Fitzgerald smiled back. 'His name is Fergus,' she told Joice.

A few days later Mrs Fitzgerald greeted Joice and said that Mrs O'Grady had told her that she was a writer from Australia, a country that had given shelter to many Irish patriots. She invited Joice into her apartment and over a cup of coffee she explained that she and her husband had spent two years in an artists' and writers' commune in Brittany. Not surprisingly, Mabel Fitzgerald and Joice discovered they had mutual friends in George Russell's circle of writers and artists.[6]

A friendship grew between the two women. Talking with Mabel, Joice learned to understand the Republican point of view more clearly. A dedicated member of the Cumann na mBan, the women's branch of the Irish Republican Army, Mabel spent most of her time writing press releases for her husband's Department, explaining why Ireland must become a Republic.

Mabel Fitzgerald had lost her home and seen her furniture and possessions smashed by the Black and Tans. Fearing the Tans might harm them, she had sent her two eldest boys to boarding school. She was terrified that her husband might be shot at any moment. She had difficulty sleeping, scarcely ate and was losing weight. Feeling a sense of comradeship with a fellow writer, she confided to Joice that she risked imprisonment by carrying in her handbag her husband's press releases, which she typed up at night. She also campaigned on behalf of Sinn Fein members in Irish jails and tried to raise money for the Irish White Cross—the equivalent of the British Red Cross. Fortunately, as yet the police and the Black and Tans were not allowed to search women. Ireland was a devoutly Catholic country with a peculiarly prudish attitude to sexuality. Sinn Fein and the Republican Army exploited this loophole, using wives and girlfriends to carry messages, bombs and guns for them.

Towards the end of the year, Father Flanagan, Acting President of the Irish Republic in the absence of de Valera, who was in America raising funds for the cause, telegraphed a letter to Mr Lloyd George, the British Prime Minister, stating that the IRA were ready to make peace and asking him what measures he proposed.

Christmas 1920 came and went, and still the British did not know what Michael Collins looked like. Mabel Fitzgerald described him as tall, athletic and square-jawed. Once, the Black and Tans raided a 'safe' house where he and his gang had been working and found his signature on a cheque, the ink still wet. As always Collins had managed to escape over the rooftops and continue his work from another 'safe' house. He was rumoured to have a complete wardrobe of disguises. Joice wondered if Mrs Slaney's house had ever harboured him.

In January 1921 de Valera slipped back into Ireland from America, his return hailed in the Irish press as a triumph for Sinn Fein. Major X told Sydney that the British Government did not want to jail de Valera, since they felt they might be able to negotiate with him. The newspapers announced that Michael Collins had ordered that all British and Northern Ireland goods in the shops were to be boycotted by the Irish.

Mrs O'Grady hinted darkly that yet another Sinn Fein leader, the novelist, journalist and gun-runner Darrell Figgis, used Mrs Slaney's top-floor apartment as an office for his banned newspaper, the *Irish Republican*, whenever it became too risky to work in his own office. 'Mr Figgis is here whenever you see a light under the door at the top floor at night,' she told Joice.

Joice had seen copies of Figgis' clandestine newspaper lying around Mrs Slaney's breakfast room and had taken some copies to use as background material for their book, storing them away in her desk drawer.

One evening when Sydney was out watching the Black and Tans raid a house, Joice was visited by Mrs Slaney bearing a tray with a coffee pot. After drinking the coffee, Joice insisted on carrying the tray back upstairs. She was intrigued to know whether Darrell Figgis was using the place as his office at that very moment.

She saw a light under the door that led to Mrs Slaney's apartment and remembered Mrs O'Grady's words. Opening the door, Joice beheld a tall man with a golden beard who reminded her of a Viking warrior, hunched over a typewriter. Surely this was Darrell Figgis. He looked up, and Joice saw that he had deep blue eyes. He smiled and said 'Good evening' before Mrs Slaney appeared hard on Joice's heels, apologised for the intrusion, made no effort to introduce them and bustled her out of the room.

Major X was now living in Dublin Castle. Joice found it amazing that he was still unharmed. Sydney no longer met him around the pubs because he thought it too dangerous for them to be seen together. Now their brief clandestine meetings took place in Dublin's Botanical Gardens. The Major complained bitterly that many of the new batch of British Intelligence agents sent to replace the murdered ones were unprofessional; he feared that they would soon be murdered as well. Sydney and Joice had always intended their book should be impartial and objective, explaining the Irish case for independence as well as the British point of view. However, they found it was difficult to remain impartial in a country where political and religious hatreds abounded after seven centuries of British rule, under which the Irish had suffered famine, poverty, torture and dispossession.

One night a pounding from the heavy front-door knocker heralded the arrival of the Black and Tans to search Mrs Slaney's house. Mrs Slaney had been enjoying a smoke and one of her 'good craiks' in the Lochs' sitting room. Her hand flew to her heart. 'Holy Mother of God, who's that?' She ran out of Joice's sitting room and started up the stairs, but then she seemed to change her mind. She turned back, sat on the sofa and folded her hands demurely.

Polly the little maid went to open the front door. From the landing Joice peered down into the hallway. Through the half-opened doorway of Mabel Fitzgerald's apartment she could see baby Fergus in his nappy being passed around by some Black and Tans, who were tickling him under the chin and saying how handsome he was. Meanwhile one soldier searched his cot, a favourite hiding-place for IRA guns. Suddenly Joice remembered that Mabel had told her she would hide any incriminating Sinn Fein documents in Fergus' nappy if they were searched.

At that moment Mabel came out and called up through the stair-well. 'Will someone please look after my baby?'

Joice immediately rushed downstairs. She took Fergus into her sitting-room and tucked him under a rug on their sofa. His nappy bulged and crackled in a disconcerting way. Documents, their contents probably enough to hang his father if they were found, were obviously hidden there.

Mrs Slaney made things worse by going on the attack with the Tans. 'Are youse the blackguards who murdered those unfortunate boys at Drumcondra the other night?' she hissed. A shiver ran down Joice's spine. If *anyone* could get them all arrested it would be Mrs Slaney.

'You are Mrs Slaney, owner of this house,' the officer confirmed. 'Perhaps you can explain why you rented rooms to Desmond Fitzgerald, an IRA rebel and a wanted man. You are in a serious position, Mrs Slaney. Do you know the penalty for harbouring rebels?'

'I let rooms to Mrs Fitzgerald. Sometimes Mr Fitzgerald has his meals here—that's all,' Mrs Slaney told the officer defiantly.

After an hour of fruitless searching the Black and Tans departed empty-handed. As soon as the door banged behind them, Mabel Fitzgerald retrieved Fergus and the precious papers. But it was obvious to the Lochs that from now on the Tans and British Intelligence officers would be watching the house.

A week later, returning from a meeting with some Irish journalists, Sydney found two Army lorries blocking the road outside Mrs Slaney's front door. Black and Tans and Auxiliary officers, guns at the ready, were milling around in the street. A neighbour called out: 'They've raided Mrs Slaney's house!'

Joice, Mrs Fitzgerald and Mrs Slaney were standing on the doorstep watching as the Tans ordered Desmond Fitzgerald, wearing handcuffs, into a lorry, then drove away, presumably to jail him in Dublin Castle.

Mabel Fitzgerald was surprisingly calm. 'Desmond's safer in Dublin Castle than being at large,' she said. 'As long as the newspapers are informed he has been taken prisoner, the British won't dare to touch a Minister of the Irish Provisional Government. There was more chance that he might have been shot in the street.' She added: 'I shall go on writing his press releases.' Then she sat down to type up the story of her husband's arrest, and took it to a newspaper office in time to appear the following day.

Next morning, Mrs O'Grady warned Joice about Polly, the maid. 'One moment she's walking out with a Black and Tan and the next with a Sinn Feiner. That girl talks too much. She could get us all in trouble, the way she changes her affections.'

Mrs O'Grady's foreboding came true.

Mrs Slaney received a message that the Black and Tans, acting on a tip, had raided Darrell Figgis' new apartment in Molesworth Street, broken his typewriters, robbed his files and carried away all the back numbers of his *Irish Republican* newspaper to Dublin Castle. Figgis was incriminated up to his golden beard. Now he was on the run, but nobody expected him to remain a free man unless Michael Collins could smuggle him away somewhere.[7]

Fearing Mrs Slaney's house would be searched again, Mabel Fitzgerald paid a man to remove her own typewriter and some

Republican Army files hidden in an old sack. She decided it was no longer safe to remain at Mrs Slaney's and arranged to stay with some old friends.

Joice and Sydney also contemplated moving but by this time they had spent most of the publisher's advance and cheap apartments like Mrs Slaney's were not easy to find. Ely Place was convenient and central and Mabel Fitzgerald had offered them a chance to rent her much larger fully furnished apartment, containing her beautiful antiques and paintings. As a hot-bed of Republican intrigue, the Lochs realised that their time at the 'safe house' in Ely Place had given them some excellent material for their book.

9 'IRELAND IN TRAVAIL'— THE FINAL CHAPTERS

The evening before Mrs Fitzgerald was due to move out, Joice and Sydney heard the sound of approaching lorries, followed by the squeal of brakes. From their window they watched the Black and Tans charge up Mrs Slaney's stone steps, guns in hand. Joice's main worry was for her typed manuscript, which was highly critical of the Black and Tans. If they found it, would it be confiscated or destroyed?

'Open up or we'll break the door down!'

Joice hastily bundled together her notes, the typescript and its carbon copy. Where could she hide them?

It was too late. Three Black and Tans in jack boots and an Auxiliary officer burst into their sitting-room.

'Where's Darrell Figgis?' the officer in charge demanded.

'Haven't seen him for months,' Sydney said, trying to look casual, sprawled on the sofa, long legs out in front of him.

The officer demanded to see their passports. 'Oh... an Orstralian. What on earth are you doing *here?*' he asked Joice, who replied that she was trying to establish a child adoption scheme. Then, before she could warn Sydney, he explained that writing a book about Ireland was their main reason for being in Dublin. She glared at Sydney but it was too late. The officer picked up her typescript and issued a curt command to the Tans to search the ground floor and basement.

Joice still had some back issues of Darrell Figgis' *Irish Republic* newspaper in the bottom drawer of her desk. She realised with horror that Figgis was a wanted man, a former Secretary to Sinn Fein. If they found copies of his politically subversive newspaper, she and Sydney would be seen as Sinn Fein or even Irish Republican Army members. They must appear cooperative to the British Army major who was now leafing through her typescript. She must try to deflect his attention before he read the part about the drunkenness of the Black and Tans and how they terrorised and tortured the Irish.

How could she stop him? Joice knew from experience that even the keenest readers easily lose enthusiasm reading typescripts bristling with corrections. 'Please, officer, take the manuscript with you. Read the whole thing,' she said, smiling. 'I'd welcome your opinion. Did you know my husband published an excellent history of the fighting at Gallipoli?' Keeping her hand steady, she poured a cup of coffee and offered it to the major.

He glanced briefly at her typescript, covered with crossings-out and handwritten corrections, saw that reading it would mean a lot of work, lost interest and handed it back to her. He then sat down to drink his coffee and lit up a cigarette. Ignoring Joice, he chatted away to Sydney, confiding that while on leave from the Indian Army, he had seen an advertisement for officers in a special force being raised for service in Ireland—the Auxiliaries. The pay was higher than he received in the Indian Army, and he had enlisted. Now he bitterly regretted it. He hadn't thought working with the Black and Tans would be so tough. 'All I want is to get back to Poona, once we've beaten the Shinners.' From the floor above came a series of bumps and bangs and what sounded like the smashing of china. The Black and Tans were searching Mrs Slaney's rooms.

A high-pitched scream reverberated down the stairwell. Had Mrs Slaney insulted the Black and Tans? Had they found hidden guns?

Heavy footsteps clumped down the stairs. The major went outside. Joice could not make out a word of their muttered conversation. After some minutes the major returned. His smile had faded. He turned on Sydney aggressively. 'You're coming with us.'

Sydney looked amazed at the major's change in attitude.

'They've found guns and ammo in Mrs Slaney's bedroom. We're taking in every male in this house for questioning. Harbouring ammunition is a very serious offence in times of civil unrest.'

In vain Sydney protested while Joice backed him up.

Then Mrs Slaney appeared in a red flannel nightdress, dragged along by two huge soldiers. Her face was mottled red and white with rage. 'It's monstrous,' she hissed at the officer. 'Monstrous. All this fuss over a few war trophies. They belong to my son. He's a major in the British Army, the same as yourself.'

Clearly the major did not believe her. He told Mrs Slaney she was extremely fortunate that he was not allowed to search or arrest a woman. The men in the house would be held responsible and taken to jail. They could be tried. If found guilty they could be shot for treason.

Joice felt slightly sick. She wrapped a warm scarf round Sydney's neck and gave him a quick hug before the two soldiers jammed a gun in his back and frog-marched him downstairs.

In the front hall they found Mrs Fitzgerald attempting to calm the tearful Mrs O'Grady. Mr O'Grady, in a shabby bowler hat and a long, threadbare black overcoat looked as abject as a whippet in the wind.

A Black and Tan prodded Sydney with his bayonet. 'Move it,' he said harshly. 'We're off to the Castle.'

Joice looked on aghast as Sydney and Mr O'Grady were forced into an open Army lorry covered with chicken wire. The soldiers roped them to the central hitching post bolted to the floor. With anguish Joice realised that Sydney and Mr O'Grady were being used as hostages to prevent the IRA throwing bombs at the lorry.

The small fleet of Army transports revved up their engines and roared off into the night as Mrs Slaney screamed curses at their rear lights.

Joice tried to comfort Mrs O'Grady, who recovered herself sufficiently to turn on her employer. 'May God forgive you, Mrs Slaney, for I never will. You're wicked, d'you hear me? Wicked. You knew those bullets and guns were there all the time!'

'Hush now, Mrs O'Grady,' Joice urged. She remembered that Mrs Slaney had one son murdered by the British while the other had joined the British Army. 'We must have a talk, try to sort things out.'

'And how can I hush with himself perishing of the cold and a cruel cough on his chest,' Mrs O'Grady lamented. 'It's dead he'll be, the poor man, before they even start their torturing.'

'Pull yourself together, Mrs O'Grady,' ordered Mrs Slaney, who had regained her own composure. 'O'Grady will come to no harm. It will be good for the two of them to experience what hundreds of heroic Irishmen go through. Come upstairs now, I'll make us all a nice cup of tea. Trials and tribulations like this are uniting Ireland.'

They trooped up to the top floor. In Mrs Slaney's sitting room there was a mess of overturned little tables, aspidistras spilling earth from their pots and smashed china ornaments. Surprisingly, the usually volatile Mrs Slaney seemed unmoved by the chaos. She bustled about making tea and brought it to them in a Belleek teapot covered with shamrocks. Poor Mrs O'Grady slumped in her chair, clutching a shawl around her.

Mabel Fitzgerald, who had lived through several similar experiences, gave Joice practical advice: 'Go up to the Castle first thing tomorrow. If you can't get your husband out, find a good Protestant and Unionist solicitor. It's no good me getting any of our legal friends to help—they're on the side of Sinn Fein.'

Pressed by Joice and Mrs Fitzgerald, Mrs Slaney agreed to send a telegram to her son at Catterick Camp in England, asking him to confirm that the ammunition was his. Joice reflected again on the bitter irony that Mrs Slaney should have one son serving as a British officer while the other had been killed during an IRA raid on a barracks. High unemployment in Ireland had brought strange consequences to the Slaney family.

But at breakfast next morning, Mrs Slaney had totally changed her tune and now refused to contact her son. 'I'll just have a word with one or two grand men in our Republican Army. They'll sort it out, have no fear.'

'How? With more guns?' Joice asked with a shudder.

'We'll let Mick Collins know,' insisted her landlady.

'No, please, Mrs Slaney. Collins' Twelve Apostles going out with their guns and shooting *more* British officers would only make things worse. Much worse. You must send a telegram to your son, asking him to identify the guns and ammunition as his. I'm sure he wouldn't like to think he'd got two innocent men arrested.'

'I have to protect my son. He's highly strung—shell shock in France,' Mrs Slaney lied.

'Send the telegram, please. Time's running out. We can't leave my husband and O'Grady to rot in a cell.' Joice paused. 'Unless you wire your son, I'll have to tell my solicitor you're running an IRA "safe house".'[1]

At this threat, Mrs Slaney caved in. Reluctantly she produced a telegraph form and addressed it to Major Slaney, Royal Artillery, Catterick Camp. Joice took it to the Post Office.

Having sent it, she walked briskly through the city to Dublin Castle, the administrative centre of the British Government in Ireland. Challenged by an armed guard, Joice gave her name, which the guard wrote down. She walked across the castle's vast forecourt and entered a second, larger yard, above which loomed a vast bell tower. A line of white chalked arrows directed her down a stone-flagged passageway which reeked of damp.

On her right a door opened. She was ushered into an office lined from floor to ceiling with brown manila files. A soldier smiled and handed her a printed form. 'Please fill this out, ma'am.' It was a job application for women to search Irish female suspects! Discovering that Joice was visiting a prisoner suspected of harbouring ammunition, the soldier's expression changed. His smile faded. 'Get out of here, yer feckin' Sinn Fein bitch.'

Hastily Joice backed out. She entered the next office, only to find no one knew anything at all about prisoners. The word 'ammunition' aroused fear in everyone she met.

An hour later, after tramping down countless more stone passageways and making more fruitless enquiries, she was shown into yet another dimly-lit office. The officer in charge consulted a wall chart on which Sydney was shown as sharing a cell with a Sinn Fein gunman and a cat burglar.

Joice was furious. 'My husband's an innocent man. You've put him in a cell with a murderer. He could be killed.'

The officer smiled wearily. 'You women are all the same. You come in here crying and pleading your husbands' innocence.' Joice exploded. 'I'm *not* crying. My husband *is* innocent!' The officer spoke grimly. 'Mrs Loch, your lodging house has a very bad reputation. Darrell Figgis, editor of an underground Sinn Fein newspaper, was caught there, and Desmond Fitzgerald, Sinn Fein's Minister of Information, was arrested there. Michael Collins and his gunmen have used it as a safe house. Why *should* we believe your husband is innocent. Good God! Darrell Figgis was working at Mrs Slaney's only two days ago. All four of you typing away at subversive material while British soldiers are being assassinated by Michael Collins and his men.'

Joice felt trapped in a nightmare. She tried to clear her throat. 'We're nothing to do with Mr Figgis,' she croaked. 'My husband and I are working on a book. We rent rooms at Mrs Slaney's. Nothing more.'

The officer pointed to a file on his desk. 'Damn it, woman, our intelligence agents have dossiers on you and all your IRA friends.'

'Mrs Slaney's my landlady, not my friend. And if storing ammunition is treason, then why not arrest Mrs Slaney?' Joice demanded, regaining her voice. 'That way, you'd earn the thanks of us all.'

The officer sighed. 'We can't. The British public are so sentimental. Arresting a woman means endless questions at Westminster. We know Sinn Fein women are up to their necks in gun-running. But until we get female searchers working for us, we've orders to leave the women alone.'

'I see,' said Joice.

'If, and only if, Mrs Slaney's son communicates with us and lays claim to the stuff, then we can release your husband, providing someone we trust here vouches for him.'

Joice mentioned Major X, giving the Intelligence Officer's full name and adding that after Bloody Sunday he had moved from the Gresham Hotel to the Castle.

The officer looked up from his notes with interest. 'He's away on a mission in Belfast. Won't be back for weeks. If Major X vouches for your husband, everything's all right.'

'Away for *weeks*! My husband could be dead by then. He's in a cell with a convicted murderer!'

'Directly Mrs Slaney's son claims the ammunition we'll let your husband go. I promise.'

'Can a solicitor see him?'

'Of course.'

Joice took Mrs Fitzgerald's advice and telephoned Dublin's best known Unionist solicitor, requesting an appointment the same day.

At the solicitor's office, she was shown into a large well-furnished room with a picture of King George V on the wall. The corpulent solicitor behind his enormous mahogany desk seemed reluctant to visit Sydney.

'Michael Collins' Republican Army watch the Castle day and night,' he said. 'They take down the names of everyone who goes in. If I go there, I could be shot. Now about my fees . . .' He named a huge sum. Joice thought quickly. She would give the lawyers what money remained in their savings account, and earn the rest by writing articles for Lord Northcliffe and any other Fleet Street papers about the IRA and Sydney's arrest. If needs be she would offer to wash dishes and sweep floors at Mrs Slaney's . . . absolutely anything to get Sydney out of jail.

'Don't worry, you'll get your money,' she said firmly. 'But in three instalments. I'll write the first cheque now.'

At the mention of a cheque, the lawyer suddenly became most helpful. Of course he would visit Sydney in jail tomorrow. And he would wire Mrs Slaney's son in Britain, asking him to confirm the guns and ammunition were his. Joice felt slightly happier.

But that night, alone in their lumpy double bed, she could not sleep. Was Sydney being tortured? She had heard from Mrs Slaney that the Black and Tans removed prisoners' finger nails with pliers if they suspected information was being withheld. One o'clock, two o'clock, three o'clock chimed before she finally dozed off into a restless sleep.

It was still dark when she awoke with the sensation someone else was in the room. She lay motionless, hardly daring to breathe. Through half-closed eyelids she saw a man in a black Balaclava thumbing through the papers on her desk. Was he searching for her manuscript? Did Michael Collins' men want it, fearing it would incriminate them? Turning, he bent down and ran expert fingers through the long drawers under her wardrobe.

Joice watched through her eyelashes as the man padded cat-like around her bedroom, a pistol protruding from his leather belt. Rummaging through her suitcase he pricked himself on a needle and cursed in a rich Irish brogue. Joice kept her breathing regular, pretending to be sleeping. He ignored her purse—obviously it was not money he was after.

After what seemed like an eternity, unable to find what he sought, the man climbed out of the sash window. Like a shadow he disappeared across the rooftops. Had he been sent by Michael Collins?

The next morning Joice wired Guy Innes in Fleet Street. She offered him the exclusive story of Sydney's arrest, provided it did not appear under her by-line. It could be dangerous to reveal details about the boarding house and its connections with the IRA, so she changed Mrs Slaney's name and address. She realised Sinn Fein or the IRA would have no compunction about shooting her. The article would help to earn the solicitor's enormous fee. She stopped only for meals, which were grim affairs. Mrs O'Grady was in tears over her absent husband as she served watery Irish stew or the inevitable stewed prunes and custard. 'No one cares for folk who've no money to pay for justice,' she complained.

Joice promised to let Mrs O'Grady know just as soon as she received any news. She hoped her solicitor might arrange O'Grady's release as well.

The following afternoon Joice received a phone call from the solicitor. Her husband would be freed shortly. And Sydney had demanded O'Grady's release along with his own. He had been interrogated for three hours but was unharmed. Military Intelligence had wired Belfast and Major X had vouched for him. That was sufficient for his release. (Apparently Major Slaney had not replied to the telegram.) Sydney and O'Grady would be at the solicitor's office the next morning. Joice informed Mrs O'Grady, who called down blessings on her head.

Early next morning Joice was at the solicitor's office. Sydney, unshaved, his shirt grubby and jacket torn, was already there. Beside him stood little Mr O'Grady, coughing his lungs out. Sydney apologised to the solicitor for his dishevelled appearance. Their cell had been filthy. His tweed jacket had been torn when he was arrested. The solicitor looked pained but Joice did not care. Overjoyed, she hugged Sydney. The man she adored was safe, nothing else in the world mattered.[2]

When the Lochs and Mr O'Grady returned to Ely Place, Mrs Slaney and Mrs O'Grady were waiting in the front hall. Mrs O'Grady cried with relief as she clasped her husband. 'Blessings on your head, Mr Loch! Sure and it's a grand man ye'are.'

'Mr Loch, now you can write the truth about what happens to Irishmen in captivity,' Mrs Slaney exclaimed jubilantly.

In her employer's absence, Mrs O'Grady whispered the disturbing news that when clearing up the mess left by the Black and Tans, she had discovered gelignite behind Mrs Slaney's wardrobe. When Joice questioned her landlady, Mrs Slaney had the nerve to claim she was only keeping gelignite because it made her pot plants grow better!

Joice paid another visit to Mabel Fitzgerald, now installed in her friends' cottage on the city outskirts. When Mabel heard about the gelignite she was furious. Apparently Michael Collins insisted that only carefully selected people were allowed to keep bomb-making material. Mrs Slaney occupied a very humble position in the IRA's pecking order. She could have been asked to store a gun and ammunition for the IRA, but was certainly not authorised to keep gelignite. Mabel said she would see that Mrs Slaney received orders to get rid of it immediately. She told Joice that she was being watched by British Intelligence. After her last visit the 'privilege' of visiting her husband in jail had been withdrawn.

Over the next few weeks, Joice typed articles and news reports for Fleet Street while Sydney worked on the final draft of *Ireland in Travail*. John Murray wanted to bring the book out for Christmas next year. The question of Home Rule for Ireland and whether Ireland would be partitioned was on everyone's lips.

An election for a new Southern Irish Parliament or Dail took place. Sinn Fein, backed by the elderly and ailing Arthur Griffith, with de Valera in the shadows behind him, swept into power. The newly elected members would form the Second Dail or Irish Provisional Government.

On the afternoon of 21 May 1921, as the lilacs came into bloom in St Stephen's Green, Eamon de Valera's supporters celebrated their election by setting fire to the Customs House. Joice was horrified to hear the announcement crackle out over the radio. The Customs

House, a superb example of Georgian architecture, housed nine British Government Departments, including the Customs Service. Like the Post Office it had been chosen for destruction because it was a symbol of British imperialism.

Mabel Fitzgerald hinted that de Valera feared his authority over the IRA was waning and was now very jealous of Michael Collins. 'Perhaps Dev ordered the Customs House to be destroyed to see if Collins' men would obey his orders,' Mabel suggested.[3]

Joice and Sydney decided to go to the Customs House. A chill wind had sprung up and the huge fire burned fiercely. Half Dublin seemed to be there. Slowly the portico, with its magnificent baroque ornaments, collapsed and the huge dome caved in. Flames licked through stone crevices, leapt out of windows and roared through the roof. Pieces of charred material floated down around them. Unaccountably the huge clock on the building still continued to tick.

Joice scribbled away in her notebook, realising she could sell an eyewitness account to Fleet Street and pay off some more of her debt to the lawyer.

Mrs Slaney materialised as if by magic, a battered pair of field-glasses around her neck. 'It was the most beautiful building in Ireland,' she said grimly. Even she seemed embarrassed by such wanton destruction; but then, remembering her murdered husband and son, her hatred of the British flared up and she added, 'The Customs House represented British oppression in Ireland. England is to blame for the ruin of this place.'

Joice, busy taking notes, made no reply. Nothing she could say would make any difference.

Fireman were swarming up ladders but seemed powerless to do anything as the wind fanned the flames. Fire-hoses like grey sea serpents rose from the river Liffey. As fast as the fireman quenched the flames in one place so the wind fanned a new section of the blaze into life. Armoured cars roared around, loudspeakers blaring.

Beside Joice a bystander exclaimed, 'Holy Mother of God, 'tis a grander sight even than the burning of the Post Office!'

Finally the metal framework supporting the vast dome crumpled, leaving one of Ireland's architectural masterpieces a smoking ruin.

Sydney turned to find Major X at his elbow, unshaven and disguised in a cloth cap and shabby raincoat. He had aged visibly since the murder of his colleagues on Bloody Sunday.

Sydney was surprised to see him. 'I thought you were still in Belfast,' he said. 'When did they start the fire?'

'Around lunch time,' replied the Major. 'They took the staff completely by surprise—there was no resistance. They dismantled the telephones, herded the clerks to one end of the building, chucked paraffin and straw on the floors and set it alight.'

'Anyone killed?'

'Quite a few.'

At that moment a platoon of Black and Tans roared up in armoured cars. Two of them got out and insisted everyone move along. Major X melted away among the crowd. Joice was pleased to see that he had become much better at making himself inconspicuous.

The Lochs walked back to Ely Place past the Post Office, where Joice telegraphed an account of the fire to the Melbourne and London papers. This extra article meant she would have almost paid off the lawyer. Sydney was filled with admiration for the way his wife had master-minded his release from Dublin Castle. Her determined action had subtly changed the balance of their relationship: from this moment they were equal partners, something of a rarity in matrimony of this period.

Spring 1921 brought rumours of peace. But still the Black and Tans were driving around, guns at the ready. Rumours said the IRA were at the end of their tether. Sydney went to get a haircut round the corner one day and found his barber had just cut Michael Collins' hair and given him a shave.

The next day the Lochs' apartment was searched yet again. It was eight o'clock in the morning and Mrs Slaney had left for Mass. This time, as the Black and Tans bounded up the steps and banged on the front door, Joice hid the typescript of *Ireland in Travail* and her notes in a suitcase. Mrs O'Grady opened the door and the Black and Tans stormed into their sitting room demanding Mabel Fitzgerald's address.

'I don't know. She's been gone for months,' Joice told them. The officer in charge asked to see their passports. He looked round the room with its few pieces of good antique furniture, all that remained after most of the Fitzgeralds' possessions had been smashed by the Black and Tans.

The officer consulted an inventory. 'Seems that some of this furniture belongs to Mrs Fitzgerald,' he said, appraising the room like an auctioneer.

'Mrs Fitzgerald kindly left some of hers behind when we took over her apartment,' Joice said. 'She didn't leave a forwarding address but said she'd let us know when she'd got a place of her own so we could send the furniture on to her.'

The officer went into the bedroom, where the Black and Tans were poking their bayonets under every piece of furniture. 'Stop searching,' the officer said. 'You won't find Mrs Fitzgerald under the bed!'[4]

On 22 June 1921, King George V opened the new Northern Irish Parliament in Belfast, Ireland's most prosperous city with its shipyards, linen mills and rope works. From Belfast the King addressed a message of peace to all Ireland, calling on them to 'stretch out the hand of forbearance and conciliation, to forgive and forget'.

But he was talking to a deeply divided nation. Donegal, Monaghan and Cavan, once part of the north, contained Protestant settlers 'planted' by the British. The fact that these counties were to remain part of Southern Ireland aroused even more hostility between the north and the south of Ireland.

'They are ours by right,' Mrs Slaney declared. 'We'll show the British! Even if we have to plant bombs in northern Ireland as well.' From Monday, 11 July 1921, peace descended on Dublin as a limited transfer of power got under way.

The weather turned blisteringly hot. Joice wrote a news item for Fleet Street describing the Black and Tans driving out to Dublin's beaches in armoured cars with coloured beach towels hung over the chicken wire, smiling and laughing as though they were on holiday. It seemed the 'Irish War of Independence' was over at last.

Major X, once again wearing his khaki uniform, came to say goodbye on the way to catch the boat to England. He told the Lochs he was being sent on a special undercover mission to the Balkans. His cover in Ireland had been blown. Given his pathetic attempts at imitating an Irish brogue, Joice wondered why it had taken the IRA so long. Before the Major left, Sydney told him about the unsolved mystery of the nocturnal intruder in their apartment.

Major X looked worried. 'I'd hand in your manuscript and get out of Britain pretty damn quick. The IRA probably think Sydney squealed on them to Military Intelligence to get his release from the Castle. On top of that there's the fact that if they don't like something in your book, it could be disastrous for you both. Why not write a book on Russia or the Balkans or somewhere equally remote.'

He shook hands with Sydney, kissed Joice on the cheek and was gone, his parting words lingering in their minds.

In October 1921, Michael Collins and an ailing Arthur Griffith, 'the Father of Irish Republicanism', went to London to negotiate a truce with the British. Eamon de Valera refused to attend, fearing the talks would fail and his credibility be diminished as a result. Michael Collins was worried that the British press would be able to photograph him; he flew privately to London. But even then there were still a few photographs in the British press, revealing him as a square-jawed, clean-shaven youngish man. His anonymity was now a thing of the past.

The British negotiating team was composed of Prime Minister Lloyd George, Lord Birkenhead and Home Secretary Winston Churchill. The Irish delegates soon realised there was no chance that Ireland would be allowed to leave the Empire. Churchill and his colleagues insisted that a new Irish Government, like the newly-created Dominion of Canada, must swear an oath of allegiance to the British Crown. Collins saw this course as an abandonment of a great deal of what his Irish Republican Army had fought for. He foresaw civil war if militant young Republicans refused to swear allegiance to a British King. However, he knew that the Irish forces had only enough arms and ammunition to hold out against British troops for another couple of weeks at most. Desmond Fitzgerald, Minister of Information in the Dail, was still imprisoned in Dublin Castle. His wife was working day and night churning out press releases on behalf of the Irish Republican Government. Mabel Fitzgerald visited Ely Place to see the Lochs—she explained that if the talks failed to reach an agreement, martial law would be declared in Ireland and the killings would start all over again. After nearly two months of discussion, Michael Collins and his delegation finally signed their acceptance of an Irish Free State on what would become famous (or infamous) as the Anglo-Irish Treaty. Fearing the deadline given them for signature of the Treaty would expire, Collins, Griffith and the others signed before they had received the approval of a full meeting of the Dail Eirann in Dublin. The Treaty enraged fanatical members of the IRA. Mrs Slaney and her friends felt betrayed by Collins and complained to the Lochs that the new Irish State would remain part of the Commonwealth; members of the Dail must swear that the Irish Free State would be 'faithful to King George V, his heirs and successors at law'. 'The IRA will fight on till they get a *proper* Republic,' she told the Lochs. The day the terms of the Anglo-

Irish Treaty were announced on the radio and in the papers, Joice took her usual afternoon walk in St Stephen's Green, looking forward to hearing the military band that played there. The weather was warm and the sun shone. Mothers wheeled their babies in prams; nursemaids in white aprons escorted smiling children carrying teddy bears or bowling hoops along the paths. Everyone was converging towards the iron-lace bandstand. Suddenly, out of the corner of her eye, Joice saw a man hurl some object at a pram, then fling himself flat on the grass. A deafening blast followed, sweeping Joice off her feet. Her world spun around, then went black. When she regained consciousness she found herself lying face upwards on the grass surrounded by screaming women and children. Some had broken limbs, others lay still, blood trickling from their mouths. The Black and Tans appeared, shooting wildly. The pram at which the man had thrown the bomb was shattered, the baby inside a pulpy mass of blood and brains. As the Black and Tans dashed through the crowd, firing at random and pushing aside the screaming toddlers, mothers cradled their babies protectively.

Joice got to her feet, her head aching with the force of the blast. Beside her an abandoned toddler had what seemed to be a fit, then fell to the ground. She picked the infant up and cuddled him. The little boy turned purple, unable to breathe. Joice feared he would die and slapped him hard on the back. The sudden shock made him start breathing again.

A mother wheeling a pram approached Joice, claimed the little boy and thanked her in a voice cracking with emotion. Beside them another mother vented her feelings by exclaiming, 'Sinn Fein should be ashamed of themselves, throwing bombs at babies.' 'Them poor Shinners are only doing their duty for Ireland,' declared a nursemaid. 'In the name of God, why do them Black and Tans shoot back when it's only babies they hit.'

'And aren't the Black and Tans doin' their duty too?' responded the mother of the terrified child still clinging to Joice. Ignoring the screaming mothers, the Black and Tans herded together all the men in the Gardens and searched them at gun point. One soldier was delegated to guard the mothers and nursemaids. Another soldier took Joice's details along with those of the rest of the women. Then they were free to go. Stretcher bearers arrived to take away the wounded and the dead. Shaking with delayed shock, Joice hurried back to Ely Place.

Mrs O'Grady was standing at the front door, peering anxiously down the street, alongside Mrs Slaney. 'Mrs Loch, mum, are you all right? I was saying a rosary for you this very minute. Where have you been?' 'In St Stephen's Green, they threw a bomb—two babies were killed and others wounded, mothers and nursemaids'.

Mrs Slaney seemed unconcerned. 'The Tans shot one of the babies, not the Irish. That dreadful Treaty is wrong. It's a Republic or nothing for us. Write an article for the British and Australian press, Mrs Loch, explain the Treaty means that Ireland stays under the yoke of the British Monarchy. We Republicans *must* fight on if we want freedom.' Joice felt sick. How did Mrs Slaney know about the baby being shot by the Tans—could the bomber himself have told her? She understood the reasons why the IRA were bitter, but killing and maiming babies solved nothing.

'I *saw* the man who threw the bomb,' she said, shaking. 'Could he by any chance have come here for shelter?'

Mrs Slaney spluttered something inaudible and rushed inside the house.

That evening, Mabel Fitzgerald appeared with chubby Fergus in her arms and a holdall containing Fergus's pyjamas and washing things. Could Joice possibly mind him overnight? Mabel was very upset by the news of the dead babies and injured women. She blamed it on hotheads in the IRA who refused to swear allegiance to a British King. They had apparently vowed to continue the fight by any means available, 'fair or foul'. And she was worried about Michael Collins. He felt he had had no option but to sign the Anglo-Irish Treaty, but when he did so he had said: 'I've just signed my own death warrant.'[5]

The next day Joice still had a splitting headache. Fearing another raid by the Black and Tans in search of the bomber, she and Sydney decided it was an ideal time to visit Belfast, about to become the capital of the new Dominion of Ulster.

They found wealthy, Protestant Belfast totally different to bomb-scarred, impoverished Catholic Dublin. Belfast was a city of some 400,000 people. Its solid Victorian buildings provided evidence of the wealth acquired from its shipbuilding industry and linen mills. Outside Belfast's City Hall, statues of a glum-looking Queen Victoria and an even glummer Edward Harland, founder of the Harland and Wolff shipyards, glowered down on passers-by.

The Lochs interviewed Protestants and Catholics to obtain the feelings of both sides about the Anglo-Irish Treaty and the partition of

Ireland. Joice summed up her own feelings about the north and the south, describing how 'The Protestant Church, offering a stern Biblical version of a father's love, fitted the self-reliant Orange temperament. In Eire, the Catholic Church, which held out a mother's arms and embraced mysteries and miracles and saints appealed to the more mystical Celtic spirit. Strangers found the religious bigotry of Ireland astonishing and positively medieval in its religious intolerance'.

They watched an Orangemen's procession. Men in orange sashes, beating drums, carried embroidered banners bearing the portrait of William of Orange. Orange flags hung from the windows. Sydney observed that the stern God of the Irish Protestants obviously had entirely different ideas on decoration from those of the Catholic God. The situation in Ulster was growing uglier by the day as Catholics and Protestants launched a series of bitter attacks on each other.

The Lochs returned to Ely Place, where Mrs Slaney refused to discuss the affair of the mystery bomber in St Stephen's Green.

Mabel Fitzgerald brought Fergus round and had afternoon tea. Joice thought she was looking younger and happier than Joice had ever seen her. Now that the Treaty was signed, her husband would be released from jail. In the course of their conversation she made a rather mysterious remark. 'I don't blame Michael Collins,' she told Joice and Sydney in a confidential tone, 'but I don't approve of *every* aspect of his personal life.'

Joice asked her whether she meant Collins was a homosexual. Mabel laughed. 'Not at all!' Apparently not one but *two* married women were desperately in love with him and he was supposed to be 'very close indeed' with both of them, and he had been criticised for spending evenings with beautiful Hazel Lavery, the Irish-born wife of the elderly painter, Sir James Lavery. Mabel's friend Moya Llewellyn-Davies was supposed to be another of the women in Collins' life; she had been arrested hiding guns for Collins in a hat-box. She would do anything for him and his cause and had allowed premises to be rented under her name for Desmond's Propaganda Department.

Joice found it incredible that while negotiating a treaty, Michael Collins found time to carry on such liaisons. Mabel Fitzgerald mentioned a third woman, an Irish working-class girl, whom he talked of marrying.

When Joice told Sydney about Michael Collins carrying on with *three* women, he shrugged and said men were like that. 'If women proffer sex, most men take it.'

Joice had hoped to write about the feud between Eamon de Valera and Michael Collins, but no one wanted to provide her with details. There were rumours that de Valera was now playing a Machiavellian role in trying to overthrow the Treaty and undermine Collins' popularity.

In search of more information, the Lochs visited a close friend of Mabel's, American-born Mrs Molly Erskine Childers, whose home was known as the 'rock of Republicanism'. Molly walked with a stick due to a childhood skating accident. Years ago, in spite of her disability, she had risked her life to run guns into Ireland on a yacht manned by her husband and Darrell Figgis.[6] Mrs Childers was rumoured to have sheltered Collins when he was on the run and to have had a falling-out with de Valera. Joice enquired tactfully about the supposed feud, but Molly Childers discreetly glossed over any difficulties between them. She did, however, express her fears that now photos of Michael Collins had appeared in the press, his life could be in danger from an assassination attempt.

In the first week of January 1922, the Lochs were given two sought after entry tickets to the Press Gallery for the first public session of the Dail Eiraan. The tickets were sent by Desmond Fitzgerald as the Dail's official Minister for Propaganda, recently released from Dublin Castle. Mabel told Joice a secret. After all the fuss about the Treaty had died down, it would be announced that Desmond was to be appointed Irish Minister for Foreign Affairs.[7]

At Dublin's Mansion House Joice described how 'the whole city seemed to be lining up trying to get inside. Waiting in line, Sydney narrowly avoided being arrested for the second time, this time by Sinn Fein. They picked on Sydney because he was tall, wearing a dark suit and an old school tie. He looked and sounded very English'.

Two men had Sydney in an arm lock and wrestled him to the ground. Fortunately, Desmond Fitzgerald arrived in the nick of time and told them Mr Loch was a foreign journalist and they must let him go. Sydney smoothed down his hair, adjusted his tie and took his seat in the Press Gallery beside Joice.

The hall was packed with delegates and observers for this important moment in Irish history.[8] Guy Innes had commissioned Joice to wire the outcome of the Dail's historic meeting for the following morning's paper. She described Eamon de Valera as 'A tall stern man with a slim figure, born in New York of Spanish-Irish parentage'. De Valera had by now resigned as President, leaving Collins as leader of a divided

Southern Irish Free State with Dominion status, rather than a Republic. The ancient Gaelic name of Eire, which Sinn Fein had wanted, had not been granted to them at this stage.

On de Valera's right hand sat Arthur Griffith, 'the Father of Sinn Fein'. Joice recalled the talks they had had at George Russell's Sunday evening parties and thought how much he had aged. Beside Griffith sat Professor Douglas Hyde, author of *The Literary History of Ireland*. On his right was Michael Collins—'the legendary Michael Collins', Joice wrote, 'on whose head there had been a reward of four thousand pounds'. (A small fortune at that time.)[9]

Collins argued persuasively for the Anglo-Irish Treaty. Joice thought he looked more like an office worker than a freedom fighter. She whispered to Sydney that one reason Major X and the Black and Tans had never caught Collins was because they were hunting for a murderer in a cloth cap and baggy trousers. Collins had fooled them all by dressing like a conservative businessman. Today he wore a dark grey suit, white shirt and tie. Joice described him as 'an athletic young man on the verge of running to corpulence. His skin had a deadly pallor about it. His face was large, square and handsome. Now and then he tossed his head back with all the charm of a boy'.[10] Beneath his well-cut grey suit, Collins' shoulders were broad and muscular. Joice wondered how such a tall and masculine man had sometimes been able to disguise himself as a woman.

She was impressed by Michael Collins' speech. He raised powerful reasons why Eire should accept the Anglo-Irish Treaty and revealed that Lloyd George had threatened to send even more troops to wage 'immediate and terrible war' had he and the other delegates refused to sign the Treaty. Collins told his audience he had wanted to save Ireland from war. The Anglo-Irish Treaty was a stepping-stone to the Republic and would bring economic security to the Irish Free State. He went on to outline valuable tax concessions and agricultural assistance schemes they had managed to secure from the British Government, an important factor for lowering Ireland's high rate of unemployment. He concluded by saying the Irish must stand by the Treaty and try to build economic stability so that the new Irish Free State would prosper and Irishmen would be able to find jobs at home rather than having to emigrate overseas. There was only one alternative to the Treaty: outright war with the British Empire and the deaths of huge numbers of Irish men, women and children.

Although de Valera objected strongly, on 7 January, 1922, the Dail accepted the Anglo-Irish Treaty by sixty-four to fifty-seven votes.[11] When the result was announced, Eamon de Valera broke down in tears and resigned.

Shortly after that historic session of the Dail, Arthur Griffith collapsed and died. Michael Collins, as military chief and Prime Minister of the new Irish Free State, took over control of Dublin Castle, together with its guns and armoured cars from Lord FitzRoy, the retiring Viceroy of Ireland. At the take-over Lord FitzRoy remarked coldly, 'You're seven minutes late, Mr Collins,' to which Michael Collins retorted that the Irish had been waiting seven hundred years for their independence.

The British Army and the Black and Tans made their final march through Dublin's crowded streets to the ferries that would take them home. Most of the Irish were delighted to see them go. 'Thieves and murderers!' they called out as they passed by. But those who had made money out of the Black and Tans were not so happy; the British soldiers had spent their pay freely in Dublin. Joice wrote that 'Dublin flower sellers covered their heads with their aprons and wept as they did at wakes or funerals . . . 'Ach, what shall we do now?' The shopkeepers also wailed for they would lose a great deal of business . . .' She added: 'The Irish dearly love a battle and many it seemed had enjoyed all the plotting and the excitement.'[12]

10   OFF ON A MISSION

Did Desmond or Mabel Fitzgerald tell Joice that Sinn Fein believed Sydney had turned 'informer' to secure his release from Dublin Castle? Possibly this, coupled with Major X's previous warning, was the reason the Lochs left Dublin shortly after Sydney's confrontation with Sinn Fein outside the Dail. Certainly their book *Ireland In Travail* has an abrupt ending. The ensuing Irish War of Independence would not end until April the following year.[1]

Mrs Slaney was not sorry to see the Lochs leave, but Mrs O'Grady embraced Joice and shook Sydney warmly by the hand. 'To be sure, I feel as if my own children are walking out of the house,' she told them. Hanging over the stern rail of the ferry, the Lochs watched the shoreline of Ireland merge into a haze, then disappear as they farewelled that 'beautiful but tormented country', as Joice described it.

She had added an ironic postscript to the book about English prejudice against the Irish; an English cousin of hers had commented, 'You were so brave to stay in Dublin when that dreadful Sinn Fein regiment, the Black and Tans, were murdering so many women there.' Joice had corrected her cousin: 'The Black and Tans were *British* murderers.' But her cousin refused to believe the truth. 'The Black and Tans were *Irish*,' she insisted. 'It must be true, I read it in the papers.'

'Many Black and Tans were Irishmen, but the *British* paid them, *not* the Irish,' Joice replied but still her cousin refused to believe her.[2] These and other biased comments by the British made Joice realise that history was formed out of 'a whirlpool of lies, misunderstandings, distortions, passions and inaccuracies'.[3]

One day in August 1922, the Lochs were busy correcting the page proofs of their book when they heard a radio announcement that Michael Collins had been assassinated. The reports of his death were confused. The radio announcement the Lochs heard was wrong. In the confusion following his assassination it was given out that Collins had been killed in Dublin, rather than ambushed on a lonely road in remote West Cork, outside the village of Bael na mBlath.

Joice telephoned their publisher immediately, asking that the news of Collins' death be inserted on the last page of the book. There was only room for one brief sentence, which was duly added.

At the time of his assassination, Michael Collins was just thirty-one.

He had been Head of the new Irish Free State for a mere ten days. With him went the last hope of reconciliation between the Irish Free State and the IRA. Ironically, he had been killed because he tried to remove the gun from Irish politics. The identity of his assassin would become the great unsolved mystery of Ireland.[4]

John Murray published *Ireland in Travail* in hardback in autumn 1922 under the Lochs' joint names.[5] (Few women at that time wrote political books; 'women's writing' was characterised as fiction and children's stories.) They had proved their ability to work skilfully on a joint project. Sir John Murray was pleased with the book and suggested they write a second one, taking Russia as their subject—a country which, under Lenin, was arousing enormous interest. He assured them that a book titled *Inside Lenin's Russia* would find an excellent market throughout the English-speaking world, including America, where sales could be huge. The idea appealed to both Joice and Sydney, and they decided this should be their second joint book. They would also be far away from any chance of revenge from the Irish Republicans following publication of *Ireland in Travail*.

At this time Russia was visited by few foreigners; visas were hard to obtain. The country, so recently emerged from the fierce and bloody revolution of 1917, was in the grip of a terrible famine. How were they to get to Russia to see it for themselves from the inside, rather than obtaining some sanitised version presented by the Russian Government? The Lochs would not receive royalties from *Ireland in Travail* for another six months and had almost no capital. Lacking money and with visas difficult to obtain, it seemed almost impossible to spend enough time in Russia to write a serious book. On the other hand, living in London was both expensive and potentially dangerous, if indeed Sinn Fein or the IRA were after Sydney. It was time to move on.

After their return from Ireland the Lochs stayed with various friends and relations. The Russian project was at the forefront of their minds during a visit to Joice's cousins the Rogers, who lived in Cornwall. Mrs Rogers took them to visit Mrs Hitchens, an elderly Quaker friend, who suggested that they might consider volunteering to work in Russia for the Quaker Famine Relief organisation. She promptly wrote what Joice called 'a firm note' to Ruth Fry, who directed the work of Quaker Famine Relief units in both Poland and Russia.

The Czar's troops had invaded Poland at the outbreak of World War I. After the 1917 Revolution, Lenin had continued the Russian policy of destroying Polish and Ukrainian farms, and huge numbers of Poles and Ukrainians residing in what was then Polish territory had been driven east to the Volga Basin. To feed them the Quakers had set up several Mission stations in the Volga Basin area. Joice and Sydney aimed to work in the largest camp at Buzuluk, near the port of Samara.

In the wake of the devastation of World War I, the Quakers (The Religious Society of Friends) had raised funds to establish their own welfare agency, as an expression of their 'concern' and religious faith; now they ran aid missions and refugee camps all over Europe recruiting suitable volunteers who worked without pay. A few camps employed doctors, others relied on the unpaid labour of nurses or medical orderlies. Quakers were non-sectarian and believed in giving aid where it was needed, regardless of race, religion or political conviction. Joice and Sydney knew very little about the Society of Friends, beyond the fact that strict rules governed their speech and behaviour, and that they were teetotallers. The Society of Friends had been founded by William Penn, who left England for America in the seventeenth century in search of religious tolerance. Joice had seen pictures of Quaker Elizabeth Fry in history books, visiting convict women in Newgate Jail before they were put on transports to America and Australia. She learned that Miss Ruth Fry was a direct descendant of Elizabeth Fry.

Would the Quakers be prepared to send to Russia a pair of liberal-minded authors who enjoyed a good bottle of wine and the odd pint of Guinness?

Joice and Sydney were summoned to an interview with Ruth Fry at Friends House in Euston Road, the Quakers' London headquarters. Joice, who saw herself as a liberated woman, had her dark blonde hair cut quite short. For her interview she wore the latest fashion: a sleeveless, short-skirted, bright cotton dress. Mrs Hitchens had omitted to warn Joice that Quakers were severe in dress and not famous for their sense of humour.[6] Joice described entering the presence of Miss Fry. 'It was chilling. Quakers of that era were never warmly enthusiastic. We didn't look anything like do-gooders.' Miss Fry stared unwinkingly at the Lochs through her plain steel-rimmed glasses. Her grey uniform, buttoned to the chin, reached to her ankles. She had iron-grey hair and wore no make-up. Her look of disapproval as she observed the Lochs made Joice fear they would not be accepted as Quaker volunteers for Russia.

'Mr and Mrs Loch, are you *Friends*?' demanded Miss Fry, her voice harsh with disapproval.

The Lochs were unaware of the use of the word 'Friend' in Quaker terminology, meaning 'one of us—a member of the Society of Friends'. Sydney totally misunderstood the question and thought Miss Fry was asking if they were close friends of Mrs Hitchens. He had never met a Quaker before and was suffering from mild shock. Polite as ever, he smiled at Miss Fry and replied helpfully, 'No, not friends, merely acquaintances.'

Miss Fry withered Sydney with a glare and replied frostily, 'I'm afraid our Russian Aid unit is full at present.'

'And on this note,' Joice wrote later, 'We lost Russia.' On their file Miss Fry wrote that the Lochs were 'frivolous and unlikely to be good mixers with Quakers'.

Beneath her stern exterior, Ruth Fry was a tireless worker for humanitarian causes. She belonged to the famous Quaker family which, in the hope of preventing members of the British working-class from drinking themselves to death on gin and beer, had introduced the beverage known as cocoa. Although she had clearly disapproved of Joice's style of dress and Sydney's seeming flippancy, Miss Fry was astute enough to realise that the Lochs, as writers, could help raise funds with articles about Quaker-funded missions and refugee camps. Their Polish Missions or Aid Centres for Refugees were severely under-funded, and many volunteers were dying of typhus and malaria. A few weeks later she summoned them to another interview. 'Do you have a concern for Poland?' she asked. 'Help is urgently needed there.'

The Lochs knew that Poland was another of the world's trouble spots but that was about all. Neither did they understand the term 'concern' as used in the Quaker sense, meaning a 'God-given spiritual hunger to help the welfare of certain peoples'. They wanted to leave Britain for various reasons: here was a way of doing it with all expenses paid. They listened politely as Miss Fry proposed the Quakers should pay their fares to Poland and provide bed and board if they would work with Polish refugees and write about the crisis in their refugee camps for the British newspapers.

It was agreed the Lochs would go by train to Warsaw for a brief induction period. Miss Fry had recently made an inspection tour of Poland. She explained that the Head of State was Marshal Pilsudski, a war hero, that the new Polish Republic was almost bankrupt and not one country would lend its Government money. As a result, Friends

War Relief in Britain and America was raising funds to save over a million Poles from starvation.

Miss Fry warned them they would be working in eastern Poland near the vast Pripet Marshes where malaria presented a grave threat.[7] They would be given quinine tablets when possible. But roads and transport were almost non-existent, so food and medicines were in short supply. Thousands of refugees were dying each week. She hoped they would highlight the desperate need for donations to save as many Poles as possible. As funds were so short, in return for bed and board *all* moneys they earned from freelance journalism must be handed over to the Friends.

At this, Sydney looked at Joice with one eyebrow raised. Should they leave now? But Joice calmly nodded her acceptance of Miss Fry's terms and conditions. The idea of bringing aid to refugees appealed to her ever-present desire to help the under-privileged.

The irony of their situation did not escape them. Sydney, brought up in the Church of Scotland, was verging on agnosticism and Joice, although confirmed into the Anglican Church, detested the bigotry of most organised religion. Now she had agreed they would work for one of the strictest religious organisations of all, without pay.

By this time the Lochs had secured a contract and a small advance from the British publishers Allen and Unwin to write a book about war-torn Poland. Sir Stanley Unwin had commissioned the Lochs' book on Poland because he was a dedicated pacifist. In World War I he had been a conscientious objector, serving as a stretcher bearer. He supported the Quakers' aims and wanted to publicise the work being done by the Society of Friends in Poland.

Ruth Fry had told the Lochs that as farmland in eastern Poland had been devastated under Lenin's 'scorched earth policy' and all the livestock killed, fresh vegetables, meat, eggs and milk were only obtainable at black market prices. At times they would have to eat the refugees' diet of black or acorn bread, cabbage, wild herb soup and black tea. Each month Friends House hired a special goods train and filled it with crates of Bovril, condensed milk, baby formula, high-energy biscuits and tinned sardines and sent it through Germany to Poland.

So many volunteer aid workers, nurses and doctors had fallen sick or died working in Poland that before Miss Fry confirmed their appointment, she insisted they pass a medical examination. Joice passed her medical with flying colours. 'Sound as a bell,' the doctor told her, listening to her heart through his stethoscope. He advised

Sydney that his blood pressure was high and he should take life more easily—a warning Sydney totally failed to heed.

The doctor warned them that three previously healthy Quaker volunteers, Gertrude Powicke, Richard Ball and Florence Witherington had died the previous year from typhus. Working with refugees who were covered in lice could cause typhus infection in any small cuts or open sores the aid workers might have.[8] At that time vaccines against typhus were in their infancy. Dysentery was another cause of death among aid workers. The doctor told them to boil their drinking water whenever possible. And he gave them a year's supply of quinine tablets. His gloomy prognosis of a shortened life expectancy failed to deter the Lochs: they were determined to go to Poland.

Before their departure, the Lochs were given the uniforms provided to volunteer workers. 'Ugh!' Joice exclaimed as she tried on the grey suit and thick grey cotton stockings. Coming from Australia with its bright sunlight, she loved bright colours and detested the thought of wearing a uniform. 'What a *dreadful* hat,' she complained to Sydney. 'It *is* a bit like a pancake,' Sydney said helpfully. Joice snatched off the hat and bashed it with the back of her hairbrush, trying to make it a more flattering shape.

Silver-haired Carl Heath, Secretary of Friends' International Division, asked the Lochs to come to his office for a final talk. He explained that Quakers believed it was vital to give aid to *all* refugees. Volunteers from many nations were working with the Quakers in Poland, as well as others from the British and American Red Cross, and some American church workers. 'Over ten thousand sick and emaciated refugees return to Poland each *week* from Siberia, the Volga Basin and Bielorussia only to find their villages burnt to the ground, their livestock and farm implements gone,' he told them. The Friends' War Relief Committee had established five Refugee Aid Centres, four in eastern Poland and one in Galicia, to feed the refugees and help them re-establish themselves on their farms.

Joice had a sincere admiration for the Quakers and their dedication to helping others, but she could not help worrying how she and Sydney, given to expressive language in moments of stress, would fit in with Quaker rules and regulations.

As Head of Publicity for the Polish Mission, Joice visited Fleet Street editors hoping to be given commissions for articles on Poland, rather than just sending in stories as a freelance. She was told that British people had little interest in Polish victims of Russian brutality; public sympathy lay with the Russians, who had overthrown the tyranny of the Tsars.

The left-wing press was totally uninterested. In 1921, writers, intellectuals, artists, all those who called themselves progressive or Socialists, were convinced that Communism offered mankind a far more just society than capitalism. Normally keen to support humanitarian causes, any editors with Socialist leanings said their readers did not want to hear about atrocities Lenin's Army had committed against Poles and Ukrainians. Communism under Lenin was going to solve the world's problems.

Fortunately the Melbourne *Evening Herald*, which had published Joice's articles on Ireland, agreed to take a story about Polish war victims. At their London office Guy Innes gave her permission to carry out research on Poland and Russia in their cuttings library and promised to do his best to place a Polish famine story. Joice pored over reports from the American papers; America, with its large Polish migrant population, had run several stories on Poland.

She learned that the rich dark soil of eastern Poland, the 'bread basket of Europe' had for centuries been fought over by Poles, Ukrainians, Austrians, Lithuanians, Bielorussians, Hungarians and Russians. Recently there had been two waves of invasion, the first in 1914-15 when the Tsar's troops had invaded and driven three million peasants into slave labour in Siberia. The second took place in the Soviet-Polish war of 1919, largely ignored by Britain. The eastern Polish province of Volhynia (now part of western Ukraine) was invaded by the Russian Bolshevik armies. Some eight million terrified Polish and Ukrainian peasants placed their children, pigs and chickens on carts and fled from their prosperous farms as Lenin's forces advanced, conducting his 'scorched earth' policy.

Lenin's Red Cavalry had expected to be at the gates of Paris before the summer was out. On 31 August, 1920 the victorious Red Cavalry was defeated at Zamosc.[9] This great battle halted Lenin's troops and saved Europe from becoming one vast Communist camp. The Treaty of Riga gave the newly formed Republic of Poland large slices of Russia, including magnificent forests that had once belonged to the Tsars.

But the fighting in eastern Poland had turned fertile fields into a wasteland. Those farmers who had managed to return found their homes destroyed and their livestock gone. Many were camping out, waiting to rebuild their houses and re-plough their fields, but they and their children were dying of starvation. Restoring eastern Poland was the vital task in which the Lochs would become deeply involved.

The day before their departure, the Lochs revisited Friends Headquarters and were given second-class rail tickets from London to Warsaw. Miss Fry seemed as forbidding as before. She explained that the Friends were able to conduct famine relief because, unlike most religious groups, they did not spend their money on priests, parsons or churches. Instead they relied on their conscience and the Bible to know what was right. Miss Fry added, 'We take the commands of the Lord *very* seriously. Quaker volunteers have segregated sleeping quarters and even our married volunteers sleep apart.'

Joice looked at Sydney and resisted the urge to laugh. Separate rooms? Miss Fry must be joking! Here they were, married only a couple of years and very much in love. If marital sex was not on the Quaker agenda, she wondered how Quakers managed to reproduce. However, having lost the chance to go to Russia, Joice kept silent. Somehow they would find a way to be together.

The Lochs would receive five shillings a week for necessary expenses, which didn't seem much. In return they were expected to work ten hours a day, seven days a week. They had already signed a contract confirming that all moneys earned from their freelance journalism would be handed over to the Quakers. Miss Fry gave them a wintry smile. They were now part of the Friend's War Relief, but as volunteers rather than Quakers.

They had already said their goodbyes. Joice's English relatives were worried that once again, she and her husband were going somewhere very risky. Sydney's relatives, on the other hand, 'appeared totally uninterested whether we lived or died in Poland,' Joice wrote.

11   A PALACE IN WARSAW

From the train the Lochs glimpsed meadows where the snow had almost thawed, ancient wooden houses and a few onion-domed churches with greenish copper roofs, shuttered and deserted. The linden trees that bordered long avenues were still budding. Western Poland appeared relatively unscathed.

The farther east they went, the flatter the land became. As they approached Warsaw they passed fields that stood unploughed and deserted, and the burnt-out ruins of once pleasant farmhouses and barns. Peasants and farmers in ragged clothing were forlornly attempting to dig their land, using old tins or bits of metal.

On Warsaw's crowded railway station the Lochs were met by a tall, mournful man with a drooping walrus moustache who introduced himself as Prince Menshikov, interpreter for the Friends Polish Unit. He wore an ancient overcoat with a huge, moth-eaten fur collar. The Prince told them he had fled from Russia to Warsaw in November 1917 when Lenin's troops had stormed the Winter Palace in St Petersburg, looting its treasures and sweeping away the old order. His English governess had taught him her language; now he spoke five languages and the Quakers paid him a modest salary as an interpreter.

Pointing out a train on which refugees clung like limpets to the carriage roofs, the Prince explained these were yet more of the half million Ukrainian and Polish peasants and farmers who had been deported to Russia. Now they were returning, starving and diseased, to farmhouses and cottages that no longer existed.

Soldiers with rifles herded the refugees onto another train bound for Powalski, a huge refugee camp and de-lousing station on the outskirts of Warsaw, staffed by volunteers from the Quakers and the International Red Cross. There they would receive a good square meal, and those who were too weak to walk would be given a bed. The rest had to walk back to their ruined villages as best they could.

Prince Menshikov hailed a horse-drawn cab and took them to Friends' Headquarters in the former Radziwill Palace. 'Are we both staying here?' Sydney asked him.

'Alas, dear boy, the Quakers have strange ideas. Your charming wife will sleep in the women's hostel, while you and the rest of us sleep here.'

He told them that the Quakers had been given the loan of the Palace from old Princess Radziwill, who calculated that lending her home free of charge to the Quakers for charitable purposes would save the palace if Warsaw was invaded by the Red Army. The Princess had taken most of the palace contents with her when she left—the Radziwill gold plates, her Old Masters and her antique French furniture. 'Far cleverer than my Papa,' the Prince said gloomily. 'He left everything in *our* palace in St Petersburg for the Bolsheviks to steal or destroy.'

Quaker administrators and volunteers were now camped in every bedroom and even in the corridors, which were crowded with rolled up Persian rugs. Men's jackets and trousers hung from lengths of string suspended between two nails. There was no fuel to heat the water in the bathrooms or run the central heating.

The Lochs met their co-workers over a Spartan lunch of corned beef and peas, served by one of the Princess's elderly retainers. While the white shirts and business suits of the paid administrators were unrumpled, the volunteer field workers in their crumpled grey lice-proof uniforms seemed badly in need of a good hot bath. They were camping in primitive village houses without bathrooms or inside sanitation.

Trying to see if they could obtain a relaxation of the rule which decreed they must sleep apart, Joice and Sydney had their first meeting with the head of Friends Relief, Florence Barrow. Like the Lochs, Florence was not a Quaker. She was in her early thirties, an attractive woman with clear grey eyes and a quiet unhurried manner. She and Joice took to each other immediately.[2] Florence, like Joice, was down-to-earth yet imaginative, excellent at managing people and modern in her outlook.

In the 1920s few educated women were allowed careers or responsible executive positions. However, since Friends War Relief relied on volunteers to run their organisation, they were happy to promote such women, so long as they did not have to pay them. The Friends owed a huge debt to non-Quaker women like Florence Barrow, Dr Hilda Clark and Joice Loch.

Florence presided over a mixed bag of volunteers, some of whom had strange and totally impractical ideas. She thought the Lochs' skills and practical approach would be an excellent addition to the Polish

Unit. She apologised for the fact they had to sleep separately. She could not change the rules, as that would upset their more conservative supporters and she could not risk alienating the older Quaker families, some of whom were paying for entire train-loads of food and medical supplies.

To Florence's relief Joice assured her she understood her position. Judging from Miss Fry's letter, Florence had feared Joice Loch would be difficult.

The person who did turn out to be 'difficult' was Richard Watts, a dapper young Englishman, the Polish Unit's accountant and office manager. He insisted on expense accounts and receipts for everything. Joice was bad at figures and loathed book-keeping. She and Richard Watt detested each other from the start. He was to write to Miss Fry in London complaining that 'Mrs Loch makes excessive use of Quaker stationery and is unable to keep proper accounts'.[3]

Florence explained that the Polish Unit contained British, American, Commonwealth and European volunteer workers. It had three doctors, some nurses and a few medical orderlies to deal with thousands of sick and dying people. Every member was totally overworked.

They spoke about the newspaper articles the Lochs hoped to write, and Joice had to tell Florence there was little interest in Britain about famine in Poland; the British were much more fascinated by Lenin's Russia.

Florence sighed. 'Unfortunately, the Russian propaganda is excellent. Lenin's Hands-off-Russia campaign and his support from Europe's Socialists masks the horror of his crimes in Poland.' She explained that the Quakers followed an ancient Chinese precept: 'If you give a man a sum of money it can feed him and his family for a week—if you give him a fishing rod or a plough, he can feed his family for life.' But many more donations were needed to achieve that goal.

Florence suggested the Lochs take a few days to explore Warsaw before starting work, and an interpreter called Pani Bianki (*Pani* meaning Madame in Polish) was provided as their guide. She showed them both sides of Warsaw, the beautiful painted old houses in the Stare Miasto (old town) and the alleyways behind them where emaciated men, women and children begged for money—in sharp contrast to the elegant shoppers in the main streets. Pani Bianki, an impoverished war widow, scowled at the well-dressed men and women. 'All black marketeers,' she hissed.

She introduced them to fellow writers, including Melchior Wankowicz who would become a close friend to the Lochs, as well as to Polish princes, counts and countesses, many of whom had lost almost everything in the war. Joice found the proliferation of Polish titles amazing until she learned that unlike the English aristocracy, each son and daughter of a Polish nobleman bore the same titles as their parents. Pani Bianki told them how 'the miracle of the Vistula', had saved Poland from the Red cavalry and Russian invasion. The Poles, who regarded Russia as their traditional enemy, had been rallied by Marshal Pilsudski, whom Pani Bianki described as a national hero. '*Nie damy sie*!'—'We will not surrender!' the Polish soldiers cried. They fought so fiercely at Zamosc that they won their freedom. It was Europe's last great cavalry battle.

On the final day of their sightseeing, they were joined by a Professor from Oxford, who was writing a book about Warsaw. In his honour Pani Bianki arranged a visit to the wine cellar of a family friend, an elderly count, who offered each of them a glass of wine from a dust-covered bottle. The label bore the date 1720.

'Remarkable!' exclaimed the Professor. 'Are you *sure* this wine is so old?'

'Certainly,' exclaimed the count. 'This cellar has been owned by our family since the seventeenth century. I am the last of the line and when I die, the contents will go to our President, to be served at official banquets.'[4]

Emerging from the dark of the wine cellar onto the street, the Professor collided with a malnourished young woman carrying a bundle in her arms. She shot them a furtive glance, then drew back a grimy shawl to show a baby with a wizened face and puny limbs. Pani Bianki explained that the girl was trying to sell the child, but was scared she might be arrested. 'Girls who have been raped or have babies out of wedlock receive a small feeding allowance which is meant to last them for six months. When they run out of money they sell their babies to other girls, who then get an additional feeding allowance.'

'So they pass these poor malnourished babies around like parcels. Who feeds them when they get older?' Joice asked. She recalled the orphans in the slums of Dublin, and her abandoned adoption plan. 'These girls have no homes, no jobs, no money. When their babies turn six months they often leave them on the steps of the Foundling Hospital—or sell them to a foreigner, as this girl is trying to do.'

Deeply moved by the girl's plight, the Professor took out his wallet and slipped a wad of banknotes into her hand. She murmured her thanks and tried to push the child into his arms. Embarrassed, he waved her away and made signs she should use the money to feed herself and the child. Speaking through Pani Bianki, Joice suggested the girl come to Quaker headquarters to get powdered milk formula and clothes for her baby.

Poland had endured centuries of war, invasion and devastation but its inhabitants seemed to have a talent for survival. Most had retained their keen sense of humour and their capacity to make the best of life. During her stay in Poland Joice grew to admire the Poles more and more.

When Sydney mentioned his years of experience with horses in Australia, Florence Barrow asked him to take charge of the aid program in which horses, hired from the Polish Army, were being loaned to peasants to plough their land. Previously the Polish Unit had loaned one horse to each farmer for two or three days, then sent a groom to collect the animal. The grooms found that many horses had been severely overworked and often flogged nearly to death, so desperate were the farmers to get their fields ploughed in the brief period the horses were on loan to them. Sydney suggested that in the long term, it would be far more economical if a large number of the horses, formerly used to pull gun-carriages, be purchased instead of hired from the Polish Army. After some discussion his plan was adopted as the horses were no longer needed for Army service. Over a thousand horses were purchased for a nominal sum.[5] To protect the animals trained handlers accompanied teams of horses to each village.

When the days became longer Sydney was sent on an extensive tour to inspect the first results of his horse-and-plough loan scheme, accompanied by Joice. They took with them three horse-drawn *furmankas* and a motorised truck fitted with bunk beds and kitchen equipment, donated by Friends in London. They toured eastern and central Poland, making notes and writing reports.

In the late afternoon of a warm June day they drove across a bridge to an island in the Vistula, and found themselves in a village which seemed almost unscathed by the war. It was the highlight of the village year, the eve of the feast day of St John, its patron saint, which fell on midsummer day, 21st June. The village seemed full of well-fed people enjoying themselves, eating sausages and black bread from market stalls and drinking mugs of beer.

At twilight they saw village girls in brightly flowered head-scarves, white linen blouses and skirts with bands of brilliant embroidery. The girls looked healthy, blue-eyed, magnolia-skinned and many had woven scarlet poppies and blue cornflowers through their long blonde hair.

This was traditionally the night for courting and betrothals. Girls and boys were floating gaily decorated boughs down the dark waters of the Vistula, and the river was bright with these toy boats, decked with flowers and lighted candles. The Lochs were told that if a boat made by a girl bumped against one decorated by a boy, it was a good omen for a Catholic marriage.

Here in this village the Lochs found themselves in the Poland of old, a totally different world from the misery in the Stochod Valley.

Joice knew that in pre-Christian times, midsummer day was devoted to pagan celebrations of the summer solstice. The scene before them, officially in honour of St John, had obvious pagan roots, which became more evident as night fell and fires were lit along the banks of the Vistula. The young men, dashing in their short jackets flung like capes around their shoulders and hats with a peacock feather placed at a jaunty angle, leapt and danced through the fires, bringing exclamations of fear and admiration from the girls. Then each dancer found the girl whose boat had bumped into his own and took her into the woods.

It was an unforgettable experience which inspired one of Joice's best poems, *The Eve of Saint John*:

> *This is the night of St John,*
> *Set candles alight on the rafts,*
> *The Vistula calls,*
> *Bright shafts of light*
> *Slide into the water*
> *Bring forth your lovers and daughters,*
> *This is a night for lovers,*
> *Dance through the fires*
> *Hands on their hips,*
> *The wide river slips,*
> *Silent and deep,*
> *Send forth your ships,*
> *Your brave little craft,*
> *Dancers alight with desire.*

To implement his horse-and-plough loan scheme, Sydney was put in charge of a small command post in the valley of the Stochod River.

Because of its innumerable loops, twists and turns the local peasants called it 'The River of a Thousand Ways'.

Joice, meanwhile, went off to Powalski's de-lousing station and quarantine camp for a month, in order to write about conditions there. She was given an old railway compartment as her office and sleeping quarters.

The camp was so overcrowded that refugees had to build themselves wigwams out of tree branches. Once-fertile fields around the camp had become a wasteland of shell-holes, barbed wire and skeletons. In the bitter cold of the previous winter many Polish, Ukrainian, Bielorussian and Jewish refugees had starved or frozen to death; others had died of typhus, dysentery or tuberculosis.

Members of the Mission's typhus units stood by week after week in their de-lousing stations, clad in black rubber boots and silver mackintoshes, earning for themselves the title 'silver ladies'. They were armed with clippers, razors and bottles of disinfectant. They lived in a world of steam, surrounded by naked patients, some skeletally thin, others with swollen stomachs that masked starvation. All the hair had to be shaved off the patients' heads and bodies to get rid of the lice, which swarmed so thickly that 'at times the horrible creatures had to be removed with the blade of a knife'.[6]

Joice found she needed her irreverent Aussie sense of humour on occasion when she joined in this task, de-lousing, steaming clothes, helping refugees to pick the nits out of armholes, then killing them with a lighted cigarette. She gave a graphic description of the refugees camping in their bough shelters in the forests, drainage ditches or in former Army dugouts, looking as though they were covered in a 'white moving curtain of lice'. It was not work for the fainthearted or squeamish, but Joice bore it all without complaining. Food was desperately short. Each day thousands more starving refugees streamed through the Powalski de-lousing station. Joice had no wish to take food out of the mouths of refugees, and denied herself breakfast and lunch. She would work all day, her only source of energy a glass of black tea and one piece of black bread. Each evening she returned to her railway carriage and lit the oil lamp. When the nights were chilly she would wrap herself in an old fur coat she had bought in Warsaw's flea market and type up that day's notes and her press releases. By that time she was hungry for the black bread and tinned sardines she had brought from Quaker headquarters. She rationed her supply carefully; her single meal consisted of one slice of black bread and half a tin of sardines.

Sometimes, exhausted by working in the de-lousing station, she fell asleep over the typewriter. Once she was woken by a band of starving children, clad in rags, who banged on the doors of the railway carriage, which Joice had been warned to keep locked. The emaciated children had been told she had food for them. She wound down the window a little and with sign language and her few words of Polish tried to make them understand she had no food to give them. Desperately hungry, the children beat their fists on the walls and windows of the railway carriage until Joice was reduced to tears of frustration and despair that she was unable to help them.[7]

Obtaining timber for reconstruction work was another problem Sydney was asked to tackle. In principle each farmer could obtain a permit to chop down thirty-five cubic metres of timber from State-owned forests to rebuild his house and barn. But Poland's Public Service worked extremely slowly. Printing the application forms and sending them out to the provinces took so long that many children died of cold before their parents obtained the required permit.

Appalled by the human misery he encountered, Sydney tried to cut through a maze of petty bureaucratic restrictions and asked the Polish Government if, in return for a licence fee, Friends' War Relief could organise the printing and distribution of the application forms. He finally won his battle: Friends Polish Unit was allowed to set up a printing press to print the forms.

What was needed now was for Sydney to organise a huge timber cutting program, using the Army horses he had obtained to haul timber out of the forest and transport it to the villages. The area granted by the Polish Government for this vital reconstruction program was the huge forest of Selecz, once the hunting ground of Russian kings and princes, with a direct rail line to St Petersburg. The whole area had been handed over to Poland in war reparations.[8] Sydney's program became hugely successful during the winter when ploughing was impossible.

The Lochs attended bi-monthly Executive Meetings in the Radziwill Palace, presided over by Florence Barrow. Each meeting started with five minutes silence for prayer and meditation. Then each of the five Mission Heads suggested schemes for spending the limited funds available and told the meeting about desperate cases in their particular area. Field workers and administrators sat around the long mahogany table in the enormous ballroom with its chandeliers and rows of little gilded chairs, shrouded in dust sheets. Lunch took place at a long table in the Radziwill's former dining room. The Friends were served their meagre meal of thin soup to which some Bovril extract had been added, followed by boiled vegetables and rice. They drank water from cut-glass wine goblets and were waited on by an elderly butler and an ancient footman in a frogged jacket and knee-breeches, relics of the Radziwills' former splendour.

Joice realised she must make her first story about famine in Poland so appealing that hard-boiled Fleet Street editors would have to print it. She must think up an unusual angle and get good photos. She asked Richard Watts, the accountant, for bars of chocolate and some second-hand toys. Initially he refused. Joice insisted it was vital she had them to take photos which would, in the long run, get them more aid money to buy food. Grudgingly Watts complied with her wishes.

Joice, Prince Menshikov and a peroxide blonde, wife of an American Senator who might donate funds to their cause, took the train to Powursk Mission. Joice had managed to wrap the precious chocolate bars and toys in some gift paper. In the train the Senator's wife, who had a deep Southern drawl, chatted away about the famous and titled people she had met in Europe. She showed photographs of herself with a Polish countess who ran an orphanage she had visited.

They were met by a driver with a *furmanka* and driven to what had once been a prosperous farming village. They saw emaciated children in ragged clothing with sandals made of strips of birch bark wrapped round their feet. They had lost their homes as well as their parents and were camping in Army dugouts or ruined cattle sheds. As the excited children swarmed around her, Joice did her best to share out her gifts. Choking back an impulse to cry, she photographed the children as they tore open the small parcels.

The Senator's wife from Alabama now revealed her true colours. Faced with emaciated children in rags, she recoiled in horror.

'But didn't you say you hugged and kissed those children in the countess's orphanage?' Joice asked her sarcastically.

'Aw honey, those were *aristocrat*'s children, not snotty little peasants,' the American replied. She then asked Joice to photograph her standing beside Prince Menshikov. 'Fancy all the folks back home seeing *me* with a real live Prince!' she exclaimed, wrapping her mink coat around her and sidling closer to the astonished Prince.

Joice shot her a look that would have stripped paint. 'We're here to raise money and help starving children,' she said, 'not to get in the society pages.'

'Geez honey, I doan' have the money with me but I'll get my husband to talk to the President,' the Senator's wife promised, fluttering her eyelashes at the mournful Prince, who had never been seen to smile since he left Russia. Neither he nor Joice spoke a word to the American woman on the return journey to Warsaw, and neither of them were surprised when no donation was ever received from the Senator or his wife.

On her return to the women's hostel, Joice used an empty crate for a desk and typed up her article about starving and homeless children who would be lucky if they lived until the New Year, unless the British public donated tinned food and money to the Society of Friends Polish Relief Fund.

To date, her numerous press releases to Fleet Street editors had not been published. Yet stories pleading for funds for starving children in Russia appeared regularly in British newspapers. Surely her heart-breaking feature article about starving Polish war victims and their children, living in water-logged dugouts, would get into the newspapers and attract much needed funds. Joice added the photographs to her piece, sealed the envelope and sent it to her old friend Guy Innes.

The article did appear in the British press and succeeded in arousing a great deal of interest in the work of the Quakers in Poland, as well as many donations of food and money for Polish children. An entire goods train filled with chocolate bars, second-hand clothing, dolls and toys was on its way out to Poland well before Christmas. And Joice even received a letter of congratulation from Miss Fry.

12   WOLVES IN THE BLIZZARD

By the autumn the Lochs were working at Powursk Mission, the smallest and most remote of the Society of Friends' five Refugee Aid Centres. One benefit of leaving Warsaw was that at Powursk they had a tiny unheated bedroom to themselves.

Mission staff stayed in one of the few houses left standing in the once prosperous farming village of Powursk. They allocated food, clothing and medical assistance to an area lying south and west of the wide Pripet River and its marshes and tributary, the Stochod River. This was that fertile land once known as 'the bread basket of Europe' for its acres of cornfields.

In the 1920s the area then known in Polish as Volhynia or in Ukrainian as Volhin and its surrounding provinces formed a part of the ethnic melting-pot of Marshal Pilsudski's brand-new Polish Republic.[1] Most of the landless agricultural workers and tenant farmers spoke Polish or Ukrainian, a third much smaller group spoke Bielorussian [White Russian]—languages with certain similarities so that each could comprehend most of what the other was saying. While a small minority owned their land, for centuries most of them had been bound in serfdom to wealthy Polish landlords. A large proportion were illiterate. The Poles were devout Catholics, the Ukrainians Orthodox Christians.

In the recent Soviet-Polish war the landlords had fled for their lives from the Red Cavalry to Warsaw; Lenin's scorched-earth policy meant that they had not been able to return to their burned-down homes and churches and devastated farmlands. Many unfortunate peasants had no means of escape. They had been trapped in their farmhouses and incinerated by the soldiers of the Red Army. Others had been nailed to barn doors and burned with the barns; now those who had managed to escape were returning to claim what was nothing more than a scorched wasteland.

The Relief Unit at Powursk distributed standard anti-famine packs of tinned sardines, evaporated milk and packets of biscuits to starving families. Joice helped to give out food, blankets and second-hand clothing to villagers camping in Army dugouts or bark huts deep in the huge pine forests. Travelling there in a horse-drawn *furmanka* and hearing the wolves howling was a terrifying experience.[2]

Prince Menshikov, his long threadbare coat flapping around his ankles, soon left for Warsaw and was replaced by a younger man, Prince Alexander Makinsky, another dispossessed White Russian. Prince Alexander also spoke five languages and was far more adaptable to changed circumstances and entertaining than the tragic and gloomy Prince Menshikov with his reminiscences of past splendour in the Menshikov Palace.

With Prince Makinsky acting as his interpreter, Sydney was away for weeks at a time supervising his extensive horse-and-plough loan scheme. Ploughing continued even in autumn so that the fields would be ready for sowing flax, corn and wheat in spring. Sydney used the Mission at Powursk as his base. He had a small office there where he drew up schedules for each horse team, under its own controller, to be sent to different areas to plough overgrown fields. Sydney's plan ensured each peasant farmer was loaned two horses with their own groom or horse-handler to see to their food and welfare. In addition a plough was donated to each family participating in the scheme, as well as seed corn, flax seed to produce linen woven by the women of the family and a small iron cooking stove. The ploughs and stoves were manufactured in a Quaker-owned factory in Poland.

Sydney's many relief teams operated over a huge and devastated agricultural area of what was then eastern Poland, stretching as far north as Vilnius and around to Pinsk and Brest-Litovsk. Florence Barrow would later testify that Sydney's plan was of enormous help in saving a large area of eastern Poland from starvation.

When the poplar trees started to drop their leaves, Joice was asked by the head of the Publicity Department in Warsaw to accompany a visiting photographer who was to make a film on the work of Friends War Relief.

As soon as the bearded photographer opened his mouth she recognised that familiar Aussie twang. He turned out to be the celebrated polar explorer Hubert Wilkins (who would eventually be knighted for his exploits as a member of Shackleton's last Antarctic expedition). Hubert Wilkins was not a Quaker but, like the Lochs, he sympathised with the aims of their War Victims Relief. Having made a very successful documentary on polar exploration, he had volunteered to make another at his own expense to help the Quakers raise more funds for war victims, showing the devastation in eastern Poland. He had also come to Poland hoping to obtain a visa to visit Lenin's Russia, and planned to make a documentary there before returning to Australia.

Their interpreter for this trip was another dispossessed aristocrat, Count Tarnowski, a member of one of Poland's oldest and most distinguished families. Before the Russian invasion the Count's family had owned a castle with a fine library and art collection but everything had been destroyed or looted by the Russians and his castle left in ruins. The Quakers could not let Joice, even as a married woman, stay overnight in a tent with two men plus a male driver. A recently arrived French volunteer, Marie Dupont, was detailed to accompany them as Joice's chaperone.

By now it was late autumn. Joice, Marie Dupont, Count Tarnowski, Hubert Wilkins and a Polish *furmanka* driver set off to film returned refugees living along the barbed-wire entanglements and dugouts of the old Curzon line, marking the border between Poland and Russia. Some of the dugouts were flooded by autumn rain. These peasants and their hungry children were some of the most unfortunate war victims in Poland.

On the third day of shooting the temperature dropped to sub-zero and it became impossible to continue. The tracks over which they bumped were so deeply rutted that Hubert Wilkins' camera lens cracked, causing him to curse and fume in a highly un-Quaker-like manner. Snow started to fall, first gently but gradually turning into a blizzard. Their exhausted horses could not continue and they led them into a nearby barn. The blizzard increased in fury. The driver told them they would be lucky to get out alive. In a lean-to shed next to the barn they heard the lowing of calves. Joice described how 'Rats squirmed over us in the pitch dark. We were hungry but found the Polish horse conveyer had forgotten to pack any of the black bread'.

As they grew hungrier, all they could talk about was food. Joice described her mother's Sunday dinner of roast beef, roast potatoes and Yorkshire pudding in the Australian bush. All they had to feed themselves were two tins of frozen sardines. In the howling blizzard it was impossible to return to the *furmanka* for provisions. They were still cold in spite of wearing Cossack boots lined with sheepskin and long sheepskin coats. Icicles formed on their eyebrows—the scarves they wore over their faces froze solid. They ransacked the barn but could find nothing edible. They lacked matches or any sort of cooking pot or pan to follow Hubert Wilkins' suggestion that they should boil up the horse harnesses and chew the leather.

Through a chink in the log walls of the barn they glimpsed red-eyed wolves loping towards them through the blizzard. Then came a series of crashes as the huge creatures broke through the flimsy wooden lean-to shed where the calves were stabled. The calves squealed piteously as the wolves tore into them. Frozen with cold, they listened in horror. Without guns they were powerless to drive the wolves away.

'Do you think the wolves can smell us?' Joice whispered.

Hubert Wilkins did not reply but grabbed one of the pitchforks which hung on the walls. Joice followed his example. With a sinking heart she remembered a dying gypsy she had nursed who told her, 'You'll never leave Poland. You will die here'. Would she see Sydney again? How would he know what had happened to them? She wrote her husband a farewell note on a page torn out of her diary and placed it on a shelf, propped against a rusty can of oil.

After two days with no food or drink apart from handfuls of snow which blew in through the cracks between the log walls, the blizzard abated. The farmers who owned the calves arrived and were horrified to find their precious animals eaten by wolves. By now Joice and the others were weak with hunger. They had just enough strength to call out.

'You're lucky to be alive,' their rescuers told them.

The five travellers were overjoyed to leave the barn. Outside, their breath rose in clouds on the cold air. Dark forests etched in snow stretched away to a pink and mauve horizon. Around them were waves of snow with crests ruffled like foam. To Joice, who had grown up in the Australian bush, the vast expanse of pristine white snow was staggeringly beautiful.

The villagers were magnificent. They took the wheels off the *furmanka* and replaced them with sledge runners. One peasant, undernourished himself, insisted on going back to his dug-out and returned with the only food he had—a plate of cold fried potatoes. The four of them fell on the potatoes, ravenous with hunger. To Joice nothing had ever tasted so good. They raided the *furmanka* and in gratitude gave the peasants all the tinned sardines, bottles of Bovril and seed corn in the wagon. Their unfortunate horses had been so badly affected by frost-bite that they could scarcely walk. The peasants then harnessed themselves like dogs to the *furmanka* and pulled the giant sledge several kilometres until they reached Powursk Mission.

Powursk Mission, run by six British, Australian and American volunteers and a groom, was overwhelmed by demands for medical services and emergency food supplies and severely under-staffed for the huge amount of relief work that faced it. By now Joice had handed over to an American journalist the thankless task of trying to publicise the plight of Friends War Service in Poland in the press. He hoped to attract donations from his wealthy compatriots. Joice preferred the more active role, helping refugees rather than writing press releases to British and Australian newspapers which were only mildly interested in their plight or were firmly on the side of Communist Russia and would not run her stories.

Sister Hetty Meadows ran the medical services at Powursk single-handed and needed all the help she could get. As one of the few Quaker volunteers with some medical experience, Joice was asked to assist her. Having had a great deal of practice in delivering calves and lambs, Joice was confident that she could easily learn how to deliver babies. At this period the Quakers had only three paid doctors, all of them grossly overworked. In addition the Refugee Missions used female *doktorikas* (similar to China's 'barefoot doctors') who had been trained by doctors to stitch up wounds, deliver babies and deal with the most common infectious diseases. The Society of Friends in London and America provided *doktorikas* and doctors with bandages, basic drugs and other medical supplies.

Sister Meadows had arrived in Poland a year before Joice and had been coping alone for twelve months. She found Joice's calm and practical approach a great help and soon realised her new assistant possessed extraordinary manual dexterity allied to a quick brain. Joice was very good at operating and stitching wounds. Sister Hetty, a highly experienced nurse and midwife, taught Joice medical and surgical techniques and birthing procedures which were to prove invaluable for the rest of her life.

Joice soon learned to recognise the symptoms of typhus: high fever, a rash of red spots on the chest and abdomen and severe diarrhoea, enough to kill undernourished refugees whose immune systems were already weakened by poor diet and unsanitary living conditions in prison camps or settlements in Russia.

Writing notes for their book on Poland, Joice described Quaker-funded relief teams as 'do-gooders on the grand scale. We ministered to the starving, to those sick with typhus and dysentery, to swarms of homeless reduced to camping in old army dugouts and trenches. Hundreds of people, thousands of people, until they stumbled into our dreams. Snow heaped over their hovels and dugouts melted with the heat of the iron stoves with which we supplied them'.

Once the daily out-patients clinic was finished it was time for house visits. Joice and Sister Meadows were driven in one of the straw-lined *furmankas*, converted into a horse-drawn sleigh to cope with the heavy snow on the roads. Each week they seemed to be surrounded by more and more starving people. Refugees flocked out of the pine woods, crying and holding out their hands for food and medicines. The *furmanka* would start out laden with tined food from their storeroom, but there was never enough for all those outstretched hands. They had to be very careful when distributing food in case fights broke out.

Joice found that allocating scarce famine relief was an extremely difficult job. Through the interpreter, each man or woman told a heartrending story. Gaunt mothers went down on their knees and prayed for food for their children. It was harrowing for both Joice and Sydney; they had to decide who should have the ploughs, the loan of horses, or share in the limited supplies of tinned food that arrived by special train from Britain each month.

Joice remained unshaken by the sight of blood. She was eager to gain as much medical knowledge as she could. Each night by the light of an oil lamp she pored over her uncle's old medical books, the two-volume set of Cassells' Complete Companion to Medicine and her even more ancient copy of Household Surgery, or Hints on Emergencies by Dr J.F. South. Sister Hetty lent her some more recent textbooks. Joice was virtually undergoing a practical 'internship' in basic medicine. There were no antibiotics or complex drugs at this time. Disinfecting was done with EUSOL—Edinburgh Solution of Lime. Sassafras oil was used against ringworm, aspirin widely prescribed for a variety of conditions and iodine was the universal panacea for wounds. Occasionally they were lucky enough to be visited briefly by doctors or surgeons from Britain or America, working as Quaker volunteers in their vacations. From them, Joice learned even more about crisis intervention, stitching complex wounds and giving first-aid. She learned how to inoculate adults and children, splint legs and recognise many more diseases.

Administering famine relief and learning so many medical and nursing procedures marked a turning point in Joice's life. She had come to Poland as an impartial journalist and narrative writer, intending to assist the Quakers as a way of obtaining background for a book on war-torn Poland. Now she found herself becoming more and more emotionally involved in humanitarian and para-medical work for the refugees. In times of crisis this concern would become even more important to her than writing.

For their book, Joice wanted to obtain an insight into what gave the Quakers the necessary strength and motivation to continue their work. Occasionally she attended prayer sessions, when the Quakers read a section from the Bible and prayed aloud for spiritual strength to face their enormous task. At their meetings the Quakers did not rely on a priest or minister, but took their inspiration from the text for the day. Although Joice never became a Quaker she regarded herself as a 'fellow traveller' and drew strength from attending their meetings. She rarely talked about God or religion and always insisted that 'kindness to others' regardless of religion or creed was the highest form of good. She was convinced God manifested Himself in many ways, through many different faiths.

Miss Fry's censorious statement that the Lochs would not mix well with the Quakers had preceded them. At first the more traditional Quakers, who addressed each other as 'thee' and 'thou' and abhorred 'the works of the Devil', as they termed dancing and alcohol, found the Lochs too 'modern' and did not appreciate Joice's down-to-earth sense of humour. However, after getting to know them better, even the strictest Quakers revised their opinion and came to respect the Lochs for their dedication to the welfare of suffering refugees, for their imaginative ideas and their endless capacity for continuing their work under the most stressful and uncomfortable living conditions.

Towards the end of November food supplies for famine relief and for the relief workers themselves were running low. They still had a few bottles of Bovril left but had finished the tins of sardines and condensed milk. New food supplies, along with seed corn, flax seed and more stoves and ploughs to distribute were not due to arrive for a number of weeks yet. When eventually the Mission ran out of tinned food, many starving refugees had to survive on a thin soup made from boiled grass and leaves, while Mission staff were now down to one meal a day, a bowl of watery cabbage soup and a piece of black bread. Breakfast was a mug of weak black tea—there was no milk. Formerly they had had two ounces of chicken each week, but all the chickens had been eaten, so there were no fresh eggs either.

That winter several volunteers at Powursk died from the combined effects of overwork, malnutrition and typhoid. The saying 'You'll never get out of here alive' became a black joke. Eventually the death toll of Quaker volunteer workers would become so high that the League of Nations paid a Scottish doctor to tour eastern Poland and write a report on their working conditions. He recommended that the Quakers should employ a health worker whose sole task would be to monitor the health of volunteer field workers and check that they were receiving a reasonable diet.

So many refugees had dysentery and typhus that it was impossible to avoid catching some disease. Eventually Joice came down with dysentery and was confined to bed, weakened by diarrhoea and vomiting. She almost died. Miraculously, Sister Meadows was not affected and nursed her through, helped by one of the doctors from another Quaker Mission. When Joice recovered she was so thin that when she put on her grey serge uniform again the skirt slid over her hips and landed around her ankles. It took several weeks before she was well enough to start work once more. Sister Meadows was now so overworked without Joice's help that a former Army medical orderly was sent from Warsaw to assist her.

In the long winter of 1922 the famine seemed never-ending. However many winter clothes the volunteers distributed from the bundles that arrived on the specially chartered goods trains labelled 'Hilfe' [Aid Relief], there were never enough to go round. Many peasants still wore potato sacks tied with string around their waists and primitive birch-bark sandals.

By now it was so cold that whenever the staff went outside the Mission house, icicles crusted along their eyebrows and their breath formed white clouds and hung on the air. Sydney returned from the command post on the Stochod Valley at least once a month for a few days. Their time alone together was precious.

It was now that Joice discovered she was pregnant. She had turned thirty-five, well past the age that doctors of that period recommended having a first child. At that time childbirth was still hazardous, even for younger women, but the idea of bearing a child thrilled her. It was a time of hope, happiness and excitement—the pregnancy Joice and Sydney had longed for but never thought would happen.

13 'THE FOURTEEN THUMBS OF ST PETER'

Joice was worn out after months of working long hours seven days a week without a break. As she was pregnant, she cut back her hours and was given increased rations of powdered milk. For the sake of the baby she thought of leaving Powursk and returning to Warsaw where the aid workers' diet was better. Then the thing she had dreaded most in the world happened: she lost her baby.

Losing a deeply-wanted child had an immense psychological effect on Joice. She could not eat or sleep and became deeply depressed. Coping with famine, death and disaster coupled with the shock of the miscarriage took a heavy toll. Normally caring, optimistic, vivacious and well-balanced, she became withdrawn, silent and morose.

She was urged to rest but could not sleep. Thinking work would help she returned to assist Sister Hetty in the medical centre, but found she could no longer cope with lines of sobbing women and starving children; the sight of a sick or dying baby would immediately trigger her emotions. Unable to weep in front of the patients, she would leave the room and rush to her bedroom, where, control abandoned, she would weep for hours.[1]

Sydney was extremely worried. Administering his aid relief meant spending long periods away from Joice at the central control post along the Stochod River. And just as Joice needed him most, his second-in-command, Prince Alexander Makinsky, was offered a job by the Rockefeller Foundation and departed. However, at this critical moment the Prince decided to take a drop in salary and return, preferring to work with Sydney, a man who always inspired loyalty and affection from his helpers.[2]

It was late winter. The ground was frozen solid, so no work could be done in the fields. It was generally agreed that Joice needed a holiday. Sydney was given compassionate leave to accompany her on a brief working holiday in Russia, all expenses paid. Quaker Famine Relief in Moscow secured them hard-to-get visas to enter Russia, the country they had wanted to visit for so long.

Under the auspices of the Quakers the Lochs were able to see 'the real Russia', a rare privilege. Usually foreign writers saw only the sights the Russian Government deemed suitable for 'approved' (left-wing) visitors, those unlikely to criticise the regime. Lenin's Bolshevik Revolution was a social experiment that fascinated intellectuals and workers all over the world. The selected group of writers granted visas to the Union of Soviet Socialist Republics were not told that millions of Russians were slaughtered in purges, sent to gulags, or, in areas such as the Volga Basin, left to starve. Most writers failed to ask the right questions, their critical faculties undermined by the false belief that Russia was a workers' Utopia.

For that reason alone Joice's lively and candid account of life under Lenin is historically important.[3] This chance to visit the exotic country she had longed to see revived her spirits. As she and Sydney had worked without pay for over a year and donated their earnings from journalism to the Quakers they would be able to stay free of charge in the large house in central Moscow used as a hostel for Quaker volunteers. They were given train tickets from Warsaw to Moscow and set off on the long trip. By order of Lenin, Moscow had become Russia's new capital instead of the more Europeanised city of St Petersburg, which had recently been renamed Leningrad.

After leaving Minsk the train slowed down and then ground to a halt amid vast steppes covered in snow as far as the eye could reach. The engine driver, his face black with grease and grime, visited each compartment asking the passengers to give him money for what he called 'speed'. In the Lochs' compartment sat an attractive Russian girl with dark eyes and waist-length black hair, who spoke a little English. She explained they must give the driver money to buy wood for the engine, as Russian railways were short of funds to run the trains. Although the Lochs considered this a form of blackmail, it was not worth risking being stranded in the middle of deserted steppes, miles from anywhere. So they parted with some money and in due course the journey continued.[4]

'Gigantic Russia! Vast distances, vast steppes like travelling across the sea; the pine forests, peasants on the stations wearing thick woollen coats from their heads to their heels'—these were Joice's first impressions.

After another few hours travelling they witnessed a most distressing incident. The Russian girl who had interpreted for them was arrested by Red Army soldiers, who handcuffed her and dragged her screaming from the train. Powerless to help, they watched as the soldiers bundled the girl and her baggage into an Army lorry. According to the train conductor, who had had the story from the officer in charge, the unfortunate girl was returning from London. It seemed she had been paid large sums by members of the Russian Orthodox church there to smuggle gold and silver icons and reliquaries containing the bones of saints out of Russia for safe-keeping.

Sydney looked thoughtful when he heard this and said it could be true. 'There is a Russian church in London, just off the Bayswater Road . . . in St Petersburg Place—apt name, really.' He asked the conductor, who spoke a little English, what would happen to the poor girl. The conductor passed a finger across his throat and gave a grimace. Also in their compartment was a well-dressed and equally well-educated Englishman with an unusual walking stick, which had a carved snake as its handle. He told the Lochs he was going to Moscow for a Trade Fair at which he would be selling combine harvesters and threshing machines to the Russians. He would be staying in a hotel reserved for Party functionaries and trade visitors. He told Joice that he had stayed there before and knew that much of the hotel's fine antiques and fittings had been looted in the Revolution. It lacked central heating and sometimes there was no hot water in the bathrooms.

'You're lucky that you're officially working for the Quakers,' the English businessman said dryly. 'The secret police won't follow you around the way they do most foreigners. With any luck they won't give you an "interpreter" who's actually a member of Lenin's secret police.'

The Lochs realised their stay in Russia would not be long enough to write the Russian travel book John Murray had originally wanted to commission. Instead, Joice planned to use their visit to plot a novel set in Russia. She had already decided that the plot would hinge on a British spy at work in Lenin's Moscow. Possibly she was aware of the British spy Sydney Reilly, who worked in Russia in 1918. To help with the monotony of their long journey, Joice fantasised that the unfortunate Russian girl who had been arrested, and the English businessman in their compartment with his unusual walking stick might be incorporated as characters into her novel.

There was no restaurant car on the train. At some stations peasants sold bread rolls filled with meat. At others stick-thin children begged for scraps of food, and there was nothing but a samovar of boiling water to which passengers took their own drinking vessels and made tea.

When the Lochs arrived in Moscow they were met by Ruth Pennington, the liaison officer from the Quaker Mission. In response to Sydney's question, she confirmed they would not be given one of Lenin's 'interpreters'. Ruth drove a battered little Ford owned by the Mission. Across the river they gained a good view of the red walls of the Kremlin, the setting sun reflected on snow-covered glittering domes, surmounted with gilded crosses and spires.5 Moscow was so beautiful that Joice could see why Napoleon had sacrificed the lives of half a million soldiers in his greed to possess this extraordinary city.

The rambling old building which housed the representatives of the Quakers and various American Missions was once the residence of an aristocrat. All the furniture had been removed and they slept on camp beds. Meals were provided by an English housekeeper.

Next day, rested and refreshed by a good night's sleep and a cooked breakfast, the Lochs walked across the huge paved expanse of Red Square where cohorts of soldiers were drilling. To be allowed to visit the Kremlin, its churches and cathedrals, they hired an official guide who spoke reasonable English. He showed them the fantastic gilded domes, resembling a Grand Vizier's turban, of the fifteenth-century Cathedral of Vassili the Blessed with its painted interior. Red Army soldiers had stripped bare the interiors of this and other churches; their Byzantine-inspired icons, gold altar crosses and richly embroidered vestments were now displayed to a mocking public in special museums. Inside one Kremlin museum, the guide showed them rooms piled from floor to ceiling with church artworks and gold and silver treasures, including thousands of jewelled icons and a life-size Virgin made entirely of silver. Robes embroidered for Orthodox priests had been so richly encrusted with jewels that the garments stood up stiffly by themselves.6 Their guide seemed proud of the fact that the Bolsheviks had put these items on display rather than destroying them. Joice was fascinated by Russian icons depicting bearded saints, the stern face of Christ Pantocrator and the suffering Mother of God with her baby, often depicted as a tiny wizened little man.

Russian Orthodox cathedrals had huge domes on which a Christ Pantocrator triumphed, finger upraised in warning, surrounded by vast pyramids of saints and martyrs with golden haloes, a vast hierarchy filled with doom and foreboding. It was a far cry from the gentle Jesus meek and mild in the stained-glass windows of the Anglican churches of Joice's youth with their neat flower arrangements and pretty Christmas crib complete with a Madonna and a cuddly baby Jesus. Did these stern images represent something dark and gloomy in the Russian soul, like the plays of Chekov, she wondered.

After their guided tour they returned to Friends headquarters, where the capable Ruth Pennington took them under her wing. Ruth was also liaison officer of the Mission's International Aid Committee, run by the famous Polar explorer, Dr Fridtjof Nansen. His public appeals for funds to feed starving Russian children brought in enough money to buy trainloads of seed corn from well-wishers all over Europe.

Nevertheless, Ruth explained that Dr Nansen's appeals in the Western press for funds for famine relief had not been as successful as they had hoped. Money had been raised and corn bought, but the Russian railways were so hopelessly antiquated and so short of fuel that it was almost impossible to get the corn to those areas where it was needed most. Many areas that did receive seed corn found that it did not germinate during the terrible drought of 1921. As a consequence, there was starvation the following winter. Now, in the spring of 1922, the peasants in the Volga Basin and other areas faced a famine of huge proportions, as well as epidemics of typhus, cholera and malaria.

It was like eastern Poland all over again, Joice thought with despair. The Quakers were doing their best to cope under terrible conditions, shipping out ploughs and seed corn from London but they had many other demands on their relief services: hungry refugees in war-torn countries like Austria, Hungary and Serbia.

Dr Nansen's Committee was also experiencing difficulties trying to seek out and repatriate half a million Hungarian, Austrian, Polish and German prisoners-of-war from slave-labour camps in Siberia, held there in direct contravention of the terms of the Geneva Convention. Lenin refused to recognise the League of Nations or any of its directives, so it was extremely difficult to enter the gulags. Although the Aid Committee had finally succeeded, they found that many of the starving prisoners had died of malnutrition and lack of medical care. The average survival period for a prisoner in a Siberian slave-labour camp was one winter. The International Aid Committee knew that by now most of the men and women on their list of missing prisoners would be dead. This was the first time the Lochs had heard about gulags and slave labour; it was a far cry from the fulsome compliments they had read in the press about Lenin's achievement in liberating the peasants and forming the new Union of Soviet Socialist Republics.

A strange assortment of people shared the huge Mission house, from devout Quaker volunteers to disillusioned former Communists.

The latter had come to Russia to help feed the starving; they now realised Communist Party officials were making huge profits reselling much of the food donated for famine relief, while Lenin's government was trying to play down the fact that famine existed at all.

The Quakers were also providing food and aid to the starving in Astrakhan and Kirov. The Society of Friends in Britain and America were sending medicines to establish four children's hospitals. When the supply trains arrived in Moscow, delivery of the medicines direct to the hospitals was the responsibility of staff working for the Moscow Mission.

Ruth Pennington and Tolstoy's grandson Ilya had just returned from a trip to Siberia to buy ponies, which were to be donated to farmers in the Volga basin. These farmers lacked transport of any kind; their horses and oxen had been slaughtered and eaten during the previous winter's famine.

Ruth told the Lochs: 'On the surface the Communist experiment seems to be working. Few people in Britain or Europe understand that although Communism has created a prosperous new class of bureaucrats, hundreds of thousands of small farmers and middle-class professionals are dying of starvation. They're classed as "non-people" and denied ration cards.'

Joice nodded. 'The *real* story doesn't get into *any* newspapers, Russian *or* foreign. Fleet Street and Australian editors just don't want to hear it, all they want are positive, upbeat stories about Communism.' Ruth sighed. 'We know the truth but we dare not publish it for fear of jeopardising our relief work.'

Huge posters in Moscow streets bore blow-ups of Lenin's face. Others showed *kulaks*, the former prosperous peasant farmers and property owners, as pig-like brutes riding on the backs of the workers or being pulled by them in rickshaws. These images were simple and easily understood; like icons, they were ideal for presenting ideas to peasants who could neither read nor write.

The food situation in Moscow worsened each day. Food shops had bare shelves. Long queues formed at the mere rumour that a shop had food to sell. Any trees in the streets or parks had been stripped of leaves and the grass growing round them plucked out so that people could boil it up for soup. Many *kulaks* and aristocrats, lacking ration cards, collapsed from hunger and lay dying in the streets. Red soldiers were given the job of tying their legs together, which made it easier to bury them—often rigor mortis set in before the burial parties reached them.[7] Huge rats swarmed everywhere, gnawing on the corpses. Refuse disposal was non-existent. Bands of street children dug in the huge piles of rubbish in a desperate attempt to find food, or prostituted themselves for the price of a meal.[8]

Every worker was forced to donate forty-five per cent of their earnings to the State, including prostitutes, who still managed to ply their trade even though money was short. Some were girls of 'good' families, hiring out their bodies for a loaf of bread or a bar of chocolate. Their best clients were Party members, known as 'Nepmen' after Lenin's NEP (New Economic Policy Programme). NEP policies were just starting to be encouraged: by now Lenin was appalled at the financial mess his policies had created.

For Nepmen and high-ranking Party officials and their fur-clad wives, who made big money out of the new regime, the black market provided some relief from the famine. At the kerbside elderly women in head-scarves sold hard-boiled eggs and rye bread topped with salted herring at very high prices. Occasionally the bread was topped with pearls of black or red caviar. Apparently waiters or minor Party officials smuggled out the caviar in their pockets after Communist party functions and sold it on the black market.[9]

Abandoned timber homes were stripped to provide wood for the bonfires that burned every night on street corners. Men and women in ankle-length coats and fur hats warmed themselves and cooked what little food they had in frying pans held over these communal fires. To keep the fires going, soldiers dragged handcarts piled with carved oak panelling and handsome mahogany doors out of abandoned buildings. During the previous winter Muscovites had burned most of their furniture trying to keep warm.

On Sundays, aristocrats (officially non-existent since they lacked ration cards) were allowed to sell off their possessions and use the money to buy food on the black market. At street stalls former Grand Dukes and Countesses displayed what remained of their jewels, their Fabergé Easter eggs or table silver, which they sold piece by piece in order to live. Sydney bought a superbly crafted solid gold watch and chain and a Voigtlander camera from a Grand Duke for a pittance. He felt embarrassed when the owner thanked him as though Sydney had done him a great favour. Several of the British and American Quaker volunteers had by now purchased valuable Persian rugs to take home. Antique icons could be bought very cheaply, some stolen from the churches by criminals, others sold off by aristocrats or *kulaks*. Street traders offered gold wedding rings looped together on iron hoops.

Some aristocrats had nothing left to sell, and, though they might have a title and be able to speak seven or eight languages, there was no work for them; they were reduced to begging in order to eat. The sight of elderly, distinguished-looking men and women begging for scraps of food from passers-by was harrowing. Joice saw men in battered coats with fur collars: she saw a couple who reminded her of Prince Menshikov—perhaps they were Princes too.

Not everything was harrowing in Moscow. In the creative arts it was a time of hope and excitement. The Russian revolution marked the start of a wave of artistic and musical experimentation as talented young artists and designers poured their creativity into working for the Party. Joice queued for hours and managed to buy cheap tickets to attend the Bolshoi Ballet; the performance thrilled her. She and Sydney also attended an avant-garde performance of *Lohengrin* by the Moscow State Opera, a 'modern interpretation with Cubist-inspired scenery'. She marvelled at the brilliant costumes designed by Leon Bakst or his imitators. The burning creative force was overwhelming. Tickets were incredibly cheap to encourage factory workers and other manual labourers to attend the ballet and opera.

One evening the Lochs visited one of the few restaurants still open during the food shortage, once famous for its French cuisine. The decorative fountains, emptied of water, were now filled with cigarette butts, the accumulation of several years. The restaurant was thronged with the new rich, Nepmen and their wives, the latter swathed in furs and bedecked with diamonds.

While they were there, a frail, emaciated woman entered, supporting herself with a stick. Her features were aristocratic and her style of dress indicated she had once been rich. She wandered around the tables, begging for food from the Nepmen and Party officials. Contemptuously one of them flung her a plate of lobster shells, from which she vainly attempted to suck some nourishment. Meanwhile his colleagues and their bejewelled wives roared with laughter at the spectacle of another aristocrat in distress.[10]

Unlike many foreign writers who visited Russia and were lavishly entertained by the Communists, Joice maintained a strong sense of reality and described the good alongside the bad. The Lochs, unbiased and politically unattached, were able to see for themselves that Ruth Pennington's analysis of the situation was correct. The Russian economy *was* in crisis. Ironically, some parts of the vast Soviet Union had a surplus of food, but because of the rundown transport system it could not reach the famine-stricken areas. By now, Joice was highly sceptical of political or religious fanaticism of *any* persuasion.

After some weeks in Moscow the Lochs visited the Friends Famine Relief mission in the village of Buzuluk, near the large port of Samara on the Volga River. They travelled there by a slow train on the Moscow-Siberia line. The trip took three days.

They passed through undulating grasslands with scattered birch trees and pines, log cabins and sometimes a monastery or a fortress enclosed by a wall, like a miniature Kremlin. They traversed a vast wasteland designated as an industrial zone, soon to be known as Stalinsk in honour of Lenin's successor. *Kulaks* and political prisoners would be used to help build the foundations of the great steel factories of Stalinsk, Novokuznetsk and Kuznetsk in southern Siberia. Thousands of these slave-labourers were destined to die amid ice and snow. Later they would be replaced by volunteer workers, whose photographs appeared in glowing articles about 'the people's labour'.[11] The train continued to Samara (under Stalin it would be known as Kuybyshev) and finally the Lochs arrived at the Quaker Mission in Buzuluk.

Buzuluk, a small rural town, had been established during the lifetime of Count Tolstoy, author of *War and Peace*, who had worked with the Quakers. Tolstoy had Socialist aims and believed in the Quaker credo that 'help should be given without political, racial or religious discrimination'. Aided by a few members of the Tolstoy family, the Quaker Mission had dispensed soup and clothing to Russians, Ukrainians, Poles and Tartars at Buzuluk long before the Bolshevik Revolution and had been allowed to remain there when other foreigners were ordered to leave.

Samara had been classified by the League of Nations as a disaster area, but Lenin denied entry visas to their relief workers. Thousands more could have been saved if the League of Nations had been allowed to carry out relief work. Instead, the Quakers carried the entire burden.

Two remarkable women, Anna Haines from London and Anna Louise Strong from America, were in charge of Quaker famine relief in Buzuluk. The Quaker aid programs they had organised over the past three years had fed and kept alive over 16,000 starving children.[12]

Civil war in Russia had lasted for three years following the 1917 Revolution, and huge areas of crops and livestock had been destroyed. The *kulaks* had killed their livestock rather than hand it over to collective farms, thus aggravating the famine. Following the poor harvest of 1920 and renewed drought of 1921, Red Army soldiers had requisitioned the meagre amounts of grain left in the peasants' storage barns, leaving them to starve.[13] The harvest of 1922 was not much better. Desperate for food to feed their families, the peasants ground acorns into flour, mixed it with sawdust and baked the bitter-tasting famine bread. They made soup from grass and any wild herbs that had survived the winter. There were whispered stories of cannibalism, of corpses of young children, usually the first to die of malnutrition, being cut up, boiled and eaten so that their siblings and parents could survive.[14] Those who died during the severe winters could not be buried in the frozen ground; corpses piled up awaiting the spring when the ground would be soft enough to dig. The morgues were filled with more corpses and it was rumoured that many of those had been stolen and eaten.[15]

Following the Revolution, almost five million *kulaks* had their homes and livestock confiscated along with their hard-earned savings. As a reward for thrift and hard work they were now homeless outcasts in their own country, described by Lenin as 'enemies of the State'. Most had been deported to the gulags. The Quakers were attempting to feed those who remained.

Sydney gave Anna Haines and the Famine Relief Committee at Buzuluk some of the Polish Unit's ideas for relief schemes. Joice helped deliver emergency packs of tinned food to peasant homes and when necessary gave medical advice or delivered babies. She was interested in the work of what the Russians called *feldschers*, highly trained medical orderlies or 'barefoot doctors'. They had received a similar training to hers as a *doktorika* and did the same kind of work.

The peasants in the Samara region lived in log cottages. Their water supply came from huge barrels which in winter were placed in their living rooms to prevent the water freezing solid. Malaria was prevalent as mosquito larvae bred in the barrels in summer. The young and the very old slept on top of the stove. The smell of wet sheepskins, unwashed bodies and tightly swaddled babies was overwhelming. The small houses swarmed with *tarakans*, insects that resembled huge black cockroaches. Joice even found a *tarakan* in the sour brew of pumpkin-rind tea that one woman offered her.

In some areas where food was not such a problem, Communist volunteers toured peasants' homes teaching them to read and write and spreading propaganda for the regime. Centuries of regimentation by the Tsars had made many Russians easy prey for totalitarian regimes. Subsequent psychologists and sociologists, influenced by the theories of Geoffrey Gorer, have attributed the Russians' strong desire for conformity of thought to the custom of being kept immobile in swaddling clothes as babies. Joice wrote: 'Russians as a nation have a strong tradition of thinking alike. In Tsarist times it was abnormal to be a Russian without being of the Russian Orthodox religion. The Communist Government has taken over what was once a Tsarist view of correct or right thinking. The effect of all this on the life of the country is profound.'[16]

The Lochs saw how many of the evils of the old Tsarist regime were being reproduced by Communism. High-ranking Communist Party officials and Nepmen adopted Tsarist powers and privileges, founding a so-called democracy based on purging all opposition to their policies. Anyone who dared to question Lenin's authority could end up as slave labour. Stalin would continue this practice. (Years later Joice commented that Lenin and Stalin committed more atrocities against their own people than all the Romanovs put together.) The Lochs spent a few weeks at Buzuluk. They accompanied Anna Haines, delivering emergency packs of foods to orphanages filled with anaemic, emaciated children clad in rags. These visits had a profound effect on Joice. In Dublin she had thought about adopting an orphaned baby. Following her miscarriage she had decided that if she could not have a child of her own she would do everything in her power to help as many orphans as possible.

On their return to Moscow, they visited an exhibition of icons and holy relics, put together by the editor of *Bez Boznic*, an atheist propaganda newspaper funded by the Communist Party,[17] designed to shake the faith of devout peasants in the Orthodox church. A huge range of exhibits removed from churches by Red Army soldiers revealed for the first time that as many as fourteen thumb-bones of St Peter in gold and silver caskets had been venerated in various churches, along with three different versions of the shroud of Christ. Joice was fascinated to see how the minds of simple people could so easily be manipulated by Orthodox priests and political commissars alike. The Lochs saw at first-hand how the Communists capitalised on the harsh life of the Russian peasant. Poverty-stricken people needed a deep, almost mystic faith to help them survive famine, deprivation and sickness. Belief in the Bolshevik version of Marxism was being promoted by Lenin in the same way that the leaders of the Russian Orthodox Church had manipulated the peasants. Joice asked herself whether this hunger for belief was an integral part of the Russian soul.

One day in Moscow, the Lochs watched as a workman climbed the onion dome of the huge Church of the Redeemer, ordered by the

Communists to smash the gold cross on top. The man slipped and fell onto the pavement a hundred feet below, broke his back and lay screaming in agony. Abruptly, the mood of the crowd, which had been applauding the destruction of the cross, changed. Their deeply ingrained faith reasserted itself as they wept, wailed and crossed themselves, demanding a priest to give the dying man the last rites.

Sparked by the girl smuggler's arrest on the train, by meeting the English businessman with the carved walking stick and by visiting the Government-sponsored exhibition of stolen relics, Joice's creative skill and sense of irony returned and she created the synopsis and characters of her novel, *The Fourteen Thumbs of St Peter*. The protagonist is the unnamed narrator, a young unmarried English girl who, having volunteered to work for the Quaker Mission to Moscow, is unwittingly drawn into a plot to steal the fourteen thumb-bones of St Peter. The bones go on show at an exhibition of holy relics master-minded by the evil Piotr Pavlovich, editor of an atheist newspaper, who receives his orders direct from Lenin. Then the dubious thumb-bones are stolen by Mr Crowe, an English businessman whom the heroine meets by chance on her journey to Moscow. At the request of the Russian Orthodox Church in London, who fear their beliefs are being damaged by spurious relics exhibited for public ridicule, Crowe smuggles the thumb-bones out of Russia by train, hidden in a hollow-walking stick with a carved snake as its handle.

Meanwhile Pavlovich kidnaps the heroine and tries to force her to reveal who stole the bones from his exhibition. She refuses and is about to be tortured when Pavlovich receives a message from Stalin that Lenin is dead. Stalin orders Pavlovich to drop everything and mount a huge international publicity campaign announcing the forthcoming public display of Lenin's embalmed body in Red Square. The girl is dumped back at the Quaker Mission unharmed.

Joice's novel ends on an ironic note. Lenin's embalmed corpse in its glass casket goes on display in Red Square, surrounded by adoring peasants who, after Pavlovich's huge publicity campaign, turn Lenin into an object of veneration. His mummified corpse in its glass casket replaces the bones of the saints in their gold reliquaries that past generations of Russians worshipped.

In Stalin's time writers who visited Russia and were seen as sympathetic to Communism received substantial royalties for Russian editions of their works. Needless to say, *The Fourteen Thumbs of St Peter*, published in London in 1927, never had a Russian edition.

Visiting the Swallow children at Hambledon plantation. Joice NanKivell, is the second child from left, standing beside Daisy in her white nursemaid's uniform. *(Hambledon Album, John Oxley Library, State Library of Queensland).*

Between 1880 and 1890 plantation life in north Queensland was luxurious. Edith NanKivell, always elegantly dressed, in her pony cart visits her sister-in-law at Hemsleigh plantation. *(Hemsleigh Homestead file, John Oxley Library, State Library of Queensland).*

Indentured Pacific Island cane workers around Ingham, Queensland, 1890. (*John Oxley Library, State Library of Queensland*).

Portrait by John Longstaff of Joice's favourite aunt, the famous Ellis Rowan [née Ryan]. Ellis, a talented artist and writer encouraged Joice to write books. (*National Library of Australia, Canberra*).

Following their bankruptcy, Edith NanKivell and her family went from a spacious Queensland homestead to a dirt-floored hut in the Gippsland forest. *(Private collection).*

These two little girls would be friends for life: Joice NanKivell (left) and Estelle Simson (right). *(Photographed by E Humphrey of 264 Collins Street, c. 1900, courtesy Joyce Welsh).*

Sydney's friend, Major X from British Intelligence and his colleagues, disguised as Dublin working men. A double agent stole this historic photograph from security files in Dublin Castle. Michael Collins' men numbered the men as suitable targets for IRA marksmen: most of them would be shot on 'Bloody Sunday'. (*Hilton-Getty Picture Library*).

On 25 May 1921, Dublin's Customs House, symbol of British authority, was burned to the ground by Republican supporters. Joice was there and wrote up the story for a London newspaper. (*State Archives, Dublin*).

Above: Joice's press office and sleeping quarters in an abandoned railway carriage bear a sign 'Society of Friends: Anglo-American Mission to Poland'. Joice wept when bands of starving children beat on the doors of the carriage demanding food, because she had none to give them.
(Sydney Loch).

Right: Portrait of Joice Loch, wearing a grey sweater bought in London and a fur hat bought second-hand in a street market in Warsaw. The photograph was taken when she was working for the Quakers in Poland.
(© Pandanus Press).

Polish and Ukrainian war victims, fed and clothed by the Society of Friends, open Christmas presents from Britain, received after Joice's newspaper story about the plight of refugee children in eastern Poland. *(Sydney Loch)*.

Above: Victorious Turkish cavalry take possession of Smyrna. (*From the collection of Joice Loch*)

Below: Greek Orthodox refugees carrying their few remaining possessions wrapped in sheets or pillow cases. (*Commander J. G. Adamson, RN, MBE. © Pandanus Press*)

Above: Refugees without money desperate to escape wait at the Quayside hoping Greek naval ships will take them to the mainland of Greece. The wealthy Greek and Levantine residents have already left on private yachts or their own merchant vessels

Below: The Greek port of Smyrna (Izmir), 14 September 1922. Following the massacre of its inhabitants by Ataturk's troops two days previously, the Greek port set alight by order of Ataturk continues to burn. The wharves are deserted: many thousands of Greeks have fled to the Greek mainland in fishing boats or sought safety aboard French and Italian battleships, while British and American warships had orders only to rescue those with British or American passports. Thousands more have drowned, been shot, incinerated or held prisoner by Turkish soldiers. *(Photographed from a British warship by the author's father, Commander J. G. Adamson, RN, MBE. © Pandanus Press).*

Marines and naval officers including my father go ashore. This is now dangerous as Turkish soldiers and Balkan *chettes* are murdering so many people. They take pistols with them and bring rescued Greeks to safety on HMS *King George V* and HMS *Iron Duke*.
© *Pirgos Press*

Below: HMS Iron Duke photographed at night from HMS King George V. Smoke obscures the burning buildings along Quayside. Refugees stand there hoping ships will rescue them and screaming for help. Their screams echo across the water to the battleships who cannot intervene as they have orders from Whitehall forbidding them to become involved. The British Government does not want to offend Mustafa Kemal as he now controls the valuable Mesopotamian oil concessions.

Above: Boarding HMS King George V are staff and families from the British consulate and British passport holders. They are placed on a chartered vessel bound for Malta. The 2,000 Greek refugees who have spent two days and nights on the upper and mess decks are transferred to a British merchant vessel whose charter fee is paid by Sir Henry Lamb, the British consul out of Government funds, and this humanitarian rescue although somewhat tardy is recorded in the Naval Section of the British National Archives at Kew.

Below: Watched by the crew of the King George V the chartered British merchant vessels head off for Athens with a load of refugees on board. When they arrive at Piraeus they find refugee camps overloaded with refugees and have to go north to Thessaloniki. Here Joice Loch will record what happens as she cares for wounded Greek refugees and those suffering from typhoid in the camp's medical centre.

Landing at Thessaloniki at the end of September some refugees from Smyrna bring crates or bundles of possessions. Some who have fled from ethnic cleansing in other parts of Turkey own nothing but the clothes they wear. Some refugees are ill as they had to drink polluted water as they waited on the waterfront at Smyrna. *(From the collection of Joice Loch)*

Below: The Quakers supply transport for refugees to the camp at Thessaloniki where Joice Loch will work in the medical centre. *(From the collection of Joice Loch)*

The rugged tower of Prosforion, built centuries previously by a Byzantine emperor, became 'home' to the Lochs in 1926. *(Sydney Loch).*

Joice Loch in her tower sitting room, circa 1929. The man sitting on the sofa with a cat on his lap, opposite Joice, is Sydney Loch. Furniture made by the village carpenter can be seen; one of Joice's Pirgos rugs is on the wall. *(Estelle Slater, courtesy Joyce Welsh).*

Monks from Athos harvesting olives. These well-established olive groves behind the village would soon be taken away from the control of the monasteries by the starving villagers of Ouranoupolis. *(Sydney Loch).*

Father Meletios, the librarian at Vatopedi, talks to Paraskevoula, midwife and matchmaker. *(Sydney Loch).*

In charge of a refugee camp in Palestine, Joice encouraged Polish women to earn income and gain self-respect making and then selling dolls in national costume. *(Sydney Loch)*.

Joice and Sydney enjoying a rare moment of relaxation from the worries of running two huge refugee camps in World War Two. *(Joice Loch collection)*.

One sad result of the Greek Civil War, were the many orphaned girls trying to 'mother younger siblings without a breadwinner in the family. To help them Joice set up classes in childcare and nutrition at the American Farm School and taught some of them to weave rugs to earn income. *(Joice Loch collection).*

Half-starved orphans are now well-fed and wear good second hand clothes donated by Australian and Canadian families on Joice's initiative. Above the loom is Joice's design for those Byzantine mythical beasts named gryphons. *(Sydney Loch).*

Joice's original caption reads 'A rug made in Ouranopolis'. Modesty prevented her from adding that she had designed the rug herself. *(Sydney Loch)*.

Joice wrote under this photograph, 'Sydney and I with Theodore Litsas, Manager of the American Farm School'. *(Joice Loch collection, courtesy Martha Handschin).*

Below left, Fani Mitropoulou as a young widow. Joice wrote, 'Fani runs me and the tower'. At right, Fani's son Nikos in 1958. Nikos and Fani were models for Christophilos and his widowed mother in Joice's books *Tales of Christophilos* and *Again Christophilos*. *(Courtesy Fani Mitropoulou).*

Left: Joice Loch in mid-life, possibly on her second visit to Warsaw. *(Courtesy Fani Mitropoulou)*.

Below left: Joice at her typewriter with one of her cats, descendants of the original Sylvia and Mustapha. *(Courtesy Martha Handschin)*.

Below right: In World War Two Madame Sophia asked friends of the Lochs on Athos to care for Joice's cats. Strict laws banned all female creatures from Athos, Garden of the Mother of God. The monks failed to investigate too closely and were surprised when several of the cats had kittens. *(Sydney Loch)*.

15 RIBBONS OF BLUE THAT BIND FOREVER

Snow was melting in the streets of Warsaw by the time the Lochs returned to Poland.

During their absence a letter had arrived from Joice's mother with sad news: Aunt Ellis Rowan had died from a recurrence of malaria, which she had originally caught in New Guinea on one of her flower-hunting expeditions. She had been devotedly nursed by her sister, dear Aunt Blanche. Joice wept over the news, remembering her aunt's kindness to her as a child and her wish that Joice should become a professional author. Yet another link with Australia and the past was gone.

Joice wrote a letter of consolation to Aunt Blanche and another to her mother, telling her about the trip to Russia and how all the hard work in Poland was taking effect. Things were improving. The horse-loan scheme Sydney had organised the previous year was a great success. This, together with the large-scale distribution of seed corn, seed potatoes and flax seed meant that hundreds of acres of eastern Poland were once more under cultivation. Now, in the Lochs' second Polish year, vast tracts of land were already turning green. The harvest was expected to be good.

Donations from Friends in America and Britain had paid for hundreds of calves and hens and vast amounts of vegetable seeds, flax seeds and spinning wheels, all distributed by the five Polish aid units. Former battlefields had been restored to pastures where cattle would soon graze. Most rural families could now look forward to fresh milk, eggs, vegetables from their own gardens and a chicken in the pot on Sundays. Linen would be made from the harvested flax and embroidered by the women. The Government's donation of timber to the farmers and Sydney's timber-hauling scheme meant that over a thousand new homes were springing up, their roofs thatched in traditional eastern Polish style. The worst of the Polish famine would soon be over.

Joice and Sydney made several lifelong friends during their sojourn in Poland; they included the writer Melchior Wankowicz, Prince Makinsky and their interpreters Pani Bianki and Count Tarnowski.

The Count was an amateur historian with a fund of entertaining stories about Poland's history of bitter glory, triumphs, heroism, invasions and defeats down the centuries. 'We Polish are resilient,' Count Tarnowski told the Lochs. 'We have had to be.'

He accompanied Joice in the *furmanka* one day when she went out to deliver a baby to a woman who was still living in a damp Army dugout. On the return journey, knowing Joice's interest in history, the Count showed her the vast Narocz Lake, one of the Masurian Lakes which had been the site of a great battle in World War 1 between the invading forces of Germany's General Hindenburg and the army of the Russian Tsar Nicholas. Count Tarnowski told her that in the spring of 1916, when the Germans appeared to be winning, 60,000 young Russian conscripts from the Tsar's Army had sought to escape and return home across the frozen waters of Lake Narocz. But it was spring, and their horses crashed through the melting ice, many pulling their riders down with them. Thousands of young Russian soldiers drowned in their desperate attempt to escape from the advancing German army. Now their corpses lay among the weeds at the bottom of the lake where huge pikes lurked.

Around the lake, silver-birch saplings had sprung up through the heaped skeletons of German and Russian soldiers. The whole area and parts of the Stochod Valley were vast graveyards filled with bleached bones. Joice stumbled over some skulls; she could see the bullet holes in them. Corpses were everywhere, even in the birch forests through which she and Count Tarnowski were walking. She heard a sound like crackling twigs. With horror she realised these were not birch twigs but the outstretched fingers of long-dead soldiers beneath her feet.

That night she wrote an epitaph in blank verse for those 60,000 young men who lay at the bottom of Lake Narocz.[1]

Springtime along the valley of the Stochod River inspired her to write another poem, about the arrival of the storks. After the snow had melted, thousands of birds migrated north to Poland to build their nests. To the peasants the birds were an omen that good harvests would return in spite of the desolation. 'Look, Pani Loch, a stork!' they shouted out excitedly. 'And another! And another!' The storks, with legs red as sealing wax, folded their black-barred wings and glided down into the marshy fields as the women laughed and hugged their children to them.

Count Tarnowski told Joice that when he was a child every farmhouse and cottage had a stork's nest on its thatched roof. During the fighting, by some strange sixth sense, the birds had stayed away.

Now, as a result of the scorched-earth policies of the invading Russian army, there were so few roofs on which the huge birds could build their nests that they were forced to use the tops of Army dugouts. He said that once autumn came, to avoid the cold the storks would fly away to the vast delta of the Danube. There they lived for several months on the abundant supplies of fish in its shallow waters before continuing their journey south to Africa, where they would winter before returning once again to Poland.

Joice gazed at the storks, delighted that their arrival brought hope to the war victims. 'It's a beautiful sight,' she said. 'How I would love to follow their migration south.'

When she returned to Warsaw, Joice was presented with two crested envelopes containing letters from Marshal Pilsudski. She and Sydney had each been awarded the Polish Gold Cross of Merit. They were invited to an evening reception at the Presidential Palace. Other important members of the famine relief teams, including Joice's friends Alizon Fox and Florence Barrow, had already received their medals at a daytime investiture held while the Lochs were in Russia. The Polish Government were aware of the enormous debt they owed to the British and American Quaker volunteers, several of whom had given their lives working for the Polish people.

The evening the Lochs received their medals was a memorable one. Sydney wore a borrowed evening suit and Joice her only formal dress, which had remained at the bottom of her suitcase ever since leaving London: a slim sheath of black silk, its matching stole fringed with an intricate pattern of sky-blue ribbons. France's General Foch was in Warsaw and an official dinner was being held in his honour after the investiture, to which the Lochs were also invited.

At the investiture Joice and Sydney went forward in turn to have their medals pinned on them by Marshal Pilsudski. Later, in his speech at the formal dinner, the Acting President referred to the remarkable achievements of Quaker volunteers who had helped to rebuild and restock the farms, with the result that now almost a million returned refugees were working their land again. Joice was proud to think that Sydney, with his genius for organisation, had played such a significant part in this achievement.

At the dinner table Joice sat opposite Marshal Pilsudski and next to Count Markiewicz, who turned out to be the husband abandoned by Constance Markiewicz, the Irish Revolutionary, whom she had met at George Russell's literary evenings in Dublin. Joice said what a coincidence it was that she had met his wife in Dublin and how much she admired Constance Markiewicz for her courage. 'Don't speak to me about that she-devil!' the Count responded angrily. He turned away from Joice and gave his whole attention to the lady sitting next to him.

On Joice's other side was a silver-haired Polish general with beautiful manners who was both gallant and entertaining. Like most educated Poles, he spoke fluent English and French and was well-read in both languages. He and Joice discussed literature animatedly, and Joice told him about the book on eastern Poland she and Sydney intended to write. The General showed great enthusiasm for the project.

From time to time Joice glanced over to Sydney, who was seated between the elderly wives of two dignitaries, struggling hard to talk in Polish to them. After the main course there was a short interlude: Paderewski, the famous Polish pianist, now an old man, gave a recital of Chopin Polonaises to tremendous applause.

By the time dessert was served, Joice and the Polish General were chatting away like old friends. He asked about the Lochs' plans after they left Poland. Joice told him they wanted to go somewhere relatively inexpensive and write full-time. They dreamed of living in a good climate: Spain, Southern Italy or a Greek island were all possibilities. The General fingered his moustache thoughtfully and wondered if they would be able to break their links with the Quakers entirely after their experiences in Poland.

Joice laughed. She said that first and foremost she and Sydney were writers; she explained how their experiences in Ireland and the possibility of retaliation against them by the IRA had brought about their involvement with the Quakers.

The General asked whether the blue ribbons that fringed her stole held any special significance. 'Not really, it's simply that blue is my favourite colour,' Joice replied.

President Pilsudski, overhearing their conversation, leaned across the table and remarked that according to the Old Testament, blue ribbons on a garment indicated that the wearer was devoted to serving God. He quoted a verse from the Bible about the Children of God fringing their garments with ribbons of blue to show that they followed the commandments of the Lord rather than those of their own hearts.

'Perhaps your choice of a blue fringe is an omen that you'll *never* escape from Quaker service,' the General said with a twinkle in his eye.[2]

'Oh no!' Joice exclaimed. 'My heart's set on writing. I'm going to be a full-time author and so is my husband.' She found the conversation amusing but did not take the General's prediction seriously. Superstition held no place in her philosophy.

By now several of the Refugee Missions were being wound down. Sister Hetty and other volunteers returned to their homes and families. It was something of a shock for the Lochs to realise that, unlike most of their fellow volunteers, they had no permanent home and owned very little apart from their books.

Their writer friend Melchior Wankowicz tried to persuade them to stay in Poland. They found the Polish countryside breathtakingly beautiful—especially in autumn, when the linden trees turned from gold to red, and in spring when the fields were filled with wild flowers. However, both Joice and Sydney longed to live in a warmer climate, preferably beside the sea. They both loved Australia but it was too remote for aspiring writers at a time when most publishing took place in London or New York. Britain was out of the question due to its chilly wet winters and fogs. So where *should* they go? They talked endlessly about the possibilities, and Joice spoke with longing about Greece and the blue Aegean Sea or a villa on the Spanish coast.

Every now and then Joice smiled to herself as she recalled the General's bantering remark that perhaps she would never escape from Quaker service. She had enormous respect for the Quakers. British Quakers were not a large Society in terms of numbers, but they had played a huge role in raising funds for Polish, Ukrainian, Bielorussian and Russian war victims without reference to nationality, colour or creed. They had done similar work in other parts of Europe, being almost the only charitable organisation involved with refugees at that time.[3]

Joice found it very hard to understand how Quakers could firmly believe that God had a plan for the world, when He permitted the suffering and deaths of so many innocent people. To express her doubt about her belief in an Almighty God, she had written a poem in a dark moment during her stay at Powursk. She had sent the poem, called *The Face of God*, to Florence Barrow, a non-Quaker like herself:

And if you see the face of God,
can you read what lies upon it?
I can only see a long steep hill,
with a broken cross upon it.
And if you see the face of God
can you read what tears are on it?
You say the untroubled face of God
has tears of love upon it
Then have I looked too long
that I find no answers on it?

For Joice, religions, creeds and nationalities would always seem relatively unimportant. She often said that what really counted was not whether someone was Orthodox, Catholic, Protestant, Muslim, Russian or Hottentot: 'the kindness of one human being to another' was what she deemed important.

In that spring of 1923, the Polish Government was able to take over many of the welfare organisations the Society of Friends had established. Now the Friends Welfare Committee in London prepared to send their volunteers returning from Poland to other areas with grave problems. Only a few were left behind. Sydney Loch was one of these, involved in setting up a Farm School for orphaned boys and girls near Brest-Litovsk, a task that would occupy the next six months. It was agreed with the Polish Government that the Friends would hand over the Mission buildings, the factory that made ploughs and other farm implements and their horses and equipment to a newly constituted Eastern Borders Committee, which would continue their work in eastern Poland.

Joice, who was staying at the Friends Women's Hostel in Warsaw, planned to help out as a medical orderly until Sydney had finished his work at Brest-Litovsk. But fate has a way of interfering with plans. The Lochs were invited to attend a farewell meeting in Warsaw, held to express thanks to all the volunteers. Dr Hilda Clark, who ran the Vienna Mission, was to address the meeting, and Joice and Sydney also met Nancy Brunton Lauder there, an amusing American who shared many of their interests. Nancy was not a member of the Religious Society of Friends. Having been born to great wealth, she felt she should give back something to the less fortunate, and the Friends Missions enabled her to do this.

Hilda Clark was a legend in Quaker circles. She had renounced a brilliant career in medicine to run Friends War Relief in Vienna.[4] She was a striking-looking woman, tall and graceful; her lustrous black hair was pulled back from a centre parting and she had a beautiful smile. She thanked them all for their heroic efforts and went on to give an inspiring speech, telling them that Greece was the new world trouble spot where Quakers were providing aid to refugees. Joice and Sydney listened, absorbed, as Dr Clark described the recent catastrophic events that had taken place.

She explained that for centuries, millions of Greeks had been permitted to live under Turkish rule in Asia Minor. During World War I, the Greeks had remained neutral until 1917, when they entered the conflict and fought bravely on the side of the British, French and Serbians against the Turks and Germans . . . so bravely that Britain and France had given the Greek Government a mandate to invade Turkey. The declining Ottoman Empire, traditional enemy and occupier of Greece, was ruled by an elderly and corrupt Sultan and appeared to be on the verge of collapse.

Hilda Clark knew how to capture her listeners: like a true storyteller, she related how for centuries Greeks had dreamed of recapturing territories that had once been part of the vast Greek-speaking Empire of Byzantium. Now they had their chance. When the Ottoman Sultan finally surrendered, it seemed that at last, Greece had attained her ambition.

In May 1919, the Greek Army landed troops at the big Turkish port of Smyrna, and marched north. As the second largest Greek Orthodox city in the world, Smyrna had been virtually controlled by Greeks, and now, under the mandate granted by their allies, it was *their* city and a major port.

After a dramatic pause, Dr Clark went on to the next phase of the story. In 1922 a new Ottoman force unexpectedly emerged. Under the command of its dynamic leader Kemal Ataturk—'Leader of the Turks'—it repulsed the advancing Greek Army. President Venizelos of Greece, certain of the support of his wartime allies, refused to negotiate with Ataturk. But no support was forthcoming and the Greek army retreated to Smyrna.[5] Chasing after the defeated Greek soldiers, who were exhausted after four years of desert fighting on a meagre diet, were both the Turkish troops who had defeated them in Anatolia and an unruly band of Balkan brigands on horseback. Greek residents of Smyrna who had previously welcomed the invading Greek army feared reprisals by the Turks. Violence began in the Armenian quarter where homes were looted, money demanded from householders and their daughters raped, first by the Balkan *chettes* who were soon then joined by Turkish soldiers. By the following day the violence had spread to the Greek quarter where many hundreds of Greek residents were murdered.

Dr Clark's audience listened intently as she related this major crime against humanity in which hundreds of thousands of Greeks and Armenians were killed in revenge for Turks killed in the Greek-Turkish war. She explained how Turkish soldiers and Balkan *chettes* or bandits, aided by some Turkish residents of Smyrna set fire to the wooden houses in the Armenian and Greek quarters, using petrol to accelerate the flames with the householders locked inside their homes so that they perished in the flames. The fire spread rapidly across both the Greek and Armenian Quarters as the fire hoses had been cut by persons unknown.

Eventually the blaze reached the consulates and warehouses that lined the long boulevard known as Quayside. Here some 2,000 Greek refugees from Anatolia and the hinterland of Smyrna were camping hoping to find a ship to take them to the Greek mainland and were distraught to find no ships were available. The violence spread to the Quayside where armed soldiers manhandled the refugees, robbing them of the few valuables they still possessed, killed all young men and at gunpoint continued raping girls and young widows. The exits from the Quayside were blocked by machine guns so the refugees could not escape. Many were widows and children whose ancestors had always lived in Greece. During the four year Greek-Turkish war fought in the Turkish province of Anatolia, Turkish soldiers had killed their husbands or taken them prisoner and marched them into the desert to die.

The fire spread rapidly carried by the prevailing wind. It lasted for more than three days in which the magnificent city of Smyrna was reduced to rubble and ashes. The heat on the Quayside was suffocating and some refugees died of thirst. They prayed for ships that would take them to Greece. The fire was headline news in the overseas press but none of the assembled warships were allowed to help the refugees.

British, American and French battleships, riding at anchor off Smyrna, received orders not to become involved. Greece's former allies had pursued Turkey under an elderly and ailing Sultan, but they were unwilling to oppose Kemal Ataturk; they hoped he would negotiate favourable oil concessions with them from the Mesopotamian oilfield in which Turkey had a share. The discovery of valuable oilfields in Turkish-owned Mesopotamia had changed the policy of the British and American governments towards Kemal and his nationalist government: they had no wish to turn Kemal into an enemy.

Orders were given to the waiting navies not to intervene. They were allowed to rescue only their own nationals. Helplessly the naval officers watched through binoculars as thousands of terrified Greeks swarmed onto the quayside. Still the Turks advanced upon their panic-stricken victims as they fought for places on the quayside, hoping the foreign vessels would rescue them. Those at the front were pushed relentlessly into the sea. Women, the aged and infirm, thousands of children . . . screaming, crying, swimming, drowning.

An estimated 200,000 Orthodox Christians managed to reach the quay at Smyrna and stood there in a line almost two miles long. Some 25,000 unarmed Greeks were trampled underfoot or slaughtered where they stood by members of the Turkish cavalry. Most of the young Greek men perished. Those who were left were widows, orphaned children and elderly parents and it was these unfortunate people, many of whom had been saved by warships from the British navy and an American Baptist minister who had chartered vessels to bring them to Thessaloniki, who the volunteers would be caring for in the new Quaker-run camp at Thessaloniki.

Dr Clark paused again before she related what followed. False propaganda implied that the Greeks and Armenians had set fire to Smyrna before evacuating the city and that they had killed many Turks. The result was a Muslim uprising against Greek Orthodox villagers throughout Asia Minor and Muslim Bulgaria. Thousands more Greek homes were burned, thousands more Greek women and girls raped.

Briskly Dr Clark went on to outline the present position. The League of Nations had ratified a formal 'Exchange of Populations' whereby 1,500,000 Greeks would be exchanged for 400,000 Turks residing in Greece. Thousands upon thousands of Greek Orthodox refugees were pouring into camps all over Greece, carrying the few possessions they had managed to snatch up as they fled.

Britain, in part responsible for encouraging the Greeks to invade Turkey, had donated only a small sum to build refugee camps, and these were now grossly overcrowded. The Greek Government, one of the poorest in the world, lacked funds to feed and house the refugees. The British Society of Friends, supported by old Quaker families like the Frys, Cadburys and Rowntrees, were donating money, as were American Quakers. Quaker-trained *doktorikas* were desperately needed, as well as teachers: many of the children were orphans and special schools were to be set up for them.

Hilda Clark ended her speech by saying that if anyone, especially those who had received practical instruction as medical orderlies, felt a special 'concern' for Greece, now was the time to go there and help save the lives of over a million Greek men, women and children, many of whom were desperately sick. She paused dramatically and waited.

Joice looked at Sydney. Dr Clark's speech had moved her deeply. Having studied Greek history and culture, it had always been one of her dreams to visit Greece.

Nancy Brunton Lauder raised her hand to volunteer. Joice knew that if she volunteered, Sydney would do the same. He was aware of her feelings about Greece, feelings that he shared. He always seemed to know her thoughts; now, as she glanced towards him, he gave a gentle nod by way of response. When Hilda Clark asked, 'Any more volunteers?' Joice raised her hand. 'I'll go,' she said. How could she refuse the needs of so many crying out for care and compassion? She would be by herself to begin with; for the next six months Sydney would be busy setting up the Farm School and Orphanage at Brest-Litovsk; after that he could join her in Greece. Their book about working in refugee camps in Poland would have to wait.

Dr Clark told them that improved vaccines against typhoid were being shipped out by the American Friends. Volunteers were at risk from cholera, malaria, blackwater fever, typhoid and typhus. Anyone who wanted to withdraw could do so. Not a single hand was raised.

The Lochs, still relatively young, were united in their desire to help Greece. And perhaps Greece was the place in the sun where they would eventually be able to settle down to write full-time. At Quaker headquarters in London, Carl Heath was delighted they were to join the Quaker Relief team in Greece. Sydney confirmed his intention to join Joice as soon as his duties in Poland ended. Carl Heath said that Joice could travel by train from Warsaw to Thessaloniki whenever she was ready. Work as a *doktorika* and part-time journalist would be available immediately at a huge refugee camp which had been set up in the grounds of the American Farm School, near Thessaloniki.

Soon it was time for fond goodbyes until their reunion six months hence. For better or worse the Lochs were no longer just observers and journalists but had become deeply involved with the Quakers. The Polish General's words to Joice had come true. 'Ribbons of blue' were a sign that her life was now inextricably linked with Quaker aid to refugees. Sydney's experiences at Gallipoli and Geoff's death in France had made both of them aware of the brevity of human life. Material success was certainly not their most important goal. During the past two years, dealing with poverty and death as a daily occurrence had convinced them that it is not what one owns in life but how one lives that counts.

Their decision delayed completion of *The River of a Hundred Ways: Life in War-torn Poland*. When the manuscript was finally ready, Joice asked Florence Barrow to write an Introduction to the book, which was eventually published in London in 1926. In her Introduction, Florence Barrow outlined the facts about Friends' aid to eastern Poland. Over 30,000 acres of fallow and devastated land had been ploughed using their own horse teams and Quaker-made ploughs; 32,182 cubic metres of timber had been hauled out of the forest to build 1,600 new homes; 2,500 tons of flax seed had been distributed by aid teams. The flax had been made into linen, hand-embroidered by Polish and Ukrainian women, and sold at a Quaker-run shop in London, the proceeds used to benefit Polish families.

Three qualified doctors and a dozen *doktorikas* or medical orderlies (one of whom was Joice) had saved the lives of thousands of refugees and delivered many hundreds of babies. And once again the Polish people had demonstrated their ability to survive.

16 GREECE—THE DREAM AND THE REALITY

On a warm evening in May 1923, Joice climbed down from the train onto the crowded platform of Thessaloniki station. She wore a simple cotton frock. Having sold off their furniture to avoid paying storage charges, the same battered suitcase she had taken to Ireland and Poland held all her worldly possessions—her Quaker uniform, a few civilian clothes, a portable typewriter, her dictionary and medical books, tools of the trade for a journalist turned humanitarian aid-worker.

Thessaloniki station was soot-stained, noisy and swarming with adults and crying children. Everywhere Joice saw distressed groups of women, elderly men and children, refugees from Turkey and Asia Minor. She noted the lack of young men of fighting age, and realised that the Turks had killed most of them.

These sad survivors had always lived in Asia Minor—some of their families had been there since the days of the Greek-speaking Byzantine Empire. Now here they were in Greece under the auspices of the League of Nations' compulsory 'exchange of populations' scheme. Almost a million had already arrived; more were to follow. The numbers were so vast and money so short that Greek officials could do little to help them.

The refugees carried bundles and pillowcases containing their few possessions and most wandered around aimlessly. Many spoke Turkish and, like Joice, knew only a few words of Greek or spoke in Pontic Greek, an ancient dialect unintelligible to mainland Greeks. The women wore baggy Turkish-style trousers, their hair and the lower part of their face covered by scarves, as Turkish custom demanded.

With her blonde hair and fair skin, it was obvious Joice was a foreigner. Even before the advent of mass tourism, most Greek men were fascinated by foreign women, especially blondes. Hordes of potential Romeos surrounded her, hoping to change her money and offering trays of *filo* pastry triangles filled with spinach or honey and nuts.

A young man touting for local hotels, wearing a cheap shiny suit over natty two-tone shoes, mimed the action of laying his head on a pillow. '*Angliki?*' he asked.

'No, *Australiki*,' Joice replied proudly. The Greek word for 'Australian' was one of the few words of modern Greek she knew. She had studied classical Greek at university.

The tout latched onto Joice's arm in a vain attempt to lead her to one of 'his' hotels.

Joice shrugged off his hand. 'No,' she said firmly and shook her head, not realising this gesture meant 'yes' to Greeks. Encouraged, the man moved so close she could smell the garlic and tobacco on his breath.

Unfortunately, Joice's classical Greek was about as intelligible to the tout as words written by Chaucer would be to most Australians. 'Begone, shameful varlet,' she admonished him, 'I have a hostelry already and seek only a chariot for hire.'

Bewildered by her vocabulary, the tout turned to his companions, tapped his head and muttered a few words that made them burst out laughing. Obviously the language of Homer, Euripides and Sophocles did *not* work in twentieth-century Greece.

Dodging the jeering men she lugged her suitcase to the exit. Instead of a row of taxis she found a few ancient horse-drawn carriages for hire. The state of the horses, their ribs protruding like toast-racks, horrified her. She selected the fittest looking animal and asked its driver to take her to the Majestic Hotel, where overnight accommodation had been pre-booked by Quaker headquarters. The Majestic sounded surprisingly grand for the Society of Friends, who generally housed their volunteer workers as cheaply as possible.

The horse clip-clopped down cobbled streets crowded with beggars and refugees, many of whom had long since given up hope of finding work and squatted immobile on the pavement. This ancient part of the city was a maze of winding alleyways. Wooden houses built by the former Turkish occupiers had balconies enclosed with lattice that jutted across the narrow streets. They passed by gaudily painted cafes where policemen and soldiers in Greek uniforms lounged with a proprietal air drinking *ouzo*, delighted that at long last Thessaloniki was Greek rather than Turkish. Ten years ago, Greek victory in the Balkan wars had ensured that most of the Turkish and Bulgarian occupiers of Macedonia had departed.[1] Then, during World War 1, British troops had poured through this city which they called Salonika.

Greece—The Dream and the Reality

Rabbis wearing black hats and robes strode through crowded thoroughfares filled with donkeys, mules and clanging trams. Joice had read that Thessaloniki had a population of some 60,000 Sephardic Jews, refugees from Spain. Street stalls offered wooden tubs of *feta* cheese, barrels of black olives and stacks of *baklava* dripping with honey. On their heads women bore trays of pale loaves on their way to the public ovens.

Thessaloniki was a clanging, teeming city, throbbing with life. The din became even louder as they passed under the great triumphal arch built by the Emperor Galerius and entered the portion of the city traditionally reserved for metalworkers. In open-fronted workshops men sweated over glowing embers and anvils, hammering out pots and kettles.

Joice was enthralled by the huge domed churches built long ago, when Thessaloniki was second in importance to Constantinople, capital of the Byzantine Empire. Slender minarets had been added later by the Turks, who turned them into mosques; following their departure the churches were now re-consecrated to Greek Orthodoxy. Her driver stopped in front of a row of crumbling houses bearing signs proclaiming they were the Hotel Imperial (24 rooms), Hotel Olympus (20 rooms) and Hotel Splendide (24 rooms). The Hotel Majestic was the last one in the row, distinguished by its sagging balconies.

Joice pulled out some drachmae notes given her at Friends Relief Headquarters in Warsaw and offered them to the driver. To her surprise he flew into a rage and flung them back at her. She added a good tip. The driver became even more enraged, pointing at the banknotes and yelling.

Luckily for Joice, an English-speaking businessman passing by took pity on her. He explained that under new State of Emergency laws to combat inflation, all Greek banknotes had only yesterday been devalued by one-third. He took from his wallet a 'new', devalued bank note, which was in fact an old note with one corner cut off and three words stamped in red across its face. Now Joice understood. She apologised to the driver and gave him sufficient 'old' notes until he was satisfied.

An elderly porter from the Hotel Majestic picked up her case and they went inside. Joice thought 'Hotel Squalid' would have been a more appropriate name. However, there were clean sheets on her bed and a mosquito net. She remembered the dire warnings about malaria.

Waking early next morning, she went downstairs and was given a cup of coffee with grounds fine as sand and a bowl of creamy yoghurt with a spoonful of golden honey. She paid her bill with another stack of 'old' banknotes and asked the porter if any of the cab drivers spoke English. She hoped to acquire some background knowledge on her way to the refugee camp set up on the campus of the American Farm School.

The porter signalled to the third cab on the rank. 'Yanni has spent much time in New York. He will look after you.' 'Do you know the American Farm School?' Joice asked the driver. 'It's about six miles from here.'

'Sure thing, lady,' he responded in a flat Bronx accent. As they set off, he explained that he had been born Yanni, but was always called Johnny, the name the Americans had bestowed on him.

The cab trotted through unpaved streets filled with barefoot children clad in rags. As they journeyed, Joice asked questions about the recent events in Greece. Johnny told her that not only had thousands of Slav and Albanian refugees flocked to Greece's northern provinces after the Balkan Wars, but now Thessaloniki was attempting to absorb the hundreds of thousands more from Turkey and Asia Minor. He sounded angry and bitter. 'More than a million Greeks are being forced out of their homes and vineyards and "exchanged" like cattle for a much smaller number of Turks,' he said. 'It's crazy. Why should they be allowed to come here? There's not enough work for them. They should go to Athens. These goddamn refugees bring nothing with them except diseases which can kill our children.'

Joice was amazed by his anger. She had believed the Greeks in Thessaloniki would be sympathetic to their compatriots. But she realised it was useless to speak up in defence of the refugees. Yanni, or Johnny, was a poor man; of course he felt threatened by inflation, soaring food prices and the prospect of epidemics of cholera and dysentery. She told him she was working on an article about Greek refugees for the British press, and wanted to visit the port in Thessaloniki to see them arriving. Johnny said he could make a detour and changed direction.

As they approached the port Joice felt she had been swept into a dejected tide of human flotsam and jetsam. They passed a huge Byzantine watch-tower built of white stone above a quay where fishing boats were unloading more fugitives from the villages and towns of Asia Minor. Many carried their possessions wrapped in sheets. Some had been able to bring with them a few hens in coops, a goat or two or a pig.

'You, *kyria* [lady] and other foreigners have come to help the thousands of starving refugees, but who is coming to help *us*? The price of bread rises daily. I have seven mouths to feed. Are my children to starve as well?'

Johnny told her he was a widower and had returned to Thessaloniki from New York with his five children to find himself a new wife. In the meantime, his sister was helping to look after the children. He had never intended to stay, and was desperate to return to America. But now the immigration laws had changed and return was impossible. 'Everything has changed,' he complained bitterly, describing how France and Britain had divided Macedonia between Greece and the new Kingdom of Serbia, Croatia and Slovenia (later to be known as Yugoslavia). From the way he talked, it was obvious he loathed Serbs, Bulgarians and Turks as well as the Greek Government in Athens. 'They are deluging us with Greek refugees to make us more Hellenic,' he complained. 'Most houses in this city lack running water or sanitation. What we need from Athens is more money, not more *refugees*.'

Joice tried another tack. 'But these refugees are Orthodox Christians, just like you and your children.'

Johnny raised his eyes to heaven. 'They have been corrupted by living among Muslims,' he said, cracking his whip over the horse's ears. 'Some of them even speak Turkish, not Greek.'

Listening to Johnny, Joice realised anew the enormity of the problem that she and her co-workers from Quaker Welfare and the Red Cross faced. As they left the port and headed out beyond the city, she sat in silence, wishing that Sydney was with her and hoping that his arrival in Greece would not be delayed by any unforeseen event.

The paved road turned into a dirt track over which the carriage bumped and swayed. On their right, Joice glimpsed a makeshift refugee camp where adults and children huddled forlornly against a barbed wire fence. Johnny explained they would stay there until land was requisitioned by the Government to establish a refugee village.

They passed through the hamlet of Charilaos. Johnny told Joice that during the Great War, the French and British had established a military aerodrome here. Now, Joice was appalled to see that the old airfield was being used to hold huge piles of naked corpses. An overwhelming stench hung on the air. She felt sick. As they drove on, they passed more decaying bodies swarming with flies that lay beside the track. Dead children lay beside their parents, their bodies left to rot.[2]

'Refugees from Turkey, robbed and murdered by brigands. Others drank bad water, got swamp fever, collapsed and died here,' Johnny informed her grimly.

Joice shuddered. 'Swamp fever' meant the killer disease Blackwater Fever. This nightmarish place resembled something out of Dante's Inferno.

Johnny whipped his skinny horse into a canter. Only her sense of duty prevented Joice from ordering him to turn around and head back to the port, to board a ship which would take her to Britain or Australia—out of the nightmare. But she told herself that Sydney wouldn't give up if he had to face a few hundred corpses. She was here to do something positive. No turning round now.

Gradually the piles of reeking corpses were left behind. They were travelling through an arid, flat wasteland with a distant backdrop of mountains silhouetted on the skyline. Then suddenly, abruptly, the landscape changed to an oasis of flowering almond trees with pink blossoms, ploughed but unfenced fields and rows of neatly-tended vines. A faded sign proclaimed they were entering the grounds of 'The Thessaloniki Agricultural and Industrial Institute and Farm School'. The Stars and Stripes fluttered in the breeze beside the blue-and-white flag of Greece.

Today the Farm School is a huge, handsome campus on 375 acres of land beside Thessaloniki Airport. In 1923 there were only cow barns, a big vegetable garden, a few wooden or mud-brick cottages for the staff, an infirmary, a blacksmith's forge and a huge concrete storehouse. A long barrack-like building served as a combined kitchen-dining room with accommodation for male pupils above it. Beyond it lay the latrine block, communal washhouse and a laundry with stone wash-tubs.

Joice had been told she would sleep above the storehouse, known by the aid workers of the various relief missions as 'The Ark'. As they drove up to it, suddenly Joice recognised the elegant socialite Nancy Brunton-Lauder, wearing men's dungarees and a cotton head-scarf, emptying a bucket over the balcony. The sight of one of America's wealthiest heiresses dressed like a workman appealed to Joice's sense of humour. She was fond of Nancy, who was both witty and worldly. Like Joice, she enjoyed a glass of wine or a cocktail, something which shocked the older Friends back at Quaker Headquarters.

On seeing Joice, Nancy let out a squawk of pleasure and rushed down the outside stairway. 'Thank God you've come!' she greeted her.

Joice jumped down from the carriage and Nancy enfolded her in a hug before Johnny came up to collect his fare.

Joice disentangled herself from Nancy's grasp, picked up a bucket of water and gave the poor horse a drink. Johnny demanded a huge sum which she paid him willingly, adding a good tip. Like the refugees he resented so much, he faced an uncertain future.

Talking nineteen to the dozen in her soft Southern drawl, Nancy grabbed Joice's case and led her up to the top floor. She apologised that Joice's small, box-like room would be barely big enough once Sydney arrived. But at least, thanks to the Bible Mission Societies, they had somewhere to sleep and to store clothing and medicines for the refugees.

Joice dumped her case beside her folding bed and followed Nancy back down the stairs to the central store. Here bales of second-hand clothing, tinned food and medical supplies were unloaded, checked and donated to refugees who possessed only the clothes they stood up in. Stocks of blankets and quilts had apparently run out; until the next supply train arrived from London, unfortunate new arrivals had to huddle together under newspaper, cardboard and spare clothes. It seemed that the Quakers, the International Red Cross and several British charities were providing money, second-hand clothing and bedding, as well as quinine and vaccines—these, however, were expensive and demand exceeded supply. Other major donors, besides the American Bible Missions, included the Lord Mayor of London's Fund and the Save Greece Fund. The Farm School helped out by providing free flour and vegetables.

Then Nancy took Joice on an orientation tour of the campus. They walked to the periphery, where the large deserted barracks built by the French Army during the Great War had been allowed to fall into disrepair, its windows broken. But Nancy reassured Joice that the roof was still good: this was the only suitable place to house over a thousand refugees, who slept in rows on the floor.

Those who could not find places in the barracks slept out in large khaki tents sent by the American Society of Friends or provided by the Greek Army. Blankets and quilts were what they desperately needed. Joice made a mental note to add this important fact to one of the articles she would tap out on her portable typewriter late at night, once she had finished her aid work each day. She would get the refugees blankets by hook or by crook.

Like Joice, Nancy had gained practical experience of nursing, first-aid and minor surgical procedures working for Quaker Relief on the

Polish-Russian border. Her husky voice dropped to a whisper as she told Joice that a substantial proportion of the women and girls had been gang-raped by Turkish soldiers before they left their former villages. Belonging to a culture that placed a very high value on female virginity, the shame this engendered had resulted in a number of suicides.

'Greece is such a mixture. Some things are so strange, others so familiar. I admire the Greeks, they have a capacity for survival that we Americans simply can't understand.'

Joice agreed wholeheartedly. 'The Professor of Classics I worked for in Melbourne used to say "at heart all of us are Greeks. Our architecture, our language, our philosophy, our concepts of beauty, art and sculpture, our sense of tragedy and comedy, our literature, are all based on those of ancient Greece"—he said it so often I know his speech by heart. The Greeks have given us far more than we imagine.'

'And now *we're* giving something back,' Nancy responded, half-serious, half-joking. 'The sad thing is that as fast as relief workers construct more cesspits, latrines and washrooms, more refugees arrive with cholera, dysentery, diphtheria, malaria, and/or half-blinded by eye disease. We don't have nearly enough doctors or vaccines to cope. I'm paying for some vaccines out of my Trust Fund, and the Friends promise to send us another doctor soon.'

Joice said she would help Nancy to implement her health programs as soon as she had finished her current newspaper article.

Soon after Joice's arrival, Nancy took her to meet Dr John House, cofounder of the Farm School, and Susan, his serene, youthful-looking wife, known to everyone on campus as 'Mother' House. John House was a silver-haired, dignified man in his seventies. He was hoping to retire for the second time and hand over the reins to his son, Charlie, who had studied Civil Engineering at Harvard. He explained that Charlie was away at present on a tour for the Greek Government, prospecting for suitable sites to build refugee villages. Dr House's first retirement had been from running a Mission station. Shortly afterwards, convinced that agricultural prosperity was what the poverty-stricken Greeks needed more than Bibles, he had struggled to establish the Farm School as a Christian technical college. Starting with only a small hut and a caretaker, he and his family had raised the money to build up the Farm School campus, which also housed a meteorological station.

Boys entered the school at fourteen and were trained to become competent farmers using the latest methods. There were fifty-four students, Greeks, Albanians, Serbs, Armenian and White Russian refugees, some fee-paying, others on scholarships provided by Dr and Mrs House and their supporters. Many of the brightest students had been granted scholarships to attend university in America. The largest group of orphaned children had been rescued from Smyrna by an American naval vessel and brought to the school by the ship's captain.[3]

'We look on all the orphans here as our own children,' Susan House said quietly.

The huge influx of refugees was largely responsible for the fact that the Farm School was still in debt, in spite of loyal support from its American trustees. Many of the students would in time become teachers or farming instructors themselves. Joice thought it a pity there was no school to house and educate girls and was pleased to learn that a girls' school was being planned.

The Houses were known for their warm hospitality and their religious tolerance. They invited Joice and Nancy to stay for dinner, and during the course of conversation 'Mother' House revealed that they were hoping Charlie would soon marry a teacher he had met on an America-wide fund-raising tour for new dormitories at the Farm School. She said that as soon as Charlie returned from his present trip, he planned to employ as many refugees as possible to help him build the dormitory block. This would give the refugees some much-needed income. The block was to be named Princeton Hall, after Dr House's alma mater. Princeton graduates had donated a major share of the money for the new building.

Conversation was wide-ranging. Joice explained that she had arrived ahead of her husband because her work in Warsaw had come to an end, but Sydney would not be able to leave Poland until he had set up a smaller version of the Houses' Farm School in eastern Poland. In her amusing manner, she made a good story of her encounter with the hotel tout at Thessaloniki station, and deplored her inability to speak modern Greek. Immediately Dr House offered to arrange language lessons with a Greek staff member at the Farm School.

The Houses were people after Joice's own heart—warm-hearted, well-travelled, intensely practical in their outlook on life, and with a love of books that equalled her own. Their daughter, Ruth, who was not with them at dinner, was matron of the Farm School as well as accounts secretary and general factotum. She continually worried about the finances, whereas Dr and 'Mother' House believed that God would find a way to provide whatever was needed.

John House told Joice he had enormous confidence in the abilities of the Greek people, admiring them for their diligence, their deep sense of family loyalty and their ingenuity at being able to survive under harsh conditions. With a twinkle in his eye he added: 'I have yet to meet an American able to support a wife and six children from a few stony *stremmas* [a Greek measurement of land] the way a Greek can. If we can get them into new homes, however basic, and give them some farming instruction, most of the million or so refugees will survive.' He paused, looking searchingly at Joice and Nancy. 'It's easy enough to find the magnitude of the task daunting. But just consider that I started this Farm School on land without any water supply whatsoever. Everyone said I was mad, but land without water was all a retired missionary could afford.' He looked across at his wife. 'Susan and I have a motto: "We Specialise in the Impossible".' He grinned in an almost boyish way. 'And our motto works!'

Dr House had sensed that Joice and Nancy were discouraged at the enormity of the refugee problem and the slender resources at their disposal. 'Just remember that all human beings need new challenges,' he told them quietly.

Joice would never forget his words. She too loved a challenge and thought Dr House was right: the only way to confront what seemed insurmountable was to refuse to be beaten. From that moment she adopted the Houses' motto as her own.[4]

Besides the conversation classes in modern Greek arranged by Dr House, working in the stores and giving out clothes to refugees, Joice spent a few days in the delousing station, staffed by Red Cross volunteers, to get more background to the newspaper story she was writing. Once it was completed, she began to help Nancy with her vaccinations and the aid program she had set up to eradicate eye disease amongst the refugees.

At lunch time and in the evenings both women worked in the canteen, wielding gigantic ladles to serve long lines of refugees with herb soup and black bread. As wheat was scarce acorns had been added to the dough, which made the bread taste bitter. For the evening meal they doled out tin plates of fresh fish with *horta*, which included a salad of tomato, *feta*, olives and wild herbs such as boiled pigweed, a preventative against scurvy. This was followed by creamy yoghurt made from goat's milk, with honey and a slice of bread. Discipline for the aid workers was very strict. Only when the refugees had finished eating could the volunteers eat whatever was left. After several aid workers died from malnutrition this policy was eventually changed.[5]

At breakfast they ate yoghurt sweetened with honey, bread, tomatoes and olive oil. Fresh eggs were a luxury, meat unobtainable. Nothing was wasted by the peasant women who cooked for the refugees and staff. The campus had been picked bare of herbs and weeds by this time, and whenever the Farm School's only truck was free, some of the women would clamber aboard and set off into the surrounding countryside to pick nettles, dandelions and other weeds. Even the water in which the herbs and greens were boiled was made into a nutritious soup.

The most nutritious of the herbs was pigweed. Joice recalled how, when she was a child in the Gippsland bush, her mother used to send her off to collect it for salads. Edith had called it 'purslane'. This was one small example of the way her own experience of loss and dislocation following her parents' descent into rural poverty gave her an empathy with the homeless and downtrodden. Most of all, Joice could not bear the thought of thousands of Greek children dying. As children she and Geoff had dreamed of visiting Greece. Now that dream had become her reality, in a way she had never imagined.

17 'THE ART OF BEING KIND'

Joice's experience in emergency surgery meant that she was promoted to assist Arthur Bertholf, a Protestant missionary and teacher who had been relieved of his Farm School duties to run the refugee aid program.[1]

Everyone on campus said Bertholf was a saint; Joice soon discovered that 'saints' were not the easiest of people to work with. Her first encounter with the Bertholf family occurred one evening when she visited their cottage and found the family seated around the dinner table: Mrs Bertholf, French, chic and delightful; Rachael, a tiny girl in a white bib, and a little boy named John.

Rachel, her spoon halfway to her mouth, stared at Joice as she entered the room. The next moment the door that led into the kitchen was flung open and a tall, lean man with dark burning eyes came running in. He snatched Rachel and John's plates away from them. The children yelled out: 'Daddy, Daddy, *don't*' then burst into tears as their father ran off through the kitchen. Mrs Bertholf raced out after the disappearing plates and found that her saintly husband had given his own children's dinner to some refugee children begging for food at the back door. Witnessing this unhappy incident, perhaps Joice remembered an evening long ago in Gippsland, when she and Geoff were banished to the kitchen while unexpected guests ate their share of rabbit and roast potatoes.

Nancy warned Joice that Bertholf had no idea about budgeting and would cheerfully spend an entire month's aid budget in a single week, leaving the Farm School staff and pupils existing on bread and water for the rest of the month. She thought that Charlie House would have been a better choice to run the aid program. 'But he's too busy finding sites for refugee villages and building on campus,' she added.

Nancy loved a good gossip. Charlie's fiancée, Anne Kellogg, a pretty young widow, would soon be arriving from America. She had a graduate diploma in teaching and Nancy predicted she would be marrying the Farm School as well as Charlie—who, it seemed, was a workaholic.

'THE ART OF BEING KIND'

To get the refugees out of the camps, under State of Emergency laws the Greek Government was repossessing vacant land from private owners and monasteries, often in isolated, low-lying malaria-infested areas that no one else wanted. The Army was mobilised to help build two-room 'sugar cube' houses from concrete blocks. (These were the 'basic houses' Dr House had referred to.) Able-bodied men were given tools and materials and instructed by Army engineers in the techniques of construction. Soldiers built homes for the many widows and orphans, as well as for the elderly and infirm. Hundreds of thousands of refugees waited in camps behind barbed-wire, enduring primitive conditions until village wells could be sunk. Over one hundred new villages were planned but as yet most of them lacked piped water or sanitation. As a result, the refugees were dying in epidemics of cholera, malaria and blackwater fever.

Joice watched them depart in groups on the long trek to their new homes, carrying their belongings on their backs or pushing hand-carts. She knew that if they died, the refugee problem was so vast their deaths would be unrecorded.

The team of aid-workers at the Farm School refugee camp included a few Scottish and Swiss volunteer doctors, some medical orderlies (one of whom died of malaria), Ethel Cooper, always known as 'Pharaoh', an eccentric middle-aged Australian archaeologist, with whom Joice and Nancy Brunton-Lauder had worked in Warsaw, British-born Alizon Fox and Lilian Shrimpton, who had also worked with Joice and Sydney in eastern Poland, and Arthur Bertholf, assisted by his team of twenty Greek Boy Scouts from the Farm School. The boys were allowed time off from lessons to help out with sick refugees and bury the dead. There was no transport so Joice, Nancy and Pharaoh bought themselves sad-eyed little donkeys to ride around the huge campus. Joice named hers Menelaus and fed him up on scraps she saved from her portions at meals.

By now the team was totally overworked. Fortunately several more volunteers arrived from Britain and America, including a wealthy British Quaker named Dorothea Hughes, who donated large sums to set up a laboratory to research the cause of blackwater or 'swamp' fever and bought the Farm School a much-needed new van. Dorothea Hughes also shared Joice's interest in setting up a school for girls on campus.[2]

The refugee crisis seemed never-ending: more and more refugees, widows and children and old people, poured in each week.[3] The former military barracks where they were housed now had missing roof tiles. The rooms were damp, cold and lacked any furniture. The plight of the children and mothers in the barracks distressed Joice, who did everything in her power for them. She was horrified to see orphaned girls as young as ten desperately attempting to feed, raise and discipline their younger siblings.

With the assistance of an interpreter, Joice organised classes to help the young orphans from Turkey survive life in Greece. As Nancy had warned her, she discovered that some of the girls had been gang-raped by Turkish soldiers. They had seen their homes burned down and their parents murdered. Alone in a strange land, they turned to Joice for comfort. Due to the lowly position of women in a male-dominated society, most of the girls had been kept at home and denied any chance of education; the majority were illiterate or semi-literate. Joice dreamed that one day it might be possible to set up some sort of school for them on campus if only the funding could be obtained. She longed to talk over her new experiences with Sydney, missing him badly.

Meanwhile, Charlie House returned to take over the running of the Farm School from his father. Charlie had a truly Christian spirit but belonged to no particular religious sect or denomination. He was extroverted, ebullient, wiry in build with twinkling blue eyes and an infectious grin.[4] Taking the Sermon on the Mount literally, Charlie wore second-hand clothes so that he could give more money to refugees. There was always a slide rule protruding from a pocket of his battered suit. He was happiest of all discussing building plans for some project like a new blacksmith's shop on campus.

John and Susan House regularly invited Joice, Nancy and Alizon to simple meals in their home, where they ate the same Spartan diet as the refugees. Around the dinner table they met some of the agricultural specialists recruited by Dr House to teach the boys modern farming techniques in addition to the good all-round education the other teachers sought to give them.

Charlie House, like the Lochs, was first and foremost a humanist. He was an excellent organiser, a doer as well as a thinker, a talented linguist, tough enough to dominate rough men on building sites by the force of his personality, and, if the occasion demanded, good with his fists. There was much about Charlie that reminded Joice of Sydney. Earlier, Charlie had been something of a black sheep, and had surprised his family by deciding that his life's work did not lie in establishing himself as a professional civil engineer in America. Instead, he made the decision to return to Greece and follow what he felt to be God's plan for his life—to take over the administration of the Farm School from his father.

Mother House told Joice she felt that Anne Kellogg was the ideal person for her son. Their wedding was scheduled to take place quite soon.

On one occasion, Joice suggested to Charlie that it was a pity that his father had placed the Farm School on parched wasteland without any water supply. (Over the years, Charlie had sunk two wells and put in cisterns to store rain.) 'Dr House told me it was all he could afford,' she said, 'but maybe he could have found a few more donations.' Charlie laughed. 'The Greeks thought my father was crazy to buy land here. But really, he had no option. It was parched land or nothing. And he was right to choose it. It's the sort of land our boys will eventually have to work, the sort of land where those poor refugees will have to live and support families.'[6]

Finally Anne Kellogg arrived. She was slim and dark-haired, attractive both in looks and personality. Tragedy was narrowly averted a few weeks after her arrival at the Farm School, when she suffered a burst appendix and almost died. During her lengthy convalescence, she and Joice grew very close. As soon as she was well again, Anne and Charlie were married by Dr House in a simple ceremony at the Farm School.

Encouraged by Anne, Joice worked long hours with a Greek interpreter, teaching the female refugees survival skills such as cooking, sewing, reading and writing. She also taught them home nursing, so that they would be better equipped to care for younger siblings and other sick relatives.

Joice was saddened by the fact that some of the missionaries she worked with appeared so blinkered by the dogma of their own Christian creed. Bertholf, for example, was eager to convert members of the Greek Orthodox Church to Protestantism. Joice thought that Greek Orthodoxy with its liturgies and ancient ceremonies brought colour to the sad lives of refugees, many of whom had been relatively prosperous in their former lives in Asia Minor, central Turkey or the Princes Islands near Constantinople, where they had owned farmhouses, fertile land and vineyards. Now, through no fault of their own, everything they had worked for and valued had been taken from them. She felt strongly that their faith in the Orthodox church and in their icons helped them to face desperate poverty, the loss of loved ones and all they had held dear. She resented Bertholf's attempts to convert Orthodox Greeks, some of whom were illiterate, to his own austere version of the Word of God.

Dr House, on the other hand, was extremely tolerant and allowed the Farm School boys to worship in the Orthodox or Protestant creeds. Whenever Joice herself was asked what religion or creed she followed, she would recite the following verse:

So many Gods, so many creeds,
So many paths that wind and wind,
When just the art of being kind
Is all this sad world needs.

Again, while Charlie House and the Lochs enjoyed a drink with a meal, Bertholf and others were rabid teetotallers who regarded all wine as 'the demon drink'. Joice thought some of the missionaries, as well as the Quakers, were extremely bigoted when they insisted that their God viewed drinking wine as a sin, completely ignoring the fact that for the Greeks, tending their vineyards and drinking wine was a vital part of their culture.

Only once did Joice reveal her true feelings to the zealous Arthur Bertholf. One morning, exhausted after having spent all night with a dying baby, she set off with him to look for a family of refugees reported to be dying on the same dirt track that Joice had taken when she arrived at the Farm School.

They walked for about a mile under blazing sun until they found them. The father was already dead, his face covered in flies; the mother was in an advanced stage of typhoid fever, coughing and delirious. As yet the children did not appear to be affected by the disease.

Bertholf inoculated the children. The mother lay without moving beside the dirt track, her eyes glazed. At her withered breast a baby wailed, vainly attempting to suckle milk. While Joice tried to soothe the crying baby, Bertholf attempted to comfort the dying mother by telling her that he saw 'the hand and will of God among this suffering'. Then he read her some verses in English from his Bible. The woman gazed up at him blankly, unable to comprehend a single word.

Joice was aghast, aware that, as an Orthodox Greek, the woman would have preferred to have an icon or crucifix in front of her eyes in her last moments. By now Joice was on the verge of burn-out. She remembered the starving children in Poland whose homes had been burned to the ground by the Russians, dying from starvation in drainage ditches and army dugouts. She remembered how many refugees from

'THE ART OF BEING KIND'

Turkey had already died of tuberculosis, typhoid, cholera, malaria . . . The death of this poor woman with her baby at her breast was the final straw.

Her normal self-control snapped. Cradling the crying baby she shouted at Bertholf: 'Maybe *you* can see the hand of God here. All I see are starving children and a dying woman. How can your precious God want *this*?'

Stunned by the force of her anger, Bertholf remained silent.

By now the mother was dead, her baby still crying from hunger, desperately searching for her nipple. Tears of rage and pity poured down Joice's cheeks. She shouted, 'Don't be so *smug*. If there really was a God, *nothing* like this could ever happen.'

Bertholf looked at her open-mouthed but said nothing. He probably realised that working ten hours a day, seven days a week in such stressful conditions, Joice had reached her limit. And she was only too aware from her experiences in Poland and Russia that as fast as she and her co-workers nursed one batch of refugees back to health, they would be replaced by another equally tragic group.

Immediately she had vented her feelings Joice felt sorry: she had not intended to hurt Bertholf. Bigoted though he might be, she knew he was a kind and caring man. Embarrassed, she turned from him and walked away, cuddling the sick baby. Perhaps she would be able to find some milk formula to save it from dying as well. Meanwhile, two of Bertholf's Boy Scout troop arrived with handcarts to wheel the corpses to the Farm School campus for burial in the cemetery.

Back at the Farm School, Anne House took charge of the baby and begged Joice to get some rest. Joice protested. How could she rest with so few aid workers to help? Aiming for the impossible needed superhuman strength. Sometimes Joice was so tired she was unable to sleep, thinking of all the children she had grown fond of who had died in her arms. Once again overwork meant she suffered from outbursts of weeping and food tasted like ashes in her mouth.

It was extremely fortunate that Sydney arrived a few days later, bringing with him a new sense of hope and mission. He had managed to persuade two senior Greek Army officers to drive him out to the Farm School in a lorry, which was loaded to the roof with tinned food and medicines. Joice was overjoyed. She hugged Sydney to her, delighted he was safe and well.

Teaming up with Sydney again was like a tonic. Joice gained comfort from the belief that when they worked together they could achieve so much more to help the refugees. Sydney, anxious about her exhaustion, insisted that she take a holiday, and Charlie lent them the Farm School's battered old van (known as 'Tin Lizzie') for a weekend away by themselves.

Sydney and Charlie became friends, which pleased Joice, who had developed such a warm rapport with Anne House.

Joice described how 'a love of God and of people shone through everything the House family did. They had an excellent sense of humour, loved books and the company of congenial people. Anne's Saturday "high teas" at the Farm School attracted everyone in the English and American expatriate community for the fun and entertainment they provided. Even the gossip on which expatriate communities always thrive was the friendliest of gossip'.[7]

As the summer wore on, at long last they began to win the long battle against typhoid and blackwater fever in the camp, though these diseases would continue to plague the three hundred refugee villages that sprang up across northern Greece in the sparsely populated provinces of Macedonia and Thrace.

Then an epidemic of malaria broke out among the refugees in their tents: the land on which the Farm School was built was infested with *Anopheles* mosquitoes. The medical centre did not have enough quinine tablets to go round. The wells often dried out, leaving them to rely on storage cisterns for drinking and washing water. In a desperate effort to control the mosquito's breeding cycle, each night Bertholf's Boy Scout troop was instructed to pour kerosene on the surface of the water in the cisterns, to kill the larvae or wrigglers.

Charlie House had read in a scientific magazine about gambuzia fish—it seemed they devoured mosquito larvae and bred very rapidly. Sydney suggested asking Friends Welfare Service to set up a fund to buy gambuzia fish, as well as mosquito netting for the school's dormitories and the infirmary. A member of staff was sent to Italy to bring back thousands of tiny gambuzia fish in tanks. These were released into the storage cisterns with the exception of ten fish, which Joice placed in a small observation pond. Fish had always interested her since her days in Gippsland when she had wanted to start a fish farm.

Unfortunately the impractical Bertholf failed to tell his Boy Scouts about the gambuzia fish. The next night they went out as usual and poured kerosene over the water in the storage cisterns, with the result that all the precious gambuzia fish died. Only the ten in Joice's observation pond were left. However, gambuzia fish do breed extremely rapidly. Joice, by now regarded as the expert on the species, supervised the breeding of new stock. Soon she had several breeding ponds, all stocked from the ten surviving fish. The Farm School eradicated its mosquitoes and earned much-needed income by selling gambuzia fish to other Governments and charities. Joice's gambuzia breeding programme would eventually save hundreds of thousands of people throughout Greece, Serbia and the Middle East from malaria. It was later discovered that gambuzia fish eat smaller species of fishes. Barrie Jamieson, Emeritus Professor of Marine Zoology at the University of Queensland, states that their use caused some harm to the ecology. However, in poorer countries in the years before aerial mosquito spray programs could be used, millions of lives were saved by the use of gambuzia fish.

She was awarded the Order of St Sava from the King of Serbia for her part in the gambuzia malaria prevention program, and from the Greeks she received the Order of the Phoenix, a decoration awarded to foreigners of distinction, established when Greece became a republic in 1924.[8]

To her delight, Joice was now put in charge of an intensive teaching program for the girls on the campus, some of whom had never been to school, while others had had their education interrupted by the refugee crisis. With the aid of an interpreter, she taught them to read and write and do simple sums, as well as basic survival skills. Many still wore the baggy harem pants, pointed velvet slippers and heavy silver necklaces their mothers and grandmothers had worn. Some spoke no Greek at all and had to be given lessons by a member of the Farm School staff who spoke both Turkish and Greek. So great was the fear of the girls' parents that they might meet the Farm School boys that their schoolroom had to be located at a considerable distance from the rest of the classrooms. Following Turkish custom, most of these girls had never been allowed out of their homes unchaperoned and were totally innocent about the opposite sex. With the exception of instruction in the Moslem faith, they had been raised as Turks.

The girls also learned agricultural skills from the Farm School instructors. Some of the new arrivals came from cities such as Istanbul and predominantly Pontic Greek towns like ancient Trebizond on the Black Sea—their families had inhabited that part of the world for centuries. Now they had to learn to raise pigs and chickens, grow maize, chickpeas, lettuce and tomatoes and which wild herbs and weeds could be picked to make a weed soup, knowledge that Greek village women took for granted.

Joice became devoted to her students. When they had finished their courses, she did her best to find employment for those who needed it, realising they could help their families survive if they had paid work.

Greeks had a long tradition of emigration, and to begin with this was seen as a solution to the refugee problem. But the American Government, fearing mass unemployment, put up barriers against it—and after 1929 the Great Depression caused America to reject migrants for years. During the 1920s the Australian Government's infamous 'White Australia', pro-Anglo-Saxon policy made Australia reluctant to accept a huge influx of Greeks. Joice taught 'her' girls about the natural beauty of Australia, and told them it was a land of individual freedom, religious tolerance and equality of opportunity. Years later, some of these girls did migrate to Australia, where they married and made new lives.

Joice was supposed to travel to Serbia to collect the medal awarded to her for the gambuzia breeding program, but she found it impossible to leave her teaching duties with the girls. Although Greece and Serbia were not on friendly terms, a high-ranking Serbian official was sent to Thessaloniki to present her with the gold sunburst medal of the Order of St Sava. He told her that Sava had been a member of the Serbian royal family who took his vows as a priest and went to live in a Serbian endowed monastery on Mount Athos. He said that the Republic of Athos, founded in the tenth century, was a veritable Shangri-La, possessing art treasures that had been brought there by monks fleeing from the sack of Byzantium by the Venetians and members of the Fourth Crusade in the year 1204, or else gifted by Czars, Kings and Princes.

The Lochs, with their journalistic instincts, thought that gold and jewels from Byzantium, hidden away in the monasteries of Mount Athos for centuries after the fall of Constantinople, sounded like a fascinating story. The Serbian official filled in more details for them.

The Greek Orthodox Empire of Byzantium (known as the eastern Roman Empire) had been plundered of much of its treasure, first by the Crusaders at the end of the Middle Ages and then two centuries later by the Ottoman Turks. Initially the Crusaders and their Venetian allies, claiming they were 'liberating' the city, stripped Constantinople of ecclesiastic altar vessels, jewelled crucifixes and icons, gold and silver plate, illuminated manuscripts and jewelled reliquaries in three days and nights of pillage. Terrified, the monks and priests had fled with whatever treasures and embroidered vestments they could carry and sailed off to Thessaloniki, the second most important city in the

Byzantine Empire. They paid their fares by selling off gold and jewels, then disappeared with the rest of their treasures into the vast mediaeval monasteries of Athos, where they kept alive the traditions of Byzantium.

Joice and Sydney listened spellbound. Athos, it seemed, was a timeless land lacking all modern development, where no women or 'beardless creatures' were permitted by an Imperial decree dating from Byzantine days. Realising that such a tale of plunder and hidden treasures could provide an excellent topic for their next book, they vowed to escape to this fascinating area just as soon as they could manage it.

18 IN THE SHADOW OF THE HOLY MOUNTAIN

In the summer of 1925, the Lochs set off with Nancy Lauder Brunton, Alizon Fox and two other friends on a camping holiday to the head of the Athos peninsula, taking a small collapsible boat with them.

In those days reaching the coast of Prosforion, the area immediately north of Mount Athos, meant a two-day journey. The potholed road from Thessaloniki petered out at the town of Arnea. From there travellers and pilgrims bound for the monasteries of Athos rode along a rough mule track which wound its way through eighty-six kilometres of forest to the white-painted rock known as the Tripiti. Travellers would cover the rock with their coats and light a fire to attract the attention of the ferryman, who rowed across to pick them up, then ferried them to the refugee settlement known as Pirgos, the last village in Greece, five kilometres down a dirt track from the frontier of the independent Republic of Athos. From the Tripiti a mule-driver took the animals back to Arnea, having arranged to collect the party in ten days' time.

When the Lochs and their friends arrived at the coast of Prosforion they were awed by the distant view of snow-covered Mount Athos, whose tree-clad slopes seemed to rise straight out of the sea. Dr House had told the Lochs that the peninsula was named after Athos, son of the sea god Poseidon. The original settlers of Athos worshipped pagan gods who they believed lived at the top of the sacred mountain. There were two main settlements in the area in classical times: the village of Acte, long since destroyed, which had been famous for its huge statues of Poseidon and Apollo, God of Music; and a large city buried beneath the ocean.

According to local tradition, in the year 49AD, the Panagia or Virgin Mary and St John the Divine were on their way to visit Lazarus—who, having been raised from the dead, had been appointed Bishop of Cyprus—when their ship was blown off-course. The ship's captain mistook the tip of the Athos peninsula for the island of Cyprus and landed there. At the sight of the Panagia, the huge pagan idols fell from their pedestals and shattered. The people of Athos, realising their gods were powerless to save them, converted to Christianity and implored St John and the Mother of God to stay and protect them from pirates. But the Panagia explained that she and St John must continue their journey to Cyprus. Enchanted by the beauty of the wooded peninsula with its masses of wildflowers, she asked that it be named 'the Garden of the Mother of God' in her honour. No other woman should be allowed to land there.

The Lochs knew that monks and hermits had been living in caves and small huts on Athos since the fourth century. The first enormous fortress-cum-monastery, known as the Great Lavra, was built between 961-963 by St Athanasios with financial support from the Emperor Nicholas II of Byzantium. Over the centuries, Kings, Tsars and Emperors had endowed thirty-nine more monasteries, enjoining the monks to say masses for their souls. Only twenty of these remained, most of them veritable museums of Byzantine and post-Byzantine art. Some of the earliest monks broke the Virgin Mary's command and imported women: in the year 1060 news of orgies on Athos reached the Emperor Constantine Monomachos in far away Byzantium. (At that time, Athos and the entire province of Macedonia were part of the Byzantine Empire.) The Emperor flew into a rage and it was then he issued the Imperial edict banning all women from Athos, whether resident or transient, as well as 'beardless men' and carts or carriages which 'run on wheels'.[1]

Much later, several monasteries were plundered by Catalan pirates, and during the Greek War of Independence (1825–29), more were ravaged by Muslim Turks. Lacking any sealed road or regular ferry service, the Athonite Republic on its sea-girt peninsula remained largely unknown, a lost world, where time was measured thirteen days behind the rest of Europe.

In 1924, the Greek Government granted the monks a new constitution and certain privileges in return for handing over land lacking water outside the boundaries of Athos. This had now become the site of the refugee village of Pirgos. However, some of the monks still farmed the richer areas close by.[2]

The Lochs and their friends pitched their tents on Donkey Island, directly opposite Pirgos, which lay north of a huge *pirgos* or watchtower. Today, as then, the island is unspoiled and uninhabited. No one lives there and on its long sandy beaches herds of wild donkeys roam. As the camping party swam in the warm, clear peacock-blue sea, dolphins wheeled and jumped beside them. Far away down the peninsula, silhouetted against the sky was the snow-covered peak of the mystic Holy Mountain. They had found an earthly Paradise.

Each day Sydney rowed across to Pirgos to buy goat's milk. One morning he met a black-bearded monk in a conical hat who introduced himself as Brother Anaphronos, a Bielorussian from the huge monastery of St Panteleimon, which had been founded by the Tsars. He had come down to the new settlement to buy goat's milk and eggs; because of the lack of any female creature in the timeless world of Athos, these were unobtainable on the Holy Mountain.

Brother Anaphronos clearly relished an opportunity to practise speaking English. He told Sydney that the watchtower beside the new refugee settlement had once belonged to the monastery of Vatopedi; it had been confiscated from Athos by the Greek Government along with the land on which the refugees had built their straggle of little concrete houses. The monk expressed his fears for their future, and his doubts that they would be able to survive by farming. He told Sydney the ground was hard as iron; under the thin layer of topsoil lay a thick substratum of granite.

Eleni, a young woman from the Princes Islands near Istanbul, sold Sydney a jug of goat's milk and told him that she, her husband and their young children had walked for five days from their camp outside Thessaloniki to get here. Soldiers had sunk three wells at Pirgos and then helped them build a two-room cottage. The Greek Government could not afford to pay welfare benefits. They had given each family a few olive saplings, some cord to make a fishing-net and a trident for octopus fishing and left them to survive as best they could. Due to the current drought, most of the seeds and cuttings planted by the refugees had died.

The refugee settlement lacked shops, a taverna or a *kaphenion* serving coffee. Brother Anaphronos was delighted when Sydney offered to row him back to Donkey Island for a cup of real coffee. As the monk sat with the campers, he told them how a hundred thousand monks had once lived and prayed in the shadow of the Holy Mountain. Now they were down to five thousand. A year ago, the new constitution of Athos had made each monk a Greek citizen, but the Parliament or Holy Council at Karyes, the capital of Athos, was responsible for internal administration, sending representatives of the Republic to Thessaloniki and Athens.

Sydney paid Nanou, a fisherman, to sail them around the peninsula of Athos in his fishing *kaïki*. From the sea they saw vast forests of chestnut, beech, oak and walnut trees and monasteries huge as fortresses, connected to the outside world by private jetties from which the occasional *kaïki* plied between Athos and Thessaloniki or Athens.

On their second meeting with Brother Anaphronos, Sydney and Joice learned that the twenty Athonite monasteries no longer received support from kings and emperors. Their income was supplied by selling timber. The monks made their own wine and grew olives from which they pressed an exceptionally fine pale-green virgin oil. There was no electricity and no doctor on the Holy Mountain, only a herbalist named Father Klemens, who went from monastery to monastery on his donkey.

For his part, Brother Anaphronos listened with interest as the Lochs told him about their journey to Moscow in 1922 and the work of the Quaker mission at Samara. He was distressed when they told him about the Russian aristocrats reduced to begging in the streets of Moscow and revealed that before the Revolution he had been a prince. He had fled Russia and, lacking skills to earn a living, had fulfilled a childhood ambition to become a monk. As a Prince he had owned vast estates. Now he had a small apartment in the monastery of St Pantilemion and a faithful servant who had remained in his service to look after him. He said he was happy to be working in the monastery's magnificent library and caring for the illuminated manuscripts and ancient printed books it held.

Sydney's meeting with Brother Anaphronos was hugely fortuitous.

He was invited to visit the monastery overnight for a guided tour. Nanou sailed him down the coast to the monastery's private jetty, leaving him there while he sailed off to collect timber from another monastery.

At St Panteleimon Sydney was greeted by Brother Anaphronos. Over a glass of Russian tea, the monk told him that the huge building with its green onion-shaped domes topped by golden crosses had originally been built to house one thousand monks. Now it was inhabited by a mere tenth of that number, many of them old and frail. He showed Sydney frescoes of the Panagia in robes of blue, the colour produced by grinding lapis lazuli to a powder, and pointed out the subtle differences between Greek and Russian icons.

Brother Anaphronos then showed his guest the monastery's combined library and treasure-house. It contained over 2,000 books in richly jewelled covers, 600 Slavic manuscripts and over 1,000 Greek illuminated manuscripts, many produced in the libraries of ancient Byzantium.[3] These were not solely religious works. Many of the library's treasures were from the era of classical Greece; their preservation on Athos had been a significant factor in the spread of classical literature to Florence during the Renaissance.

Sydney was especially intrigued by the large collection of Romanov portraits in heavy gold frames, including those of the late Tsar Nicholas and Tsarina Alexandra, murdered by Lenin's order in the cellar of the 'House of Special Purpose' at Ekaterinburg, in western Siberia. Brother Anaphronos told Sydney that the monk Rasputin, who later gained such enormous influence over the Tsarina, had walked from Siberia to Athos in his youth and stayed for a while in the Russian-endowed monastery.

The following day Nanou returned to collect Sydney and they sailed to the Greek monastery of Xenophontos, where Nanou was to load more timber. Here they were greeted with small glasses of a homebrewed version of *ouzo* known as *tsipouro*.

Xenophontos, built in the tenth century, resembled a crusader's castle. Its stone walls were a metre thick. Sydney asked the monks why the ground floor lacked windows. He was told it was to prevent pirates forcing their way in to plunder the monastery's gold and art treasures. On Athos, between them the Greek, Serbian and Russian monasteries owned more than 20,000 icons. Sydney realised that these were very valuable, not only as aids to devotion—'windows to heaven' as the monks called them, but as rare early Christian artworks, some dating back to the twelfth and thirteenth centuries.

Above and below the monastery small groups of monks lived in *sketai* or small monastic 'outhouses' sharing a simple routine of work and prayer. Others, who found the discipline of the monastery repugnant, preferred to live as hermits in the many caves that honeycombed the steep cliffs of Athos. Their only link with the outside world was a basket of food lowered down each month on a rope. All the monks lived in a time warp of the Middle Ages. Some of the hermits would best be described as eccentrics, but a number of the monks living in the monasteries were highly educated men who delighted in talking to Sydney in English.

By now Sydney was completely fascinated by the lost world of Athos, and made up his mind to return here. He was fired with enthusiasm to write a book about the Holy Mountain, and hoped to illustrate it with photographs.

Later that summer the Lochs came on a second holiday to the coast of Prosforion, this time camping on the beach by the medieval watchtower rather than on Donkey Island, because this made it easier to enter Athos. This time Sydney tried to meet as many of the monks who came down to the village as he could. One of them, a Greek monk named Brother Meletios, would become a lifelong friend of both the Lochs. He was a keen reader and asked them if they could lend him any books in English. It transpired that he was the librarian at the monastery of Vatopedi, built in the eleventh century, on whose land the refugee settlement was built. Vatopedi was one of the oldest and most important of the monasteries, and the only one to have converted from the Gregorian to the 'modern' Julian calendar.

Sydney was invited to visit Vatopedi. This time he walked the five kilometres to the frontier, crossed over the low stone wall that separated the Athonite Republic from the Greek mainland and went through forests where deer and wild boar roamed. Suddenly, the monastery rose before him, its walls painted a deep Venetian red to remind the monks of the blood of Christ shed for them.

After the customary glass of *tsipouro*, accompanied by home-grown olives, Brother Meletios unlocked the treasure tower. He told Sydney there were three ancient keys for three different locks, each one kept by a different monk to lessen the risk of robbery. He showed Sydney a finely worked gold casket set with jewels, an exquisite example of the craftsmanship of Byzantine jewellers. In the casket was a holy relic: the girdle of the Panagia. It had once held an honoured position in the great Byzantine cathedral of Hagia Sophia in Constantinople, which the Turks had turned into a mosque. Brother Meletios told Sydney that the girdle of the Mother of God had such healing power that during the Middle Ages it had been loaned to several cities under threat from bubonic plague.

Among the other treasures were golden candlesticks and jewelled altar crosses salvaged from the churches of Byzantium, and hundreds of icons and illuminated manuscripts of parchment or vellum, held between heavy covers of gold or silver studded with emeralds and rubies.

There were many fewer monks than in the past. Their cells or small apartments were in the upper storeys of the monastery. The lower storeys held kitchens, pantries, storehouses and workshops. Like most of the other monasteries, the windows were heavily barred to guard against pirate attacks.

Each morning the monks chanted matins followed by liturgy. They took their main meal, at which no meat was allowed, at midday. Fish could be eaten provided it was caught by the monks themselves. In the afternoons they helped clean and maintain the building, made candles or worked in the fields. Compline was between six and seven. A few went to bed early while others conducted all-night vigils in chapels constructed when William the Conqueror ruled England.[4]

Sydney learned that in recent years the monks' ancient tradition of providing hospitality to guests had been abused—often valuable pages had been ripped out of illuminated manuscripts. These thefts had taught the monks to be wary of foreign 'book lovers'. However, out of gratitude for the medical advice and aspirins that Joice gave to the monks met at Pirgos, and because the monks knew the Lochs were working at a refugee camp, Sydney became one of very few westerners allowed to take photographs in their treasure-houses. He was specially interested in artefacts from the Byzantine era in gold, silver and carved ivory, with their wonderful jewelled ornamentation. He saw gold and silver altar vessels and bishops' rods studded with jewels and richly embroidered vestments in the Byzantine tradition.

In the days when the monasteries had been well-endowed they had employed skilled wood-carvers, gilders and fresco painters to decorate their chapels and refectories. Stone masons had embellished fountains and fonts of honey-coloured stone with sculpted deer, doves of peace and double-headed eagles—symbols with which the Emperors of Byzantium had enriched the previously severe art of the early Christian fathers, who were terrified of committing the sin of 'making graven images'.

Returning to Thessaloniki, Sydney had his films developed and sent a selection of large-format black-and-white prints, taken with his Voigtlander camera, together with a synopsis of the book he proposed to write about Athos to several British publishers.

For months he heard nothing. Then, via the farm school, he received a letter and a contract from Lutterworth Press, who liked his ideas for an illustrated book on Mount Athos. Pleased to have signed the contract, he returned to Athos, determined to visit every monastery on the peninsula. Joice accompanied him, camping close beside the refugee settlement of Pirgos and working on her Russian spy novel, *The Fourteen Thumbs of St Peter*, which also dealt with treasures, saints' bones and skulls from monasteries.

As sunbathing or swimming was unheard of among refugees from Muslim countries, where women never showed even the hair of their heads or their bare arms in public, she used to swim at the small, secluded sandy beach beside the massive stone watchtower that dominated the village. The tower or *pirgos* fascinated Joice. Brother Meletios had told her that it was built in the tenth century by the

Byzantine Emperor Andronicus Paelogus the Second. In mid-life he had renounced the Imperial crown, taken his vows at the monastery of Vatopedi and had built the watchtower to house his grieving wife, who came to visit him there every summer. The tower's foundation stones had come from the ruins of the pagan city now submerged beneath the sea in front of the tower.

The tower of Prosforion (the name of the area at the head of the peninsula) was built from honey-coloured stone, with walls over a metre thick. Above its massive iron-hinged oak door was an opening through which boiling oil could be poured onto the heads of unwelcome visitors. To please his wife, the Emperor Andronicus had a wooden balcony erected on the top floor of the tower. According to legend, he and his Empress would sit there together, holding hands and watching the sea. When the Emperor died he bequeathed the tower to the monastery of Vatopedi, so that sick monks could convalesce there.

This is how Joice described the tower: 'It rose mystic, wonderful, gleaming bluish-white under the full moon, its ancient stone walls stained pink by the setting sun. On the seaward side was a tiny beach, lapped by small waves.[5] Swallows and swifts wheeled there, pelting noisily in and out of the corbels that supported the roof. Little screech owls danced over the moss-covered slated roof: swallows poured in and out of its eves on currents of air that streamed through the glassless windows and stuck their nests to the enormous beams that supported the roof and locked the joints of the ancient tower together.'[6]

Joice was fascinated by the centuries of history the *pirgos* represented, including the legend of the ghost of a monk murdered by pirates, who haunted the top floor. A romantic at heart, she was longing to settle down in a permanent home. Perhaps even now she dreamed that the tower might one day become the place of refuge that she and Sydney had craved for so long.

19   WILD HERBS AND BITTER BREAD

While Sydney was away on Mount Athos, Joice made friends with Eleni and other women of Pirgos, from whom she bought goat's milk and eggs. She was saddened to see how many of the refugee children had stick-like arms and spindly legs bowed by rickets, due to a diet low in vitamins. The poorest families could not afford meat or chicken, and eggs from their hens were sold to the monks to bring in money. Their staple diet was fried octopus, *horta* or weed soup and a greyish, bitter bread in which what little flour they had was supplemented by ground acorns gathered in stealth on the slopes of Mount Athos.

There was no Government doctor and since there was no access to the village by road, it seemed unlikely one would ever be sent there. The Lochs knew that it would take years for the surviving olive saplings planted by the villagers to bear fruit for oil; the poorest villagers would be on the verge of starvation for a long time to come.

The wells dug by the Army had been placed too close to the backs of the cottages, where the villagers stabled their mules and donkeys, so that they became polluted with ordure and rubbish after rain. To make matters worse, hens, goats or dogs would sometimes fall into the wells, and this led to more outbreaks of typhoid, dysentery and blackwater fever.

Appalled that so many children seemed undernourished and covered in sores and ringworm, Joice brought simple remedies and malaria vaccines with her when she and Sydney made their next visit to the refugee village, as well as a supply of calcium tablets. Joice stressed to the mothers to whom she gave the calcium tablets that they would prevent rickets, warning them that girls with severe cases of rickets could suffer terrible agonies or even die in childbirth.

Although most of the tiny whitewashed cottages were shining clean inside, there was as yet no rubbish collection or sanitation. Behind the cottages rat-infested piles of rubbish and open drains swarmed with flies. Huge mosquitoes hung in clouds after rain and the poorest villagers had no mosquito netting or screens.

As there was no pharmacy or community health centre, on her second visit Joice, a trained *doktorika*, decided to use the nursing and medical experience she had gained with Sister Hetty in Poland to help the refugees. She wrote: 'Most of the people had arrived with malaria. I was faced with the appalling situation of whole families down with it at once, the floors of stricken houses became vast beds where people shivered and sweated with fever under heaps of blankets. It would have been impossible to find ten aspirins, or ten quinine tablets or a single roll of cotton wool had we searched the entire village.'[1]

At Pirgos the summers were scorchingly hot while winter was harsh: the thermometer could soar to 35_ for days at a time during the long waterless summers. There were no trees, hence no shade in the houses nor for the women working their small vegetable plots. The inhabitants broiled in summer and froze in the winter snowdrifts and blizzards.

As Brother Anaphronos had told them, the area known as Prosforion at the head of the Athos peninsula was based on granite and grew nothing but scrub and prickly pear. The only fertile land in the area was farmed by monks from Chilandari and Vatopedi, whose abbots had already agreed in principle to hand over this ploughed land rich in olive trees and vegetables to the refugees, but Government negotiations over the precise terms of the handover were delayed. This meant that Pirgos was virtually a village under sentence of death.

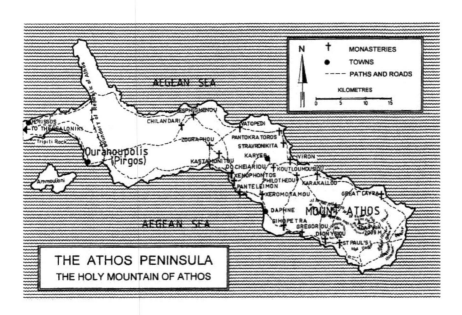

THE ATHOS PENINSULA
THE HOLY MOUNTAIN OF ATHOS

As always the poor lacked privacy. Family rows were overheard by neighbours and gossiped over around the well, where the housewives or their daughters met each morning to draw the day's supply of brackish cloudy water for drinking or washing. More gossip came from black-robed grandmothers or *yar-yars*. They sat on packing crates outside their front doors, crocheting or mending torn garments, reminiscing about the old days back in Turkey or Asia Minor, or talking about young women who looked too long and hard at one particular man.

The huge crescent of white sand in front of the cottages was dirty and filled with rubbish; here barefoot children in ragged clothes guarded scrawny goats, pigs and feather-duster hens to prevent them from being killed by the wolves or wild boars that could emerge from the woods of Athos.

Most of the villagers had only recently arrived at Pirgos settlement. They could never return to their former homes and had spent several years in refugee camps around Thessaloniki since leaving Turkey or Asia Minor. The Lochs soon discovered that the refugee settlement named Pirgos ('Tower') was a place of despair, desolation and enforced exile.[2]

Suffering had failed to unite the refugees, who were divided into two hostile groups with scant sympathy for each other.[3] Greeks who had fled from relatively prosperous areas like the Princes Islands, close to Istanbul, could usually read and write; many had left behind well-tended homes, prosperous farms or fishing boats.[4] This group spoke and wrote Greek and had been to school until they were fifteen or sixteen. They despised the often illiterate Turkish-speaking refugees from poverty-stricken central Turkey and around the Black Sea, who were formerly artisans and rug weavers. The only thing that connected these two widely differing groups was their fervent belief in the Orthodox Church and the idea that they were Greek. Both groups had brought their favourite icons with them and would not dream of selling them, even if it meant going without food.

Those villagers allowed time by the Turks to plan their exodus had brought their savings and livestock with them. They were economic survivors, as were those, like Eleni and her husband Sophocles, with relatives in Greece who had lent them money. Armed with capital, a few of the refugees saw an opportunity for trading and bought fishing boats or *kaï̈kis* to transport timber and olive oil for the Athonite monasteries to sell in Thessaloniki or built crushing mills for olives.

Other refugees, threatened by Muslim mob violence, had fled with nothing but the clothes on their backs; unable to find paid work of any kind, their diet was so poor they were prey to a host of diseases.

Although the monks of Mount Athos felt pity for the refugees on their doorstep, they did not have the funds to employ all of them, and religious observance constrained them against selling off their valuable historic treasures to feed the starving. Most of the monasteries were asset-rich but short of cash, so they paid the refugees with jars of honey, olive oil, or perhaps a magnificently carved Russian cupboard or table which the recipient would carry down to Pirgos on his back.

Because most of the vines and the olive saplings given to villagers by the Government were dying in the stony and infertile soil, Joice also brought to the village seeds of selected hardy plants such as pumpkin, melon, chickpea and spinach. She told the villagers that when these seeds had grown in their vegetable patches they should add them to their *horta* soup along with the wild purslane or pigweed, which was rich in vitamins, especially vitamin C.

Some refugees had brought their savings with them in the form of rugs woven in Islamic patterns, usually in silk. One man, known as the Rug Miser, had put all his savings into one superb silk rug. He boasted it was the most valuable rug in the world. Once every three months he placed it outside his cottage to be admired, stroking it 'like the hair of a woman' as the villagers said. Others kept gold coins in a bridal chest, hoping that with good dowries Paraskevoula, the matchmaker, would be able to arrange suitable weddings for their daughters. Some villagers conserved their wealth in the form of silver *piastres* set into ornamental head-dresses and necklaces. A few hid their bank notes in hollow walls—but sometimes the rats that swarmed around the mounds of garbage would use them to make nests.

Joice saw a strong contrast between the relatively affluent and the poorest villagers who had so little, lacking even mattresses or bedrolls. They slept wrapped in a blanket on the floor, their only furniture a low table or packing case off which they ate their meals. The wife's duty was to tend the cooking fire, which must never go out, which prevented her from leaving the home for any length of time. Their way of life had not changed down the centuries. Many husbands only allowed their wives out of the house to draw water from the well or to hoe the maize and chickpeas in their stony vegetable plots. Most of the women went barefoot to the well and by ancient custom kept their heads covered. Like the men, they wore baggy cotton harem-style trousers, usually black.

The village had no trees, no shops, no *kafenion* and no church, all things dear to the hearts of Greeks. It was very difficult for the inhabitants to obtain everyday commodities or agricultural implements. Without an access road and motorised transport it deserved its nickname: 'the village at the end of the world.'

Donkeys, rather than mules, provided much of the transport because they were freely available from the wild herds on Donkey Island. It infuriated Joice when villagers flogged or starved their poor little sad-eyed donkeys. When she protested they claimed that donkeys were animals of the Devil. If the poor beast died they would simply catch another one on Ammouliani and beat it into submission. She was horrified to learn about the many cruel superstitions the villagers had brought with them from Asia Minor. In an attempt to break the second successive drought, they sacrificed a male donkey, burying it alive in the dried-up bed of a stream, believing that the wretched creature's cries of distress would cause God to send rain. Joice threatened to withhold her medical services if they ever sacrificed another donkey.

Some of the villagers tried to make shoes from donkey or mule skins, but found that they became stiff in the rain and were so uncomfortable that they wore them only on festive or name days. Most village children went barefoot.

Many of the poorer refugees were illiterate; when they needed a letter written they approached Joice or the village schoolmaster. But it was not all poverty and desperation in Pirgos. On name days or saints' days the wealthier villagers put on their best costumes, visited each other's homes and danced to the music of fiddle and drum or sang the bitter-sweet songs of separation and loss.

By now Joice had made friends with several refugee families. She enlisted the help of Charlie and Anne House, who gave her Quaker staples such as tinned sardines, packets of biscuits, aspirin and iodine from the Farm School stores—and, in view of the flies and the smell, plenty of disinfectant.

Blackwater fever was rife in a large number of the refugee villages in the province of Halkidiki and caused many deaths, especially among young children. In the research laboratory Dorothea Hughes had funded at the Farm School it was soon discovered that the cause of blackwater fever was drinking water from wells polluted with ordure after rainstorms, and work began on a vaccine.

Once the village numbered five hundred people, it was agreed it should be given a more imposing name than Pirgos. No one wanted to live in a place that was simply called 'Tower'. The village council, presided over by the Mayor, agreed to petition the Government to let the village adopt the ancient name of 'Ouranoupolis', after a Greek city dating back to the days of Alexander the Great and his father, Philip of Macedon. The first Ouranoupolis, which had dominated the area beyond the neighbouring village of Ierissos, had been destroyed in an earthquake many centuries previously, but no one seemed to consider this a bad omen. Nor did anyone comment on the irony of naming this straggle of two-room dwellings after a particularly large and prosperous city. (However, a few diehards persisted in going against the trend and obstinately went on calling the refugee settlement 'Pirgos'.)

The Mayor or President of Pirgos was a black-bearded giant from Kayseri in central Turkey who looked more like a Turk than a Greek in his white turban and black baggy trousers. He set off on the long and difficult journey to Thessaloniki for an audience with the Governor of Macedonia. When he returned, he bore the good news that the Governor had agreed the village of 'Pirgos' would from now on be known by the grander and more sonorous name of 'Ouranoupolis'.

It was whispered that the Mayor's brother kept an antique shop in Thessaloniki, frequented by foreign visitors and wealthy city dwellers. The villagers were certain that the Mayor's large and comfortably furnished home owed a great deal to the fact that he acted as a selling agent for a couple of avaricious monks, who were said to bring down to him from Athos pages from some of the medieval illuminated manuscripts in their libraries. It was rumoured that the deals were brokered in the antique shop. Whether this was true (or whether the Mayor had managed to bring a substantial sum of money with him from Turkey), Joice never attempted to discover.

One thing became clear: shared disaster and the loss of their former homelands had not given the wealthier villagers a sense of fellow-feeling. The rich did not wish to share their worldly goods with the impoverished.

Ouranoupolis was one of dozens of refugee villages that had sprung up in the province of Halkidiki. For centuries the area had been part of Macedonia and fought over by Turks and Slavs. The Greek Government in Athens was only too happy to 'Hellenise' it by filling it with Greek refugees . . . provided this could be done at minimum cost. The Government, desperately short of money, could provide no more welfare benefits for refugees. Since the refugee crisis the populations of Athens and Thessaloniki had doubled, and the authorities were desperately trying to build enough apartment blocks to house them all.

By 1926 most of the refugee camps in Greece were almost empty and Friends War Victims Relief at the American Farm School was being wound down. The Lochs faced a problem. Like most full-time writers everywhere, their income was hazardous and irregular. All those years spent caring for others as unpaid aid workers meant they lacked savings or capital to buy a home. Renting somewhere inexpensive seemed their only option.

The black-bearded Mayor of Ouranoupolis came to the rescue. He invited Joice and Sydney to a cup of strong Turkish-style coffee in his well-furnished two-storey home. It was followed by small glasses of *tsipouro*, the homemade *ouzo* which burned the throat like a tracer-bullet. To show respect to the host it must be swallowed in a single gulp.

'Just one more glass to kill the microbes—*Dia na skotosome to mikrovio!*'—a suitable toast indeed for a village with a polluted water supply, Joice thought. This was followed by a third glass—and as the male guest, Sydney now had to toast the health of the Mayor.

The purpose of the visit became clear: the Mayor asked Sydney, who owned an old German rifle, if he would shoot a couple of wild boars that were killing the villagers' hens and baby goats. He suggested the Lochs should set up camp in the courtyard of the watch-tower while Sydney tried to kill the wild boars. Perhaps it was the *tsipouro*, but somehow Sydney found himself agreeing to this proposition. Over yet another glass, it was arranged that next day they would move into the courtyard. The tower had a well and its water, unlike that of the wells in the village, did not taste sulphurous and brackish.

Finally, the Mayor said that if the Lochs were interested, he could put in a good word to the Government to grant them a long lease on the tower at a low rent. He told them that under the 1922 State of Emergency laws the monks of Vatopedi, the monastery to which the tower had belonged, had been banned from living in it. He explained that as soon as the Greek Government was able to provide the money, it hoped to restore the historic Byzantine Tower of Prosforion and possibly convert it into a museum.

By now the Lochs had established an excellent reputation with the Greek Government for their aid relief and their classes at the American Farm School. They loved the idea of making their home in the tower by the sea. It would be a dream come true. Elated at the prospect and buoyed up by *tsipouro*, they left the Mayor's house.

Sydney, a crack shot, killed the two wild boars, saving the villagers' hens and young goats. The Mayor was now determined to ensure that Kyrie and Kyria Loch would come to live amongst them.

Tremendously excited by the prospect of a home of their own overlooking the sea, the Lochs returned to the Farm School and continued their work for the Quakers until the last of the 1,500 or so refugees who had passed through the camp had been re-housed.

When finally they were able to make the tiring journey back to Ouranoupolis, the Mayor invited them for another glass of *tsipouro* and told them that the Governor of Macedonia had recently paid an inspection visit to the Prosforion area. It was all agreed. In return for a token rent and an undertaking to carry out some structural repairs, the old Byzantine tower could become their new home. A lease would be drawn up by the Government-sponsored Agricultural Bank of Greece.

Sydney observed that a Byzantine tower overlooking the sea *must* be the ideal place to write a book on Mount Athos. Joice agreed enthusiastically. Turning the tower into their home presented quite a challenge. There was no plumbing or electricity. The lower floor reeked of donkey manure. But Joice, who had grown up in the bush in wooden shacks with dirt floors and no electricity, was convinced they could make the tower liveable.

The devout had prayed to their icons that the Holy Mother of God would perform one of the miracles for which Mount Athos was famous and save them from starvation. Now this miracle was about to happen. In 1926, two years after the first cottages had been built, two 'foreign' writers, both with a strong social conscience, arrived to live in Ouranoupolis. The villagers were convinced their prayers had been answered: Kyrie and Kyria Loch had obviously been sent from Heaven to save them.

The Lochs paid a young boy named Yanni to help them whitewash the walls of a few rooms and remove the donkey manure. Villagers to whom they had given free medical assistance and Quaker friends from the Farm School helped. Soon the tower had clean rooms with scrubbed floorboards. They now had a huge home of their own, filled with centuries of history.

They moved in their few possessions and commissioned the village carpenter to make eight handsome oak dining chairs, a matching oblong dining table and bookshelves for their precious books. Once their books were arranged on the shelves, the dining-room had a unique atmosphere.

There was no electrician or plumber in Ouranoupolis, so they had to bring out an electrician by boat from Thessaloniki. He connected a small generator which would provide electric light to two rooms. This was all they could afford until their books brought in enough money to install electricity to each floor.

Once the Lochs had moved into the tower they soon discovered another drawback: the high ceilings were ideal during the summer but in winter it was impossible to heat the rooms adequately. Water for drinking or for washing had to be drawn from the well in the courtyard and brought twice a day to the stone-flagged kitchen and heated on the cast-iron wood-burning stove. Next door was the dining-room, with windows set in whitewashed walls overlooking the Aegean and distant islands. Joice felt that this glorious view more than compensated for medieval inconveniences. She turned one of the lower rooms into a study for herself, commissioning a desk from the local carpenter. An oak tree was brought down from Mount Athos, cut into planks and steeped in manure to age it. When her desk was finished, Joice placed the miniature Australian flag which Edith had given her beside her portable typewriter.

Then, with a room of her own but without a guaranteed income, at a time when relatively few women writers were published—and several years before Virginia Woolf would write *A Room of One's Own*, with its message that women needed 'a room of one's own' and a regular income in order to write seriously—Joice Loch sat down to begin her first novel. Unlike the two books she and Sydney had written together, she had as yet no publisher for it. She worked hard on a plot with an ironic ending and typed up a long synopsis. Since she was known as a narrative writer rather than a novelist, she decided to write the first ten chapters and send them, plus the synopsis, to John Murray in London.

Next she wrote up her notes on Poland for *The River of a Thousand Ways: Life in War Torn Poland* and wrote a series of articles called 'Modern Athonians' for *Blackwood's Magazine* about the Halkidiki area and the refugee villagers. She also acted as Greek correspondent for whichever paper her old friend Guy Innes was editing. Although she received a good rate when the papers bought her stories, getting them to London via the haphazard Greek postal system presented a problem and without a phone there was no way of knowing if they arrived safely. Sydney received payment for part-time teaching at the Farm School which helped support them.

It was not long before sick or injured villagers came to the tower for medical assistance. Desperate for help, mothers of sick children, women with splitting headaches or men carrying an injured fisherman in a blanket would knock on the heavy wooden door of the tower by day or night. Joice would rise from her bed and treat them as best she could. The villagers called her 'our doctor'—she was the only form of medical assistance they had. When a little boy flattened his finger to the bone between two fishing boats he was brought to Joice screaming with pain. She disinfected the wound with iodine and stitched the finger. It healed.

Gradually Kyria Loch became known around that part of the province of Halkidiki as 'our great doctor'. In vain Joice protested that she was a writer, not a doctor, and had been trained merely as a medical orderly or *doktorika*. Illiterate and simple people refused to believe her. By now Joice was earning a reasonable sum from freelance journalism but used a good deal of her income to buy medicines and dressings for the villagers. She looked forward to the day when children would no longer die of typhoid due to polluted water from the wells.

For those who visit Ouranoupolis today it is hard to visualise the bleak refugee settlement filled with black-clothed widows as the Lochs first saw it three-quarters of a century ago. Today's Ouranoupolis is a friendly holiday village set amid groves of olives with a crescent-shaped beach. The long jetty makes it the last port before Mount Athos and an overnight stop for visitors to the monasteries. The two-room concrete cottages of the original refugees have long since been extended or replaced by two-storey homes. Certain streets are still unpaved and it lacks a bank, but Ouranoupolis now has food shops, *pensiones*, a tourist agency selling boat trips for visitors to sail around the coast, souvenir shops, *kafenions* and a street lined with small family-run restaurants with brightly coloured awnings.

20 THE TOWER BY THE AEGEAN SEA

The news spread around the monasteries of Athos that two writers were living in the Tower of Prosforion who had many modern books in English and were prepared to loan them. Soon monks in charge of the vast libraries at Vatopedi, St Panteleimon, Chilandari and Dionysiou started coming to the tower to borrow books. They had lived relatively sophisticated lives before taking their vows and enjoyed the luxury of real coffee, stimulating conversation and news of the outside world.

Some of the less sophisticated monks, who could neither read nor write and were unable to speak English also visited the tower, asking for aspirin and other medicines. Conversations with them took place in the Lochs' unique blend of modern and ancient Greek. These monks were simple men possessed of strong faith. They boasted of the miracles performed by their icons, which for them were sacred objects of reverence rather than works of art, the saints they depicted to be kissed and worshipped.

The old Byzantine tower had enough rooms for friends from Britain, Australia and Poland to stay in summer when the cool sea breezes made it comfortable. Among the many friends who came to visit were Prince Makinsky, the writer Melchior Wankowicz and Estelle Slater (nee Simson) and her husband from Melbourne.

At first the Lochs employed a village woman to prepare their meals, but she proved to be unreliable—and a terrible cook. Then Brother Anaphronos told them he was looking for a job for Madame Sofia Topolski, the widow of one of his former friends. She too was a White Russian refugee, in desperate need of a home for herself and her little son, Michael. Apparently she was an excellent cook. She came to see the Lochs and they took to each other immediately. Madame Sofia was tall, with upswept hair, an ample figure and a warm smile. She and her son moved in the next day.

Madame Sophia, a doctor's daughter, was well-educated and spoke excellent French and English. She had lost her husband and everything she possessed in the Bolshevik Revolution—except for a silver samovar which she installed in the tower kitchen; it continually bubbled away with water for coffee and Russian tea. Once Madame

The Tower by the Aegean Sea

Sophia took over everything ran smoothly. She became part of the Lochs' lives: soon they could not imagine life without her.

As Sydney and Joice lay in bed in their room high up in the tower, they looked down on the deep blue sea below. From the rear windows of the tower they could see the thickly wooded slopes rising to the snow-covered peak of Mount Athos, which imparted a never-ending sense of awe.

This ancient tower by the sea seemed idyllic enough for the Lochs to remain there for the rest of their lives, devoting themselves to writing. In this remote corner of Greece they had found everything a writer needed.

They realised, however, that for the refugee villagers of Ouranoupolis, life was far from idyllic. Joice had by now become *doktorika* to an entire village on an unpaid basis, buying the medicines and vaccines from funds donated by charity organisations or out of the earnings from her writing. A doctor friend in Melbourne bought what she needed and shipped out the medicines and vaccines to Thessaloniki. There they were collected from the Farm School. Each evening villagers would come to the tower with various ailments and Joice would dress injuries and hand out medications from her capacious medicine chest.

The village women worked very hard: rearing their children, keeping the home fires going, baking, cleaning, drawing water from the well, washing and tending their vegetable patches as well as hoeing rows of maize in the fields. Once the drought was over and the soil started to bear seeds again, young girls and married women would rise at four each morning and set off for their fields or vegetable patches and work there until eleven. In winter they lit their way with pine torches.

The Lochs tried to help the village carpenter by persuading friends who admired their rustic furniture to commission pieces from him.[1] In Poland, self-help schemes such as providing flax to make linen which the peasant women embroidered and sold, had worked well. They discussed encouraging a furniture industry at Ouranoupolis, using the fine timbers from Mount Athos. But without a sealed road or a regular ferry service transport presented severe problems: cupboards and dining tables could not be carried long distances on the back of a donkey.

Joice's fame as the village *doktorika* spread. More and more of the inhabitants fell into the habit of calling in at the tower for medical assistance. A ground floor room in the tower became the village medical centre and Joice the 'barefoot doctor'. By now she was experienced in diagnosing and treating most of the usual childhood ailments. In the 1920s there were relatively few drugs available and antibiotics had not been discovered; the practice of medicine was far less specialised than it is today. Before antibiotics became available even minor infections were dangerous. Patients could die from what today would be regarded as a relatively minor cut if it were left untreated. Joice provided iodine, bandages, Eusol and aspirin, offered burn ointments and dressings, oil of sassafras to cure ringworm, and, whenever possible, the latest vaccines.

Many village women suffered from a disability common among those who work barefoot in stony fields. In Greek this ailment is known as 'the hitting by stones'. Sufferers develop a sore under the toughened soles of their feet, which becomes infected. Joice dealt with this successfully by lancing the sore place with a sterilised razor blade and applying iodine or Eusol to disinfect the wound.

On one occasion a man with four daughters who particularly wanted a son asked for Joice's help when his pregnant wife began to miscarry. There was nothing Joice could do to prevent the miscarriage. Neighbours crowded into the house, wailing and crying, for the embryo was male. The father, who had been waiting outside, demanded to see the child, but the foetus had disappeared. He beat his head, wailing 'My son! Where is my son!' Fearing the cat might have eaten it, his neighbours told him the Devil had taken the embryo.

Finally the man asked his wife's deaf *yar-yar* or grandmother where the foetus was. 'In the bread cupboard. I put it there so that the cat would not eat it,' she replied. She rushed from the room and returned bearing the foetus in a soup plate, proudly showing it off to all the neighbours. Privacy was unthinkable in the village. The entire family and most of the neighbours were always present at births and deaths.

Kyria Loch was often called out night and day to advise or 'be the luck-bringer' at difficult births. To begin with Paraskevoula, the village matchmaker and midwife, distrusted Joice. She had always acted as the local wise woman-cum-witch and viewed Joice as a rival.

Paraskevoula, who habitually wore baggy, bloodstained trousers which were seldom washed, had fled from the poorest region of Caesaria. She could neither read nor write, but had a deep knowledge of herbal cures. The villagers credited her with magic powers and many demanded her services whenever there was a baby to be delivered. Paraskevoula sold headache cures made from dried and powdered seahorses. As a remedy for sexual dysfunction and fading virility she sold the sun-dried testicles of otters, pounded to a powder by her mortar and pestle. To cure burns and bites she sold 'mouse oil'—olive oil in which a mouse had been steeped. Her other magic medicines included oil in which the herb yarrow had been steeped, to soothe earache or sore or cracked nipples caused by breast feeding.

Villagers who lacked money paid Paraskevoula in kind. She charged one loaf of bread or its equivalent to deliver a baby, provided the labour was not a difficult one. If a baby was 'lying badly' and the labour became prolonged, Paraskevoula would brace herself back-to-back with the pregnant woman, hooking her arms firmly around the mother's. Then she would toss her patient in the air and bring her down heavily on her feet, repeating this drastic action until the baby was forced out. If the baby appeared before the *yar-yar* arrived (who traditionally blessed the child by spitting on it), Paraskevoula would try to delay the birth by forcing the head in again, a practice Joice tried hard to stop. Coping with a difficult birth, Paraskevoula would sometimes tie a live octopus to the woman's stomach; this she called 'bringing on the baby quickly'. After cutting the umbilical cord she placed crushed garlic on the baby's navel as an antiseptic. It seemed to work better than the manure poultices which many villagers persisted in using.

In her role as healer-cum-midwife, Paraskevoula had a rival, a stout dark-haired widow named Marigo, who was more avaricious than Paraskevoula and demanded higher fees. Both midwives insisted that the afterbirth be bound to the mother's stomach for three days 'to keep away the evil eye'. The villagers firmly believed that bad luck would follow if this custom were not followed. They also believed that if anyone blasphemed against the Panagia, the Mother of God, in the presence of a pregnant woman, her baby would be born with a harelip. Marigo told Joice stories of women who had delivered babies with long ears like hares, and other hideous deformities. Like Paraskevoula, initially Marigo refused to have anything to do with Kyria Loch. But after the deaths of two babies Paraskevoula claimed were 'lying badly', she swallowed her pride and began to seek Joice's opinion in difficult cases.

Joice realised she had to take things slowly if she were to succeed in modernising such primitive birthing procedures, though many women enduring long and painful labour asked for her help. When she was called out to assist at a difficult birth she would always go; if she refused, she knew that Paraskevoula or Marigo might apply one of their more awful methods. After providing wise birthing counsel, she was often asked to be the *koumba'ra* or godmother. (In years to come she and Sydney would pay the fees for some of her numerous godchildren to attend the Farm School).

Marigo was not only more mercenary than Paraskevoula, she was far less competent and relied much more heavily on witchcraft and magic potions to ward off the evil eye, selling her patients amulets with huge painted eyes and strings of garlic to hang by the front door. Serious trouble ensued when Marigo learned that a pregnant woman who had been told to expect a difficult birth had gone by mule to Arnea and caught the bus to Thessaloniki's only private hospital to be 'cut open' by Caesarean section. Marigo decided she could do the 'cutting open' operation herself and earn a fat fee.

Shortly afterwards, a village woman undergoing a long and difficult labour had her stomach cut open by Marigo with a rusty old Turkish bayonet. There was no anaesthetic. The young mother died in agony, her baby cut in half. This death by 'cutting open' became the talk of the village. Women no longer invited Marigo to deliver their babies, preferring the combination of Paraskevoula and Kyria Loch instead.

One day Joice rescued a baby owl from being drowned by some of the local children. It had been stoned and had lost an eye and a toe. She took the little owl back to the tower and fed it with an eye-dropper. The owl became very fond of Joice and used to sit on her shoulder; even after it had recovered it refused to fly away, and she kept it as a pet. Once the villagers' olives and vines were established and the threat of starvation removed, Joice did her best to stop the villagers killing blue tits, robins and baby owls for food.

Whenever she found kittens stoned to death or birds, trapped in nets, that had died from starvation, Joice tried her best to educate the village children to be kind to animals. She told herself they did not know any better. Their ancestors had suffered terrible cruelty under the Turks for four hundred years: that history of suffering and death had left a strain of cruelty in their souls.

Cats were Joice's favourite pets. Soon after she and Sydney moved into the tower she was given a grey Angora kitten she named Sylvia. Over the years she had quite a few Angoras, and for the rest of her life she would sit at her typewriter with a cat beside her while she worked.

In what little spare time she had, Joice managed to complete the manuscript of her novel *The Fourteen Thumbs of St Peter*.[2] Posting anything to London was a problem; several of her newspaper articles had been lost in the mail. John Murray were due to pay an advance on her novel on receipt of the first chapters, and she posted two copies of these to London from Thessaloniki. For months she heard nothing.

Finally she received a letter from Murray asking for the material. It had been scheduled for publication early the following year in Britain and America and they were waiting for her typescript.

Joice decided there was only one thing to do. The manuscript was now completed. She must take it to London herself. She planned to be away for at least two months while Sydney stayed in Ouranoupolis working on his book about Athos. She hoped to visit Quaker Headquarters in London and return with some desperately needed money to buy medicines and enable her to start some self-help scheme that would provide the poorest villagers with an income.

From Thessaloniki she travelled steerage on a passenger liner bound for London, where she stayed at the Lyceum Club in Piccadilly.[3] She took in the manuscript of *The Fourteen Thumbs of St Peter* to John Murray's office and received a good advance. It would be published in New York by Morrow, who promised a large print run. America was in the midst of a boom, the stock market was soaring and books were doing well. Everything looked rosy for Joice's new career as a novelist.

In London she visited Friends House and talked to the Quakers about the problem of rickets and dysentery in the refugee villages. She spoke persuasively, asking for donations for health education programmes and medical drugs for Ouranoupolis. But the Society of Friends still had huge demands for its welfare services in Britain, war-torn France, Austria and Belgium; they regretted that they could only provide part of the money needed. This meant that Joice would have to continue funding most of the medicines herself.

On her return to Greece, she was confronted by a general strike of the Communists in Thessaloniki and noisy and violent street marches. The strike aggravated previous problems with the Greek postal service, which was now so unreliable and chaotic that Joice wrote to John Murray asking for the galley proofs of her novel to be corrected in England, rather than sending them to her. Her publishers did this and sent the subsequent page proofs to Joice via another of their authors, Dr Philip Sherrard, who was coming to Athens to work at the School of Archaeology. So began a lifelong friendship between the Lochs and Philip Sherrard and his family, who often stayed with them at the tower.

During one of their visits, Dr Sherrard's daughter firmly believed she had seen the ghostly monk said to haunt the top floor of the tower, where the bones and skulls of monks had been stored since ancient times. This particular monk was believed to have been murdered by pirates in the sixteenth century. In search of gold and silver icons the pirates had battered down the great oak door and ransacked the tower. The ghost carried a lighted candle; its wavering light could sometimes be glimpsed through the top windows of the tower. Over the years several of the Lochs' guests were convinced they had seen the ghost; they all said that they 'felt' someone passing by them on the stairs at night. Joice believed the ghostly monk was a friendly, protective phenomenon.[4]

The refugees at Pirgos were fortunate to have a devout and devoted Archimandrite priest. A village church was under construction, and in the meantime services for the entire village were held on the top floor of the tower, in the very room where the bones of dead monks (including those of the ghost) were stored in a special bone-cupboard. To conceal the bone-cupboard a wooden screen had been erected, originally hung with icons of Christ Pantocrator, the Holy Mother of God and various saints. After the church building was completed, the village carpenter removed the screen piece by piece and re-erected it in the church.

Joice was delighted to learn that film rights for *The Fourteen Thumbs of St Peter* had been optioned by a Hollywood producer. Like most of her earnings, the option payment rapidly disappeared into ointments, iodine, aspirin, vaccines and quinine tablets for the villagers. She was excited by the prospect of the film. On 25 April, 1929, when the American stock market was soaring in price each day, she wrote to John Murray, saying that during the move to the tower she had lost her copy of the contract for her novel. She wanted to know 'how she stood with them over the film rights'. She saw the film deal with Hollywood as something 'which could be used to help the village get on its feet'.

Unfortunately she never received more than the option money. In the devastating stock-market crash of September 1929, the film producer was bankrupted so *The Fourteen Thumbs of St Peter* never reached the silver screen. America, Britain and Australia slid into depression and high unemployment.[5] It was not an ideal time to be an international author, still less one trying to support so many poverty-stricken refugees and run a free medical service.

Undaunted, Joice started making notes for a book of short stories based on some memorable characters in the refugee village. She jotted down the story of Stavros, who owned the oil mill. He was a miser who refused to donate one drachma to starving families and stored his bank notes in one of the hollow mud-brick walls of his mill. One day he ran into the street, howling like a dog and shaking his walking stick. 'The rich rats have devoured all my money! Oh! How I would like to kill those rich rats!' His son came to the tower with a handkerchief filled with minced fragments of drachmae notes and implored Sydney to achieve the impossible, to persuade the bank in Thessaloniki to accept them and give his father new notes in exchange. Needless to say, this was a task Sydney declined.

Because of the other demands on her time, these tales would remain dormant in Joice's fertile mind and in note form for decades. Since her girlhood she had possessed a true passion, a compulsion to write creatively, but all those other demands, including her journalism, deprived her of the opportunity to become a full-time literary writer. Joice Loch's ambitions were divided between her humanitarian aims and her writing, and selfishness was an element entirely missing in her make-up. Her natural inclination was always to attend to the needs of others before her own. When she did manage to sit down at her desk to write creatively, she was always professional, producing as much as she could before yet another interruption forced her to put down her pen. She did not abandon projects.

The Fourteen Thumbs of St Peter remained her only novel. It had a clever plot and an ironic ending. For a first novel written under difficult conditions, it was a real achievement. One may speculate on the literary reputation she might have achieved if she had written more fiction. Joice NanKivell Loch possessed a flair for narrative description, particularly in her vivid and vibrant impressions of nature, which often reflect the lyricism of some of her poems. She wrote with clarity, wit and perceptive feeling and in her own distinctive voice. Her verse has a more variable and emotional quality than her prose, which never revealed her emotions. Her best poems convey a real passion and lyrical talent and linger in the mind. Although she was always known as 'Kyria' or 'Mrs Loch', Joice still wrote her newspaper articles and some of her books under her maiden name of NanKivell.

That same year, 1929, the villagers, weary of trying to cultivate iron-hard ground and despairing that they would ever receive the fertile land the Greek Government was supposed to be repossessing from Athos, took up their shovels and mattocks and marched out to take over the land by force from the startled monks who were busy ploughing it. The Government ratified the takeover and suddenly people in the village who gained fertile land felt rich. Girls without dowries had previously been forced by their families to marry older men with money, some of whom came from America to seek a 'traditional Greek wife': the girls married men they scarcely knew. Now, thanks to the land takeover, these girls were able to marry their sweethearts, who now had fertile land and were perceived by the village mothers and the matchmaker as 'good husbands'.

Other couples were not so lucky; some young men who tried to thwart their parents' wishes and marry for love rather than for dowries paid a high price. These 'love' marriages were usually doomed as they were thought to shame the parents of the bride. At this time, any girl who slept with her betrothed before the wedding was deemed 'a fallen woman', one who had 'lost her honour', and the betrothal would be broken. How could the husband ever trust his wife again, knowing she was a woman of 'easy virtue', the *yar-yars* demanded. However, by tradition a man who got a girl pregnant and refused to marry her could be killed by the girl's father or by her brothers as a way of preserving the family's honour. Joice despaired of these entrenched attitudes. She was convinced that better educational opportunities were the only hope of improving life for village girls.

By now the Mayor of Ouranoupolis was extending his house, enlarging both the lower and upper storeys and filling it with still more handsome furniture. The rumours continued that his home extensions were the result of dealing in stolen artefacts from Mount Athos. Wisely, Joice decided it was not a good idea to write one of her short stories about this. Living in such a small community with its fierce blood feuds, it would be easy to spark a vendetta that could end in murder.

Instead she wrote a wry story about Eleni, one of the village women. Joice met Eleni when she and Sydney first visited the village. Eleni was married to Sophocles, a grim man who had made her work like a mule ever since she had come to him as a bride of fifteen. She worked day and night, pausing only to cross herself when the church bell rang for prayers. She had borne her grumpy old husband two children, a son whom she adored and a daughter who had married one of those wealthy, elderly Greeks who came from America to find a 'traditional' wife. The daughter had met him only two days before the wedding. She was her father's favourite child, and he provided lavish nuptials. Since then, she had returned from America for a visit every five years.

Eleni had slaved away believing that her much-loved and hard-working only son, now married and living with her and her husband, would inherit the family home and livestock. She nursed her husband devotedly, and when he died she gave him as important a funeral as she could manage within her slender means. After the funeral, when Sophocles' will was read aloud, Eleni was furious to learn that her husband had left everything, including the house and livestock, to his wealthy daughter in America. He had made no financial provision whatsoever for his wife, son or daughter-in-law. Eleni, the traditional Greek widow in black, mourned no more. She raced to the recently dug grave wielding a huge stick and beat the earth with all her strength. 'Take that, false husband!' she cried, 'that will crack your skull!' As a poor village woman she had no legal rights; angry and frustrated, she then vented her feelings by urinating on his grave until scandalised villagers pulled her away. Four years later Eleni took her revenge. She refused to follow the Orthodox custom of exhuming her late husband's bones, washing them in wine and storing them in the bone house. This meant that the grave could not be used again. Her neighbours were so outraged that finally they dug up and washed the bones themselves.

Ancient and pagan superstitions thrived in Ouranoupolis, handed down from generation to generation. Many villagers believed that crushed garlic bound to a limb would repel the evil eye; that the breath of a dying mule would bless those who inhaled it; that poultices of chicken manure would heal a wound far better than the iodine Joice gave them. (Joice would recount with a certain amusement that sometimes, just to be certain, her patients used both the manure and the iodine.) Tales of vampires who sucked the blood of sleeping babies and succubi or ghosts who demanded sex from young girls were whispered by the fireside. Women who were menstruating were deemed 'impure' and forbidden to enter the church until menstruation had ceased.

Joice wanted to bring change and give the women an income, thus increasing their self-esteem (many were regarded by their husbands as a poor second to their donkeys, and worked as hard). But she did not know how to achieve this. And how could she find the time? She was kept busy attending to the villagers' medical problems, writing letters and witnessing documents for the illiterate, trying to raise funds to bring the village a supply of unpolluted water and a road.

The Lochs made an effort to help those refugees who wanted to learn deep-sea fishing but lacked the skill or had no reliable boats. The Aegean, so peaceful and blue in summer, could just as suddenly blow up and become dangerous; the sudden storms around the coast of Athos were known as Poseidon's revenge. Several of the village men, fishing from leaky cockleshells they had built themselves, had drowned in freak storms.

Joice and Sydney wrote to Hatchard's bookshop in London, asking for the latest textbooks on building boats suitable for fishing in Mediterranean or Aegean waters. When the parcel of books arrived, the Lochs persuaded the village schoolmaster to provide Greek translations, so that villagers who could read would have the chance to learn the latest fishing techniques and try to build their own boats. Joice's hugely successful Russian novel helped to supply funds for the project, and with the aid of Alexis the carpenter several families built their own boats.

By now the Lochs so closely identified with the villagers and their struggles to survive that nearly all their money and their efforts went on self-help schemes. Years later Joice would describe how 'for two writers to set out to achieve the impossible and to help an entire village to exist seems fantastic; but perhaps we were fantastic, and impractical, inasmuch as the enormous financial difficulties involved did not seem to dawn on us'.[6]

In the late 1920s Greece was so poor that it was impossible for the Greek Government to pay widows' or unemployment pensions. The Lochs valiantly undertook the responsibility for feeding the widows and children in the village, those most in need. They sent out dozens of letters to charities in Britain, America and Australia asking for funds to help the villagers become self-sufficient. They asked for a school, for piped water and electricity—amenities Ouranoupolis desperately needed. But in that time of world-wide depression, most charities and businesses did not reply. Others wrote back to say that their funds were already fully committed. Only the Society of Friends in America and Britain remained steadfast in supporting the Lochs' efforts to keep the refugee village alive and healthy.

'Please, Kyria Loch, give us work,' was the cry Joice heard on all sides. Most of the refugees had a fierce pride which prevented them from begging. It would still take several years for the olive saplings that had survived the drought to bear fruit, so that the green virgin oil could be milled in Stavros' new oil mill and sold. The supply of fish was slowly improving but meat was scarce and expensive. No one wanted to kill off goats which gave milk for *feta* cheese and yoghurt, which could be sold to the monks.

Joice continued to rack her brains, desperately looking for a viable self-help scheme for the poorer villagers and widows. There must be some way of harnessing their skills.

21   RUG WEAVING SAVES A VILLAGE

The solution to the problem of self-help for the village presented itself in a most unexpected way.

One day a charcoal burner's wife arrived at the tower asking to see Kyria Loch urgently. Joice muttered a few words under her breath, but put aside the article she was typing and accompanied the woman to her spotlessly clean concrete cottage. Inside she noticed an icon in the corner of the room with a tiny lighted wick floating in a glass of oil. Dyed sacking covered the dirt floor. Lying on his bed roll on the floor was an elderly man bathed in sweat. He had high fever and diarrhoea, clear symptoms of dysentery. She examined him closely and found his gums were bleeding. The woman admitted that her father had great trouble eating. Joice had seen the signs of scurvy during droughts in Gippsland when families lacked fresh vegetables. It was clear the old man was suffering from lack of vitamins as well as from dysentery.

Joice questioned his daughter about his diet. In response the woman hung her head and revealed that she and her father lived on a porridge of bread bulked out by bitter acorns, milk from their goat and *horta* soup, made from the herbs and weeds that grew close by. Every scrap of meat, fish or octopus went to feed her children and her husband, who needed his strength for his charcoal burning for the monks of Athos. The poor woman wrung her hands in despair. 'Kyria Loch, what can I do. Meat and vegetables are expensive. My vegetable patch is on poor soil—my pumpkins died and so did my *andithia*.'

Joice feared that many other frail and elderly people might be dying in silence from malnutrition. She advised the woman to pick roots of the wild herb *anthrakala* or pigweed, rich in vitamin C, cultivate it in her vegetable patch and serve it in herb soup, or put it in a weed salad. Paraskevoula, wise in ancient lore about herbs and plants, supported Joice's advice about the pigweed. She also advised preserving it in home-made vinegar for the winter months.

The woman told Joice that when they had lived in Kayseri in central Turkey they had managed quite well because she had helped to feed the family by weaving silk and woollen rugs. In fact her father was previously a famous rug designer. The woman disappeared into the tiny bedroom and returned brandishing a pillowcase. From it she pulled out a shimmering pile of coloured silks, enough to make several rugs.

The sight of that rainbow of colour gave Joice her inspiration. She suddenly realised the possibilities presented by the woman's weaving skills. Others must possess those skills: surely rug-weaving could provide the answer to self-sufficiency in the village. She promised to get the woman a loom, commissioned a new rug from her, and gave her money to buy fish and fresh vegetables for her ailing father.

She then went to ask the village carpenter whether he could make a simple loom. Proudly he told her that he had made several looms 'back home' in Kayseri—he would be delighted to make one for Kyria Loch. Joice paid him in advance so that he could buy the timber. When the loom was completed, she gave it to the rug-designer's daughter. Now the woman could earn money by weaving rugs, just as she had done before the massacre at Smyrna and the exchange of populations.

The more Joice thought about her inspiration, the more viable it seemed. Rugs were relatively light; they could easily be transported to Thessaloniki on the back of a donkey and sold there. Why hadn't they thought of this before? Lack of communication was probably the main reason. Most of the former rug-weavers spoke nothing but Turkish, which meant the Lochs had great difficulty in understanding them.

A short time later, when Joice returned to the cottage of the charcoal-burner's wife, she found the old man sitting up and directing his daughter as she sat at the loom weaving the silk rug from an ancient Muslim-inspired design he had used in Turkey. The woman ran to Joice, kissed her hand and wept tears of happiness. Sadly, malnutrition and scurvy had taken their toll and the old man did not live to see the completion of the rug, the first to be woven in the village.

Joice discovered that many of the female refugees from central Turkey had been skilled rug-weavers and had dyed their own wool, using modern factory-made dyes. Many had managed to bring with them the tools of their trade. Now there seemed some hope for Ouranoupolis, if only Joice could raise enough money to commission looms and find a supply of ready-spun wool. (There were no sheep in the village and spinning was not one of the women's crafts.) Silk rugs would be too expensive a proposition.

She and Sydney talked it over. They decided the best idea was to use a small legacy Joice had recently received following the death of her Aunt Ada, Uncle John Turner's wife. Joice had hoped to spend the money installing electricity throughout the tower but decided that could wait.

With her usual energy and enthusiasm, she threw herself heart and soul into starting a women's weaving cooperative. She used part of her legacy to pay the carpenter to make more looms. Providing more money, she wrote to volunteer staff at the Quaker mission on the island of Chios, famous for its fine wool, to buy a large quantity and have it shipped to Thessaloniki, where she arranged to have it spun in a factory. She planned to market Pirgos Rugs as 'woven in Macedonia', their patterns incorporating design motifs from the Byzantine carvings, embroidered vestments, altar cloths and book covers Sydney had photographed in the various monasteries of Mount Athos.[1] She was determined to give 'Pirgos Rugs', as they were to be called, a distinctive Greek identity. Greeks would certainly buy these rugs. To wealthy Greeks in Athens and Thessaloniki, anything Turkish or Arabic was taboo. The Turks had enslaved the Greeks for centuries: anti-Turkish feeling was stronger than ever following the burning of Smyrna, the ethnic violence in Asia Minor and the refugee crisis.

Joice tried to get more women to join her weaving cooperative but they demurred, preferring to weave Persian and Turkish designs. She warned them that such Muslim-inspired designs would find no buyers in Greece, but persuading them was not easy. Most refugee women from Asia Minor failed to see the value of making distinctively Greek rugs, claiming they could only weave the patterns they had followed before. By this time Joice had carried out some market research and knew she was right: neither affluent Greeks nor foreign visitors would buy Greek-made Persian or Turkish-style rugs. She was also aware that Pirgos Rugs could not compete in price with the rugs woven by nomads in remote parts of Anatolia or with Greek factory-produced rugs. Pirgos Rugs must be seen as luxurious collectibles, in designs that were totally different from those obtainable elsewhere.

There was no chance the monks of Athos would let a woman into their libraries and treasure houses, but a rich source of motifs had been revealed to her when, in order to help Sydney with his book, she had carried out research into various periods of Byzantine art and seen fine examples in the great Christian basilicas of Thessaloniki. She knew that the earliest Christians had used only the cross to adorn their churches or what became a secret Christian symbol, a stylised fish, the disciples being regarded as 'fishers of men'. But since the days of the Emperor Justinian wealthy Christian Byzantines had spent a great deal of money adorning their beehive-domed churches, rich in mosaics, metalwork, embroidered wall hangings and church vestments. Those early Byzantine artists depicted motifs derived from Roman classical art such as swallows, deer, doves and peacocks. The Roman double-headed eagle, whose twin heads represented the Emperor as head of State as well as the Orthodox Church, became the logo of the vast Byzantine empire which included north Africa and northern Greece, with Thessaloniki as its second most important city.

Joice decided that Pirgos rug designs would be based on Byzantine motifs and include a range of exotic beasts such as griffins or gryphons—a cross between a lion and a dragon, originally found in Far Eastern art and incorporated into that of Byzantium. The mythical gryphon eventually gave rise to the winged lion of Byzantium, which was in turn taken over by the Venetians after their capture and sacking of Constantinople: the Byzantine gryphon became the winged lion of St Mark, the symbol of Venice.

Joice felt that one motif that belonged exclusively to Mount Athos must be used: the tiny daisy called 'Footsteps of the Panagia', found only upon the slopes of the Holy Mountain. According to the monks, these daisies sprang up wherever the Mother of God had walked. Herbalists from the Holy Mountain like Joice's friend, Father Klemens, dried them and sold them to cure people's sorrows or minor ailments.

Using Sydney's photographs as a reference source, Joice designed her own Byzantine-inspired rugs. With her love of ancient history, she was determined that Pirgos Rugs should celebrate the glories of the Byzantine Empire, and of Athos. She worked on their dining-table, drawing up her ideas on sheets of graph paper. Her favourite design was taken from a carving at Vatopedi of the *Esphigmenou* or Tree of Life, showing amongst the blossoms a bird which had eaten the flower of good and evil. The logo of Pirgos Rugs should be the Byzantine double-headed eagle, which would appear in the border of most of the rugs woven by the women's cooperative during their early years.

From Sydney's photograph of an illuminated manuscript of the Revelations of St John the Divine, which had come to Athos from the holy island of Patmos, she drew milk-white unicorns with golden horns and a sailing ship representing the one that brought the Panagia to Mount Athos and St John to Patmos. The Lochs had visited Patmos, where women were allowed into the monastery of St John, and Joice had seen the Byzantine illuminated manuscripts, embroideries and art treasures stored there.

Another design was inspired by a magnificent blue-and-white fifteenth-century fresco in the monastery of Vatopedi, showing almond trees in blossom, with Byzantine winged dragons, elephants and eagles in its border as well as the double-headed eagle. Her design 'The

Garden of Eden' was based on Sydney's photograph of an illuminated manuscript brought by monks from Byzantium to Athos in the thirteenth century. It showed peacocks—symbols of eternal life—crouching hares, deer lying down beside lions and dragons. The rug had a border of medicinal plants cultivated by some of the monks of Athos.

Joice decided it was vital Pirgos Rugs did not use factory-made dyes whose reds and blues would eventually fade, but natural hand-produced dyes that would last for decades.

Many of the former rug-weavers, all women, were keen to return to work. But the village men were stubborn and ultra-conservative. Initially they were the ones who made the decisions. They rejected Joice's dangerous 'new' ideas for Byzantine designs, even though they desperately needed the money the rugs would bring. For their womenfolk to weave rugs using Turkish designs was the only way these men could relive the past. They remembered the time when their rugs were famous all over the world and every house had its loom; even their youngest children tied in the knots. They could not forget their old lives in Asia Minor: the flat-roofed houses, the camels that carried their goods, the watermen whose brass water-pots were decorated with strings of turquoise-blue beads to ward off the evil eye. Their cosy world had collapsed when Ataturk's soldiers arrived to tell them they must leave their villages and the country in which they and their fathers and grandfathers were born.

Joice saw it was pointless to start a fight over this issue, or the women's weaving cooperative would be banned by the men and never get off the ground. She decided to take the matter gently and attempt to change prejudices by talking to the women, one by one, at her clinics.

One by one the leaders of the village came to the tower to repeat the same story: 'We are sorry, Kyria Loch, but rugs have always been Turkish. No one will buy rugs with Greek designs on them.' Some of the women insisted, 'Working with plant dyes is impossible. Manufactured dyes are far easier to handle.'

The villagers did not seem to realise the contradiction between their insistence on using ancient Turkish patterns and their wish to employ modern factory-made dyes. The uproar about 'Greek versus Turkish designs' lasted for weeks. Joice refused to give in. At her evening clinics she discussed the idea of Byzantine designs and natural dyes with her female patients, and when she helped Paraskevoula with difficult births she broached the topic with the woman who gathered

213

for the birth. Slowly and tactfully she talked them round to the idea of weaving rugs incorporating Byzantine motifs.

Paraskevoula, now Joice's warmest supporter, was the first to offer suitable plants for dyes. One morning she arrived at the tower bearing a bag of golden onion skins which she instructed Joice to boil in water and then leave for a week to allow the mixture to ferment. The midwife, her dark eyes sparkling with excitement, said she was happy to share her secrets with Joice if they would help the village to survive. 'Steep raw wool in boiled onion skins to which alum has been added to get beautiful golden yellow,' she advised, and told Joice that every single plant, herb or berry growing wild in the area as well as the bark of most trees would give colour to raw wool, ranging from pale pinkish-cream, to green, brown, purple or black. Different tones could be obtained from the same plant according to what setting agent or mordant was used.

Slowly, by trial and error, Joice learned how to make natural dyes from herbs, berries, leaves, blossom and bark. She discovered that the deepest black came from wild sloes or from the bark of the scrub oak, used for centuries by Greek and Turkish women to dye their hair. A colour resembling turquoise could be obtained from the leaves and flowers of *pistachio lentiscus* or skene. Pink and pinkish-beige were obtained from pine chips with salt added as a mordant, or from willow bark to which alum had been added. Joice soon discovered they must dry wool on which alum had been used away from the sun, otherwise it would have streaks of colour through it.[2]

To protect the village women from exploitation, the Lochs drew up contracts in which Pirgos Rugs provided an advance payment for the weaver. Two-thirds of the selling price went direct to the weaver. One-third covered the cost of the wool, the upkeep of the looms and money for the girls who helped gather the plant material and dye the wool. The first Pirgos rugs were woven in 'natural' shades, using black, white and ochre wool. Next came a soft pink produced from pine bark chips. Gradually new shades were introduced and as this happened, the market for Pirgos Rugs increased.

Earning money through Pirgos Rugs gave the village girls and women self-confidence and a measure of independence, even if they were illiterate. The women's weaving cooperative brought in a regular income to many families and paid for shoes and clothes for their children.

To the astonishment of the village men, three of the very first Pirgos Rugs designed by Joice won first prize at the International

Trade Fair held in Thessaloniki. As a result, the Laiki Techni (Technical College) in Thessaloniki decided to commission rugs from the village for re-sale. Paraskevoula continued to provide valuable advice. She and Joice found they could create different effects by steeping the wool for varying lengths of time, using roots and lichens and sometimes adding twigs and sawdust to the mix.

Intelligent girls like Fani Kollinbas, who, due to lack of money, had been forced to leave school at the age of twelve, came to Pirgos Rugs to earn money. Joice and the hard-working Fani gathered, boiled and fermented a variety of plants, blossoms and lichens from different localities throughout the year, using various mordants. Magenta and claret-red were obtained from dandelion flowers and roots or the bodies of a tiny beetle called *kermiz*. A bright green was produced by fermenting cow manure and ivy leaves; vats of human urine imparted a more brilliant tone of green to the wool. The green could be intensified even more when goat manure was added and the raw wool 'marinated' in this smelly mixture for several months. The dyeing of the wool was initially carried out in tanks in the courtyard of the tower but then moved further away.

Joice devoted an enormous amount of time to experimenting with plants and roots. Finding new dyes became a passion. She kept notes of her procedures and planned a small book on the craft of dyeing wool using natural methods. The American Board of Missions agreed to fund this, realising that it would provide other village women with an additional skill. The village women sighed with admiration over Joice's spectrum of coloured wool drying in skeins. Yet there were some who still hankered for the speed and ease of factory-produced dyes.

Over the years Joice added to her designs motifs from pre-Christian times such as the leaping dolphins she and Sydney had seen on frescoes during a visit to Knossos on the island of Crete. Joice's dolphin design, based on a fresco in the Queen's bathroom in the Palace of King Minos at Knossos has become the most valuable of all the Pirgos Rugs. The wonderful blue of the background came from the bark of the mountain ash that grew on Mount Athos.

Joice began to see her rug designs as 'history in art', helping to preserve the richness of the past.[3] With memories of her bush childhood she made certain nothing was wasted. Any short lengths of wool left over from bigger designs were used to make small wall hangings incorporating simple designs with a local theme. Two of the most popular were a view of the tower and a stylised owl, for which Joice used her own pet owl as a model.

She paid Alexis to make more looms, bought more wool, included more of the widows and poorer women in the weaving cooperative and directed the marketing and publicity for Pirgos Rugs. She enlisted the help of friends in Britain, Australia and America to buy rugs and show them to friends in order to win more commissions.

Fani Kollinbas proved highly capable and was eventually promoted to be Joice's liaison officer with the weavers. Most of the village girls and women wove their rugs at home. Often two girls sat side-by-side at a loom weaving from designs Joice copied for them on graph paper. Even girls who could not read and write were able to follow these diagrams, which they nailed above the loom. Fani recalls that it took two women working together between six weeks and two months to make one of the larger rugs. Eventually Fani would become the operations manager of Pirgos Rugs, only resigning years later when she married her long-term sweetheart, Michael Mitropoulou from Ierissos.

Joice's inspiration had paid off. The Pirgos women's weaving cooperative could not keep up with all the orders it received. It became a financial success and brought much-needed income to many families in 'the village at the end of the world'.

View from the olive groves behind the small port of Ouranoupolis, the former refugee village where Joice Loch ran Pirgos Rugs and a free medical service from her home in the historic tower of Prosforion (centre). *(Jake de Vries)*.

Having no public access by land, Mount Athos remains an unpolluted sanctuary and nature reserve. Ferries reserved for monks and their visitors leave each morning for the port of Daphni from here, as do the daily sightseeing trips round the peninsula which only run in summer. The tower of Prosforion is to the right of the jetty. *(Jake de Vries)*.

To save the villagers of Ouranoupolis from starving, Joice designed Greek rather than Turkish rugs for them to weave. Her *Tree of Life* was inspired by a Byzantine manuscript in the library of Esphigemenou monastery. Other rug designs were based on frescoes, carvings and illuminated manuscripts photographed by Sydney Loch at Vatopedi and at Dionysiou. *(Jake de Vries)*.

Above: The ancient Byzantine tower of Prosforion became Joice Loch's home and workplace for fifty years. *(Adam Editions, Athens).*

In the 1%0s, Joice, helped by Fani and Martha, finally managed to dye raw wool a magnificent shade of blue using plants that grew on Athos and indigo berries brought to the village by gipsies. The exquisite colour inspired Joice to design the most prized of all her designs, the Blue Dolphin, which took two weavers working for a month to make it. On Joice's death this beautiful rug was stored in the tower of Prosforion. *(Jake de* Vries).

Left above: A few of the many honours awarded Joice Loch. These include the Greek On:ler of Beneficence, the Greek Order of the Phoenix, a Rumanian medal for work with refugees and the Polish Cross of Virtue for saving Polish women and children from Nazi death camps. Her previous medals were stolen during the Greek Civil War and most could not be replaced. *(Jake de Vries, with thanks to Byzantine Museums, Thessaloniki)*.

Right above: After a bad fall, the indomitable Kyria Loch had to use a walking stick. She received her many friends and admirers at the Tower of *Prosforion.(Courtesy Martha Handschin)*.

Right: Inauguration of the Joice Loch Memorial, Botanical Gardens, Ingham in 2002 by Daryl Briskie, Parliamentary Secretary to the Premier of Queensland, Keith Phillips, Mayor of Ingham and Alex Freeleagus, Greek Consul for Queensland AM.

22 EARTHQUAKE

Each summer warships and destroyers from the Royal Navy's Mediterranean fleet sailed from Malta to Thessaloniki on what the British termed 'show-the-flag' manoeuvres. The Admiral of the British Fleet, a powerful figure, had read one of the Lochs' books, greatly enjoyed it and decided to visit Ouranoupolis, hoping to make their acquaintance.

After a courtesy visit to the port of Thessaloniki, where the Admiral entertained the Governor of Macedonia to dinner, the British Mediterranean Fleet anchored off Ouranoupolis and the Admiral sent over a naval rating with a letter inviting the Lochs to dine aboard his flagship.

The meal was pleasant and the conversation light-hearted. Joice was an amusing raconteur and so was the Admiral. Joice related the story of the Rug Miser and the rich rats, and told how her patients liked to take out a double insurance by using their manure poultices as well as her iodine and Eusol. The Admiral was interested to learn how, through Pirgos Rugs and other self-help schemes, the Lochs had helped the refugees of Ouranoupolis to survive typhus, cholera and famine. The ship's surgeon asked searching questions about the problems of a village without a doctor where malnutrition and rickets affected so many children.

The next day a tender arrived from the Admiral's ship. Two sailors in white uniforms brought dozens of fresh-baked loaves from the ship's ovens and tins of evaporated milk for the village children. Joice was delighted and arranged to have them distributed amongst needy families. Along with the food supplies came a note from the Admiral saying how much he had enjoyed meeting the Lochs and inviting them on board again, this time to a farewell dinner the following night.

The next morning a distraught couple arrived at the tower with their little girl, who had fallen into a cauldron of grain which, according to village custom, was being boiled for winter storage. The child was screaming with pain. Her burns were horrendous and some grains of wheat had lodged inside her ear. By now Joice was fairly practised at treating burns; each winter without fail, toddlers fell into the Turkish style charcoal braziers the villagers used to heat their homes. But this child's burns were the worst she had ever seen, and she was only too aware that her stock of medicated dressings was running low. The little girl was in agony, her eyelids and nose a mass of seared flesh. Joice feared her face would remain badly scarred, and there was a danger she might lose her sight. She despatched Nanou, who now worked as their boatman, over to the Admiral's ship with a note asking whether the surgeon could bring over to her equipment for the latest burns treatment from his surgery.

Twenty minutes later, the surgeon was rowed ashore to the jetty beside the tower. He donned an operating gown and after cleaning out the ear and doing everything possible for the injured child, he asked Joice: 'How on earth do you manage to cope with medical emergencies, run the sales side of Pirgos Rugs *and* find time to write books?'

Joice shrugged and extended both hands. 'Books and writing have to take second place to medical emergencies. Sydney and I are determined to get this village on its feet.' Then she recounted her conversation at the dinner in Warsaw, telling the surgeon how President Pilsudski and the general had related the Old Testament story of the Israelites who had woven ribbons of blue into their garments to signify that they followed the path of duty rather than their hearts' desires. Fate, she told him lightly, seemed to have placed her here to help the villagers rather than follow her own inclination to be a full-time author.

The surgeon paused for thought. He considered life as a Royal Navy surgeon hard enough. After seeing the conditions under which Joice worked entirely without payment, as well as supplying her own drugs and dressings, he felt humbled. He had a fully equipped operating theatre, trained orderlies to assist him and crates of medical equipment. He now fully appreciated just how hard Joice worked without any funding, medical back-up or a local hospital, virtually on call twenty-four hours a day.

Joice explained that she and Sydney bought what medical supplies they could afford. By now they were short of a number of medical supplies they badly needed. She added: 'All we can do is trust in Providence.'

The surgeon dryly commented that perhaps Providence was being overloaded. Back on board ship, he related everything he had observed, as well as Joice's remark about trusting to Providence to the Admiral. When the Lochs went over for the farewell dinner, the Admiral received them warmly. Once again they talked about Greek customs and folklore and foreign travel as well as books and writing but nothing was said about Joice's medical work.

Early the following morning, the Admiral's barge arrived at the jetty below the tower. Two crew members unloaded five cases filled with medical supplies. With the crates came a note from the Admiral addressed to Mrs Joice Loch; he wrote that he also trusted in Providence, but hoped, on this occasion, he could render Providence a little assistance.

Joice was overwhelmed by such generosity. She replied with a glowing letter of thanks and a copy of *The Fourteen Thumbs of St Peter* with a special dedication to the Admiral. Then she and Sydney waved the fleet goodbye as the ships steamed away in convoy. Madame Sophia and her son were away in Thessaloniki so they did not unpack the crates immediately. All five were placed on the lower floor of the tower beside some newly-washed sheets, pillowcases and towels that were waiting to be ironed on Madame Sophia's return. That same day, from ten until midday, the women in the weaving cooperative of Pirgos Rugs had their annual general meeting. Joice was kept busy chairing the meeting and discussing promotional activities and plans for the future.

During lunch with Sydney, she looked out of the dining-room window and noticed that the swallows seemed more restive than normal, and in the distance they heard the village dogs howling and donkeys braying. It was almost as if the animals had a premonition of some impending disaster...

She spent the afternoon instructing a group of girls about the dyeing process. After dinner that evening she typed up the minutes of the committee meeting of Pirgos Rugs and, exhausted, went to bed at about ten-thirty. She fell asleep immediately.

Around midnight there was a loud knocking on the weathered oak door of the tower. Sydney was sound asleep. Joice got up, threw on a dressing-gown and went downstairs. She opened the massive door to find a child in tears. The girl, who seemed slightly retarded, wanted Joice to come with her straight away, insisting that her sister was very sick. Joice, puzzled by the girl's manner, wondered why the mother had not come to ask for help at this late hour. She told the little girl to return home and said she would come first thing in the morning. By now Sydney had woken up, pulled on some clothes and come downstairs. He thought Joice should go to the little girl's home there and then and insisted on accompanying her. 'You know our motto. No matter how late it is, *never* refuse a patient,' he said.

Joice sighed, but she knew Sydney was right. There just might be something seriously wrong with the girl's sister, though her instincts made her doubt it. She stomped upstairs, pulled an old dress over her head, picked up her medical bag and headed off into the village with Sydney.

Her instincts had been right: they got to the cottage to find both the parents asleep. There was absolutely nothing wrong with the younger child. The mother was mortified to learn that her other, retarded daughter had got Kyria Loch out of bed for no reason. She said the girl was 'difficult' and had been demanding a lot of attention recently. Joice suggested tactfully that perhaps the priest or the schoolmaster could help them. She was careful not to reveal to the parents her annoyance at being called out for nothing.

It was long after midnight as they walked back to the tower. All Joice could think about was going back to bed and getting a good night's sleep. They were only a short distance from the tower before the ground under their feet started to shake. *Earthquake!* Over the centuries the province of Halkidiki had earned itself a grim reputation for devastating earthquakes.

They heard what sounded like gun shots, followed by a distant rumbling. A heavy chimney-pot crashed to the ground, narrowly missing Sydney's head. They watched in horror as huge cracks appeared in the tower's massive walls and wondered whether their home would crash to the ground in front of their eyes. Above their heads the owls and bats roosting in the eaves of the tower fled into the night. The village dogs were howling in chorus, while from their cottages women and children were screaming in fear. The Lochs turned round and hurried back to the village to give whatever help they could.

Screams continued to sweep through the village as the earth rocked and split the little concrete houses, reducing some of them to rubble. Only the newly-built wooden homes remained relatively untouched. Tremors and rumblings continued at ten-minute intervals, accompanied by the sound of collapsing walls. Roof tiles and other debris injured some adults and children.

Villagers emerged in panic from their cottages, some clutching icons of favourite saints or of the Mother of God. Panic-stricken, they offered up prayers for assistance. Some fell on their knees before the icons, praying to the saints and the Panagia to save them. Joice did her best to comfort the distressed. Several frail and elderly men and women had been thrown from their beds. Two had died. She was called away to assist a pregnant woman who had gone into premature labour. While the tremors continued, she managed to deliver the baby. In the next house she was called to see a toddler with a weak heart. The child died in Joice's arms and she had to comfort the distressed parents. By now a queue had formed for the services of *doktorika* Kyria Loch. Fortunately Joice still had her medical bag with her. Sydney helped her splint broken legs and stitch cuts. They both worked through the night without sleep.

At daybreak, a man galloped into the village on a mule whose flanks were dark with sweat. He screamed out 'Ierissos is destroyed! Hundreds have been wounded! Kyria Loch, please come!'

The homes in the neighbouring village of Ierissos were much larger than those of Ouranoupolis and made of stone—most had two storeys, making them more vulnerable in an earthquake.

Joice's medical bag was almost empty. She knew they must get those five crates donated by the Admiral out of the tower and take them to Ierissos. Tremors continued at regular intervals, almost as though the earth had a pulse. Sydney timed each tremor by his watch, recording intervals of between ten and twelve minutes. Just time to get inside the tower and bring out the crates. He marshalled a team of volunteers outside the tower. As soon as one tremor was over, they dashed inside. Part of the ceiling had collapsed and they had to clamber over stones and broken beams to reach the ground-floor room where the crates were stored.

'How lucky Madame Sophia and Michael are away!' Joice said. 'They might have been injured or killed.' Then she discovered that part of the floor above their own bedroom had come down, bringing rubble onto their bed which had collapsed under the weight. The Lochs realised that had they not answered the child's midnight call, they would certainly have been killed.

The men who had volunteered to go to Ierissos dragged out the crates of medical supplies as well as the piles of clean sheets and pillowcases to use as bandages and tourniquets, and loaded them aboard the Lochs' fishing boat. Joice, Sydney and four strong men clambered aboard. The men took it in turns to row. The limpid sea was clear and smooth as glass. With each fresh tremor myriads of minute phosphorescent creatures exploded upwards from the sea-bed like incandescent fireworks.

At the large white-painted rock known as the Tripiti, six men from Ierissos were waiting to carry the heavy crates of medical supplies. The messenger who had brought the devastating news to Ouranoupolis had returned, riding a fresh mule, to let them know that help was on its way. From the Tripiti they set out towards Ierissos. Joice described how 'The road wound through hills that split and crashed in front and behind us but never beside us.'[1] The bearers kept close beside the Lochs; only half in jest they said they had charmed lives and must be beloved of the gods.

As the rescue party approached the last hill before Ierissos, terrible moaning was heard. Joice looked around. Where was Ierissos? She remembered a large, picturesque walled village built of local stone where ancient gabled houses lined cobbled streets so narrow they could be spanned by a man. The wooden balconies that protruded from the houses were so close to their opposite neighbours that they could almost hold hands. Ierissos was one of the few villages in the province of Halkidiki to be built entirely of stone. Now stone walls, gables, balconies, entire houses had disappeared. Corpses and wounded people and animals, hideously shattered by falling debris, lay amongst the rubble, many half-buried. The destruction of the ancient village was total.

Some of the wounded were already being carried down to the beach by young soldiers from the Greek Army, who had been on training manoeuvres nearby. Their arrival in this isolated place without a road was seen as miraculous as that of the great Kyria Loch, the lady in the tower.

The Lochs were already exhausted from lack of sleep but the horror of the situation lent them renewed strength. Sydney, whose calm leadership and organising skills were formidable in a crisis, found crowbars and picks. He formed four rescue teams, each with its own leader responsible for searching for bodies in different areas, and issued instructions that one member of each team was to report to him hourly. Desperately tired, he forced himself to continue.

Two of the soldiers levered open the Admiral's crates of medical supplies and equipment. Joice selected operating instruments, surgical gloves and masks and gave instructions that some sheets should be torn up for bandages. All the equipment was carried down to the beach, where she set up an emergency 'hospital' with a large flat stone to serve as an operating table. There were no trees, no shade of any kind—by now the sun was well up and she had to work under the broiling sun in her thin cotton dress. She started operating immediately, assisted by a young Greek soldier who had worked as a medical orderly. The sheer horror of the situation gave her strength.

Rescue teams carried down a seemingly endless stream of injured adults and children they had dug out of the rubble. Corpses were taken to the burial area, where two policemen buried them in shallow graves. Joice described how, as fast as they covered the corpses with earth, renewed tremors ejected them from their newly-dug graves. The macabre scene was reminiscent of Michelangelo's dark vision of the Last Judgement. She had written an article for the Melbourne *Herald* in May 1928 about the total destruction of Corinth in an earthquake; now she was actually living through a similar catastrophe.

The young soldier put on a surgical mask, threaded needles with catgut, passed Joice instruments as she needed them and disinfected the instruments between patients as Joice attended to the wounds of those who had been injured. There was no anaesthetic in the crates, but there was some morphine. Joice told the medical orderly to give those in the greatest pain shots of morphine. At times their agony was so intense that she had to instruct two soldiers to hold down patients who struggled and screamed as she operated. The work was harrowing and she had to steel herself to continue. She would have given anything to have had a trained anaesthetist with equipment.

Almost every emergency had been catered for in the Admiral's gift. There were tourniquets by the dozen, surgical needles and cat-gut, gauze bandages, dressings, splints, heart stimulants, morphine—everything she needed. She could not help wondering whether the Admiral and his surgeon been blessed with second sight.[2]

As the hours passed more and more of the injured and dead were pulled from under the rubble—the piles of corpses mounted higher. Joice continued to work under the blazing sun. She drew upon memories of Uncle Harry Ryan, operating on their dining-room table in Gippsland and the knowledge she had acquired working as a *doktorika* with Sister Hetty in Poland. The task before her would have daunted most surgeons. However, Joice's excellent memory for the diagrams in Uncle Harry's surgical textbook and her steady hand stood her in good stead. She snipped, stitched and pulled together flesh that hung in strips. Some of the wounds were so terrible she knew she could not deal with them without proper facilities. But she was determined to save as many lives as possible. After being operated on the patients had to lie on the shadeless beach under the pitiless sun. The stench of unwashed bodies, faeces and urine and the sickly-sweet reek of death increased as the sun rose to its zenith.

Almost numb with fatigue, Joice continued to staunch bleeding wounds and stitch and bandage shredded flesh, driven on by her surging adrenaline and a strong sense of duty. As the blazing hot day wore on, her eyelids felt leaden and she longed to sleep. Her mouth was parched, her tongue swollen with thirst. She was given the last trickle of fresh water available, from an urn that had somehow remained intact. Like Ouranoupolis, Ierissos lacked piped water, and all the wells had disappeared under piles of rubble. Under the scorching midday heat her aching back was a mass of blisters. All she could do was concentrate on her patients without considering her own acute discomfort and thirst. For months afterwards she relived the horror of the scene in vivid nightmares: the screams of the wounded and the dying, the lack of shade, the blistering sun and the rigid corpses ejected from their graves with each new earth tremor.

Later she wrote: 'I did what I could, where I could. However, no doctor could have saved the poor woman with a broken back and broken legs who nursed her baby till she died. Ghastly triangles of flesh hung from heads to shoulders and had to be patched back into shape. There were cut arteries, broken legs, back wounds, stomach wounds . . . I was struck by the courage of the Greek people . . . There was no confusion or fuss. Each person took their turn. Those who were able helped the patients by brushing away flies.'[3]

One of the rescue teams found an undamaged bucket and Sydney instructed their leader to take it down to Joice on the beach. She told the medical orderly to fetch sea water to wet the clothing of the wounded so that they would dehydrate to a lesser extent. Periodically both Joice and the young orderly walked into the sea fully clothed to cool down. Their throats were parched and drinking sea water was tempting, but they both knew its dreadful consequences.

After operating for almost eight hours with only a short rest, the medical supplies finally ran out . . . just as the long line of wounded men, women and children came to an end. Totally exhausted, Joice looked down and saw, in the bottom of the fifth crate, one last finger-guard. She was so tired she gazed at it in a stupor. Her tongue stuck to her lips, making it hard to speak but finally she croaked: 'It must be here for a reason.' The young soldier who had had been assisting her held out his hand. His middle finger was badly cut. She disinfected the wound and put the finger-guard on it.

The Lochs feared that no tents or doctors would be able to reach Ierissos because of the lack of a sealed road. Joice realised that by the following day many of those she had operated on would be dead if they were left exposed to the sun. She prayed for a miracle but feared they had already used up all their luck. What was it the naval surgeon had said? Something about Providence being overloaded.

As the sun sank and darkness blanketed the scene Sydney came down to the beach. He looked completely exhausted and said that in the warm darkness it was impossible to continue the search for survivors under the rubble.

During the night, the moans and cries of the wounded men, women and children lying on the beach continued. Joice felt desperate, helpless. There was no more morphine to mask their pain. She did the rounds of the injured, offering words of comfort and reassurance. She dreaded their second day without drinking water; many would surely die.

Suddenly the night sky was criss-crossed by the brilliant white glare of searchlights. Another miracle *had* come to pass. The Admiral and his fleet had returned.

The British Fleet's tenders landed close to them with tanks of fresh water, freshly-baked bread and hospital tents. The surgeon came ashore in a larger boat bringing with him a small field operating theatre. He was horrified by the scene before him and dumbfounded by what had been achieved under such terrible conditions. He took one look at Joice and insisted that the first thing he would do was treat her badly blistered back. Then, worried that she would collapse with fatigue, he made her lie down and rest and insisted she must leave everything to his medical team. At this, Joice wept with relief.

The Admiral congratulated Sydney for his heroic efforts. Apparently one of the fleet's captains had heard an S.O.S. call from the Greek Army over his ship's radio. The Admiral's powerful radios had contacted Thessaloniki and appealed for help. More rescue agencies would be arriving.

Towards dawn a destroyer flying the Greek flag steamed in, carrying the Governor-General of Macedonia, his entourage and food, tanks of fresh water and more medical supplies and tents. Most of the wounded would now be saved. More and more ships arrived, carrying medical orderlies, supplies, tents and beds for the wounded, this time sent by the Greek Red Cross. It seemed the news of the earthquake had spread to Thessaloniki and Athens—yet Ouranoupolis, 'the village at the end of the world', lacking radio contact, had heard nothing since the messenger from Ierissos had screamed out his dreadful news the previous night.

Eventually over one thousand wounded men, women and children would be saved and the name of Kyria Loch would be famous throughout Greece.

The surgeon was worried that Joice needed more rest. The Admiral ordered a warship to take the Lochs, the four valiant rowers and their boat back to Ouranoupolis. Aboard ship they were given cabins where at last they were all able to catch up on a few hours of much-needed sleep.

Back in Ouranoupolis Joice typed up an official report suggesting that the Quakers provide them with funds to earthquake-proof all the remaining cottages. Wealthy Quaker industrialists and humanitarians like the Cadburys, the Frys and the Rowntrees sent money for damaged walls to be shored up with timber. One room in every replacement cottage was also given additional timber bracing. The same measures were applied to Ierissos.

The Governor of Macedonia had approached the Government in Athens about the restoration of the tower of Prosforion. As the Lochs were now national heroes and the tower of historical significance, it was agreed that some essential work had to take place. During the bitterly cold winter of 1933, while restorations to earthquake damage began on the medieval tower, the Lochs rented the only stone house in the village which had somehow survived the earthquake. From here, with the help of Madame Sophia and Fani Kollinbas, they ran a free soup kitchen for the villagers. Gradually the villagers of Ouranoupolis returned to their homes. Ouranoupolis was almost back to normal within a year, but the rebuilding of Ierissos took three years. During all this time, its inhabitants lived in tents supplied by the Red Cross and the Greek Army.

An official thanksgiving ceremony was held to celebrate the restoration of Ierissos, to which the Lochs were invited as guests of honour. They found all the new houses bright with paper streamers and flowers and everyone dressed in festive finery. The *retsina, ouzo* and *tsipouro* flowed freely. To the accompaniment of pipes and drums young girls wearing bright scarves over their long dark hair, striped bodices and full skirts whirled around in traditional dances. Then, after much clapping of hands, men with eyes dark as sloes and huge mustachios stepped forward, clasped each other around the waist and performed their time-honoured steps.

Finally the Mayor or Village President made a speech thanking all those who had taken part in the earthquake rescue and the reconstruction of the village. He presented the Lochs with an illuminated scroll which recorded the fact that they were awarded the Freedom of Ierissos. Joice wore her sober grey Quaker uniform, brightened by a row of medals on red and blue silk ribbons awarded by the Governments of Poland and Greece.

By now, Kyria Loch, was revered all over Macedonia and other areas of northern Greece as 'The heroine of Halkidiki'. For the part she had played in saving the earthquake victims, she had received a second Greek Order of the Phoenix.

That same year, she was invited to London to an investiture at Buckingham Palace to receive the Medal of the British Empire (MBE) from King George V. It was typical of Joice's unselfishness and modesty about her own achievements that, instead of spending money on her fare to England and accommodation in London, she should forgo the experience and contribute the money she would have spent to help fund a new village hall and schoolhouse for Ouranoupolis. The MBE award for Mrs Joice Loch, on its red-and-white ribbon, was sent to Athens in the Diplomatic Bag. At that time medals were rarely awarded to women. Poland and Greece had given Joice Loch some of their highest awards deemed suitable for foreigners. Joice NanKivell Loch's extraordinary selflessness and humanitarian endeavours ensured her a British award at the lower end of the scale; the MBE was later described as 'the secretary's medal' because so many women received it. Once again Joice went to an investiture in the British Embassy in Athens, wearing her Quaker uniform decorated with its row of medals from other nations. The Ambassador, amazed to see how many medals she had been awarded, remarked with evident surprise: 'It's unusual for a *woman* to get *one* medal, let alone *so many*.'

The Lochs dreamed of the day when Ouranoupolis would have its own doctor provided by the Greek Government, as Ierissos now had. They also hoped the Government would fund a sealed road instead of the mule track connecting Ouranoupolis to Arnea, and seal the road from Arnea to Thessaloniki. But in the 1930s depression and recession had struck even the wealthiest of countries; previously generous American and Australian church groups and private patrons had to cut back on their giving. Raising money for a road and a doctor proved impossible. Joice remained undaunted. She and Sydney would continue to work towards these goals for 'their' village.

Fortunately the devastation caused by the earthquake had only a minor impact on the rug-weaving industry of Ouranoupolis. The demand for

Pirgos Rugs was greater than ever and production was soon in full swing again. Joice's involvement remained undiminished. But by now her workload in management, marketing and publicity had become so heavy that she was contemplating handing over most of the responsibility of running the industry to the other women.

In 1938 the Lochs' work in founding, running and publicising Pirgos Rugs and providing unpaid medical assistance to Ouranoupolis was officially recognised and they were each awarded another medal from the King of the Hellenes. Joice received the Order of the Golden Fleece. At the investiture held by King Paul and Queen Frederika, the Queen told Joice that by founding Pirgos Rugs, running free clinics, providing vaccines against malaria and improving the villagers' livestock, she and her husband had saved or altered for the better the lives of hundreds of Greek men, women and children. (Later, after the end of World War 2, Sydney would receive the Order of the Redeeemer [First Class], and Joice, for 'outstanding humanitarian efforts' the Order of Beneficence, established by the King in 1948 as an award to Greek and foreign women 'for benefits to Greek society'.)

In 1939 Joice finally made the decision to hand over the responsibility for running Pirgos Rugs to the village women. She would only act as consultant when asked. This would give her more time for attending to the villagers' medical needs and she hoped it would build the self-esteem of the village women, helping to break the pattern of complete subordination to their husbands. She announced her decision at a meeting of the assembled workers, telling them that she would remain on the board and continue to help with marketing and publicity, but from now on Pirgos Rugs was their cooperative: they must run it themselves. Before she stepped down she arranged a loan from the Agricultural Bank to buy more looms and wool. The Laiki Techni in Thessaloniki continued to act as selling agents, paying the women in advance for orders they obtained.

From now on the rug weaving changed many women's lives in the village to an even greater extent. They were now responsible for earning an income entirely by their own efforts and were able to express opinions in public at their board meetings. Some even dared to remove their head-scarves and felt free to leave their houses when they wished, without asking their husbands' permission. They no longer remained silent in the presence of their men-folk. (After World War 2, the boldest—and the youngest—greatly daring in breaking with centuries of tradition, replaced their long black skirts for shorts like those Joice wore, when they dyed the raw wool at the vats.)[4]

EARTHQUAKE

At long last Joice had more time for relaxation, reading and writing. Each summer, friends from various parts of Europe and Australia arrived as guests. Other visitors included friends from the Farm School and the British Legation. Sometimes visiting yachtsmen would arrive unexpectedly and always be invited to one of Madame Sophia Topolski's delicious meals. They ate around the long refectory table in the tower dining room with its windows overlooking the sea. The whitewashed walls were now broken by the brilliant blues, greens and soft pinks of the intricate Pirgos rugs.

This was the happiest and most fulfilling period of Joice's life; it seemed as though the good times would never end.

Joice's close friend Estelle (now Mrs Slater) arrived from Melbourne to stay at the tower and as always Joice was overjoyed to see her childhood friend again. Estelle and her husband, enthusiastic about the rugs and the aims of the cooperative, helped by promoting Pirgos Rugs in Melbourne. Gradually the fame of Pirgos rugs spread and they were sought out by buyers in London, Europe and Australia.

Sydney continued to teach part-time at the Farm School, initiating several more imaginative aid schemes sponsored by the Society of Friends Relief services. One scheme provided for the import of pedigree goats and pigs to Ouranoupolis and other refugee villages on the neighbouring peninsulas of Sithonia and Kassandra.

Without the dedicated work of the Lochs there would be no pretty little holiday resort at Ouranoupolis today. The only memorial to the refugee settlement could well have been a row of wooden crosses embedded in the iron-hard soil.

For the first decade of the village's existence, not one single inhabitant other than the Lochs possessed a radio. Weddings and church processions held on feast days and religious holidays were the only form of public entertainment. Every four months the women would carry their icons around the village and their priest would walk before them swinging his silver incense burner inside each cottage to purify it and expurgate evil spirits.

Weddings provided the best free entertainment of all. When the parents of the bride were not too poor, the celebrations could last as long as three days. If the bride was marrying a man from another village a cord was placed at the entrance to the village; symbolically the bridegroom had to cut the cord in front of all the villagers before he and his family could enter Ouranoupolis.

There was an age-old pattern of betrothal and marriage. First a suitable dowry was negotiated between both sets of parents, using the services of Paraskevoula as matchmaker. Then, before the wedding, everyone was invited to admire the bride's dowry of gold coins, embroidered linen and bed-roll covers. Another essential item was a hand-embroidered baby sling or *trokni*, which enabled young mothers to carry their babies on their backs. Refreshments were served and friends of the bride threw rice on the bedroll, symbolising luck and fertility.

Early on a Sunday morning, unmarried girls went to the bride's house to dress her and accompany her to the church. At the reception that followed the marriage ceremony they presented the bride with a spoonful of jam, a loaf of bread and a jug of wine, symbols of prosperity. A huge feast was provided by the bride's family. Speeches were made and toasts drunk to the health of the bride and groom and to the parents of both families, and plates were smashed according to custom.

Group weddings came about after the dramatic events of another day when the villagers, tired of waiting for the Government to fulfil its promises, again took the law into their own hands and invaded the last of the Greek fertile land owned by Athos. The Greek Government had taken over all the monastic property on Greek land lying beyond the wall that divided it from Athos, except for the large and fertile farm that belonged to the Serbian-endowed monastery of Chilandari. Negotiations had been proceeding for a decade but nothing had happened.

One morning the Lochs looked out of the tower and saw men armed with spades and axes advancing down the road. They followed the marchers, who broke into the farm that still belonged to Chilandari, shouting to the seven monks who worked it: 'Get out! This is our land now!' And they proceeded to set about them with spades and sticks until the terrified monks fled back to their monastery. The Abbot of Chilandari appealed to the Yugoslav consul in Thessaloniki, who represented the Serbs. The Serbian consul came out to Ouranoupolis, intending to order the land to be given back to Chilindari. Fortunately, he was a good friend of the Farm School, where he had previously met the Lochs. They invited the consul to have coffee with them in the tower and explained the promise made to the villagers that they would given the land which belonged to Greece.

In due course that fertile land with its magnificent grove of olive trees became the property of Ouranoupolis by law. It was subdivided into plots and assigned to individual householders. Once again, possession of good farmland, olive trees and a crushing mill meant dowries for many girls and young men and led to a rash of betrothals.

At the mass wedding that followed the repossession of the lands of Chilindar, Elena, daughter of the widow who ran the [*kafenion*]— described by Joice as 'beautiful as Helen of Troy' with her long-lashed dark eyes and golden skin, led a line of girls in a wild and ancient dance. Accompanied by musicians on pipes and drums, the guests sang the *rembetika*, the sad haunting songs of dispossession from their villages in Turkey or Asia Minor. Married women formed a circle and danced the leaping *liarigovnes* dance, wearing white blouses, brightly embroidered waistcoats and necklaces of coins which tinkled as they moved and red or blue silk kerchiefs on their heads. Then the young men performed 'the threshing dance' in memory of Greeks slaughtered by the Turks. Wearing black waistcoats ornamented with coins and black breeches and holding their hands high above their heads they whirled and twirled before passing beneath the crossed arms of two male dancers, who made chopping movements to imitate the knives of Turkish executioners.

This was by far the largest wedding ever held in the village; it lasted for three days. Everyone rejoiced: the days of poverty, hunger and despair were forgotten. Hopes for a bright future with olive groves, new fields and oil mills were on everyone's lips. None of the villagers could have realised that the coming conflict in Europe would mean the ruin of all their high hopes and plans.

23 THE RAPE OF POLAND

As the autumn of 1939 approached, the Lochs listened each day to the BBC's Foreign Service broadcasts, fearing a German invasion of Poland. They heard with distress and foreboding that Hitler had invaded Czechoslovakia and increased his demands for *lebensraum* in the east, while the British Prime Minister, Neville Chamberlain, followed his policy of appeasement and pleaded for 'peace in our time'.

Hitler and Stalin appeared diametrically opposed. No one was aware that Russia and Germany had made a secret pact to carve up Poland. The British and French Governments gave Poland worthless guarantees which they could not honour while Hitler and his generals plotted to remove that country from the map of Europe. Poland's hero Marshal Pilsudski, the man who had awarded the Lochs their medals, was dead. Polish friends like Pani Bianki and Melchior Wankowicz wrote complaining that his successor lacked his strong-minded and experienced direction of national affairs.

On 23 August 1939, Hitler and Stalin signed a treaty of mutual support with secret clauses detailing which Polish territories each of them would annex. From the moment the ink was dry on the paper, the Polish Republic with its outdated army and military equipment was doomed. From Warsaw, Melchior Wankowicz wrote that in a bid to defend Poland's borders, thousands of middle-class and professional men had enlisted as reserve officers. They were told they would be issued with guns to repel the forces of Nazi Germany should Hitler attempt to invade. Meanwhile, Britain's Prime Minister implored the Polish Government *not* to call up those thousands of reserve officers and soldiers.[1]

In August 1939 Melchior Wankowicz wrote again, describing how 'for months every able-bodied Pole has waited for a call-up notice, believing that once the harvest is in, the Germans will attack. Our problem is that we lack guns'.[2]

On 1 September German tanks invaded the northern borders of Poland through East Prussia and entered from the south-west through Slovakia. Some 30,000 men in the Polish Army reserve, who still had not received call-up papers, made unsuccessful attempts to obtain guns. 'As fast as they reached what they understood was a recruiting centre, they found the centre had removed itself elsewhere,' Melchior wrote in the last letter the Lochs would receive from him for years.[3]

Early in September, the Lochs listened as the BBC announced that Britain and France had declared war against Germany. In spite of their guarantees of support, neither Britain nor France had sent the Poles the planes, guns and ammunition they had requested.

Deserted by those who claimed to be their Allies, the regular Polish Army fought like lions using outdated equipment. They held out against Hitler's overwhelming tank force, but the clear September weather proved ideal for Germany's Luftwaffe. The Germans bombed Poland's airports and destroyed her limited fleet of planes. Warsaw, left defenceless, was bombed until the historic city was virtually a heap of rubble. The entire Polish Parliament or *Sejim* fled to neutral Rumania, taking with them Poland's reserves of gold bullion.

On 17 September, Stalin's troops entered eastern Poland planning to meet up with the Germans at Brest-Litovsk. Any reserve officers they found were taken prisoner and shipped to Russia where they planned to send as many Poles as possible, repeating the forcible evacuation of eastern Poland begun by the Tsarist forces in World War I and continued by Lenin during the Soviet-Polish war. Realising that Poland was defeated, hundreds of thousands of Polish families and the widows of regular soldiers or reserve officers of the Polish Army climbed into cars or trucks and drove to neutral Rumania or to Hungary in a mass exodus.

Germany was Rumania's most important trading partner, the largest consumer of Rumanian corn and oil. Fearing a German invasion, King Carol II of Rumania had recently issued orders that all male Polish refugees in his country were to be interned, so that Hitler would not accuse him of harbouring a huge fighting force which could be used to attack Germany.[4] Members of the Polish Parliament, with the exception of the Polish Cabinet, which had fled to Angers, in northern France, drove to Rumania expecting to be received as honoured guests.

Instead they found themselves confined in two huge internment camps, alongside those reserve officers who had been unable to secure guns to fight their enemies. King Carol refused to allow the exiled members of Parliament to place their gold in Rumania's banks, directing that it must be sent to Swiss banks instead.[5] The King hoped to use Rumanian oil and wheat as bargaining counters with Hitler; he deluded himself that he could remain friends with both Germany and Britain, and was convinced that as long as he kept all Polish men of fighting age in the internment camps, Rumania would not be drawn into war with Hitler.[6]

The Lochs, deeply worried about the fate of the interned Poles, wrote to Friends War Relief in London volunteering to help. They were told that as soon as the Secretary, Roger Wilson, returned from an inspection tour of Bucharest they would be advised in what capacity their services could be used.[7]

Stalin's plan to remove Poland from the map included forcible evacuation of its ethnic population on a vast scale. The Russians killed or shipped to Siberia all educated Poles who might present a threat to Stalin's Communist regime. The Germans followed the same plan in Western Poland, starving Jews to death in their ghettos and shipping able-bodied Poles to German labour camps where they were used as slave labour.

Some 20,000 Polish reserve officers, soldiers and priests taken prisoner by the Russians were sent to three huge prisoner-of-war camps at Smolensk. Their wives and children interned in Rumania waited for news of them, never dreaming that every one of them would soon be shot on Stalin's orders in the woods of Katyn—a silent massacre that would not be revealed for years.[8]

Meanwhile, from Northern France the Polish politician and military leader General Sikorski, with the help of those members of the cabinet who had escaped, organised the formation of the Free Polish Army.[9] The Polish soldiers interned in Rumania were desperate to leave their camps and join General Sikorski's new Polish Army. Those without money pawned their wrist-watches to pay for 'black market' visas to leave Rumania and escape through neutral countries to France. Those who had money bribed corrupt Rumanian officials into granting them exit visas.

As the weather turned colder and Christmas approached, the Lochs went to stay with Charlie and Anne House at the American Farm School. They were on the Farm School campus when they received the telegram appointing Sydney Head of a new Friends Relief Mission to Polish civilians in Rumania.[10] Joice was to be responsible for delivering humanitarian aid to Polish women and children. The British Consul at Thessaloniki would provide them with rail tickets to Bucharest and they would be met on arrival by a representative of the British Legation. They were to work in close contact with the Legation in Bucharest.

The Lochs were now in their early fifties. 'Kindness to others is what counts' was their motto. Now was the time to show it.

Greece remained neutral during the Polish conflict. Emotionally she had links to Britain but she exported the bulk of her tobacco and fruit to Germany. Most people thought that Hitler would see no advantage in invading a desperately poor country where there was no oil or manufacturing industry.

The Lochs said goodbye to the House family and returned to Ouranoupolis to pack and farewell their friends. 'We'll be back soon,' they said. 'Don't worry about us.' Like most of the Allies at the beginning of World War 2, they thought Hitler would be defeated within a year or eighteen months. They filled their suitcases with things they considered would come in handy, their choices indicative of their personalities.

Joice took her portable typewriter, her old Quaker uniform, warm underwear, pyjamas, a favourite grey lambs-wool sweater which she always found useful because it had pockets, some skirts, the fur coat and hat she had bought in Poland decades earlier, a couple of favourite photos, and her well-thumbed copy of *The Complete Companion to Medicine*. At the last moment she picked up from her desk the little Australian flag her mother had given her and which she had brought with her from Melbourne so long ago and placed that in her suitcase as well. It symbolised a link with the country of her birth and the strong, enduring bond between herself and her mother.

Sydney, who never bothered about clothes, took a battered Harris tweed overcoat which had belonged to his grandfather, his favourite brown walking shoes, a large umbrella, a Swiss Army knife, a grey Homburg hat, two pairs of trousers and a Polish-English dictionary. At Joice's insistence he packed more shirts and underwear.

Without a thought for their own safety the Lochs left their home in the tower, their possessions, their precious writers' notebooks and manuscripts and their personal collection of Pirgos rugs. Joyce entrusted her beloved Angora cats to Madame Sophia Topolski, who would remain living in the tower with her brother, a Russian doctor who had fled from the Communists. He promised to continue the tower's policy of providing free medical service to the villagers. Madame Sophia was authorised to draw on the Lochs' bank account for expenses and for her salary.

'We'll write,' they told Madame Sophia and their many friends from the monasteries of Mount Athos. 'We'll be back within a year at most.'

At Thessaloniki railway station the Lochs were met by the British Consul, who gave them train tickets to Bucharest. As all the *couchettes* were booked they were forced to spend the night sitting up in a crowded compartment. At Sofia they changed trains for Bucharest.

After crossing the Bulgarian/Rumanian border, they traversed the Carpathian mountains. The scenery was like something out of a folk-tale—snow-covered peaks descending to pine forests, vast crumbling castles, wooden houses with balconies and slanting roof beams like those on cuckoo clocks.

Below the snow line the scenery changed. Their train clattered past lush green valleys dotted by villages built around shingle-roofed churches with bronze onion domes, green with age. Joice knew that Rumania was a country of devout Orthodox peasants. As they neared their destination, they passed by vast cornfields and miles of orchards and market gardens.

At Bucharest a very tall young man with a lock of blond hair falling over his forehead stood beside a uniformed chauffeur who held a placard bearing their names. The tall young man introduced himself as Nigel Fox-Something-or-Other, the latter half of his surname drowned out by the whistle of a steam engine.

As they emerged from the station gypsies with outstretched hands crowded around them. *'Mi-e foame, foame!'* they shrilled, pointing at their mouths. *'Dâ-me ban.'*[11] The stench of unwashed bodies was overwhelming. With a skill born of practice, Nigel Fox-What's-it handed out small coins to the waiting hands, opened a rear door of the Legation's black limousine and ushered the Lochs inside, then took his seat in the front beside the chauffeur.

Ever since she had first set eyes on him, Joice thought that Nigel reminded her of someone she disliked. Now she remembered. It was Percy B, the wealthy Tasmanian who had pestered her to marry him all those years ago!

They drove off smoothly, scattering the gypsies who jumped out of their way. Looking out of the window, Joice saw shops laden with luxury goods, enticing restaurants and cafes and sleek, well-dressed citizens going about their business, ignoring the groups of shivering women and children begging at street corners.

'Rumania is supposed to be a wealthy oil-producing country—so why are there so many people begging?' Joice asked Nigel.

'It's a *nouveau riche* country with a huge national debt and Hitler as its main trading partner,' Nigel replied in a world-weary manner. 'The Rumanian Army pays its soldiers so little that some of their wives are reduced to begging. Stalin's demanding the return of parts of Russia, Bulgaria and Germany that Rumania was granted by the League of

Nations after World War 1. Russia's desperate for Bessarabia because it's got oil wells. She could invade and take them by force.'

'Can the Rumanian Army stop her?'

'Not a chance. Most Legation wives have been sent home already in case of invasion. The Foreign Office are working on escape plans for us but take no responsibility for the Polish internees or for volunteer workers like yourselves. You'll have to find your own way out if we are invaded.'

Nigel turned to Joice, perhaps to assess whether she was up to the job she had been sent to carry out. 'Mrs Loch, you're a colonial, I believe,' he drawled in his upper-crust accent, somehow indicating a superiority to mere 'colonials' which made Joice's blood boil. He went on: 'Do you speak Polish or any other foreign language? Have you any knowledge of Rumanian or Polish culture? I read Eastern European languages at Oxford, and I find that Latin is the only language that helps with Rumanian. Did you study Latin in Orstraylia?'

I won't be patronised by some toffee-nosed Englishman half my age, Joice vowed to herself. She told him firmly: 'We volunteered for this job because we've worked with Poles before. We both speak some Polish as well as Greek. I'll manage Rumanian—it's a Latin language, so it should be easy to learn.' She was determined not to be patronised by this arrogant young man. In fact, like most Australians of her period Joice *did* have difficulty with foreign languages, but she wasn't going to tell Nigel this. She told herself she must not lose her temper with him; they had to establish a reasonable working relationship for the sake of the Polish refugees. But in order to achieve this, she must dent Nigel's innate sense of superiority to 'colonials' or he would be impossible to work with.

'We're not complete hicks in Australia, you know,' she said, attempting to speak lightly. 'We do know which knife and fork to use and I studied ancient Greek and Latin at university. The Classics Department at Melbourne is highly regarded by scholars everywhere.' Nigel was used to dealing with diplomats' wives who gave dinner parties and lived in the shadow of their husbands. He was unaccustomed to women who stood up for themselves. He glared at Joice but said nothing.

'You were telling us about King Carol,' Sydney interjected, trying to ease the situation.

Nigel explained that the King held divided loyalties, but was generally considered pro-British: his mother was British, and neither he nor his late father, the German-born Prince Karl of Hohenzollern, spoke Rumanian as well as they spoke German and English. He had a Jewish mistress, Magda Lupescu, and had banned the military wing of the powerful and anti-Semitic Rumanian Fascist Party, the Iron Guard.

When the Iron Guard murdered one of his Prime Ministers, the King had their leader, Captain Codreanu, arrested.

'I read that Codreanu was murdered,' Sydney said.

Nigel shrugged and explained that officially Codreanu had been shot 'escaping from jail'. 'But everyone knows the soldiers were acting on the King's orders,' he said. 'Codreanu's second-in-command, Hora Simia, fled to Germany where he's running an internment camp for Jews and political prisoners. If the Iron Guard came to power they would murder all the Jews, possibly the Poles as well, as enemies of Germany.'

The Embassy limousine crossed the Calea Viktorei with its elegant shops and pavement cafes, entered Episkopi Street, then turned off into an enormous square. Nigel pointed out the new Royal Palace, guarded by soldiers in scarlet uniforms covered in gold braid. Joice thought they looked like musical comedy soldiers; they certainly didn't inspire confidence.

On the opposite corner of the square was another huge building with an orange neon sign flashing the message *Athenée Palace Hotel*. From a third-floor balcony the French flag and the Union Jack hung alongside the Rumanian flag, directly above the hotel's imposing entrance.

They drove to the far side of the square and passed under a wide archway into a cobbled courtyard, stopping beside the modest entrance to a much smaller hostelry. Nigel explained their hotel had once been a coaching inn, which was why its main entrance was at the rear.

Sydney got out and helped the Legation's chauffeur to remove their luggage from the boot while Nigel uncoiled his long legs and stepped onto the cobbles. 'Good spot, this, right in the centre of everything. The English Bar at the Athenée Palace just across the square is where all the British journalists and diplomats gather to get the latest news.— I'll just check everything's in order,' he added, and disappeared inside the hotel.

'Nigel went to Eton, which explains a lot,' Sydney murmured, who had recognised Nigel's Old Etonian tie.

Joice frowned. 'Who cares? He's a terrible snob. I don't happen to think that where you went to school matters one bit,' she retorted.

Nigel reappeared. Their room was ready. The hotel's owner had agreed to send the account to the British Legation for settlement. And two other Quaker volunteers from London, both young women, had just arrived. He looked at Joice. 'The Polish wives and widows are going to need a lot of help. Do you think you'll be able to cope?'

Joice barely managed to restrain her exasperation at his patronising tone. 'Well, back in 1922 I helped hundreds of Polish refugees using an old railway carriage as an office and living on black bread and tea for weeks. Living in a nice hotel like this should make the task a great deal easier,' she replied evenly, walking past Nigel to shake the outstretched hand of the hotel's owner.

Doamna Elena Popescu was an attractive dark-haired woman in her fifties. Her plump fingers were laden with gold and diamond rings. She told the Lochs that her husband had died five years ago and she now ran their small hotel single-handed.

'You can have breakfast each day in your room or downstairs, from seven to ten o'clock,' she told them in heavily accented English.

Before Nigel left he said he would set up a meeting with the British press for the Lochs to explain what aid measures Friends War Relief would be delivering to the interned Poles and their families. 'No need to be alarmed—Press contacts are vital for charities,' he told them.

'We know,' said Joice crisply. 'Both of us happen to be accredited journalists.'

Nigel looked crestfallen. Obviously he hadn't been made aware of that fact.

Sydney, diplomatic as ever, thanked Nigel for meeting them, and they agreed to meet for a pre-dinner drink in the English Bar at the Athenée Palace the following day. Nigel, his job done, departed.

Doamna Popescu took them up a huge polished wood staircase that suggested beeswax and much elbow grease. On the first floor they walked down a corridor decorated with deer heads and antlers. She ushered them into a bedroom which smelt of freshly laundered linen. Long windows overlooked the Royal Palace. Joice's first impression was one of shining cleanliness. In the far corner gleamed a huge white-tiled stove and on the double bed lay a plump white feather-filled quilt that resembled a large meringue.

By now Joice felt exhausted. Doamna Popescu, realising the Lochs had had a tiring journey, offered to have some chicken soup brought to their room. Gratefully they accepted, too tired to go out for a meal. Ten minutes later she returned with two bowls of delicious soup and slices of rye bread. They drank the soup, unpacked their possessions, had hot baths and went to bed.

Next morning they woke to find the sun streaming through their shutters; in spite of Nigel's grim prediction of a German or Russian invasion, Joice felt ready for anything.

Downstairs, Doamna Popescu served small porcelain jugs of foaming hot chocolate and crisp rolls with butter and jam in the little breakfast room. She advised them to take a *trasura* or horse-drawn cab to the Quaker Relief Centre.

When they arrived at the small house rented by the Quakers they were welcomed by Dermod O'Donnell from London headquarters, who had set up the Mission Centre. Joice found that she had been assigned an office where she and the two new volunteers would interview the Polish wives and widows and distribute the winter clothing sent out in bales from London. Joice hoped they would also be able to organise fund-raising schemes to supplement the meagre living allowance paid to Polish women and children by the British Government.

The waiting room was filled with sad-eyed women, many of them accompanied by young children. Joice soon realised that those whose husbands had been taken away as prisoners by the Russians or the Germans were the most deeply distressed. The women whose husbands had been interned were more fortunate; they were able to visit them behind the barbed wire of the Rumanian camps. Most of the internees were planning to enlist with the British or Free Polish Armies as soon as they could obtain their exit visas. Dermod O'Donnell was about to set up an advisory service in one of the internment camps.[12] That night over dinner the Lochs discussed the huge changes in conditions for volunteers since they had last worked for Friends War Victims Relief. Quaker volunteers no longer addressed each other as 'thee' and 'thou', and the new breed of female volunteers were smartly dressed and gave the impression of being quite worldly young women. Married volunteers were no longer housed in single-sex dormitories but in comfortable hotels. And Dermod O'Donnell had informed them that instead of living on the tinned rations of former days, they would receive a meals allowance so that they could eat out in restaurants.

'Thank God, no more tinned sardines and watery Bovril,' Joice said thankfully.

Unlike Joice, whose moth-eaten fur coat had been bought in a flea-market in Warsaw, the new female relief workers wore ankle-length coats of fox and mink. They gave the Lochs the impression that relief work was more a travel opportunity than a vocation.

Nigel and other members of the British Legation were enrolling as many Polish men as possible in the British Army or the Royal Air Force. Able-bodied men, including boys as young as sixteen, were given three alternatives. The first was to remain in the internment camp, which carried the risk of being shot or sent to a slave labour camps should the Russians or Germans invade. Their second choice was to bribe corrupt Rumanian officials to give them exit visas; the Legation would then provide rail tickets via Italy to France so that they could join the British or Free Polish Army forces. (At this juncture Mussolini had not yet joined forces with Hitler.) The third choice was to apply legally to the Polish Government for an exit visa that could take months to arrive. For the Polish women, the only option for those without money (the vast majority) was to stay in Rumania. No one, apart from the Quakers, cared enough to take responsibility for their welfare.

Unfortunately for the Polish internees, Rumanian Government officials were beginning to realise they could make big money out of issuing exit visas to Poles and Jews keen to leave the country. The Ministry deliberately delayed the issue of exit visas to enable senior bureaucrats to sell 'instant' visas at inflated prices. A legal exit visa cost one thousand *lei* a head, a black market visa six times this amount. The corrupt officials had even established a small office in the centre of Bucharest to sell these 'black market' visas.[13] Everything connected with the Rumanian Public Service, it seemed, worked by bribery. 'Can't the women escape and get free board and lodging by joining the armed forces?' Joice asked at their meeting the next night with Nigel and the Legation's Press Attaché´ in the English bar of the Palace Athenée.

'Not a hope,' Nigel answered curtly. In his eyes Polish women rated far lower than men. He was not interested in enlisting them in the WAAFS or the WRENS.

Joice was prepared to argue with Nigel but soon realised that most of the women, all devout Catholics, had large families. For them enlisting simply wasn't an option. She was haunted by the plight of these unfortunate wives of Reserve and career Army officers, many of whom had received no news of their missing husbands since the Russians had taken them prisoner. Some feared their husbands had been killed. Others believed they would manage to escape, and lived in hope of a speedy reunion and a return to their country once Britain and France had defeated Hitler and Stalin.

The wealthier Poles had lost jobs, status, beautiful homes, servants, orchards and livestock. All the refugees spoke wistfully of their past lives and of returning to their own homes. The few Jews among them were more realistic: they accepted the fact that they would probably never be able to return and were keen to take any form of work Joice could find. Many dreamed of going to Palestine to take part in the formation of the proposed new Jewish state of Israel. Joice could see that one of her many tasks would be to find schooling and decent accommodation for a group of Jewish orphans whose parents had been killed escaping from Poland.

Joice's first job was to find the Polish women and children and the Jewish orphans suitable accommodation in private homes, as they could not be housed in the Army camps. She also tried to get hold of teachers and textbooks for the children. The younger volunteers doled out second-hand clothing and bedding while Joice tried to counsel the women and offer financial support out of their limited budget. A Jewish clothing manufacturer in Britain kindly sent out bales of new shirts and underpants which were distributed to the men and followed this donation with bales of children's clothes. Joice contacted retired English governesses and set up English language classes for the children. It transpired that many of the more educated Polish women spoke excellent French and German and had little difficulty learning English.

At British Legation functions the Lochs met R.D. Smith, Lecturer in English Literature, who had recently married Olivia Manning, the Legation's Assistant Press Officer and general factotum. She was also hoping to write a book about her time in Bucharest. Olivia Manning Smith was one of the few British wives who insisted on remaining in Bucharest; the rest had been sent home during a previous invasion scare. Her husband was a vague but amiable academic, employed by the British Council as a Lecturer in English literature. Joice found Olivia Manning cool, distant and reserved. Unknown to the pair of them, they had much in common. They had both endured difficult childhoods, both worked as Press Officers and written books about the troubles in Ireland, although Manning's Irish novel was still unpublished. Her huge literary success would come twenty years later, with her series of novels, *The Balkan Trilogy*, which convey a vivid impression of Bucharest awaiting invasion. Her lecturer husband, R.D. Smith, was the model for the unforgettable Guy Pringle, who, as the Germans invade, puts on a performance of *Troilus and Cressida*.[14] In real life R.D. Smith was putting on a series of evening lectures on *Great English Novelists*. He showed little interest in Joice's plan to set up

English language classes for interned Polish refugees and did not provide her with any assistance.

On their first visit to the largest of the internment camps, Joice and Sydney found themselves gathered into bear-like hugs by men who had been youths with them in Poland twenty years before. Using money from Friends War Relief the Lochs brought wireless sets and powerful loudspeakers to the camps, believing that Polish language broadcasts would help to keep the prisoners' morale high.

'Pani Lok, Pani Lok, you've come to help us,' a middle-aged Polish soldier cried, tears of joy streaming down his face at seeing the Lochs again.[15] By now thousands of Polish men of fighting age had enlisted in the Free Polish or British Armies and departed. Most of the remaining internees were older men, who had formed self-help groups to assist their less educated compatriots to learn English. Some earned a little money from keeping chickens and selling eggs. Sydney established a lorry driving course in the camps. So many of them had been professional men that such practical courses would be useful to them in either the Free Polish or the British Army. Furthermore the Lochs, always practical in their aid schemes, realised that these Polish refugees' academic qualifications might not be recognised should they have to work outside Poland.

All the younger Polish men were desperate to leave Rumania and fight Hitler. 'A bullet can only kill you once,' a tall blond-haired young man told Joice. 'If I stay here in the camp, thinking of my dead comrades and my sisters imprisoned in a German labour camp, or even worse, (probably he meant working as sexual slaves for German officers as part of the Nazi Aryan breeding programme) I die a little every day.'[16]

Some of the Polish soldiers and civilians were experienced skiers. They escaped from Rumania through what Joice termed 'The Green Frontier', a secret route that twisted and turned through the high mountain passes of the free countries of Europe. The mountains were fraught with danger to those using them as an escape route, but to many brave Poles, the Green Frontier would bring safety and a new life. Heavy snow storms now concealed the outposts which guarded Rumania's borders. Only plumes of smoke betrayed the positions of the armed guards.

The Lochs obtained skis, waterproof ski clothes and knapsacks which they filled with a compass, a map and high-energy snacks like chocolate and glucose tablets for those who wanted to slip away through the deep snow to neutral Yugoslavia or Italy. From Trieste and other ports the Poles caught ships that took them to British-run Persia, Palestine or Britain, where they enlisted to fight Poland's enemies. Naturally this type of aid had to be hidden from the top brass at Quaker Headquarters in London.

Joice's placed her mother's little Australian flag on her rickety old desk at the Friends Mission. On some days it was hidden by mountains of paperwork. Clerical assistance was becoming essential if she was to get through her heavy workload. She asked Father Ambrosius and another Polish priest to find her a suitably mature Polish woman to act as her assistant in return for a small salary and accommodation and meals in their hotel.

At Christmas the Mission held a party for as many of the Polish women and children as possible. Joice especially enjoyed the excellent choir provided by the women, who stood under the Christmas tree and sang hauntingly beautiful Polish Christmas carols. Where on earth would they all be next Christmas, she wondered.

24 A MEDAL FROM KING CAROL

Joice, now in her fifties (although she looked considerably younger), imagined the new assistant she had requested would be someone of her own age, possibly a widow. When Father Ambrosius told her he had found the very person for the job, she was surprised to discover this was a young woman of twenty-two—the Countess Lushya, sole survivor of one of Poland's oldest families.

Joice sighed. 'At twenty-two no one has enough experience to cope with the harrowing situations we have to deal with,' she told the priest. 'Please, Pani Loch,' he replied. 'Talk to her for half an hour and you'll understand why the Countess Lushya *is* the right person to help you. She is very well organised and has excellent contacts. She will raise large sums of money to help Polish people here.' He paused and added gravely, 'one thing I beg is that you don't mention her family'.

Joice looked at him inquiringly.

'The Countess lost her parents and her only brother when Poland was invaded, as well as her home and all its contents when Warsaw was bombed. She is alone in the world except for an aunt in America,' Father Ambrosius told her.

'What happened?'

'As they escaped from Poland a Nazi pilot flew low over their car and strafed them with bullets. Her father was killed instantly, her mother and brother died on that terrible journey. The Countess had to continue driving with them dying in the car until she crossed the Rumanian frontier. Since she came to Bucharest she has shown enormous strength and given what remained of her money to others.'

Lushya, petite and raven-haired, presented herself for an interview. She was disarmingly honest as she answered Joice's questions. No, she couldn't type fast, she only used two fingers but hoped to improve. What she could do was organise filing systems: she used to help her father handle some of his financial affairs and she was good at figures and book-keeping.

To Joice, who hated keeping the accounts she sent to Friends House in London each month, this was a real point in Lushya's favour. She explained that she needed someone to run the office side of things as she and Sydney would be busy setting up English-language, lorry-driving and plumbing courses, even a hat-making course, all aimed towards getting Polish men and women jobs in a foreign country.

In some ways the young Countess reminded Joice of Prince Tarnowsky, the amusing aristocrat who had acted as their interpreter in Poland twenty years ago. The Countess's smile lit up Joice's dingy office. Lushya spoke French, German, Italian and Rumanian and had connections in Bucharest prepared to help with fund-raising schemes. She also showed Joice a list she had compiled of wealthy Rumanians prepared to allow Polish families to 'house-sit' their beautiful villas on the Black Sea free of charge until next summer. Privately Joice thought that the Countess's looks and vibrant personality would be a great help in charming Rumanian officials into granting visas. How many of them would be able to resist that smile or those large, slightly slanted blue eyes under the darkest of lashes?

But mere good looks were not enough. Joice asked the Countess precisely how she would tackle the fund-raising. In reply, Lushya had facts and figures at her fingertips. She told Joice she was involved with the Polish women's choir, and proposed setting up a charity committee which would include a sprinkling of Rumanian Princesses and Countesses; this would encourage the wives of bankers and industrialists to join as well. Each Committee member in turn would organise and pay for a fund-raising concert to be given in her home by the Polish women's choir, dressed in their traditional costumes. The choir did not want any money for concerts as long as the proceeds would be used to benefit Polish women and men interned in the camps.

Joice was impressed. She recalled how much she had enjoyed listening to the choir at the Christmas party. She employed the Countess on the spot, explaining that the small salary she could offer included free board at their hotel. By now Lushya was short of money; she told Joice she had been about to pawn her pearls. She was delighted to move out of her chilly lodgings and into Doamna Popescu's warm hotel.

The winter of 1940 was particularly cold. Bucharest lay under a deep blanket of snow that muffled the clip-clop of horses pulling the *trasuras* or hansom cabs along the streets, which were swept each day to allow traffic to pass freely. The children of the rich kept warm in fur coats and snow-boots, while beggars shivered in rags. Most Rumanians salved their consciences by giving every beggar they passed a small coin. Joice wanted to donate money out of the Quaker funds to help the beggars, but Dermod O'Donnell pointed out that helping the thousands of Polish refugees was the reason they were all in Bucharest.

The *crivatz*, a sub-zero wind from the Carpathian mountains, pierced even the thickest of overcoats and whistled through the thin walls of the Quaker Mission. Joice sat at her desk wearing a fur hat, woollen mittens, her old fur coat over her Quaker uniform and a huge pair of fur-lined pilot's boots over two pairs of Sydney's thickest socks. Sydney came to work in his long Harris tweed coat and a grey knitted Balaclava helmet of the type the Mission had given out to thousands of Polish would-be soldiers.

Joice and Lushya, who looked elegant in a well-cut black ski suit and high fur boots, were now on first-name terms. Joice had learned that Lushya was the Polish equivalent of the Italian 'Lucia', but must be pronounced 'Loo-shah' in the Polish way.

Before war broke out, Lushya had enjoyed a life devoted to cocktail parties, balls, winters in Davos, spring in Venice and long idyllic summers on her family's country estates, where she had acted as her father's secretary. Now she worked long hours determined to help her fellow Poles. She seemed able to charm even the most difficult people. She persuaded four Rumanian princesses and three industrialists' wives to join the Save the Poles Committee, which organised performances by the Polish women's choir in private homes, just as she had outlined to Joice at her interview. Each hostess was to provide at least a hundred guests, supply the refreshments and organise a fund-raising raffle.

The Save the Poles Committee met once a month at the Cafe Mavrodaphne. All the proceeds of their fund-raising efforts were devoted to supplementing the weekly living allowance for Polish refugees and their families, as well as some fifty or so Polish and Jewish orphans now under Joice's protection, whose school fees she paid. Rumanian Jews had organised their own aid committees to help Jewish refugees but their situation had become increasingly difficult due to threats from the anti-Semitic Iron Guard. Joice had soon realised that the Jewish orphans under her care needed as much help as the Poles. As funds poured in from the concerts, so the Lochs were able to move many of the Polish women to better accommodation.

Joice found it frustrating that well-wishers in Britain persisted in sending out large numbers of pink and blue baby layettes. This raised some ironic mirth among the Polish women: many of them had not seen their husbands for more than nine months. What they needed was warm winter clothing for themselves and their children. Joice and Lushya saw no point in storing baby clothes and gave them to pregnant Rumanian peasant women. The problem of providing overcoats and snow boots for thousands of civilian refugees was eventually solved by a grant of money from the London-based Lord Mayor's Fund as well as the fund-raising concerts.

The Lochs' resourcefulness in organising courses to help refugees readjust to their new lives was drawn to the attention of King Carol. Although he had interned the Poles for political reasons, the King was basically a kind man who had no wish to make the Poles suffer more than they had already. He was pleased with the volunteers at the Quaker Mission for caring for the Polish refugees.

The Lochs were notified through the British Legation that they had each been awarded a medal by King Carol II. Joice was to receive the Order of Elizabeth, a medal awarded to Rumanian and foreign women for outstanding service. Sydney was awarded the Order of the Star, instituted by the King's late father, Carol I, the only medal that could be awarded to male foreigners. Their investiture was to take place at the Palace in mid-April, 1940.

Three weeks before the ceremony, Joice, wearing her worn grey Quaker uniform, sat next to the old Princess Bibesco at a Save the Poles Committee lunch. Snow still lay on the ground. Inside Mavrodaphne's, the huge windows were frosted with a pattern of ice-flowers, so great was the contrast with the freezing air outside. Red silk cushions had been placed between the double-glazed panes so that not a breath of cold air could enter.

The Rumanian Princesses chattered away like birds. As far as Joice could understand them, drawing on her schoolgirl knowledge of French, their conversations consisted of whose daughter was getting engaged to whose son, gossip about the many skeletons in the cupboards of Europe's oldest families and long discussions about aristocratic bloodlines. Joice was reminded of her father choosing bulls for his cows or rams for his ewes. In place of a stud book, the Princesses had the Almanach de Gotha with its coats of arms and family trees extending back for generations.

By the time coffee topped with whipped cream was served, the conversation had turned to Joice and her forthcoming presentation to the King.

'*Enfin*, what will *you* wear, *chère Madame*? asked the elderly Princess Bibesco, whose wrinkled face and freckled hands were heavily coated with white *poudre de riz*.

'My Quaker uniform. I'm afraid I don't have a suitable dress,' Joice replied. She didn't add that she lacked both the money and time to buy an appropriate outfit. Wistfully she remembered the black silk cocktail dress she had worn for Marshal Pilsudski's investiture two decades ago in Poland, with its matching silk stole fringed with blue ribbons . . . those same blue ribbons that symbolised her lifetime decision to place duty above the inclination of her heart.

The Princesses rarely spoke Rumanian, which they regarded as the language of the peasants. Instead they used a polyglot language made up of French, English and Italian which they felt made them appear very cosmopolitan. Now, looking at Joice's shabby grey serge suit with its sagging jacket and worn cuffs, a wail of dismay arose from all four Princesses. *'Impossible, absolument impossible!'* they chorused.

Princess Bibesco looked Joice up and down to assess her size, then offered to lend her a tailored coat and skirt and matching silk blouse which had been made for her niece, 'the young Princess Bibesco'. She told Joice it was *très elegante* with a slightly military look, dark-blue with gold braid at the neck and sleeves. The suit would be *très convenable pour vous, chère Madame*', the Princess assured Joice, It seemed the young Princess Bibesco was one of Coco Chanel's best patrons but she had left this particular Chanel suit behind after making one of her flying visits to her aunt from her home in Paris. '*Naturellement* my niece would be delighted to lend you the suit, Madame.'

The other Princesses agreed that as the head of their Committee, it was *trés importante* that Madame Loch should appear *molto molto* elegante at the Palace. She must not let their Committee down by looking shabby for her Royal audience. With a shock Joice realised that, overwhelmed by work, she was indeed looking a bit rumpled in her old uniform, and tried to smooth down her worn skirt. Princess Bibesco thought they might have gone too far using the word 'shabby'. She tried to make amends by congratulating Joice on preserving her complexion and her slim figure in spite of working so hard. '*Una molta bella figura,*' she repeated, waving fingers heavy with jewelled rings in Joice's direction.

The other Princesses nodded their approval. Princess Bibesco, pleased by the vision of Joice elegant in her niece's Chanel suit, continued: 'I will tell my maid to bring it to your 'otel tomorrow.'

Joice thought it would seem ungrateful to refuse.

After the others had departed with much kissing of cheeks, she and Lushya had a quiet cup of coffee together. Lushya remarked that the Rumanians were very different to the Poles. 'We never surrender. The Rumanians are *Latinos* at heart, they enjoy life, family, friends, food. For now they just want to live and let live. They will be very kind and generous to us to try and keep a foot in both camps. But as soon as they realise that Britain will do nothing for them they'll turn to Germany to save them and abandon us. Above all they fear a Russian invasion.' She changed the conversation. 'By the way, do you know just how small the living allowance is that a Polish wife or widow gets from the British Government?'

'Not exactly. When I asked Nigel, he wouldn't quote an exact figure—he said it depended on the number of children and a few other things.'

'A Polish wife or widow with one child receives precisely one hundred *lei* a week. A little more if she has other children. One hundred *lei* is less than the cost of that pot of coffee and the cakes we have eaten. That's why these concerts are so vital. I too have lost my home, my family, the future we envisioned. As soon as the war is over I shall go to New York to stay with my widowed aunt who lives there. She says the only way to restore our Warsaw home and the family estates to their former condition is to marry money. Her plan is for me to marry an American millionaire and get him to pay. Americans love titles.' Joice wasn't certain if Lushya was serious or not. She hoped not.

The next day, as promised, a maid dropped off at the Lochs' hotel a huge glossy white box with CHANEL embossed on its lid.

Joice carried the box upstairs to their room, placed it on the bed and lifted the coat and skirt out of its layers of tissue paper. The fine wool felt soft to the touch. French navy-blue was the fashionable shade of the season, and there was a matching silk blouse with a long ribbon tie at the collar. Around the neck and cuffs of the jacket were slender bands of hand-stitched gold braid. To Joice's delight the suit fitted perfectly.

'What a beautiful woman I married!' Sydney exclaimed approvingly as he entered the room and saw her standing in front of the long mirror. 'That suit's perfect for the Palace. The King always wears specially tailored white uniforms covered with gold braid. You'll be a matching pair!'

'I just hope no one at Quaker Headquarters hears about me wearing a Chanel suit and complains. I can see the letters now: "Mrs Loch, you are far too frivolous to run a Quaker Mission." Don't you remember our first interview and Ruth Fry writing to Florence Barrow saying we would never fit in?'

'I don't think she'd say that now,' Sydney said quietly, but Joice didn't answer, too busy looking critically at herself in the glass. Princess Bibesco was right; in spite of all that hard work and those cream cakes at Mavrodaphne's cafe her figure was still good and her legs and ankles slim. The dark navy-blue set off her fair complexion. As she took off the jacket she saw a Chanel label inside the neckline and a slim but heavy gold chain attached to the inside of the collar. Inside the hem of the skirt were tiny lead weights which ensured that it would hang perfectly as the wearer walked. Scott Fitzgerald was right, Joice thought: the rich are different.

'No one could possibly call *you* frivolous, my love. You deserve something in return for all the unpaid work we're doing. I remember the investiture in Warsaw—I was quite jealous of that Polish general drooling over you. Besides, your uniform is so old it's falling apart, you can't possibly wear it to the Palace.'

Sydney borrowed a cutaway morning coat and trousers from a Legation official as tall and broad-shouldered as himself. Joice salved her conscience by slipping an official armband, embroidered with the red Quaker star, around her right sleeve.

As they left, Doamna Popescu emerged from her glass-fronted office to congratulate them. She had lent Joice a pair of navy-blue court shoes to go with the suit. They were a bit on the large side but Joice stuffed the toes with some tissue paper from the Chanel box and they were fine. 'You both look vairy 'andsome', Doamna Popescu beamed.

They crossed the huge square in front of the hotel. From far away the brand-new Royal Palace seemed most impressive. 'And so it should, King Carol spent a fortune on it,' said Sydney. However, as they approached the palace, they could see that the huge building bore all the evidence of shoddy workmanship. In places the rough red brickwork was exposed through thinly rendered plaster. In the vast reception hall an orchestra played a selection from Lehar's *Merry Widow*. White-and-gold porcelain urns filled with hot-house lilies scented the air. Flunkeys in powdered wigs and knee-breeches ushered the Lochs into the throne room, where they sat side by side on gilt chairs. King Carol, a tall man who struck Joice as far better-looking than in most of his press photographs, wore—as Sydney had prophesied—a white uniform with gold epaulettes and stood on a raised dais.

The Lochs rose and came forward one after another down a long strip of red carpet, and the King pinned on their medals. Joice's Order of Elizabeth was a gold and enamel sunburst; Sydney's Order of the Star took the form of a cross bordered in gold, its centre enamelled in brilliant blue.

Joice found the King knowledgeable about their work and very easy to talk to, but as they spoke she thought his eyes were the saddest she had ever seen. Clearly the whole situation must be terribly upsetting for him, with one side of his family English and the other German. She thought some people judged him too harshly for trying to negotiate with both Hitler and Great Britain in the effort to save his country from invasion.

During the reception that followed the ceremony, she looked around to see if the King's mistress, the red-headed Jewish divorcée, Madame Magda Lupescu, was present, but could not see her. Doamna Popescu had told Joice the somewhat Gothic tale of the King's romantic life. When he was Crown Prince, he had eloped to Russia with the daughter of a Rumanian diplomat. But his family had forced him to annul this love-match and marry Princess Helen of Greece (the mother of Crown Prince Michael), whom he had divorced a few years later. Meanwhile, he had met Magda Lupescu, the second great love of his life, and had gone to live in exile with her. When his father was dying he had been recalled and pressured to re-marry Princess Helen, which he refused to do.

Joice wondered what it would be like to marry someone for love and be forced by your parents to have the marriage annulled. It was a haunting story that lingered in her mind.

That evening the expatriates who gathered at the English Bar at the Athenée Palace toasted the Lochs. Even Nigel was pleasant to Joice. The only gloomy note came from the Reuters correspondent, a stocky Glaswegian with a drinking problem, who foretold the imminent fall of France. 'Russia and Germany are planning to squeeze their way to Rumania's oilfields. It's purely a question of who will get there first.[1] How long will the Rumanians remain pro-British once they realise we canna' protect them?' he asked.

Joice remembered that Lushya had expressed the same sentiment. In spite of the central heating in the English Bar she shivered. How could they manage to get all those thousands of Poles out of Rumania before the Germans arrived?

The Save the Poles Committee organised a fund-raising dinner at Capsa's restaurant. The champagne was French, the caviar from the Black Sea, and tickets were enormously expensive. Rumania's superrich jowled their way through mountains of food. The function was a great success. Joice was amazed at how many women they were able to help with an additional living allowance. The Polish 'Escape Fund' was building up.

One day Lushya relayed an unusual request. Some of her Army officer friends in one of the internment camps urgently wanted a printing press to produce a Polish newspaper. Would the Quaker Relief Mission donate one, or could they buy one out of the Save the Poles fund? When pressed, Lushya admitted another reason. One of the inmates of the camp was a man who, before the war, had been Poland's most brilliant forger. He could use the press to print exit visas so realistic that no one would be able to tell they were forgeries. Hundreds of Poles would be able to reach safety.

'I don't want the Quakers to know about this,' Joice told Lushya. 'We'll donate the press from all this ticket money from the dinner and ask no questions. What the eye doesn't see, you know . . . '

As the thaw set in and the snow turned to slush, the King announced an amnesty for acts of violence by the Iron Guard. He was under great pressure from Hitler as the main buyer of Rumania's oil, and as a result of business negotiations with Germany he had to agree to lift the ban on the Iron Guard and Rumania's Fascist Party. The result was that Bucharest saw an influx of strapping young men in jack boots and green uniforms who hung around street corners looking bored and sullen. The *Times* correspondent said they were a bunch of Jew-baiting thugs who, if their leader, Hora Simia returned, were likely to make a bid to gain power and get rid of the King.

Spring 1940 arrived late. By the time the chestnut trees that lined the Chaussée were decked in pink blossom and the *crivatz* had ceased to blow, King Carol had attempted to sell Rumanian oil to the British Government, but for reasons Nigel refused to disclose his offer had been turned down by Britain, who bought oil from Mexico instead.[2]

Rejected by Britain, Carol had received a demand from Hitler that Rumania's food and oil exports to Germany must be increased to seventy per cent of its overall production. The King had little choice but to accede. If Rumania stopped trading with Germany its entire economy would crash. The country was caught in an economic trap.

As a result prices rose. Doamna Popescu started to complain bitterly, telling Joice that butter and milk had almost doubled in cost and she would be forced to raise the prices of her breakfasts. The Rumanian Princesses on the Save the Poles Committee moaned that imported silks and cashmere sweaters were growing scarce in the boutiques along the Calea Victoriei. Like most wealthy Rumanians, they blamed Jewish bankers for the shortages, declaring it was all a Jewish-inspired plot.

The sadistic Hora Simia finally returned to Bucharest from his stint working in two special camps for Jews set up by the Nazis—Dachau and Buchenwald. The journalists in the English Bar deplored his return. It was rumoured he was only biding his time until he could unleash an anti-Jewish campaign. Hastily most Jews applied for visas for America and Palestine. Suddenly everything they owned was for sale or being auctioned off: homes, cars, silver, rare books, Old Master paintings, jewels, as they attempted to raise money to bribe their way out of Rumania.

Once again the Iron Guard marched through the streets. New police regulations placing restrictions on Jews were issued. Joice asked the Lochs' friend and co-worker, Mr Brown, ("Brownie") who acted as liaison officer between the American and Rumanian YMCA (known as 'ze IMCA' to the Rumanians, who had difficulty pronouncing the letter 'Y', and the combination 'TH') why America would not accept Jews in large numbers.[3] 'We're doing what we can,' he told her sadly, 'but it's a difficult time for any Government to accept large numbers of immigrants. People still remember the Depression and mass unemployment.'

By Easter 1940 the two huge barbed-wire encampments that had housed Polish soldiers and officers were nearly empty of men capable of fighting in the Free Polish Army or the British Army or Air Force. Only the middle-aged and elderly, politicians and senior Government officials and a sprinkling of University professors remained. Now France seemed to be on the point of surrender to the advancing Germans; the Free Polish Government was leaving Paris for London.

Through Friends London headquarters, the Lochs proposed to Whitehall an escape plan which would get the remaining Polish men, women and children out before the Germans or the Russians invaded Rumania. They proposed the refugees should leave from the Black Sea port of Constantza for Istanbul, Mersin and Cyprus, then take another boat to Palestine, at that time under British mandate. Although the plan was turned down, it remained in the War Office files.

The mild spring weather, when it finally arrived, transformed Bucharest into a garden city. But no sooner had the bright pavement awnings appeared and the cafe tables and chairs been set out than the papers announced Germany's invasion of Scandinavia.

The German Military Mission had rented offices to act as their Propaganda Bureau; its full-length window featured a huge map of

Europe on which German conquests were marked by black arrows. As Hitler's troops invaded Scandinavia, Holland and France, the citizens of Bucharest witnessed the black arrows advancing across the map. The Lochs and Legation officials used to walk past the Bureau after dining out and look at the map with foreboding.

At the end of May 1940, as the weather warmed up, Rumanians were devastated by the news that France, their erstwhile protector and the source of everything they considered civilised, had surrendered to Germany. The British Army in France was evacuated from Dunkirk by sea while German planes bombed them ferociously.

Under threat of invasion themselves, the Rumanians showed themselves less generous towards the Poles. They now viewed the fate of Poland with foreboding, realising the same thing could happen to them. The evacuation of the British Army from Dunkirk in a fleet of small ships and private yachts was regarded by the Rumanians as a crushing defeat, though some of the British journalists they met in the English Bar viewed it as a grim victory.

At this critical juncture, Francesca Wilson, Head of Friends War Relief in Budapest, paid a visit to Bucharest. She was a teacher with a degree in history from Cambridge and a love of adventure similar to Joice's own. She explained that the Quaker Relief Mission in Hungary was experiencing severe problems. Fear of the Germans had made moderate Hungarians turn against the Poles who had fled there, a situation exacerbated by the fact that the large German population of Hungary had never wanted the Poles to come there in the first place, viewing them as enemies. It seemed that Hungary would soon be under German rule, and Francesca was advising Polish refugees in Hungary to escape to Rumania.

Francesca was particularly impressed with the work the Lochs had done in Bucharest. She wrote: 'Sydney and Joice Loch gave to the Bucharest Mission and Friends Relief a feeling of stability I found most reassuring. Sydney Loch is the type of Englishman still to be found occasionally—kind, courteous, in every circumstance imperturbable, but in his heart unconventional and even a little romantic. His lively and attractive wife Joyce [sic] is an Australian. I don't know whether she lived in the bush there but she certainly has the practical knowledge and the gift of improvisation of someone who has done so. The Lochs' charisma had thrown a kind of magic spell over Polish civilians in Rumania. They had organised garden clubs in the villages with lectures on horticulture by experts as well as courses which provided much-needed incomes for many Polish women such as hairdressing, hat-making, First Aid and basic nursing, typewriting and other morale-raising activities. Perhaps our relief work in Hungary was just as good but the excellent relief schemes organised by the Lochs struck me as being fresher and more original.'

That fateful month of May, to celebrate her birthday Doamna Popescu invited Joice and Sydney into her office for a glass of *tzuicka*, Rumanian plum brandy. By now they were familiar with the traditional Rumanian toast: '*Noroc*'—'Good Luck'.

The *tzuicka* was strong and burned their throats. It bore a strong resemblance to the *ouzo* offered by the Mayor of Ouranoupolis and made Joice think about their old life in the tower by the sea. 'We'll be back soon,' they had assured everyone when they left Greece. Now she felt they would need all the good luck in the world to make that assurance come true.

She was jolted back to the present when their landlady said sadly, 'Domnul and Doamna Lok, we thought Britain would protect us. But no, she will not buy our oil or help us. Rumania is alone. Our Army consists of generals, privates and corporals.' She explained that the Rumanian Army was rumoured to lack middle-ranking and junior officers; well-educated or wealthy young men did not serve in the Rumanian Army because their families bribed the War Ministry to exempt them from Military Service.

One result of the defeat of France was that French fashions and perfume disappeared from the shops of Bucharest. French films were replaced by German propaganda newsreels. Joice and Sydney and members of the Legation went to see one so that the Legation could report back to the Foreign Office. It showed Hitler patting blond-haired children and blond German soldiers laughing from the turrets of Panzer tanks as they rode in triumph down the Champs Elysées. How soon would it be before German tanks were parading through Budapest, Joice wondered.

25   ESCAPE FROM THE IRON GUARD

One clear summer morning the Lochs awoke and looked out of their bedroom windows. To their consternation they saw that the Union Jack and the French tricolour had disappeared from the front of the Athenée Palace. Alongside the Rumanian flag flapped a red-and-white flag with a black swastika.

That night after dinner they walked across the square to the hotel. The English Bar was crowded with Nazis from the German Military Mission, toasting Hitler's success in *schnapps* followed by foaming mugs of beer.

Joice was desperately worried about the Polish and Jewish orphans in their care. 'Legal' exit visas were almost impossible to obtain as Hitler's diplomats had expressed a 'wish' loaded with menace to the King that no more Poles or Jews should be allowed to leave Rumania. The forger in the camp was overwhelmed with requests for the 'visas' that he printed, which so far had aroused no suspicions and had got many Poles out of the country.

The last cohort of Polish soldiers was due to depart to join the British Army. Their colonel invited the Lochs to attend a farewell dinner. There were toasts in vodka to General Sikorski and to King George VI of Britain. The Lochs joined in. A young Polish pilot on Joice's right hand, for whom Joice had found warm clothes and who had attended the English courses she had arranged, raised his glass to her and Sydney. Unable to speak a word of English when he arrived, he toasted them in fluent English: 'To our good friends, Pan and Pani Loch, who have done so much to help us I propose the toast of "Stolat"—may you live for a hundred years!'

'*Stolat! Pan Loch. Stolat! Pani Loch!*' came the reply as five hundred men raised their glasses.

What worried the Lochs most were the elderly politicians, judges, provincial Governors and other officials still in the camp. They had to get them out before the Germans arrived. They continued to bombard Friends House and the British War Office with statistics about the plight of Polish and Jewish refugees trapped in Rumania and yet more

Polish refugees arriving daily by train from the now extremely pro-German Hungary.

Finally a very senior British civil servant in London became involved and granted permission for a group of 2,000 civilian refugees from Poland to be accommodated in British-run Cyprus, provided no more than ten per cent of them were Jewish. They should cross the Black Sea to Constantinople and from there sail to the port of Mersin and on to Cyprus by chartered vessel. Should Cyprus be invaded, the Polish refugees would have to escape by sea to Palestine, although the Arabs, Britain's oil-rich allies, had made it plain they did not want more Jews flooding their country. Joice thought it strange the British should be so concerned about Arab oil, but had not taken up King Carol's offer of Rumanian oil.

On receiving the go-ahead to what Whitehall code-named Operation Swordfish, Sydney spent days drawing up escape routes for the thousands of Polish civilians in Rumania. The woman and children would not attract so much attention from the Iron Guard as the men: it was felt the families could leave by train under the guise of visiting the seaside. Joice would lead them. Her escape party was code-named Operation Pied Piper.

The Polish men would attract less attention if they left Bucharest in small groups. The British could not accept all of them in Cyprus. Some would go to British-run Persia (Iran); those whose professional skills or knowledge were specially useful to the war effort would go to Cyprus. From there they could be shipped to Britain, Palestine or British colonies in Africa where it was hoped suitable jobs would be found for them.

Joice was to have full responsibility for approximately one thousand Polish widows and wives of Reserve Army officers and their children. It was she who chose the name Operation Pied Piper, after the poem by Robert Browning about the piper with a magic flute sent to rid the town of Hamelin of a plague of rats. When the Mayor and Council of Hamelin refused to pay the piper, he piped away the town's children. Joice was told that the Rumanians believed that these 'stolen' children had later miraculously reappeared in the neighbouring Carpathian Mountains, so the name was very apt.

At this point Francesca Wilson telephoned the Lochs from Hungary: she had been forced to leave Budapest in a hurry and was about to cross the border into Rumania. Hungary and Rumania were at loggerheads over the possession of Transylvania. The Hungarians were urging refugee Poles to cross the border and seek asylum in Rumania, in order to avert Hitler's wrath from Hungary. Thousands of Polish refugees were now crossing the Hungarian-Rumanian border, terrified they could be arrested and handed over to the Germans any moment. Francesca asked Sydney to try and find emergency accommodation for them.

Francesca had been on a trip to see some Poles in the south of Hungary when she had been warned by telephone that if she returned to the Mission she would be arrested and interned. She had escaped by car through a remote part of southern Hungary. Could Joice take the train to Budapest and collect the remaining Mission funds, which had been drawn out of the bank by a Hungarian staff member who was trustworthy? He would remain at the Mission until she arrived. The money was in the safe. They could not ask a Hungarian Bank to transfer the funds to Bucharest—they could easily be confiscated by the Hungarian pro-Nazi Government. The money was enough to pay for accommodation and food for a few weeks for almost a thousand Polish people now crossing the border into Rumania, many of whom had been given the address of the Lochs' aid centre.[1]

Joice explained their difficulties in housing still more refugees. Many of the flimsy wooden huts in the Bucharest camps had now been dismantled or had collapsed under heavy snow last winter. However, there was room in an old jail at Czernowicz, capital of Bessarabia, which had accommodated several thousand Polish refugees who had now departed. The jail was dilapidated but at least it would be a roof over their heads. She would collect the funds from the Budapest Mission and use them to help Polish refugees escape on specially chartered boats down the Danube and from there via Turkey to Cyprus, where the British Army should provide for them, or to Persia, where the Shah of Persia had promised assistance.

Reassuring Francesca they would do everything possible to help, the Lochs drove to Bessarabia, some three hours away, where they arranged for the Poles arriving from Hungary to be accommodated in the old jail. On her return to Bucharest, Joice was summoned to the British Legation: Nigel, as part of British Intelligence, had discovered she was about to leave for Budapest.

'Would you mind doing the British Legation a favour while you're there?' he asked.

'Depends what it is,' Joice said warily.

'Oh, nothing much. Just take a spot of Government money to one of my contacts—or you could pay him out of Quaker funds and I'll reimburse you later,' Nigel replied nonchalantly.

'No chance. Our money's been donated to help the Poles. Why involve me of all people?' Joice asked. She distrusted Nigel and thought him a blabber-mouth, having heard him boasting about his cloak-and-dagger exploits in the English Bar. 'We're not here to do *your* dirty work.'

It seemed that what Nigel referred to as 'the Powers-that-Be' had decided this was a job that would arouse less suspicion if it were carried out by a woman. Joice was one of the few women left in Bucharest with a British passport plus a high security clearance. Joice was amazed to realise that the British Legation had security-vetted both her and Sydney.

For his part, Nigel tried hard to make his mission sound about as dangerous as a shopping trip to Harrods. But Joice realised that underneath his flippant approach, she was being asked to risk her life to smuggle money out of Bucharest into Hungary.

'Tell me the real reason for handing over the money,' she insisted.

Reluctantly Nigel admitted that a certain Polish Jew, a scientist needed by the Allies for the war effort was being 'slipped from jail'. It was obvious the money he was asking her to take out was a bribe designed for the scientist's jailer. (Recounting the story in her memoirs Joice was very modest about her role and too discreet to name the Jewish scientist.)[2]

She realised that getting this particular Jewish scientist out was important, but she also knew that if things went wrong it could jeopardise her role in getting out the funds from the Hungarian Mission to the Poles. She hesitated before replying.

'Not *scared*, are you?' asked Nigel. 'I thought Orstraylians enjoyed a bit of excitement.' He opened a desk drawer and pulled out a money-belt containing wads of ten thousand *lei* notes, enough to keep thousands of Poles in comfort for a month. Joice, trying to make up her mind, ignored his comment. Seeing he could not needle her into it, he changed tactics.

'Perhaps I should have explained what an important mission this is. Are you up to it?' he asked patronisingly.

Joice could never resist a challenge. 'Perhaps not. But who *else* have you got?' she countered crisply.

Nigel realised that this was her way of accepting. He explained that all rail lines between Bucharest and Budapest had been bombed the previous night by Rumanian partisans, furious that Transylvania was being handed back to Hungary. It was impossible to get to Budapest by train. Joice would have to fly, but with the railway out of action all commercial flights to Hungary were fully booked. The only way she could get to Budapest in time was by a privately-owned light aircraft which was accepting charter passengers at double the normal price. The Legation's travel agent duly booked her seat.

The next day, wearing her grey serge uniform with the red Quaker star on the sleeve, Joice was driven to the airport in a Legation car. She was slightly late and found herself the last to climb the gangway.

Inside the cramped plane she found her bucket seat as the door flap closed and the engines began to roar. Looking around at her twelve fellow passengers, she realised with horror that all the seats were filled by jackbooted men in long military overcoats with swastikas in their lapels. She looked across at the opposite seat and met the eyes of Herr von M, Minister of Kultur in the German Mission to Bucharest. He was the only civilian aboard the plane apart from herself.[3]

The rest of the plane had been chartered by the German Mission to transport high-ranking officers to Budapest. As an Australian Joice was travelling on a British passport—and Germany was officially at war with Britain and Australia! Under her grey uniform jacket was the money-belt containing cash to bribe a Hungarian jailer to release a Jewish prisoner. If the Germans caught her she could be shot or sent to a concentration camp; this had happened only last month when a charter plane carrying a young Englishman working for British Intelligence had been diverted to German-occupied Vienna. He was arrested by the Gestapo when the plane landed, and was now presumed dead.

Joice's palms were damp. Her stomach churned. She prayed for good weather so there was no risk the plane would be diverted to Vienna. She had met Herr von M at a diplomatic reception following a Mozart concert; he had seemed impressed when she was introduced to him as the author of several books. During the flight, the German Minister smiled at Joice and courteously pointed out the beauty of the land they were flying over—the mists swirling around mountain peaks, the huge pine forests. 'Such a *beautiful* country, do you not think, *gnädige Frau*?' Politely Joice agreed with him, praying he would not notice how nervous she was.

Then he told her that as visibility was poor, the plane might bypass Budapest and land in Vienna. Joice wondered if he suspected anything. Had there been a leak at the Legation? Were they being diverted to German occupied territory so that she could be arrested and interrogated by the Gestapo? She thought it best to pretend that she was looking forward to a brief holiday in Budapest. She prayed for the visibility to clear ... within half an hour it did.

As they approached Budapest Herr von M told her how the cities of Buda and Pest had developed entirely separately and had not been joined together by a bridge until the middle of the nineteenth century. 'The ramparts around Buda castle are wonderful,' he said. *'Mein Gott*, what a view. The best in Europe!'

Joice looked out of the tiny window and saw the silvery Danube winding far below them.

'I hope you have the time to go there and see the view, Frau Loch.'

'So do I,' Joice said with feeling.

The Minister for Kultur was politeness itself. *'Gnädige Frau*, may I offer you a lift to the centre of Pest?' he asked. She felt she could not refuse without arousing his suspicions.

The passengers left the plane and filed past Hungarian customs and passport control. Joice handed in her blue British passport, which stood out among so many green German ones. The German Minister stayed close beside her and they drove to the city in his chauffeur-driven Mercedes-Benz.

She concocted a story about having to collect a ring for a Rumanian friend from a jewellers on the Vaclav Utca, the only street name she knew in Budapest. Herr von M wound down the window that separated them from the chauffeur and told him they must drop Frau Loch there.

The car slowed and stopped. Joice thanked the Minister, waved a cheery goodbye and went into the nearest jewellers' shop to make enquiries about an imaginary gold ring left for repairs by a fictitious Rumanian lady. After a long and fruitless search she was told they had no ring answering to her description. Joice tried to look suitably surprised. Her alibi complete, she wandered around window-shopping for what seemed an age. Peering over her shoulder to check she was not being followed, she then took a horse-drawn *fiacre* to Nigel's prearranged rendez-vous, a cafe on tranquil Margaret Island. She chose an outside table under a striped awning.

Nigel had arranged she would meet his 'contact' at one o'clock. He was to carry a copy of Langenscheidt's German-English dictionary and wear a red rose in his button-hole. Joice thought it corny, as though Nigel had been reading too many third-rate spy novels. But at least having her contact carry a dictionary was a better idea than a rolled-up copy of *The Times*, as spies usually did in novels.

She ordered a pot of coffee, then waited—and waited. At a quarter to two, just as she thought something had gone wrong with Nigel's arrangements, a man arrived with a rose in his button-hole, carrying a huge dictionary. He was built like a prize fighter. He sat down opposite her, smiling with a flash of gold-capped teeth. She was reminded of the Australian expression 'flash as a rat with a gold tooth'.

A trio in black waistcoats and tight trousers played gipsy music on their violins. No one appeared to be observing their table. Gold Teeth ignored Joice, clicked his fingers to summon the waiter and demanded a glass of the most expensive Tokay on the wine list. He swallowed it as though it was lemonade and ordered another. As the gipsy trio launched into one more of their glissando-filled *csárda's* Joice's heart pounded. This was the moment.

She got up, went to the ladies' room, unbuckled the money belt, placed Nigel's banknotes in an envelope she had brought with her, put it in her handbag and returned to their table.

She sat down and said a few words to Mr Gold Teeth in English. He looked puzzled. She picked up the dictionary and opened it, pretending to be searching for the right word. Then she unfastened her big leather shoulder-bag and nonchalantly slipped the envelope containing the money between the pages of the book. She thanked Gold Teeth for lending the dictionary to her and passed it back across the table.

Gold Teeth picked up the dictionary and placed it under his chair. In fractured English he quoted the date and time his Jewish prisoner would be 'allowed to escape': on no account should Joice write down the time and place anywhere. He mimed a hand being drawn across his throat. She felt a cold shiver run down her spine—obviously Gold Teeth feared she might be captured and killed by the Germans before she could return to the British Legation with the message.

Gold Teeth drained the last drops of golden Tokay, reached under his chair, picked up the dictionary and tucked it under his arm. He stood up and without a backward glance walked away, leaving Joice to pay for his expensive glasses of wine.

Joice walked through the beautiful gardens of Margaret Island, took a bus back to the city centre and found the house that was the Quaker Mission Headquarters. She talked to the elderly Hungarian who was the last Mission volunteer left, signed for the money remaining in their funds, and was given a list of Poles who had fled to Rumania.

She recalled her conversation with Herr von M about the beautiful view over Pest from the heights of Buda. Her watch said half-past four—there was still time to watch the sun set over Pest. She took a horse-drawn *fiacre* up the steep hill to the castle ramparts of Buda. The 'Herrengasse' Herr von M had called Buda's oldest street, as though he felt Budapest was already part of Germany.

It was far more beautiful and fascinating than she had imagined. Its Hungarian name was the Uri Utca. The entire street was made up of tall houses painted in soft shades of pink, green, ochre and terracotta. The houses had arched oak doors with their former owners' coats of arms embossed in gold leaf and steeply tiled roofs with distinctive 'eyebrow' windows to light their attic rooms. A few had been turned into hostelries, their inn signs showing double-headed eagles, golden stags and roses. This was the place where she would stay but first she would see the former Hapsburg Palace, built at vast expense to house the Empress Maria Theresa, who then spent only three nights in the city, preferring to stay in Vienna.

From the ramparts of Buda Joice looked down on a magnificent panorama. Steeply terraced slopes, green with trees were crisscrossed by flights of steps, some arched and roofed like small cloisters, which descended abruptly to the wide streets that bordered the silvery loops of the Danube. Six huge bridges linked Buda with Pest. Close beside the magnificent Chain Bridge she saw Hungary's House of Parliament, its Gothic pinnacles topped by a huge dome, reminiscent of Brunileschi's Duomo in Florence or Hagia Sophia in Istanbul. Far below sprawled the nineteenth-century business and shopping centre of Pest, its wide boulevards slicing through densely packed rows of shops, offices and apartment blocks. As the last rays of the sun disappeared and the city and riverside lights came on Joice thought Herr von M had been right—it certainly was the most breathtaking view in Europe.

She returned to the Uri Utca and booked herself a room in one of the inns. Her only luggage was her big leather handbag but the concierge did not ask any questions. She slept fitfully.

The next morning Joice rang the railway station, determined not to return to Rumania on a charter plane even if she had to stay longer in Buda. To her relief, the stretch of railway line blown up by the Rumanian partisans had now been repaired. What luck! She took a *fiacre* to the station, where she telephoned Sydney, careful not to say anything that might incriminate her in case the line was tapped. She gave her expected time of arrival at Bucharest station. Sydney said he had missed her badly and would be waiting for her under the railway clock.

When the train drew in at Bucharest Joice felt her heart miss a beat as she saw him standing at the entrance to the platform, tall and distinguished in his old tweed jacket and grey flannels, an anxious look on his face as he scanned the passengers. With a pang she realised that the strain of the past weeks had deepened the lines on that beloved face. As they embraced, she felt almost light-headed with relief that her mission was accomplished. Sydney admitted he had been worried stiff. He had no faith in Nigel's organising skills.

That afternoon she rang Nigel and gave him the message from Gold Teeth. A week later they all met at a diplomatic reception at which the Lochs were representing the Quaker Mission. Nigel, glass in hand, was somewhat the worse for drink. Slurring his words, he informed Joice that the jailer had kept his side of the bargain: the Polish-Jewish scientist had been shipped back to Britain by some clandestine network. 'If I were you I wouldn't discuss such things in public,' Joice said, with a nod to indicate the foreign diplomats who surrounded them. Nigel was clearly drinking far too much. If he carried on like this he would become a security risk.

The map of Rumania was shrinking rapidly. Transylvania had gone, part of the Dobrugha district had been lopped off by the Bulgarians and the Russians were threatening to invade what they considered 'their' oilfields in Bessarabia. Meanwhile Bucharest was buzzing with rumours of the imminent collapse of Britain. Dr Goebbels' propaganda machine broadcast a barrage of anti-British propaganda. However, most Polish refugees steadfastly refused to believe the British could be beaten. Polish soldiers were earning great distinction in the British Army. The Polish Cabinet in exile, accompanied by General Sikorski, had now left France for London.

Joice and Sydney used up most of their Bucharest funds as well as those Joice had brought back from the Budapest Mission to pay for specially chartered steamers to carry thousands of Polish civilians, many of them relying on forged exit visas. The steamers ran to the port of Constantza, the first part of the Poles' long journey to British-controlled Persia or Palestine via Cyprus.

Rumours circulated among British journalists that Hitler had personally demanded King Carol cede Bessarabia and northern Bukovina to the Russians, who had been Germany's allies since the invasion of Poland.[4] Hitler now gave the King to understand that these territories would be handed back when Germany had won the war—which, Hitler asserted, would be very soon.

One evening, in search of the latest news from the foreign journalists, the Lochs crossed the square to the Athenée Palace. The foyer of the hotel was full of Germans in uniform; usually they stayed at the Minerva Hotel. Had they moved in *en masse*? The English bar was deserted. In the interior courtyard they were greeted by the Reuters correspondent, the sandy-haired Glaswegian. He was sitting with a half-empty bottle of malt whisky in front of him. Gazing morosely into his glass he asked them, 'What's my next headline? "Hitler Invades Bucharest" or "Stalin Invades Bucharest"? I must have been mad to come here. Let's all have a drink.'

By summer time Russia was on the point of invading Bessarabia, putting at imminent risk all the Polish refugees in Rumania. Twenty-four hours before the Russians arrived, Joice and Sydney drove to Czernowicz, the capital of Bessarabia. They put the Polish refugees who had sought refuge there onto a fleet of lorries and brought them back to Bucharest.[5]

The following day the Russians invaded Czernowicz. 'I was shocked to realise that many Rumanians we had talked to and had lunch with in Bessarabia would be hung from lamp-posts by the Russians. Everything movable on hoof or in store was sent back to Russia. Bessarabia was picked bare,' Joice wrote.[6]

Cars bearing Rumanian and German refugees from Bessarabia were pouring into Bucharest, which was full of horror stories of the looting and pillaging of Bessarabia. Stalin had given orders for any amount of brutality to warn the Rumanians what might happen to them. Russian troops, given large amounts of alcohol by their officers, were encouraged to rape and pillage. In contrast to the barbaric Russians, the Germans began to seem positively civilised, and it had by now become obvious that the British were not able to help. There were repercussions. At the Save the Poles Committee's Monday lunch at Mavrodaphne's, four Rumanian princesses and countesses in their chic little black dresses and pearls resigned from Joice's Committee.

'So busy, *ma chére*, so much to do, off to the country soon,' they told her. Careful not to spoil their lipstick, they pecked at Joice and Lushya's cheeks and departed. There would be no more charity concerts in Rumanian mansions. Polish refugees had become a living reproach, representing what could happen to Rumanians should the Russians arrive.

When the Lochs visited the English bar of the Athenée Palace the next evening, they found it filled with men in black-and-grey uniforms with small metal swastikas at the collar. The German Military Mission occupied every chair and bar stool, toasting each other in *schnapps* and beer, behaving in an arrogant and aggressive way. They believed the war was as good as won. Showing restraint, the British did not choose to instigate a bar-room brawl. Instead they regrouped to the chilly inner courtyard, ordering their pink gins and glasses of *tzuica* to be sent there. Instead of the cosy bar where the Germans were gathering, they were forced to sit outside on hard wooden chairs at metal tables covered in dead leaves. It seemed like a symbol of what was to come.

The Iron Guard, sinister in their dark-green uniforms and jackboots, no longer stood around on street corners looking lost but goose-stepped proudly down the Calea Viktorei, chanting slogans and holding up the traffic. Joice felt shivers run down her spine. Clearly they must get all the remaining Poles out of the country as soon as possible. Polish widows and their children were scattered through outlying Rumanian villages. Some of the women, after attending the courses Joice had organised for them, had found paying jobs which, understandably, they were reluctant to leave. Having been in an economic limbo they were now trying hard to build new lives for themselves and their children. Using Quaker funds Joice purchased a roneo-type machine. With Lushya's help, she sent out circulars advising the women of the danger they faced from an invasion and saying that the Free Polish Government in exile was urging them to flee from Rumania.

The following week the Lochs swung into their plan of action for Operation Swordfish and Operation Pied Piper. Joice, accompanied by Lushya and Father Ambrosius, was to take 450 Polish women and children and fifty Jewish children out of Bucharest by train to the Black Sea resort of Constantza, where she would pick up another 400 women and children who had been living in the holiday villas of wealthy Rumanians.

Meanwhile King Carol realised that his attempts to save the situation were clearly failing. The peasants and the working class distrusted him, resenting the fact that he spoke English and French better than Rumanian and had spent such huge sums on his new palace. Posters appeared in the streets calling for the King to resign in favour of his son by his arranged marriage to Princess Helen—Crown Prince Michael, now a handsome boy of nineteen.

The King, after his blighted first marriage and his second loveless marriage to the Greek princess, was desperate to cling to Magda

Lupescu, with whom he was very happy. The couple had already spent years of exile together in relative penury before the King's father died in 1938 and Carol had been invited to return as King. They were both aware that the Iron Guard had sworn to kill Magda because she was Jewish.

This time Magda Lupescu had absolutely no intention of living in penury. Over breakfast at the hotel, Doamna Popescu whispered to Joice and Lushya that, according to a close friend who worked at the Palace, the King was hoarding crates of jewels (Magda Lupescu's jewellery rivalled that of the Duchess of Windsor), gold bullion from the Treasury and valuable paintings, including five Goya portraits.

'How *very* Rumanian!' Lushya observed acidly.

'Our King is a good man. He doesn't like Hitler but he had to try and pacify him because Germany is the major buyer of our oil,' Doamna Popescu retorted crossly, as she placed a basket of hot rolls on the breakfast table.

Hitler, knowing he could call his own tune, demanded Rumania hand back some of the beautiful and fertile province of Bukhovina, one part to Russia, the rest to Austria. The loss of Bukhovina was a blow to the pride of all Rumanians. Joice reckoned this showed that King Carol's days were numbered. It would not be long before the Germans invaded. She had already contacted the Polish women billeted in the villages. Now she and Lushya trudged round the city to addresses where Polish women were housed, warning them that their lives and those of their children were at risk and they must leave very soon. Together with his staff, 'Brownie', as head of the American YMCA, helped Joice and Lushya in this task. The younger Quaker volunteers had now returned to Britain, fearing what might happen to them should they be caught by invading Russians or Germans.

By now final plans for the escape to Cyprus were well under way. The Polish women were told about the escape party, and warned that they would be able to take with them only one small bag, which must look as much as possible like a beach holdall, so that the Iron Guard would not suspect they were fleeing and arrest them. The loss of Bukovinia and the failure of the British to save them had now turned the populace firmly against the King, who was jeered as his chauffeur drove him through Bucharest in a bullet-plated Rolls Royce.

Rumania relied for her defence on the 'Carol Line', a series of huge trenches into which jets of oil could be pumped. In the event of an invasion these would be set alight by Rumanian soldiers. Unfortunately the plan failed. Instead of pumping oil into the trenches and lighting it, as Doamna Popescu had feared the terrified privates and corporals fled before the advancing Russian Army.

With the Carol Line of Fire out of action and without a shot being fired, the Russian troops purposely advanced only a few miles each day.

Just as he had done in Poland, Stalin made a secret pact with Hitler that Russian troops would not enter Bucharest before the Iron Guard could enjoy the glory of taking over the capital. Then the Nazis would make their move and arrest those Jews and Poles the Iron Guard had not managed to kill. Stalin was perfectly happy to let them do this in return for Bessarabia and its oil; the Germans were to take over the oil fields of Ploesti, close to Bucharest.

King Carol's old enemy, the Fascist leader General Antonescu, was appointed Minister of War in a desperate last-ditch attempt to placate the pro-German faction. Antonescu was seen by the masses as a 'strong man', Hitler's trusted ally, just the right choice to handle the crisis caused by the failure of the King's pro-British policies. Most Rumanians agreed that the King must abdicate. Overnight the word '*ABDICA*' was scrawled across street posters of the King in his elegant uniform.

King Carol, the ultimate survivor, ordered his servants to crate up everything of value in his palace so that he and Magda Lupescu could take it with them by train, as Doamna Popescu's informant had reported. He intended to set up a new home in Portugal's Estoril, home of many exiled Royals. For months he had been hoarding gold ingots from the Treasury, which were ready to be shipped out of the country with the minimum of fuss, rather than being loading onto the Royal train where the press might be watching.

The day arrived when General Antonescu, backed by the machine guns of the Iron Guard, took control of Parliament by force. In a supremely cynical gesture, the brutal Jew-baiting Hora Simia was appointed Rumania's Minister for Culture by the new Prime Minister. Shop windows were smashed: there was fighting in the streets. Corpses piled up and no one dared bury them for fear of being shot.

Guns were firing as the Lochs crossed the square in front of the Royal palace to reach their hotel. In the hallway Doamna Popescu threw herself into Sydney's arms weeping and laughing like a madwoman. Joice, having had a great deal of experience with hysterics, acted quickly. She slapped Doamna Popescu's face then coaxed her upstairs into their room overlooking the square.

Men were firing into the street from the roof of the Athenée Palace, and Sydney insisted that they lie face-down on the floor. A stray bullet winged through the long windows and embedded itself in the wardrobe. Doamna Popescu's hysterics returned.

The Palace guards in their scarlet-and-gold comic-opera uniforms disappeared, replaced by others wearing the dark-green uniform of the Iron Guard. Within an hour, Doamna Popescu's hotel had been put under surveillance by the Iron Guard. A huge man in helmet and jackboots stood guard at the front door, demanding to see the papers of everyone who went in and out.

Only then did Doamna Popescu reveal her secret to the Lochs. Her bedridden eighty-year-old mother was Jewish. Neither her father nor her late husband had Jewish blood, but under Rumanian law having a Jewish mother meant that she and her children and grandchildren were Jewish, even though they followed the Catholic faith.

'Come with me. I am taking an escape party of Polish and Jewish women to Cyprus. One or two more will make no difference,' Joice told her.

Doamna Popescu thanked her but said she could not leave her ailing mother, who was far too ill to travel. 'Doamna Lok, I am more Rumanian than Jewish. I was educated at a convent. They will not touch my mother or myself.' She sounded so convincing that Joice almost believed her.

The sporadic firing continued. At midday a man bearing a white flag emerged from the Royal Palace and declared a truce. Rumanians found it necessary to eat, revolution or no revolution. The shooting stopped; everyone went out to lunch and stacked their guns under their tables. For an hour all was calm.

'Rumanians take their stomachs much more seriously than their revolutions,' wrote Joice. 'Once the coast was clear, we poor foreigners slunk out and bought sufficient food to last us for another twenty-four hours of rage and ruin.'

Nigel had been driving around the city in his red MG sports car when the shooting started. By nightfall he had not returned so the British Legation reported him as a missing person to the Rumanian police. The following morning the police informed the Legation that the body of a young man fitting Nigel's description had been brought into the morgue. The body had been thrown from a bridge onto the cobblestones below, the spine broken on impact. The face was so badly battered it was almost unrecognisable. A Legation official was asked to go to the morgue and had no difficulty identifying Nigel, whose striped Old Etonian tie was knotted around his neck.

Joice shuddered when she heard the news. Had the Iron Guard taken revenge for Nigel's inept cloak-and-dagger work? If only he'd had the sense to keep his mouth shut rather than boasting about having masterminded the smuggling of a top-level Jewish scientist out of Hungary, he might still be alive.

Doamna Popescu was not surprised when Joice told her about Nigel. 'In 1938 the Iron Guard threw Jewish medical students to their death from ze top floor of the Medical School. My nephew, God rest his soul, vas killed zere.'

She told them that King Carol refused to abdicate until he had sold his summer palace to Antonescu's pro-German government.

Once again Lushya observed, 'How very Rumanian. It must be the first time in history a king has sold his palace *before* his abdication. What would the British have said if their Edward VIII had tried to sell off Buckingham Palace before he abdicated?'

On 6 September 1940, with demonstrators screaming for his blood outside the Royal Palace, King Carol issued a statement that he would shortly abdicate in favour of his son, who would reign under the name of King Michael of Rumania.

The Danube ferries were crowded with refugees, but the previous week Sydney had managed to charter a huge pleasure steamer for his escape party. The Polish forger at the internment camp had completed a brilliant job, producing all the exit visas and forged passports required. Now Sydney received a message from the captain that his river steamer was ready. The elderly Polish politicians were to leave Bucharest by coach and join the steamer further downriver. Operation Swordfish was under way.

Joice kissed Sydney goodbye, trying to sound unworried about the desperate adventure that lay ahead but inwardly feeling scared. It was agreed they would meet up at the small southern Turkish port of Mersin—or, should something prevent this, on the British-held island of Cyprus, where there were already several Polish refugee camps. Joice would travel from the Black Sea port of Constantza to Istanbul and thence to Mersin. If she had problems with transport she must contact the British Embassy in Ankara or the British High Commissioner in Famagusta, who would pass on messages. To avoid the messages being intercepted by the enemy she was to use her code name: 'Pied Piper'. They embraced not knowing how long it would be until they met again.

Joice cabled Friends House in London, asking for money. But the promised funds failed to arrive. Or perhaps they had gone astray—so many of the bank staff had given up their jobs and fled. The banks kept erratic hours during the present State of Emergency. Whenever they did open, there were long queues of people desperate to leave Bucharest before the Russians or the Germans arrived. Day by day the Russian troops drew nearer, heading for the vast oil fields of Ploesti, only eighty minutes drive from Bucharest.

The day before Operation Pied Piper was due to depart, the promised Friends War Relief money still had not arrived. Joice had sufficient funds to pay for tickets for everyone, but nothing to spare in case of emergencies or sickness. She prayed the money would last until they reached Cyprus, and that none of the women and children would need expensive medical treatment.

Mr Brown, the Loch's American friend and colleague, was remaining in Bucharest to act as liaison officer between the American YMCA and the Rumanian YMCA. (At this stage of the war the USA was still a neutral country.) He had kindly agreed to look after those Polish women and children who had opted to stay behind. Brownie was extremely upset that the American Government had not done more for the Poles and Jews. He insisted on taking Joice to a farewell lunch at Nestor's, a restaurant conveniently situated in the same building as his office.

It was a warm day in late September. Under the awning over Nestor's handsome door, Brownie greeted a pair of German-speaking Rumanians, who said they had been listening to the radio. They announced smugly that the German blitz on London was succeeding and Britain was on the point of surrendering to Germany. Joice and Brownie laughed. 'Don't believe Dr Goebbels' propaganda,' Joice said. 'That's all it is.'

Inside the restaurant they were shown to a window table where a well-dressed couple were already seated. Brownie introduced them as Mr and Mrs Gluckstein, of Solomon and Gluckstein's Bank. 'This is Doamna Loch, from Australia, who helps to run the Quaker Mission to Polish refugees. A woman on whom you may depend,' he told the Glucksteins.

They all shook hands. Mrs Gluckstein was from a Jewish banking dynasty, the Guttmans, owners of the famous Dresdener Bank. Her brother-in-law, who ran a branch of the family bank in Bessarabia, had been killed by the invading Russians; her sister had been gang-raped and killed by the savage Turkestaner soldiers of the Russian Army. 'We sent our chauffeur to bring my nieces to Bucharest. He hid them on the floor of the car under a rug,' Mrs Gluckstein told Joice, biting back her sobs.

Brownie had told the Glucksteins about Operation Pied Piper and asked them if they could donate money for the Jewish orphans Joice was taking out of Rumania. They had said they were happy to do this. They hoped Joice would be able to include their recently orphaned nieces and their only daughter in her party. Mrs Gluckstein had another sister living at Haifa, where there was now a large Rumanian-Jewish community. She had agreed to look after the three little girls until the Glucksteins could wind up the bank's affairs and leave the country for Palestine, which they hoped would one day become part of the projected Jewish state of Israel.

'Of course, we'll make it worth your while to take the girls to Haifa,' Mrs Gluckstein told Joice, pulling a manila envelope out of her handbag. 'Here are ten thousand *lei*,' she whispered. To Joice it seemed as if Providence had smiled again. This money would cover all emergencies during the long journey that lay before them.

'Mrs Gluckstein, please understand that I am not in this for the money,' Joice said. 'But it *would* come in handy with so many children to feed and accommodate. I worry about what happens if any of them get sick or we encounter delays.'

'Take it, take it, my dear. Get my nieces and my daughter to Palestine, that's all I ask. Otherwise the Nazis will kill them. Use the rest of the money to help the others. Mr Brown here tells me very good things about you. Please, give me your word that you will take my beloved girls to Haifa.'

'Yes, as long as their passports are in order and don't say they are Jewish.' Joice knew that prominent families like the Glucksteins were high on the Iron Guard's wanted list and could jeopardise the whole expedition.

Mrs Gluckstein reached into her handbag again and produced three British passports in the names of Sally, Susan and Janet Brown, all excellent forgeries so far as Joice could see—unless a British official been bribed to supply them. In wartime nothing was certain any more.

'Doamna Loch,' Mrs Gluckstein said nervously, 'I swear on my sister's life, no one but God himself would know these girls are Jewish. They had an English nanny. Their English is as good as yours. And their hair is so blonde they look like *shiksas*!'

Joice agreed to take the three little Jewish girls on to Haifa after leaving her party with Sydney on Cyprus. It seemed the right thing to do.[7] They arranged a meeting next morning at eight under the clock at the main railway station.

That night, as Joice made her final preparations, she thought about Sydney. By now his party must have reached Constantza, taken the ferry to Istanbul and, God willing, be at Mersin by now.

By six o'clock next morning she was ready. She bade a sad farewell to her landlady, who gave her a thermos of coffee and several rolls filled with ham for the journey.

'*La revedere*,' [the Rumanian equivalent of '*Au revoir*'] Doamna Popescu exclaimed and kissed Joice on both cheeks. Joice was heartened by the fact that Doamna Popescu obviously believed they would meet again. *I only hope she's right*, Joice thought to herself. Although she was only partly Jewish, according to the Glucksteins, Doamna Popescu's fate in Nazi-occupied Rumania was an uncertain one. And Operation Pied Piper could easily turn into a one-way journey to a concentration camp.

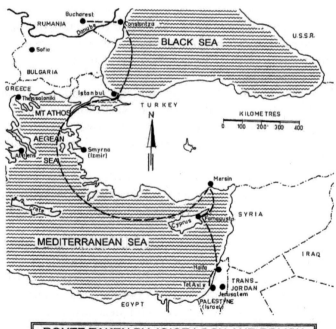

ROUTE TAKEN BY JOICE LOCH AND POLISH REFUGEES ON OPERATION PIED PIPER

26   OPERATION PIED PIPER

Operation Pied Piper started off at the main station of Bucharest on a sunny day early in September 1940.

Although Joice was totally unaware of this, by a strange coincidence this was the very day that King Carol, accompanied by the Jewish Magda Lupescu, had chosen for his grand exit from Bucharest in the Royal train. Naturally enough the attentions of the Iron Guard were entirely focused on observing the departure of the Royal party. (Later in the day, they made a dramatic assassination attempt on Magda Lupescu. A small ambush party of crack marksmen from the Iron Guard waited at the entrance to a curving railway tunnel near the Rumanian border, where the Royal train was forced to slow down. Their plan was to shoot Magda Lupescu through the window of the Royal train. The attempt failed because King Carol had the foresight to install his own team of marksmen on the train, who killed his would-be assassins.)[1]

An inner-city rally of the Iron Guards was also scheduled that day, which further distracted their attention from the ordinary travellers at the railway station. The next day Hora Simia, the Minister for Culture and his thugs would go on a killing spree: hanging their victims from meat hooks in abattoirs was to become their trademark.[2]

Most of the fifty or so unaccompanied Jewish children in Operation Pied Piper were orphans. It was vital that none of the women and children should arouse any suspicion when they boarded the train bound for Constantza. The weather was very hot that year and it was still school holidays. Joice had banked on the fact that the train would be crowded with holiday makers on their way to the splendid beaches of the Black Sea resorts Constantza and Mamounia. It had been arranged that each family should board the train separately, looking as much as possible as though they were going on holiday. Joice reckoned the Iron Guards were less likely to suspect happy children in sun-dresses and shorts, and mothers clutching beach bags.

Three bewildered little girls in smocked frocks, ankle socks and white sandals arrived at the previously arranged meeting place under the station clock, delivered by Mrs Gluckstein. They bobbed little curtsies to Joice and Lushya and announced, in beautifully enunciated

English, that their names were Zara, Magda and Dina. Joice put her arms around the little girls and promised to see that they reached their aunt and uncle in Haifa safely. The three little girls kissed Mrs Gluckstein goodbye. She burst into tears and soon all of them were crying. Then, shepherding the weeping children, Joice and Lushya boarded the train.

Leaving Lushya to comfort the girls (she reminded them that their names were now Sally, Susan and Janet and they must not answer to any others), Joice went up and down the corridors checking that all the Polish women were there. Her group included a few stolid peasants from eastern Poland but the majority were wives and widows of captured Polish officers.

For the moment it seemed they were safe, but they knew the Iron Guard might decide to board the train further down the track, inspect passports and discover that some of the children were Jewish, with terrible consequences.

A ticket inspector informed them that the train was being diverted slightly to pick up a big export consignment of Black Sea caviar and sturgeon from a processing factory at Tulcea, near the delta of the Danube. This would mean a one-hour delay in their arrival at Constantza. Joice hoped they would arrive in time to catch the afternoon ferry to Istanbul. She certainly had no wish to spend another night in Rumania.

She had exchanged her grey Quaker uniform for a bright cotton frock, sandals and a straw hat with blue ribbons. The women had only their small 'beach bags', and they had sewn any jewellery they had left into the hems of their dresses. Joice was planning to charter a large fishing boat to get them from Turkey to Cyprus. There would be little room for luggage aboard, especially with the additional four hundred Polish refugees who were to join them at Constantza.

Their steam train clattered alongside ripening fields of wheat and maize and orchards loaded with fruit. The day became oppressively hot. The journey had such a holiday feel to it that the excited, chattering children seemed oblivious of any danger. To all appearances this was a large-scale day excursion to the seaside organised by the Quaker Mission in Bucharest.

After Giurgeni the train wound along beside the wide banks of the Danube. At times the muddy waters were spliced by the mint-green waters of streams whose source lay high in the Carpathian Mountains. Looking out of the train window, Joice saw flocks of storks making their way towards the Danube delta.

Gradually the Danube grew wider and wider until they arrived at a siding beside a huge canning factory where gigantic Black Sea sturgeon were packed and their caviar tinned for consumption on the luxury market. Huge crates were loaded into the goods wagon. The whistle blew.

They set off again alongside the vast delta with its banks of reeds and fens swarming with pelicans and cormorants. The children were excited when flamingos rose into the air in clouds of salmon-pink. Joice watched the flocks of creamy-white storks with slender legs red as sealing-wax; suddenly she recalled the storks she had seen on that spring day twenty years ago in the valley of the Stochod River in Poland and the poem she had written about the beauty of their flight. She remembered Count Tarnowski telling her that each autumn the storks flew to the vast delta of the Danube and lived beside its shallow waters until the increasing cold sent them winging off to Africa.

Another, older memory surfaced: she had learned in one of her university lectures that Ovid, the Roman poet, had traversed this delta when he was sent into exile by the Emperor Augustus, banished to the port of Tomi—the ancient Greek name for Constantza.

The modern Constantza turned out to be a thriving Black Sea holiday resort with concrete Art Deco-style hotels topped with neon signs along a wide sandy beach. As previously arranged, they were joined at Constantza station by 400 more Polish women and their children, who had been 'house-sitting' the holiday villas of wealthy Rumanians. Accompanying them were a few teachers and priests who helped Joice and Lushya buy ferry tickets out of the expedition's funds. In spite of the diversion at the Danube delta, luck was on their side. The Istanbul ferry was waiting for their train.

They filed through customs apprehensively but fortunately the Rumanian officials displayed little interest in them, and once again no members of the Iron Guard were in evidence. Joice, playing the role of an English-speaking governess, steered the three little Gluckstein girls through passport control. 'We're going sight-seeing in Constantinople,' she told an official, unsure if he understood English.

He yawned and mopped his brow, sweating profusely in the heat, then stamped their passports with only a cursory glance and waved them towards the waiting ferry. The rest of the party had no problems with their forged or black-market exit visas as they filed through customs and passport control.

Joice, Lushya and the little girls climbed the gangplank. The huge Black Sea ferry reeked of engine oil, stale fish and Turkish tobacco.

Burly navvies unwound ropes as thick as their arms from huge metal bollards. Then they were moving smoothly away from the dock. They passed an enormous lighthouse. The weather had changed: now the Black Sea was grey and oleaginous under a heavy threatening sky the colour of pewter.

Just as Joice and Lushya were congratulating themselves that everything was going to plan, announcements in Rumanian and German boomed over the ship's loudspeakers. Lushya translated: 'The ferry must return to Constantza as ordered by the Iron Guard. Oh, what shall we do?'

Beads of perspiration trickled down Joice's back. Lushya's fingernails dug into her arm. The Iron Guard would be there on the dock, waiting to herd the Polish women and children into cattle trucks and despatch them to labour camps in Germany.

Back at the dockside a detachment of Iron Guards was drawn up, waiting. Joice feared the worst. The gangplank was lowered. Jack-booted Iron Guards swarmed aboard. Ignoring the Polish women who gathered their young children protectively to them, the Guards clambered up the steep companionway that led to the top deck. Joice, Lushya and the three little Jewish girls followed, keeping a safe distance.

They saw the Iron Guard gathered around eight huge wooden shipping crates, roped to metal rings inset into the deck. Was all this fuss over the sturgeon and tinned caviar that had been loaded onto the train? Surely not.

As the Iron Guards untied the ropes, the ship's captain argued with them, waving his arms and gesticulating. The officer in charge barked an order. The Iron Guards drew pistols from their holsters. The captain dropped his arms to his sides and stood very still. The boom of a crane swung over them, a huge net dangling from a hook. The crates were loaded into the net then deposited carefully on the dockside. The Iron Guard uttered cheers of delight and started to prise open the crates with crowbars. From the deck Joice caught a glimpse of something that glinted like gold bars.

'That's never tinned caviar! It's the bullion King Carol was shipping out of the country to finance his exile,' Lushya said, laughing so much that tears poured down her cheeks from sheer relief that the Iron Guard was after gold rather than Polish or Jewish refugees.

'Good on you, King Carol, you've saved our bacon!' Joice exclaimed. 'With all those millions in gold, they won't bother about inspecting passengers.' She was right. The commander of the Iron Guard waved up to the captain, indicating he could restart the ship's engines. Slowly the ferry pulled away from the dock and passed the lighthouse for the second time.

This time the crossing of the Black Sea passed without event. As they approached Istanbul, on each side of the placid waters of the Bosphurus they saw large wooden houses with pink and blue shutters and balconies overhanging the water.

They were met by a committee of Poles who had escaped from Rumania last year and were told the awful news that the German Army had marched into Bucharest a few hours previously, the signal for the Iron Guard to commence its orgy of killings.

Their bags were placed on handcarts pulled through the streets by Turkish porters. Following the luggage, they walked through street markets where men in baggy trousers and pointed slippers sold exotic-smelling spices, paper-thin pastries filled with nuts and honey and glasses of drinking water from huge copper urns they carried on their backs.

The whole group had been booked overnight into several large but inexpensive *pensiones* near the Topkapi Palace, in the old part of town known as the Sultanahmet. Lushya, exhausted by the stress, went to bed early. But Joice, with only one full day in Istanbul, the ancient city of Constantinople, centre of the Byzantine Empire, which she had always dreamed of visiting, was determined to explore the old quarter.

By moonlight she caught her first glimpse of the russet walls and huge dome of Hagia Sophia, the great Christian cathedral erected by the Emperor Constantine in the fourth century. Now it was a mosque complete with slender minarets. Her Polish guide regretted it was too late to go inside. He warned Joice that Turks and Crusaders alike had stripped Hagia Sofia almost bare but volunteered to show her over the cathedral the next day.

Next morning, she was woken by the wailing of the *muezzin*. She and Lushya breakfasted on flat rounds of Turkish bread with rose-petal jam and sweet *chay* or tea. Their Polish guide returned and Joice, Lushya and a group of the Polish women walked the short distance to Hagia Sophia and went inside.

Their guide told them how the huge gold crosses, the richly embroidered altar cloths and vestments, the gold pectorals and chalices, the relics of saints' bones in their gold and jewelled cases, so revered by the early Christians of Greek-speaking Byzantium, had been plundered by the Venetians and were now in the Treasury of San Marco. Joice thought of those other treasures Sydney had photographed in the monastic treasure houses of Mount Athos and on Patmos.

All that remained of the interior decoration of what had been the most glorious cathedral in Christendom were a few fragments of the wall mosaics: what had once been a huge mosaic of the Mother of God in her black robes and another of the Christ Pantocrator, flanked by images of the Emperor Justinian and his flighty Empress, wearing the pearl-encrusted crowns of Byzantium and richly embroidered robes with gold-embossed girdles. After the conquest of Constantinople these mosaics had been whitewashed over by the conquering Muslim Turks. They had even whitewashed the great figure of Christ Pantocrator from inside the dome. But on some walls, the whitewash was peeling and the Holy figures were emerging once more. With her love of Byzantine art Joice found the visit to Hagia Sophia a sad and disturbing experience.

They were to catch the overnight ferry for Mersin, which left Joice and her party enough time to visit the ancient palace of Topkapi. They were shown the Sultan's fabulous jewel collection, which included a faceted diamond larger than a duck's egg, jewelled daggers encrusted with rubies and emeralds and coffee cups glittering with diamonds. Their guide took them through the 'gilded cage', where the sons of various Sultans, born to his many wives, used to be confined during adolescence to prevent them being strangled or poisoned. Some of the youths had gone mad as a result.

Joice and Lushya made a head count before taking the whole party on board the ancient ferry bound for the south-eastern port of Mersin, near the border with Syria. For two nights they had to sleep on deck. On the second morning they woke stiff but tremendously exhilarated to think they had managed to escape from the Iron Guard, now in full rampage in Bucharest.

Mersin was filled with Polish refugees from Rumania and Hungary, all using this tiny port to reach Cyprus and Palestine. The numbers of refugees were so large that the British and the Germans had opened consulates there.

Joice visited the British Consulate, and learned that the Consul was ill with typhoid. She was given a letter addressed to her in Sydney's hand. Opening it, she read that he had got a very good price on three large fishing boats to take his party to Cyprus. Joice must wait at Mersin and one of the boats would return to take them to Cyprus. She should contact the Turkish Harbour Master and he would arrange everything.

Their funds were running down. After some hard bargaining with a Turkish hotel owner, Joice managed to install most of the Polish refugees in her escape party in his hotel for a nominal charge. There was only one problem. The hotel was in process of being sold and all the beds, bedding, cooking utensils, crockery and cutlery had been auctioned off. This meant that out of her diminishing funds, Joice had to replace these items as well as paying all expenses until they reached Cyprus. Once there, she assumed the British Government would contribute to the Polish women's living expenses, since so many of their husbands were now in the British Armed forces.

Joice, Lushya and a few of the older Polish women stayed at the nearby Hotel Gazelli, which fortunately had a telephone. From there Joice sent a telegram to Friends House in London, explaining that food was expensive in Mersin and they needed money to buy milk and eggs for the children.

The German consul, bald as an ostrich egg, ate his meals in the Hotel Gazelli, where, it seemed, anyone who was anyone in Mersin's diplomatic world stayed—all, it seemed, spying on one another. The dapper Italian Consul, tiny as Napoleon, pleaded dyspepsia and refused to share a table with his German counterpart, even though by now Mussolini had undergone a change of heart and entered the war as Hitler's ally. The French Consul refused to eat with either of them, but grudgingly consented to eat with Joice and Lushya. He seemed most unhappy about the entire situation. Over dinner he told Joice that the doctors believed the British Consul might die—apparently typhoid was a constant health risk in Mersin.

It was an anxious period. Mersin was scarcely a health spa and Joice feared for the health of the Polish and Jewish children. She also needed to conserve money to rent a ship with a safe water supply to take them to Cyprus. She had to try to persuade the Turks to sell them fruit, vegetables, fish, bread and fresh milk at bargain prices to feed the party. Meat was simply too expensive for their budget. The women took it in turns to cook meals in the hotel's huge kitchen, using equipment and crockery Joice bought in the market.

After a week of waiting, the largest of the three boats that Sydney had hired returned. The captain contacted the Harbour Master, knowing he was in touch with Joice. She was given a second letter from Sydney, telling her that they had had a hellish four-day voyage under sail. The wind had dropped, leaving all three sailing ships becalmed for two days. Each one had run out of drinking water. The 'modern flush toilets' promised by the Captain and the Harbour

Master turned out to be buckets filled with sand. Many of the refugees went down with food poisoning; the stench had been vile. Joice must, on no account, hire the boat of the Captain who brought her this letter. Nor should she trust the Harbour Master, who was a complete rogue and was only helping them because he received a good commission from the ships' owners. She could not run the risk of dysentery, especially with children on board, or cholera from polluted water or 'sanitary buckets'. She had to find a good modern ship. The British Consul would help.

There were many unseaworthy, picturesque old sailing boats plying for hire in Mersin harbour that the Harbour Master had recommended. The passage between Turkey and Cyprus was not long but the sea could turn rough—vessels had been shipwrecked in the past. This was a terrifying prospect. Many of the Polish children could not swim and there were no lifeboats or even life rafts on board. Joice knew she must find a modern ship to get her party to Cyprus. But how? By now she had the impression that the German consul was spying on her party to learn their destination. Was he plotting to pass on the information to the German Navy so that their ship could be attacked?

Even with unlimited money, finding a trustworthy captain prepared to take a party that included so many young children to Cyprus would have presented problems. Meanwhile the Turkish Harbour Master, fearing the loss of his introductory commission from the Lochs, insisted Madame Loch and her band of refugees should charter the first available sailing boat and leave Turkish waters immediately.

Joice was desperate. The only person who could have helped her was the British Consul and he was out of action. She sent Lushya with flowers to the Consul's home but was told he seemed on the point of death. Following the emergency plan Joice and Sydney had devised, she telephoned the British Embassy in Constantinople, giving her codename 'Pied Piper'. She was terrified her phone might be tapped by the German Consul but had to take that risk. She was put through to the Third Secretary and asked him to be kind enough to radio British Naval Command to see if they could provide a ship capable of taking her party to Cyprus. The Third Secretary sounded guarded. The British diplomatic service, like every diplomatic service in the world, was governed by strict protocols; he had definitely not been instructed by the top brass at the Foreign Office on how to deal with persistent women in charge of escape parties demanding naval vessels.

Sensing his quandary, Joice gave the name of her old friend the Admiral in charge of the Mediterranean Fleet as a reference. There was a long pause. The Third Secretary consulted someone else. There was a whispered conversation at the other end of the line. Finally Joice was asked to phone back tomorrow.

Although Joice belonged to no church or religious denomination, their situation seemed so precarious that she slipped inside the next Orthodox church she passed and prayed that God or Divine Providence would, by some miracle, protect the women and children in her care.

The following day she rang the British Embassy in Constantinople again, not overly confident that the Third Secretary would be able to help her. She was overjoyed when he told her that British Naval Command *had* found her a ship. She was called the *Warszawa*, affectionately known by the British Navy as the '*War Sow*'. She had flush toilets, water tanks and was manned by a volunteer crew whose main aim was to rescue refugees from the Nazis. Joice was amazed. It was as though all her prayers had been answered.

The *Warszawa* was due to arrive in Mersin harbour within twenty-four hours to embark Polish soldiers on their way to join the British Army in Palestine. Since she was already bound for Cyprus en route, the fare for the women and children on Operation Pied Piper would be a nominal one. There was one proviso. The ship's cook had his work cut out to provide food for the Polish soldiers and the crew. Joice must buy provisions for her group and they must cook their own meals. Joice and Lushya hugged each other at the news.

When the *Warszawa* steamed in to Mersin harbour, it was easy to see why the British Navy had nicknamed her the '*War Sow*'. She was a former coastal steamer, a battered hulk with a strong list to port, resurrected from a breaker's yard at the beginning of the war by her volunteer crew, some of whom were Polish, others British. She did have piped water but the pump-action toilets only worked intermittently and the smell was fearsome. This battered tramp steamer had saved British soldiers from the beaches of Dunkirk as well as carrying boatloads of Jews to safety. No one had given her a coat of paint for decades and she was red with rust. However, to Joice and the Polish refugees, she seemed like a luxury liner. They were overjoyed to board her and leave disease-ridden Mersin.

The plucky Polish women made the best of the situation. They rolled up their sleeves, scrubbed decks, toilets and cabins and cooked meals for themselves and their children. The Captain, who as luck would have it was Polish, handed over his cabin to Joice. 'Pani Lok, as the commander of Operation Pied Piper, you must have my cabin,' he insisted gallantly.

The Turkish Harbour Master, baulked of his commission from the sailing ship owners, was furious. He tried to delay their departure by demanding changes in their paperwork. Joice wondered if he was radioing the German Navy to tell them in what direction they were heading.

Unknown to the German Consul or the Harbour Master, the old tramp steamer stealthily loaded a large group of Polish soldiers who had escaped from Hungary and were bound for Palestine. They were smuggled aboard, singly or in pairs, under cover of darkness. The German Consul had been tipped off, probably by the Harbour Master, that the *Warszawa* should be watched. He hired a dinghy and sailed around her, keen to find out just what was going on. If he had seen any of the Poles in their khaki uniform jackets and breeches boarding the ship, he could have pressured Turkey to intern them. The ship's manifest had broken international shipping rules by not declaring they had soldiers aboard.

The *Warszawa* slipped out of Mersin harbour during the night, so quietly that not even the Harbour Master suspected her departure. Fortunately the sea was calm and they managed to avoid any German mines.

After an anxious night, Joice was relieved to see the island of Cyprus appear on the skyline. They docked at the rather grubby harbour of Famagusta, where the Union Jack was flying.[3] British Army doctors came on board. On hearing the women and children had spent some weeks in Mersin, they insisted on inspecting them for symptoms of typhoid but gave them all a clean bill of health. The old *War Sow* and her crew sailed on, taking the Polish soldiers to Palestine.

Joice and her party were escorted to a tented quarantine camp, already overflowing with Polish and Jewish refugees. She was overjoyed to find Sydney, who had been anxiously awaiting their arrival. He was accompanied by Dr Neff, Director of Health for Cyprus.

Sydney's own group had been housed in an Army camp; since so many of them were Members of the Polish Parliament they were considered official guests of the British Government until transport planes could be organised to fly most of them to Britain. However, no authority wanted to take any responsibility for the Polish women and children, financial or otherwise.

In wartime there were many empty hotels beside the beaches and beauty spots of Cyprus, but their owners refused to rent rooms to penniless refugees. After some haggling by the Lochs and the British Consul—who pointed out that these Polish refugees were educated people who would not allow their children to wreck their premises—a bulk rate was negotiated with two smaller hotels. The Lochs secured a victory when, after much discussion, it was agreed that the British Government would pay accommodation costs for the women and children on Operation Pied Piper. Sydney also managed to obtain a small weekly allowance for each refugee, plus a grant of five pounds per adult and three pounds per child for new clothes and shoes. The British Military Authorities were less than pleased to have so many women and children to care for and perhaps have to evacuate again if the Germans invaded Cyprus from Crete.

Although the Turks and the Greeks on Cyprus were traditional enemies, at this time conditions on the island were relatively calm. The odd burst of rifle fire between Turk and Greek did not worry the Lochs after the stress they had endured. British residents on the island welcomed the Lochs and were most hospitable to the Polish refugees, who were now well-housed and well-fed. A huge burden of responsibility was removed from the Lochs' shoulders.

On this beautiful island, believed by some to be the birthplace of Aphrodite, Goddess of Love, Joyce and Sydney spent what they always regarded as a second honeymoon, back in the part of the world they loved best.

By the spring of 1941, Joice was negotiating for places on a troopship to accompany the Glucksteins' little girls and the rest of the Jewish orphans to Haifa, where there was a large Rumanian-Jewish community who would take care of them. Then the Germans invaded Greece. Cyprus seemed likely to be the next area to be invaded after Crete. The Cypriots heard on the radio that the Germans had slaughtered huge numbers of British and Australian soldiers as well as Greeks suspected of being friendly to the British. What followed was a huge demand on shipping out of Greece.

Representations to Whitehall by the Polish Government in exile in London requested the British Government to evacuate *all* the Polish refugees in Cyprus to British-run Palestine, previously the destination of only Joice and the Gluckstein girls.

After an anxious period of waiting, in June 1941 the British Government sent a naval cruiser and Australian troops who had arrived on Cyprus after the battle for Crete helped load the refugees aboard the naval vessel.[4] Hearing Australian accents again made Joice feel quite homesick. The cruiser did not have sufficient rations to feed all the refugees. The Poles were given money by the Lochs (who had at long last received some funds from the Quakers) to take their own food and drink with them on the voyage, which was supposed to last just one or two days. The Lochs were so busy with last-minute arrangements, buying food and medicines for the women and children and settling outstanding hotel bills, they had no time to buy food for themselves. As the Polish refugees formed a long line and edged slowly up the gangplank, Joice and Sydney managed to get a quick cup of tea and a biscuit in an English teashop beside the harbour. When the proprietor learned they were in charge of so many refugees, she insisted on giving them four cheese sandwiches and a thermos flask of tea.

As they left Famagusta Harbour the sea was flat as glass under a scorching hot sun. The British cruiser made slow progress, twisting and turning to avoid floating mines. Father Ambrosius and the other priests on board gave lessons to the Polish children under canvas awnings while the Jewish girls and boys played under another awning and Lushya looked after those children who were sea-sick.

Joice and Sydney ate their sandwiches in the gun room, far too anxious about floating mines or German bombers to relax.

At dusk they went on deck to find the sky overcast. A cigarette butt flickered for a moment and the Captain yelled down from the bridge, 'Stop those bloody Poles smoking or the German planes will find us!'

The Lochs discovered the disturbing fact that the ship did not have enough life belts or lifeboats for all the passengers. If the ship was bombed or blown up by mines it would be a disaster. They were invited onto the bridge while Lushya stayed below to comfort the orphans. The Captain, who seemed tense and nervy, told them he had already been on two ships blown up by German mines. The next moment the wireless officer pointed at the sky. 'Are those stars or planes?' he demanded as twin points of light seemed to hurtle towards them. In the far distance came the sound of explosions. It looked as though Haifa, their destination, was being strafed by German planes. Then came the drone of engines as German planes arrived overhead. Huge waves surged around them like a maelstrom as the bombs aimed at the ship hit the water on either side. The raid seemed to last for an eternity. Then, as dawn came up, baulked of their prey the German planes flew away.

During the morning the Captain was advised by Port Control at Haifa that mines had been placed at the approaches to the harbour to destroy their ship. The Germans had succeeded in blowing up a British ship the night before as well as bombing two more which had sunk. Tenser than ever, he invited the Lochs up to the bridge again and provided tea and biscuits. Then, without any radio warning, over the horizon steamed a battered tramp ship. It was the *Warszawa*. Her list to port was now so pronounced that it seemed she might sink.

At the sight of hundreds of soldiers in Polish uniform waving and cheering from the rails of the *Warszawa*, an answering cheer went back from all the Polish refugees aboard the Lochs' ship.

'My God! it's the old *"War Sow"*. We'll be safe. She's got a charmed life. She's *never* been hit by the Germans,' the Captain said thankfully. The two ships, both bearing Polish refugees, steamed towards each other. As they came close, friends, relatives, husbands and wives, many of whom had not seen each other for years, wept for joy.

The Captain was gloomy about their chances of getting into Palestine with any Jewish children aboard. He knew that several British ships had been refused permission to land because they carried Jews. They had waited at Haifa for weeks and then sailed away again in despair. He told Joice how one captain had been so desperate he had risked a court-martial and beached his ship to get the Jews on board into Palestine—he could no longer bear the thought of carting from port to port Jewish passengers living on three feet of deck space, who could not return to their homelands, and whose relatives there were now in Nazi concentration camps.

In 1941, before the world knew the full horror of the Jewish Holocaust, it was hard to arrive anywhere with Jews aboard and gain admittance; very few countries wanted to accept them.

Joice and Sydney were determined that the Jewish orphans they had brought from Rumania would be allowed into Palestine. To their dismay the Captain told them that Palestine had demanded a reduction in the numbers of Jews entering the country. They now wanted to cut the number below the ten-per-cent level they had originally agreed. Palestine was part of the Arab bloc, mainly allies of the British, who desperately needed Arab oil to win the war. Knowing this, the Palestinians were manipulating the British over the Jewish entry provisions.

Joice believed firmly in the Quaker principle that *all* refugees regardless of religion or race *must* be saved. She had promised the Glucksteins she would deliver their daughter and orphaned nieces to Haifa. Absolutely nothing would stop her now, she vowed, even if she had to take a lifeboat and row them ashore herself.

The Captain radioed his vessel's whereabouts to the officer in charge of port control. A reply crackled back that he was to 'Cut engines, drop anchor and wait for clearance'. They followed orders, hove to and waited anxiously for more than an hour.

To pass the time and distract the children from any hint of danger, Joice and Lushya plaited the hair of the Gluckstein girls and made them change into clean dresses and ankle socks so they would look their best. The three little girls, overjoyed at the thought of seeing their aunt and uncle, chattered away nineteen to the dozen. Joice marvelled at the resilience of children. She wondered how Doamna Popescu and Mr and Mrs Gluckstein had fared in Bucharest during the dreadful rampage of the Iron Guard and the subsequent entry of the invaders.

Finally a British mine-sweeper appeared and removed the mines which the Germans had laid the previous night. They were advised by radio that it was safe to dock. British medical and port officials came on board to inspect all the passengers. To Joice's utter relief there were no difficulties about the Jewish children and no awkward questions about passports.

Once they had ushered the refugees through customs, Sydney and Joice telephoned the British High Commissioner, who had already been advised about their arrival by Whitehall. He promised that a special train would be sent to the port to deliver the refugees to two camps outside Haifa. He also invited Sydney and Joice to dine at the High Commission that night.

'What an achievement, escaping with 2,000 Poles through Turkey!' the High Commissioner exclaimed. 'I've still got a bottle of the '36 Veuve Cliquot left. We'll celebrate.'

To the Lochs, who had eaten nothing but two stale cheese sandwiches, some biscuits and a few cups of tea since leaving Cyprus almost two days before, the prospect of an excellent meal with the High Commissioner seemed magical.

Sydney hugged Joice. 'We've done it! We've got 2,500 Poles and Jews out of Rumania and *all* of them still alive. Am I looking forward to dinner! I could eat an ox.'

Joice hugged him back before dialling the number Mrs Gluckstein had given her, weeks ago, in Bucharest. The phone rang for some time before it was answered.

'This is Joice Loch. Your three nieces are safe and longing to see you. We're on the British cruiser that just came into the harbour. How soon can you collect them?'

A sharp intake of breath at the other end of the phone was followed by sobs before Mrs Gutman managed, 'Mrs Loch, forgive me. My sister and her husband were murdered by the Iron Guard three days after you left Bucharest.' Between sobs she added, 'How can we ever thank you for saving our girls?'

'Please, I don't want thanks,' said Joice, embarrassed and deeply upset by her news. Then she thought about the Jewish children who had no homes to go to and added, 'If you *really* want to thank us, please help us to find foster-homes for the other Jewish children in our party.'

'Anything, Mrs Loch, anything. We have a large Jewish community in Haifa. They will help. You have my word.'

27 THE CAMP OF A THOUSAND ORPHANS

As the High Commissioner had promised, a special train was sent to the landing stage to take the refugees to a transit camp in Haifa. Joice kissed the three little Jewish girls she had brought from Bucharest and said goodbye. A car was coming to take them to the home of their aunt and uncle. Mrs Gutman would keep her word: most of the Jewish children would find foster homes or relatives among Haifa's large Rumanian Jewish community.

Meanwhile the British Army, who ran the refugee camps, insisted that they had no funds to feed so many Polish civilians. The Quakers or the Lochs must pay for food for 'their' refugees. Once again the Lochs argued that the women's husbands were soldiers fighting for Britain; the very least the British could do for people who had suffered so much was to feed them. The colonel in charge insisted he could not feed civilians, only soldiers. *Impasse.*

By now the Lochs' aid fund was almost exhausted and the Ottoman Bank in Haifa refused to accept their letter of credit drawn up by Friends War Relief in Cyprus. This was a crisis of huge proportions. If 'their' Polish women and children were not to starve, the Lochs would have to confront the Director of the Ottoman Bank at his headquarters in Jerusalem.

Leaving Lushya and Father Ambrosius to deal with day-to-day problems, they boarded a train for the Holy City. Jerusalem swarmed with refugees—Greek, Czech, Yugoslav, Rumanian and Jewish. The Lochs had previously made a telephone appointment to see the Director of the Ottoman Bank. Apprehensive that he might prove hostile and support the refusal to honour the Quakers' letter of credit, they filed into his marble-lined office, where Joice told her story. The Director, a large bearded man in a cream tussore silk suit, turned out to be sympathetic. On learning how many women and children they had to feed, he issued instructions to the Haifa branch to pay the letter of credit immediately. Greatly relieved, the Lochs set off for the British Embassy, intending to phone Lushya from there and give her the good news.

The Embassy staff were delighted to see them. The Germans had broadcast news bulletins relating how their ship had been bombed by German planes and sunk without trace. The Embassy had believed that the Lochs and the escape party were dead. Joice remembered Oscar Wilde's famous words: 'Reports of my death have been greatly exaggerated.'

On their return to the ramshackle and overcrowded camp at Haifa, Lushya told them that large numbers of 'their' Poles had been given the chance to board a British ship bound for Nigeria, then a British colony, where work was supposedly awaiting them. Using the money now installed in a special Friends War Relief account, they arranged to transfer most of those who remained to two far larger refugee camps further south, just outside Tel-Aviv, with far better facilities than the one in Haifa. A second ship would be arriving shortly to take others who had chosen to go to Rhodesia and Kenya, where it was hoped work could be found for them in the British colonial administration.

Lushya and Father Ambrosius volunteered to remain behind in Haifa to see the Poles safely on board and to liaise with members of the Jewish community who were trying to find suitable homes for the remaining Jewish orphans. Lushya was now such an experienced interpreter that she was offered a paid job in the Haifa camp. Joice and Sydney kissed her goodbye and made plans to meet up later.

The Lochs were to lead the party bound for Tel-Aviv. When they arrived there they found that as camp commanders, they had been allocated a small apartment of their own, overlooking the sea. The British authorities, impressed by the Lochs' organisational skills, had decided they were to take charge of two adjacent new civilian refugee camps, built to house what would eventually be twelve thousand Polish women and children who had escaped from the *gulags* or labour camps in Siberia. Some Operation Pied Piper wives and widows chose to remain with the Lochs in Palestine, hoping their husbands would join them eventually, while others would soon be sent to Britain.

Hitler's decision to turn on Stalin, his former ally and invade Russia in June 1941 brought about the release of thousands of Polish men, women and children from Russian slavery. During the summer of 1941, the Germans advanced rapidly, killing hundreds of thousands of Russians. Hastily Stalin signed a treaty with Britain, which became his new ally. The British made it a condition that all Polish adults and children in labour camps or in orphanages must be released immediately. As a result, Polish men, women and children still strong enough to walk after two years of starvation diet and hard labour began to make their way south out of Russia. They left Siberia by rail, by river, on rafts they built themselves and on foot. The lucky ones managed to hitch rides on goods trains. Some went to Iran, others to British India. Many arrived in Palestine via Turkey or Cyprus and were directed to the two huge new camps on the outskirts of Tel-Aviv. At Tel-Aviv, the Lochs would eventually become responsible for the welfare of 12,000 penniless Poles, including some 9,000 widows and children, many of whom were orphaned and who had been starved almost to death in the Siberian labour camps.[1] The Lochs discovered that the Russians had followed a deliberate policy of breaking up Polish family groups in the gulags and most of the children had no idea if their parents were alive or not. All Polish men of fighting age, as soon as they were well enough, were sent to join the second Free Polish Army recently formed by General Wladisaw Anders. (In 1943 it was these men, known as 'Anders' Army' who would win a great victory at Monte Cassino as the Allies advanced northward through Italy.)

Stalin, a man whose diabolical cruelties to his own people and to the Poles has only emerged since *glasnost* and the fall of Communism, had been responsible for shipping a total of between three and four million Poles to forced labour camps or *gulags* in Siberia. Now the Lochs were caring for thousands of Stalin's victims.

This huge second wave of refugees, mainly from eastern Poland, brought with them rumours of a whole-scale massacre by Russian troops of Polish reserve officers captured and held in three internment camps near Smolensk. Much later this horror story of Stalin's treachery and cruelty would become known as the Forest of Katyn massacre.

In this vast dark forest some 15,000–20,000 Polish reserve officers (the exact number has never been established) who should have been protected as prisoners of war under the Geneva Convention, were, under orders from Stalin, ordered to dig their own graves, then shot in the head by Russian firing squads. Stalin, humiliated by the German invasion of Russia, would swear to the British that the Germans had committed the massacre.[2] The British Government, keen to remain friends with their new ally, failed to pursue the matter and buried reports like those of the Lochs deep in files at Whitehall. One result of Stalin's lies and Britain's reluctance to pursue the matter, was that many of the unfortunate women and children in the Lochs' camps in Palestine would spend agonising years hoping in vain that their husbands or fathers were still alive.[3]

A Russian-speaking Polish reserve officer arrested at the outbreak of war and transported from Poland to an internment camp at Smolensk told the Lochs how a Russian guard (with whom he played cards) had warned him to feign death 'as murder was afoot the next day'. The 'dead' Polish officer was left behind in his bunk to become the sole survivor of the Katyn massacre. The Polish reserve officers killed were not professional soldiers. They were businessmen and professionals who, as patriots, had joined the Polish Army reserve in 1939. Being educated, Stalin considered them a threat to Communism and for this reason ordered their execution. The Lochs remembered the last letter they had received from Melchior Wankowicz in Warsaw. He had told them how professional men with families, lawyers, engineers, doctors, and priests had joined the Reserve to save their country from invasion but due to disorganisation of the Polish Army commanders, many never received guns and were captured without any weapons or uniforms. Now they were all dead and their wives had no idea of what had transpired.

Enraged by Russian cruelty, Sydney relayed the Polish officer's report about the massacre of Katyn to the British War Office. The officer was now very ill and was expected to die. Sydney considered the story very important. However his report was filed away and 'lost': the War Office had no wish to jeopardise their new-found alliance with Stalin. For decades the British continued to deny that Stalin had indeed ordered the massacre at Katyn.[4] (The full horror of the Katyn massacre would not be revealed until October, 1992, first by President Gorbachov and then by President Yeltsin in a signed document. Later the ghastly evidence of the huge burial pits at Katyn would be uncovered.)

Many of the Poles from Siberia arrived with typhoid fever and died in the Tel-Aviv camp. The Lochs initially tried to buy anti-typhoid serum, but lacked the money to undertake an inoculation program for the thousands of inmates under their care.

However, a group of Poles managed to raise the money to set up a small laboratory to make their own anti-typhoid serum. They did this by giving concerts, dancing displays and puppet shows. A small hut in one camp served as the laboratory for some eminent scientists from the Universities of Warsaw and Krakow. They incubated the anti-typhoid serum in chicken embryos in a homemade incubator and made enough to inoculate everyone with whom those Poles from the Caspian Sea camps had come into contact—sailors, railway porters, shopkeepers and others—thereby ensuring that the Middle East was spared an epidemic of typhoid.

Poles who had escaped from Siberia brought children with them who were not their own, hoping that if they rescued other people's offspring someone else would save theirs. In this way the numbers of Polish orphans in the camps grew and grew. The main problems facing these children were lack of educational facilities and the misery caused by isolation from their families.

The Lochs' budget for Aid Relief came from money donated to Friends Relief Services Council and was limited by the donations Friends House received. They soon discovered that the only way the starving, ragged children could be fed and clothed by the British was to describe them on their passports as 'soldiers'. So they made sure that the magic word 'soldier' appeared on every passport, even when a child was only four or five years old. It seemed the only way to ensure the children would be fed from Army rations.

Little Katya was the first of many tiny Polish 'soldiers'. She was blonde-haired, blue-eyed and four years old. Her mother had died labouring down Siberia's salt mines, her father was a Polish general now serving with the Free Polish Army in England. After Katya's mother died, she had been looked after by a soldier who had once served under her father in the Polish Army. When the soldier left Siberia he brought Katya with him. Joice grew very fond of Katya and taught her to read and speak English. She left a year later to join her father in England but she and Joice continued to send Christmas cards to each other for years.

Sydney was kept busy negotiating better conditions for the refugees with British colonels and brigadiers. His task became easier when, due to his heroic war record at Gallipoli, the British appointed him as staff liaison officer with the acting rank of major.

Joice was now in charge of what she ironically described as 'a huge khaki-clad army of starving midgets'. These child 'soldiers' were issued with pith helmets and regulation khaki shorts. The camp now held between 8,000–10,000 children, the numbers varying from month to month as they were nursed back to health and departed for Britain, or were sent off to be reunited with their parents in Iran, Africa and other areas.[5]

To help the Friends Relief Service Council in London obtain more donations Joice wrote them an emotive report about the 'soldier' orphans: 'Picture to yourselves sloping sand dunes, not a blade of grass, not a tree and the full summer sun blazing down on dunes dotted with tents. Small boys come out of them in the early morning, dressed in men's khaki shirts and shorts which have been issued to them from Army stores. Their huge Army boots curl up at the toes as their feet only go half way down them. Some of the boys are so small that their shorts hang down around their feet and the waists have to be held up by string. In their tents they strip down to enormous men's underpants, stand their boots in tidy rows in the middle of the tents and go barefoot. We have written down the names of these unfortunate children on the Army rolls to get them food as being from ten to fourteen years, but many are much younger.'

On arrival the children's heads had been shaved by Relief workers against lice. Their thin necks were like wobbly stalks, making their heads seem much larger. Their eyes, burning with fever and starvation, stood out against their greyish-white faces. Most of the new arrivals were so ill and emaciated from hunger, scurvy and a vitamin deficiency known as pellagra that all they could do was vanish into their tents and lie there from breakfast time until the sun went down, when a slight breeze sprang up and they could creep out and walk about.

Teams of medical orderlies under Joice's control were given the responsibility of nursing these pathetic children back to health. Joice knew they must have vitamins to survive. When she confronted the British colonel in charge, he told her he had no vitamin supplements or fresh fruit for them.

Joice was furious. Here they were, living in an area of citrus groves, yet she could not get hold of oranges for 'her' children. She had always been a compassionate woman as well as a fighter for the welfare of children who had no one to defend them. The orphans needed vitamins and fresh oranges with each meal and she would get these for them. If she could only get hold of a lorry they could go to the orange groves at Jaffa and buy oranges in bulk.

She persuaded Sydney to commandeer an Army vehicle. They did this by removing the key from an astonished corporal. 'We're on a secret mission. Your truck is vital,' Joice told him.

They climbed in and Sydney started the engine. 'Tell your commanding officer we'll be back soon,' Joice called out cheerily as they drove away from the camp.

Jaffa was only an hour away by jeep. The owner of the first orange grove they visited complained he had 12,000 fruiting trees but was unable to export oranges during the war. After a hour of hard bargaining, for twenty-five pounds (a considerable amount in those days), the Lochs found themselves the owners of a year's crop.

Loading as many crates as possible into the back of the truck they returned to the camp to await a lorry which would bring the rest as soon as their cheque was cleared.

The major in charge of transport was furious and threatened to make life difficult for Sydney. Joice had to use all her charm and powers of persuasion to stop him making a official complaint to the British High Commission.

Joice told her orderlies that each child must have an orange at every meal. As though by a miracle those starved and skeletal orphans started to put on weight. They began to fool around, throw water over each other and behave like normal children once again.

Joice, with her bush upbringing, was endlessly resourceful, always dreaming up new ways to help 'her' children. She bought rope-soled shoes to act as a pattern and vast amounts of rope needles and canvas, then cajoled an instructor to teach the boys to make their own espadrilles. She knew these would be far more comfortable than the oversized Army boots issued to them. She also arranged for English tuition from retired teachers.

The Lochs established courses in tropical medicine for refugee doctors, and courses in dressmaking and doll-making for the women, to take their minds off worrying about their prisoner-of-war husbands as well as restoring their self-respect—this was especially needed for those who had been raped by Siberian guards. The Polish dolls proved very popular when offered for sale and earned their creators good money.

The Lochs met the Archimandrite Anthony, a Russian Orthodox priest in charge of the enormous orange garden that belonged to the Russian church in Jaffa. Father Anthony knew their old friend Brother Anophronos, the former Russian prince turned monk from the monastery of St Panteleimon on Athos. In spite of the fact that the Russian Orthodox and the Catholic churches were at loggerheads, the Archimandrite Anthony could not do enough for the Lochs and their Polish refugees, even though they were of different faiths. He lent the Lochs a cottage in the middle of the monastery grounds. Beside the cottage were vacant buildings which he said they could use. Joice got the women to scrub them out, bought disinfectant to kill the cockroaches and turned them into refuges where mothers and their young children could recuperate away from the stresses and overcrowding of camp life. The scheme was so successful that a bishop of the Anglican church gave Joice the use of another house at Ain-Karem for the same purpose.

The Camp of a Thousand Orphans

By now many regular Army wives had been reunited with husbands after a long period of separation. Men and women were suffering from scurvy after a Siberian duet of watery gruel, acorn bread and grass soup or porridge. Their teeth and hair were falling out with scurvy, and new mothers found it impossible to breast-feed their babies. The number of infant deaths in camp made Joice realise that these babies could not tolerate the powdered milk issued to British troops. In wartime no patent milk formulas for babies were imported into Palestine. Something must be done, or babies born to women who had survived the Siberian camps would continue to die.

Joice convened a committee of Polish and English doctors, who decided that human milk should be purchased for each baby's first nine days—the period in which most were dying—from mothers medically certified as fit. After this the babies could be fed on a diet of goat's milk, believed to be better for them than cow's milk, with mashed banana and orange pulp.

Not everyone was pleased. At the next Polish Relief Committee meeting one well-dressed woman stood up and declared that the buying of human breast milk to feed these babies must cease forthwith.

Joice's eyes flashed. Controlling her anger she asked acidly, 'If the Committee doesn't want to spend money on human milk why don't we buy a gas chamber so that these unfortunate babies can be humanely destroyed at birth? That would be more humane than letting them die slowly of starvation, don't you think?'

A collective sigh of dismay came from the Committee, signifying that Joice had won her point. The breast milk program continued: the infant death toll went down.

The plight of thousands of Polish widows in the camps posed an enormous problem. Those whose husbands had been killed at Katyn were not eligible to receive a widow's pension, since the massacre was being covered up by the British and the Russians. These women were very grateful for everything Joice did for them. A doctor's widow from Siberia, whose husband had been killed by a Russian guard as he tried to save the life of a dying woman rather than digging his quota of salt, told her: 'I am so grateful for everything you have done for us. This is the first time I have been able to get a good night's sleep. Instead of nightmares re-living my husband's death, I see the faces of the little dolls I am making.'

Appalling tales about Poles worked to death in salt mines, timber camps and on the cotton fields of Kazakstan emerged from the many widows and orphans Joice helped and counselled. One little girl described how her mother had broken her leg hauling timber. When the child ran to tell the Russian guard, he said, 'We have no doctors. Your mother can't work. She's useless.' Whereupon he took out his gun and murdered her in front of her daughter.

In Palestine, a land riven by religious and racial dissension, the Lochs' non-sectarian approach to religion made it easier to involve abbots, nuns, priests, bishops from all denominations, Anglican and Orthodox, to help the refugee children, especially the orphans, some of whom had been badly beaten and abused in Russian orphanages or labour camps.

One of the Lochs' Muslim Arab friends who shared their interest in classical music had purchased a radiogram and a large selection of classical gramophone records from Harrods in London just before the outbreak of war. These finally arrived at the same time as a group of Polish orphans who had gone blind after Russian armed guards forced them to work without hats under blazing sun in the cotton fields of Kazakstan. When the Arab heard about these blind orphans, he sent round his gramophone and records with a note for Joice: 'Their need is greater than mine.'

An Anglican Canon organised a collection of toys and games for blind Polish orphans. Meanwhile in Jerusalem the indefatigable Joice enlisted the help of Mother Maria, Abbess of the Russian Orthodox Convent of the Resurrection at Gethsemene, who turned a building in her beautiful grounds into a home and school for sixty Polish orphans.[6] A special service of thanksgiving for their arrival was held in the little church of the Convent, built around a great stone which the Abbess told Joice was where Christ had prayed during his agony in the Garden of Gethsemene. Joice wept as sixty little Polish girls knelt down to pray in front of the stone, tears streaming down their faces.

A Catholic priest whispered to Joice that every day in their Russian orphanage the girls had been told they were not Polish but Russian, that God did not exist, Stalin was their father and they would never see their parents again. But every night in their dormitory the girls would say together some prayers in Polish, weeping for their lost parents.

At a tea party given by the Abbess in her garden, as the darkening shadows turned the silvery olive trees to sombre grey, Joice talked to the girls. One of them told her, 'What the Russians told us wasn't true. One day some English and Polish officers came to the orphanage, took us away and brought us here. Our prayers *have* been answered. And a few of us have found our parents. Not many, but a few.'

Sydney was the local representative of the Polish Refugee Committee, which worked closely with the Friends Service Council. Most of the Poles had now realised it was unlikely they would ever return to their own country. They would have to make new lives for themselves after the war—in Britain, the United States, Kenya or Australia, and were eager to acquire skills that would help them as migrants. Just as they had done in the camps and villages around Bucharest, the Lochs arranged for instructors to give courses in engine maintenance, electrical repairs, bricklaying, lorry driving, sign writing—all practical trades that would help the Polish men to find jobs when they emigrated. Joice set up other courses to benefit the women, many of whom had never worked outside their homes, but who would also need jobs in their new countries.

Sydney was in the camp Post Office one day when he overheard an Army officer inquiring whether anyone knew the address of an Australian named Joice NanKivell Loch. The officer turned out to be her cousin Dick NanKivell. Sydney brought Cousin Dick back with him to their cottage. Joice had not had a letter from home for many months. Mail often went astray in wartime, and her parents still lacked a phone. Dick told Joice he had received a letter from his mother with the news that her father was dying. Joice realised she would never see her father again; it was impossible for her to return to Australia in wartime. Having grown up amidst shattered dreams, genteel poverty and bitter recriminations, she had never been close to her father, who had not been an easy man to live with. Nevertheless she mourned for him; now that she had so much experience of life, she realised the difficulties of his unsatisfactory life, which had begun with such rich promise.

After George NanKivell's death, Edith left Neerim and went to live in a small hotel in Melbourne, acting as companion to her elderly aunt Ethel Lawson. Unfortunately, Edith insisted on following the advice of her bossy elder sister, Lily, and sold the farm at Neerim very cheaply— it was hard to sell any property in wartime. She ignored the advice Joice and Sydney gave her, which was to rent out Neerim until the war was over, when she would get a far better price for it. If it had not been for the war, Joice would certainly have visited Australia when he died and have been on hand to help her mother, as she had always done in the past.

When the Lochs had left Ouranoupolis and the tower by the sea it had seemed highly unlikely that Hitler would ever invade Greece. But both Italy and Germany had invaded the country, shooting or taking hostage any male Greeks they believed to be friendly towards the British. Now Greeks were escaping by boat, making their way along the coast to Syria (now taken over by the British and French) and from there arriving in Palestine.

Joice and Sydney heard rumours that the Farm School had been taken over by German troops and that Charlie and Anne House had been interned as enemy aliens and sent to Germany. They knew that many thousands had died of hunger in Athens. They could only pray that Madame Sophia and their friends in Ouranoupolis were surviving. All letters out of Greece were censored and none were allowed to be sent to British-held Palestine or Britain.

The British had set up camps for Greek refugees near Gaza. Unable to speak English, the Greek inmates felt unhappy and isolated. The Lochs visited these camps hoping for news of the Ouranoupolis area but could not find out anything. They were distressed to discover these Greek refugees had no Relief Fund to feed them; many were already severely undernourished from years of war. They were living under depressing and insanitary conditions on food they detested. Sydney wrote a report to Friends Relief Service in London requesting donations for Greeks in Palestine and received funding to start a soup kitchen.

Joice wrote countless letters to Australian authorities asking them to accept Polish families and widows as migrants. But Australia would not change its restrictive immigration policy, and remained reluctant to admit anyone other than British migrants until 1947, when large-scale migration of Poles to Australia began.

Lushya, whose aunt had once insisted she should go to New York after the war, often came from Haifa to visit Joice and Sydney. She was enjoying her job as a camp interpreter. On one visit she hugged them both and told them she had fallen in love with a young captain in the British Army. They planned to marry and live in England. Lushya laughed as she told Joice how disappointed her aunt in New York would be, as her fiancé was certainly not rich though devastatingly handsome. The Lochs, who by now regarded Lushya like a daughter, were delighted. Joice was especially glad that Lushya had abandoned her half-joking plan to marry an American millionaire as a means to restoring her family estates in Poland.

In August 1944 the Lochs handed over responsibility for many thousands of Polish refugees in Tel-Aviv to a pair of experienced Quaker volunteers, Emily Hughes and Jean Malcolmsen.7

Joice wrote in her memoirs: 'We could not feel we were deserting the Poles, for they were still to have someone [Hughes and Malcolmsen] with them to help fight their official battles. It was the second time a large slice of our life had been spent with [Polish people].They awarded us their Gold Cross of Virtue in Jerusalem before we left, but I do think that we took more than that away with us, namely their hearts.'

After World War II came to an end the following year, Polish refugees would start leaving Palestine in huge numbers, and the women would rejoin their husbands and sons in East Africa, Britain and America.

Greece now presented the Allies with a huge Aid Relief problem: hundreds of thousands of Greeks had died of starvation under German occupation and were still suffering from malnutrition. The reestablishment of Greek agriculture destroyed by the Germans was vital. Suddenly Sydney received a letter from the American Board of Missions, offering him the job of Acting Head of the Farm School. It seemed that Charles and Anne House were in poor physical shape and had been separated by the Germans. Charlie had been interned, sent to Germany and ill-treated, and Anne had been sent to a convent in France. For the present they were in America, where they had gone to rest and recuperate.

The Farm School where he had been a part-time teacher for so long was very dear to Sydney's heart and he accepted. He was allowed to keep the rank of Military Liaison Officer to allow him to enter Greece; since the food shortage was desperate, only Army personnel were admitted.

Carl Compton, newly appointed as Head of UNRRA in Greece (the United Nations Relief and Rehabilitation Administration), wanted Joice to return and set up official aid programs to villages there as soon as possible. It was agreed she should stay on in Palestine to ensure a smooth hand-over to the new Quaker team in Tel-Aviv.

At long last the Lochs had time for a brief and carefree holiday before Sydney departed for Greece on a troopship. Joice then returned to Tel-Aviv, determined to join him there as soon as possible.

Voluntary aid workers less experienced than Joice were getting well-paid jobs with international organisations like UNRRA, which was increasing its personnel at an amazing rate. Joice, who had never received a penny for her years of volunteer work with the Quakers, was justifiably cynical about the hordes of Relief 'experts' who came forward to claim these new jobs and were given exalted ranks. She attended an UNRRA committee meeting where the allocation of Army ranks was discussed. Joice announced, tongue in cheek, that if ranks were awarded, then she should be a Field Marshal or nothing at all. It was thought out of order that 'a mere woman' should speak out of turn. Joice wrote that she remained 'a simple citizen without any rank'.

Before leaving for Thessaloniki, Carl Compton said his relief service to war victims did not need 'untrained experts'; he knew that Joice's many years of experience of setting up relief schemes in Greek villages would be invaluable.

As the war in Europe drew to a close, there was a great deal of internal unrest in Greece, led by the Andartes, Greek Communist rebels. They were rumoured to be occupying Ouranoupolis, and were said to have murdered many inhabitants and raped village girls. Carl had warned her that Communist guerrilla bands were causing mayhem in the villages.[8] Joice was desperate to rejoin Sydney. Mail was nonexistent from Greece so she had heard nothing at all from him and was very worried. Neither had she heard from Madame Sophia or anyone else in Ouranoupolis.

Carl Compton managed to secure a passage for her on a troopship bound for Athens. She feared what might await her there, but could not wait to return to Sydney and her beloved Greece.

28   RETURN TO GREECE: CIVIL WAR

On 21 November 1944, Sydney had been one of the first British civilians to enter war-ravaged Athens.

Everywhere Greeks were emaciated and starving—some 50,000 Greeks had died of starvation in Athens alone. Public transport was non-existent: railways, roads and bridges had been blown up by the retreating Germans and by Greek partisans given arms by the British to fight German invaders. The Germans had ruthlessly stripped most villagers of their livestock and ploughs and in some villages had shot all male inhabitants.

Now the partisans, known as the Andartes, had become the guerrilla fighters of the Greek Communist Party, the KKE, and were using their weapons to terrorise the villages. There was bitter fighting, Greek against Greek, brother against brother. Once again the villagers were suffering and starving.

The ancient kingdom of Macedonia had been partitioned between Greece and Communist-controlled Bulgaria, Albania and Yugoslavia. The Communist guerrillas or Andartes were in league with Marshal Tito of Yugoslavia, who planned to take over northern Greece—Macedonia and Thrace—which would thus join the Communist bloc. At this time Tito was still Stalin's friend. Bulgaria as well as Yugoslavia was providing the Andartes with arms and ammunition. The Royalist Greeks, the British and the Americans were equally determined that northern Greece should not pass behind the Iron Curtain. The British Government was backing the Royalist Government in Athens and the Greek and British armies were supporting one another.

Sydney took the first ship available to Thessaloniki. There he found the roads in a terrible condition and motor transport non-existent. He rented an ancient cart and an equally ancient horse and made his way out to the Farm School.

Realising they were losing the war, the Germans billeted at the Farm School had burned down or vandalised the wooden buildings that housed staff and students before retreating back to Germany. A huge amount of restoration and rebuilding work was needed to make the campus habitable. As Acting Head, Sydney's job was to re-establish the Farm School until Charlie and Anne House could return.

Sydney missed Joice badly but worried that the situation in Greece was far too dangerous for her to return. He had received no replies to his letters to Madame Sophia and was almost certain she had been murdered. The Andartes were supposed to be occupying Ouranoupolis, and were said to have taken over the tower as their headquarters. When Greek or British soldiers went after the Andartes they would flee into Yugoslavia, knowing that Marshal Tito would provide them with food and ammunition.[1] Securing the border with Yugoslavia was now the priority of the British and Greek armies.

Sydney wrote to Joice warning her that the situation was degenerating into civil war; until the situation improved she should remain in Palestine. Joice, fearless as ever, was determined to join him. Her passage was booked and she was not going to cancel it.

Lushya came to Tel-Aviv from Haifa to say farewell, and Jonathan, her fiancé, came with her. He was indeed very good-looking, Joice thought, as well as being amusing and an excellent linguist. The pair of them were obviously very much in love; Lushya was radiant with happiness. Joice thought how much Lushya had changed—she was no longer the often frivolous party girl but a serious-minded young woman, brimming over with happiness and plans for the future. She and Jonathan planned to live in Cambridge, where he would work in one of the colleges. He would be returning to Britain in a few days time to work at the War Office until he was demobilised, and had managed to wangle a passage for Lushya on another troopship. Having lost her father, Lushya had asked Sydney to act as her parent and 'give her away' at her marriage. Both the Lochs were very happy when Lushya suggested this, for she really had become like a daughter to them both.

The sea around Greece was full of German mines but that did not deter Joice, who left Palestine in February 1945. The defeat of Germany was announced to great rejoicing as the troopship she was on arrived at Cyprus. The capitulation of Japan and the fighting in the Pacific area would soon come to an end, following the dropping of nuclear bombs on Hiroshima and Nagasaki. Finally World War II was over.

En route to Athens the ship docked at Thessaloniki. Sydney had no way of knowing the exact time of its arrival and arranged for Joice to be met by a member of UNRRA, who drove her out to the Farm School in an UNRRA jeep.

Her joy at returning to Sydney and the Farm School was overshadowed by the horror of the situation. It was very clear, as Sydney had written, that Greece was sliding rapidly into civil war, the

Right against the Left. And Joice described the Farm School campus 'looking as though a cyclone had blown through it'.

After the first excited welcomes had been exchanged, the Greek staff broke down in sobs. Every staff member had lost one or more family members to the Germans or the Andartes. There was no meat or eggs. Bread was scarce and very expensive; once again acorns and even earth were added to the dough to make it go further. Many had relatives who were starving or had died from malnutrition. Cigarettes, rice, flour and gold were the standard methods of payment: the banks had no currency in their vaults.

Political passions, ancient family feuds, food shortages and soaring inflation made for robberies, murder, rape and other atrocities. 'Murder was afoot, and *such* murder,' Joice wrote. In the province of Halkidiki alone hundreds of innocent people had been shot or had their throats slit by the Andartes as 'enemies of Communism'. Thousands more had been tortured to reveal information. Thousands of homes had been burned. By the time the civil war ended over a million Greeks would have been murdered by their fellow Greeks, more than the total number of those killed by the Germans. Violence was now an everyday part of rural life. Corpses lay where they had been killed, rotting in fields and mountain gullies, their clothes and shoes stripped off them to be worn by their murderers.[2] Foreigners were shot or taken hostage.

At the Farm School the Lochs, together with Theo and Chrysanthe Litsas and other workers aimed to rebuild the campus; the British Army donated building materials and provided soldiers to help with the task of reconstruction, which included building a school block for girls. Joice and Sydney presided over the ceremony of laying the foundation stone.[3] Aid relief measures were paid for by UNRRA, British and American Quakers and the American Board of Missions.

In August 1947, the first load of American military aid arrived in Thessaloniki, to be followed by further aid as, very gradually, the American Government became involved in the desperate struggle to save Greece from Communism.[4]

It was vital Greek village children should acquire literacy and the latest farming techniques if they were to conquer the famine and deprivation that surrounded them. The Lochs ran the Farm School until the House family returned at the end of September 1945, and would continue to give occasional courses there for years. Initially they lived on campus in a two-room wooden hut without running water, which they jokingly named Loch Hall after Sydney's family home in

Scotland.[5] In their tiny living room Joice typed up some proposals for humanitarian aid, to which Friends Relief Services in London and America were invited to contribute.

By this time she and Sydney were convinced that Lushya must be in England, and they eagerly awaited the invitation to her wedding. Instead, Joice received a letter from Haifa bordered in black. It was from Father Ambrosius, the priest who had been with them in Bucharest. He wrote that Lushya's troopship had been blown up by German mines en route to England. Not a single passenger had been saved. Joice remembered Lushya's warm smile, her joyous peals of laughter, how her presence had seemed to light up a room, their shared jokes, the long journey with the Polish refugees from Bucharest to Palestine . . . so many memories. She wept for Lushya as she had not wept since she had lost her baby in Poland.

By the end of 1945 Anne and Charles House were back from America and had taken over the administration of the Farm School. Charlie was happy to be able to use his civil engineering skills again. Joice stayed on, teaching the girls in their new campus school. Meanwhile Sydney, accompanied by an armed escort, carried out Army liaison work, visiting villages near the Yugoslav border with aid in the form of British-made agricultural implements and tinned foods.

In most villages, the Andartes had stolen the stores of wheat, dried maize and chick peas as well as the villagers' remaining hens, goats and pigs. Survivors in the villages were thin and gaunt. Sydney discovered that in hill villages which had neither fish, meat nor eggs, the inhabitants had survived on olives, weed soup, a *horta* of herbs and weeds and the bitter famine bread made from a few grains of wheat and acorns mixed with earth. Some had caught rats, snakes and lizards and eaten their cooked flesh.

The Lochs had always admired the Greek villagers for their determination, pride and independence. They decided a good way of giving aid was to donate improved breeding stock to the depleted villages. Through the generosity of the Quakers and the American Board of Missions, it became possible to offer each family whose livestock had been stolen a pure-bred pullet, a cockerel and a pair of English pedigree pigs—the Friends Relief Committee in London contacted pig-breeding societies and arranged for pedigree boars and sows to be shipped to Thessaloniki. British soldiers collected them from the docks and took them out to isolated villages. Sydney went on some of these humanitarian aid missions. Sometimes the boars escaped, causing havoc.[6]

Gradually Joice was drawn into humanitarian relief with UNRRA, although she was never a paid UNRRA worker. In villages whose economies had been ruined by the Andartes, she instituted aid programs to plant fruit trees brought out in British Army lorries. She gave basic medical advice in remote villages that had no doctor and arranged for the donation of medical supplies to them by the Quakers. The Lochs also helped in aid schemes to distribute sure-footed sheep from the island of Chios, where a joint Friends Relief and UNRRA team was operating. Sheep from Chios had provided the wool for Pirgos Rugs, and Joice knew their milk made excellent cheese and a thick, creamy yoghurt. She was delighted with the first ewe to arrive from Chios; she christened her 'Cleopatra'.

The Lochs' second aid relief scheme was designed to help Greek fishing villages whose boats had been confiscated by the Germans and sunk or burned when they retreated. This scheme, funded by the Quakers, was based on the inexpensive but reasonably effective aid program the Greek Government had carried out in 1923-4. It involved the donation of octopus tridents and enough cord to make fishing nets so that men could catch fish to feed their hungry families.

There were still no letters from Ouranoupolis. Eventually the Lochs discovered why. Georgiu, the village postman, used to walk between Ierissos to the Tripiti rock carrying the villagers' letters. Now Georgiu was terminally ill with cancer in the public hospital at Thessaloniki. The Lochs went to visit him just before he died, and Georgiu confirmed that the Andartes had murdered Madame Sophia and her son, believing that her doctor brother from Russia had hidden gold ingots in the tower.

Their old friend Father Meletios, the librarian-curator from Vatopedi, was also brought to the British Military Hospital at Thessaloniki. When the Lochs visited him he told Joice how Madame Sophia, in the winter of 1942-3 (known as 'the winter of the great hunger') had feared Joice's beloved Angora cats would starve to death. He had agreed to care for five of them at Vatopedi, where table scraps were available, but had not thought to check the gender of the five long-haired cats before taking them there. It wasn't long before the monks discovered they were harbouring three tom-cats and two females. Now their descendants were breeding happily at Vatopedi, among them the only female creatures on the Holy Mountain . . . apart from a few hens who had also mysteriously found their way there during the war.

Joice longed to return to the tower by the sea, however great the risk. Father Meletios had told her that the Andartes had now left the village and set up camp in the surrounding forests, but they still constituted a danger. The road service to Arnea had been suspended after the Andartes had shot an entire busload of passengers.

Brooding on the situation, Joice decided to request an armed escort from the British, brave the Andartes, visit Ouranoupolis and see what had happened to their home. Sydney was away for several weeks on an aid mission with a British Army truckload of livestock; she knew he would make strenuous objections to her plan if he found out about it, so she did not tell him.

Transport was a problem, as many buses no longer ran. However the British Legation promised to send an armed guard to escort her if she could get as far as the mining town of Stratoni, north of Ierissos, on the bus. From there the guard would escort her by boat to Ouranoupolis. A returning Greek soldier took a message to the Mayor of Ouranoupolis with a rough estimate of her arrival time at the tower. Joice was aware that Nanou, Sydney's former boatman, was still away; he had sailed to Crete and from there had joined the British Army in Scotland. She asked the Greek soldier to contact Yanni, their housepainter, who had always kept a spare key to the tower, and ask him to bring bread and olives for her evening meal.

Joice caught the rickety bus to Stratoni. Armed Greek soldiers searched passengers for knives or guns. It was a dangerous journey but Joice was determined to get home and find out what was happening in their village. The bus jolted and bumped its way over the pot-holed road with two armed soldiers aboard it. Several times it was stopped by soldiers checking their papers. At intervals gaunt tattered figures with guns rose up from the roadside shouting for newspapers: those who had any threw them out of the bus. These men wore blue-and-white striped armbands to show they were the King's soldiers, guarding the road against the Andartes.

The bus made a rest stop. Joice, the driver and several other passengers got out and she drank a cup of bitter acorn coffee and ate some sweet pastries. The cafe owner recognised Joice as the woman who had saved her sister after the earthquake at Ierissos. She refused to let her pay for the coffee and pointed to a distressed-looking youth. 'Look at him. Three days ago his little sister took the goat to feed in the forest. She was caught by the Andartes, hacked to pieces and left beside the goat in revenge, because the boy had deserted them.' 'Did he have to join them?' Joice asked.

'He had no choice. The Andartes send "black" letters to young boys telling them that if they do not join them, their brothers and sisters will be murdered. That boy joined out of fear.'

Travellers for Ouranoupolis were escorted down to the seashore by armed guards and packed into a motorised patrol boat operated by the army. All the ferries had been put out of action by the Germans or the Andartes. The boat was piled high with baskets of fruit, wine barrels, guns, ammunition and bearded monks bound for various monasteries on Athos. As Joice was about to climb onto the boat, escorted by the English officer with a loaded rifle who had been instructed to act as her personal bodyguard, an old sponge diver approached them. He told Joice she had stitched up his wounds after the earthquake at Ierissos and saved his life. As he embraced her tears of joy ran down his roughened cheeks. He ran to his boat and pulled out the largest sponge Joice had ever seen. 'Yours, Kyria Loch!' he said and gave it to her. 'I wondered why the Panagia put it in my hand,' he said. 'Now I know.' Joice was moved to tears that an old man facing hunger and deprivation had given her his most prized and valuable possession.

They skirted the coast, aware of floating mines left by the Germans. The boat docked at the various small jetties below the towering monasteries, where the bearded monks disembarked. They rounded the tip of Athos, honeycombed with caves and huts where hermits lived. They passed the great craggy monastery known as Simonas Petra, the harbour of Daphni, St Panteleimon with its onion domes, Docheiariou and Xenophontos, the little islands opposite the familiar bay of Ouranoupolis and finally landed at the jetty below the tower of Prosforion. She was home at last.

It was twilight when they landed, and the jetty was packed with people come to welcome her. The British officer told her he would return the following morning to escort her back to Arnea. The patrol boat revved up its engines and sped off.

Yanni must have told everyone about her arrival. 'Kyria Loch, Kyria Loch!' they cried out in delight. Elderly women in black wept for joy, kissing her hand and said they had offered prayers for her safe return. Everyone talked at once. Joice heard that many old friends were dead. Some girls that had been unmarried when she left six years ago for Poland now had children of their own. Fani Mitropoulou, formerly Fani Kollinbas, proudly pushed forward a solemn dark-eyed toddler, whose name was Nikos, and held up a baby girl wrapped in a shawl for Joice to see.

Yanni, beaming from ear to ear, held the huge iron key to the tower's oak door. The jostling crowd nearly pushed Joice over in their eagerness to get close to her. The Mayor or Village President stood on a chair on the jetty and made a speech of welcome. It seemed everyone in the village wanted to accompany Joice to the tower.

Yanni unlocked the great wooden door. The iron bolts creaked and groaned as it swung back on its hinges. Joice, the Mayor and Yanni went inside and the rest of the villagers returned to their homes.

Fortunately the well seemed untouched. But their once beautiful home was a shambles. Personal possessions, including photograph albums, had been burned, Joice's medals in their glass case and favourite Pirgos rugs had vanished, books had been used as toilet paper and chairs chopped up for firewood by the Andartes. More books were strewn everywhere, showing muddy boot-marks where the Andartes had walked over them. Joice gazed at the walls that Yanni had started to wash down: they were spattered with blood.

The Mayor pointed to the great beams, riddled with bullet holes, grim reminders of village men and women the Andartes had tortured and killed. He told her that the King's army found it almost impossible to catch the Andartes, who retreated into Yugoslavia and returned after the soldiers had gone. One day, short of bullets, they had tied their prisoners from the village in sacks, each of which contained a live cat, and thrown them into the sea from the top floor of the tower, to die a terrible death.

They went upstairs. Yanni put down his bundle and flung open the heavy wooden shutters. Outside the waves sighed as they lapped on the beach. From far away Joice could see the top of the Holy Mountain. Yes, in spite of the horror it was good to be home.

Yanni opened up his bundle, wrapped in a tablecloth, the dinner his mother had prepared for them. Plates of grilled sardines and a cut lemon, bitter dark bread, wild pigweed salad, a bottle of rough red wine and three tumblers. Joice was touched, knowing how scarce and precious food was in the village. They ate at the oak dining table where she had designed her rugs, drank the red wine and talked.

The Mayor rolled himself a cigarette and his voice quavered as he related how Madame Sophia had died. Her elderly doctor brother had kept alive the tradition that the tower was the village's free medical centre. He was a good man, the Mayor said, who treated the villagers with medicines from Joice's chest and stitched up the wounds inflicted by the Andartes.

One dark night the Andartes came down from the mountains. They tricked Madame Sophia into opening the huge wooden door of the tower by carrying what seemed to be a wounded man in a blanket sling, in which they had cunningly concealed their rifles. The Andartes had wanted the medicines in the tower almost as much as the gold they believed the doctor had stored there, as well as Kyria Loch's gold medals, which they planned to melt down and sell. Once the door was unlocked, the Andartes burst in, shot Madame Sophia and her brother, then turned the tower upside-down trying to find the gold her brother was supposed to have brought with him from Russia.[7]

'They found nothing, of course. Only your medals and those of Kyrie Loch. You'll never get them back.'

The Mayor said the Andartes had kept Madame Sophia's son prisoner for several months, trying in vain to make him tell where his uncle's gold was hidden. Finally their leader ordered young Michael to be placed on the spit as though he was a goat about to be roasted. In drunken savagery they had then beaten him with their guns until his entire body turned black-and-blue. As he still could not tell them where the gold was they finally killed the boy.

Joice felt sick, distraught by the pointless cruelty of it all. Madame Sophia had been her much-loved friend. How could anyone treat people who had never harmed a soul in such a way, she wondered. Tears pricked her eyes for Madame Sophia, for her doctor brother, for Michael . . . and for Lushya. She buried her head in her hands, overcome by grief and fatigue.

Yanni and the Mayor fell silent, but Joice soon recovered and they exchanged more news for a half-hour. Her head was drooping with tiredness as she wished them goodnight, asking them to lock the huge oak door behind them. In her mind she saw Madame Sophia making tea from her silver samovar or baking bread, her arms white with flour, laughing and talking over the events of the day while Michael sat beside the fire doing his homework. Never again. Everything had changed. 'Never look back,' Sydney always said. 'Life must go on'. So many people needed her, she had to continue for their sakes. Wearily Joice climbed the steep wooden stairs to their old bedroom and slept.

Next morning she looked out of the window and saw a grey Angora cat, thin as a skeleton, shepherding a brace of kittens. The grey cat had a distinctive white stripe on its head. It could be the grandchild of Sylvia, her first and favourite cat.

Yanni appeared with a mop and bucket to start cleaning up. He confirmed that she had indeed seen Sylvia's progeny. Madame Sophia had given the rest of the cats to Brother Meletios but kept one kitten for Kyria Loch's return. 'After Madame Sophia was killed, that kitten went round the place mewing and howling,' he said. 'How it cried! In the end Aspasia over the road took it in. This surprised everyone—as you know, she is the kind that gives an egg and expects an elephant in return, but she fed and cared for your kitten when food was short. And here's a funny thing. It never came near the tower until I heard you were returning and started to clean up—then it came looking through the window.'

In the brief time before Joice's armed escort returned, it was impossible to sort out the jumbled contents of the tower. That would have to wait until their return, but at least Yanni would whitewash the bloodstained walls.

Old friends appeared. They told her how the Andartes had polluted the wells deliberately so that children had died of typhoid. Pirgos Rugs had run down and now there were no buyers, even if they had the wool to make new rugs. What were they to do?

'When we return, Pirgos Rugs *will* start again. I will find buyers,' Joice promised them.

She visited the lame widow, Aspasia, to thank her for saving Sylvia's last kitten. Trembling with emotion, Aspasia recounted how some village boys had found her husband's corpse on the Holy Mountain, strapped it to the back of his donkey and brought him down to her house. The first she knew of his death was the starved donkey crying his master home and a chorus of boys chanting 'Aspasia, Aspasia, your man's dead, there's a hole in his head.'

The night after that, Aspasia's door had been broken open and armed men rushed in and dragged her pretty young daughter out of bed. One man grabbed the girl and made off with her. Aspasia knew that girls taken by the Andartes were raped, 'lost their honour' and became unmarriageable outcasts in a village where young virgins were never allowed a moment alone with their suitors. She had picked up her heavy walking stick and chased after the Andartes. Her body might have been crippled but her spirit was winged. *Crash! Thwack!* went her stick on the heads of the Andartes. Aspasia's arms were like bars of iron. Guns were nothing against her fury.

The Andartes, most of whom were young enough to be her grandsons, howled in pain as Aspasia hit them over the head with her gnarled stick. By now they were short of bullets; Marshal Tito had ceased supplying them, believing the Andartes were in league with Stalin, who was now his bitter enemy. The Andartes dropped their empty guns, left the girl behind, turned tail and ran.

Other women picked up sticks, beat the young men savagely over the head or kicked them viciously in the groin. They fled to the beach and waded out to sea. Laughing the whole incident off rather than admitting they had been beaten by mere women, the Andartes walked along towards the Athos peninsula in water so deep that the women dared not follow them.

Those women who had not joined in crowded around wailing at Aspasia. 'Ayee! What have you done, Aspasia? Four rifles left behind. Ayee! The Andartes will return for them and burn the houses over our heads.'

However the Andartes did not return. Their empty guns were placed on the Holy Mountain under the tree where Aspasia's husband had been murdered. Happy to have the guns back, the freedom fighters turned bandits left the village in peace.[8]

Joice spent an hour visiting old friends and hearing their news before her guardian officer returned, as he had promised. The whole village turned out to farewell them at the jetty before they were rowed across to the Tripiti rock. From there they walked the winding mule track used for centuries by monks and pilgrims visiting Athos. Her escort kept his rifle cocked. They walked in silence, both aware of the danger that might be lurking in the forest until they reached Arnea, where an army jeep was waiting to take Joice back to the Farm School and safety.

29 'KYRIA LOCH'—THE LADY IN THE TOWER

The late 1940s and early 1950s were years of deprivation as Greece slowly recovered from civil war. Northern Greece was saved from becoming part of Yugoslavia and the Andartes were overcome.

The Lochs moved back to Ouranoupolis to live in the tower once the Andartes had been dispersed. The Society of Friends provided some money for medicines for Joice's free clinics, but food was still in short supply in the village and the children were once more in rags.

Joice wrote to many different sources requesting aid. The Canadian Society of Friends donated seven crates of second-hand children's clothes which she distributed among village families. Her Ryan relations sent money for food and crates of Australian corned beef. Several church groups in Melbourne sent donations. From Queensland, family friends the Bells, owners of Coochin-Coochin and other properties and her Stuart cousins sent clothing and money.[1]

King George of the Hellenes personally asked the Lochs to get Pirgos Rugs going again but could provide no money. All Joice's rugs, except five held at Vatopedi, had been destroyed by the Andartes, who had also burned the looms for firewood. It was not until 1950 that Joice had the money and the time to start the weaving cooperative again, paying for new looms and buying raw wool from the proceeds of her journalism. Once more she carried out the dyeing of the wool aided by Fani Mitropoulou, who was now widowed and faced an uncertain future.

Joice sat up late each night to redraw her previous rug designs from memory,[2] and made new ones based on motifs from Byzantine, Sassanid and Minoan art. To save money she packed and marketed the rugs herself so that all earnings could go to the women who wove them. However, this time it proved harder to sell Pirgos rugs, beautiful and unique as they were. Europe had been devastated by war and few people had money to spare. Fortunately the Lochs had always had many friends; some now bought or commissioned rugs. Each summer visitors came to the tower from Australia, America, Warsaw and London. Lady Norton, wife of the British Ambassador in Athens, arrived by chartered *kaïke* with a party of writers and artists including the well-known Greek artist Panos Ghika, who said that if Joice wrote her book about Ouranoupolis he would illustrate it, and this might raise funds to bring a supply of clean fresh water to the village, always Joice's dream.

Fani cooked for their many visitors. She often prepared octopus which Nanou the boatman brought to the tower. By tradition each octopus had to be beaten forty times on the rocks to tenderise it before it was grilled, otherwise it would be as rubbery as a garden hose. Far better was *oktapodi stifatho*, braised in tomatoes, onions and rosemary to keep the flesh tender. Another of Fani's specialities were red and yellow bell peppers or capsicums stuffed with rice, pine nuts and minced meat, baked in olive oil. She would prepare bream, mullet or mackerel lightly floured and fried with garlic and rosemary. Whenever Nanou had a specially good catch they enjoyed *psari plaki*. Fani's meals were enjoyed by guests in the dining-room overlooking the sea. Once again Pirgos rugs brightened the white walls.

In winter, when the wind howled around the tower and flung spray against its windows, the Lochs left to visit friends and publishers in Britain and travelled through Europe, and several times Joice returned to Australia to see her mother in Melbourne and relatives in Queensland. Edith still lived in a Melbourne boarding house with her very elderly Aunt Ethel. She had invested the money from Neerim in a small annuity. She told Joice that she was not in the least lonely and had heaps of friends. She had outgrown her migraines and her health was better than it had ever been. Edith did not need Joice to care for her, although of course she was delighted to see her whenever she came to Australia on a visit. This is how Joice described her mother on her first post-war visit to Australia: 'When I reached Melbourne, Mother was sitting up waiting with my Aunt Ethel in the large entrance of the boarding house where they lived. She sprang up from her chair . . . She was tiny and beautiful, just as she was years before! Her eyes danced, and she had wonderful white hair. How thankful I am to have seen her again then. And how she laughed and laughed and hugged me! I felt right back to ten years old, and my Mother just as fascinating. Suddenly my aunt thrust herself in by exclaiming: "How could you come all this way with no hat!" I dumped back with a crash. "I'll take you to get one tomorrow," she said firmly, "your Aunt Lena is giving a tea for you with all your aunts and cousins. You cannot go with no hat." ' Joice added: 'The tea party was wonderful in spite of the horrible hat Aunt Ethel insisted on me buying.'

In memory of Paraskevoula, who had died during the early days of the war, Joice raised money and organised a special course at the American Farm School for midwives working in remote villages to learn the latest methods of childbirth. She also gave courses in rug weaving and dyeing at the new girls' school. Both she and Sydney spent time each winter at the Farm School helping with the teaching load. Charlie and Anne House were still the Lochs' closest friends and shared many of their interests. Charlie loved designing and building and was never happier than with a slide rule in his hands, discussing new building projects for the campus with Sydney. Eventually the Farm School campus would have 400 acres of productive farmland, its own carpentry workshop, a blacksmith's forge and an arts centre.

By the 1950s, things were improving all over Greece. Villagers from Ouranoupolis were now farming the fertile fields they had repossessed from the monks in the 1930s. They sold their virgin olive oil to visiting traders and earned a good income.

In September 1951, Edith died aged eighty-five, after suffering a stroke. Her letters had arrived regularly from Australia; it was an enormous shock for Joice to realise her mother was no longer there. The small annuity on which Edith had lived came to Joice, along with a bequest from Aunt Ethel, who had died a few years previously.

Sydney always cared about others but paid little attention to his own health. Decades previously the Society of Friends doctor had told him that his blood pressure was high; at that time there was no medication to lower blood pressure. He was now in his sixties and complained that he tired more easily. Joice thought a holiday would do him good, so they spent the Christmas of 1954 with Charlie and Anne House at the Farm School, then returned to Ouranoupolis.

It was a bitterly cold winter. On 6 February the Lochs were preparing to leave for London to see their publishers when some children arrived at the tower, saying that an injured pelican was struggling in a snowdrift and needed help. Sydney went out to fetch the bird and brought it back with him. While he was recovering from the cold, sitting in front of the fire holding the injured pelican, without warning he slumped forward in his chair. Joice rushed to his aid but there was nothing she could do to help him—he died a few minutes later. His sudden death left Joice utterly devastated.

Sydney had been a member of the Church of Scotland. Burying him with the Orthodox liturgy in Ouranoupolis had problems because of the Orthodox tradition that all bones had to be removed from the grave after four or five years and placed in an ossuary. Everyone agreed it was best for him to be buried at the cemetery of the American Farm School, where he had worked for so long and done so much.

The village carpenter made a coffin. Draped in the British flag it was carried down to the tower jetty, placed on a boat and taken across to the Tripiti rock. There Charlie House, accompanied by young Hercules Jasonides, were waiting with the Farm School's jeep to take Sydney's coffin and Joice back with them to the Farm School.

The snow lay in drifts four to six feet deep and the men had to dig their way along the mule track. Progress was very slow. At one stage they thought they would have to read prayers over Sydney's body and bury him by the side of the road. Joice sat in the back of the jeep beside the coffin and slept by it at night. During that nightmare journey they had to open the coffin and shovel snow over the body to stop it decomposing. It took them three days to reach the Farm School, where the funeral ceremony was held in the Protestant chapel.[3] The funeral was so terrible for Joice that she could never talk or write about it. The awful finality of walking away from the grave of the beloved is one of the hardest things a human being has to bear.

The following year, 1955, was a bleak and lonely time for Joice, slowly coming to terms with life without her beloved husband. Living alone in the mediaeval tower and missing Sydney desperately, she started to feel her age. She was now sixty-seven. Climbing the steep wooden stairs became difficult so she moved her living quarters to the lower floor and made frequent trips to her small apartment at the Farm School where she was always welcomed as a wise counsellor.

While Sydney was alive, the tower had been a place of love and laughter, swarming with people: friends, monks from Athos and fellow writers—now Joice was alone. She no longer felt like surrounding herself with people. To keep her company, Fani Mitropoulou moved in with her children, but the old stone tower still remained a lonely place without Sydney. The first anniversary of his death renewed the anguish of her loss.

Joice now realised the people who needed her most were the villagers of Ouranoupolis. The work which she and Sydney had set out to do was still unfinished: 'the village at the end of the earth' still lacked a doctor, a community nurse and a road. Joice hated to give up on anything she had started. She decided it was vital to complete Sydney's book 'in the place where it was written' and to finish the relief work they had started in the 1920s.[4] Work was the most effective antidote against her loss and loneliness. But her most important task was to raise money for a road to connect the village to the outside world and for a larger schoolhouse to be built.

By now mass tourism was beginning to change the face of Europe. Joice dreaded the thought of tourist buses, apartments, hotels and camp sites spoiling the beauty of the coastline. However, she was convinced that although a road would inevitably bring change, it must go through to bring health and educational benefits to the villagers.

An ancient law forbade that 'any road on which a wheel can run' should approach the Athonite Republic. This suited the Greek Government which had no wish to devote precious funds to build a sealed road from Arnea to benefit one remote village and a republic of monks which did not pay taxes. The villagers were extremely resentful of the fact that for years the Government had ignored their petitions for a road. Finally, in 1956 Joice urged them to take matters into their own hands. Using picks and shovels they hacked out a primitive unsealed road over the pilgrims' route that linked the Tripiti rock to Arnea.

The first people to use the new road were an English and an American Quaker driving out to visit Joice. They had a hair-raising journey: their car narrowly escaped being flattened by a falling boulder. Clearly, the road must be widened and sealed. Joice wrote letters to the Government pressuring them to send a bulldozer, and raised funds to help the work by writing newspaper articles. After a further two years of prevarication the Government finally sent a bulldozer to level the road, but it still presented a danger to cars for long periods in winter.[5] The villagers' simple diet of bread, weed salads, maize, chick peas, grilled octopus or sardines, washed down with *ouzo* so strong it almost took the skin from the drinker's throat, soon changed. Meat and a wide variety of fresh vegetables could now be delivered by refrigerated trucks. Bottled drinks, mineral water and wines from other regions also arrived by road. Pedlars came, offering a variety of goods, including small charcoal grills on which to grill lamb chops and *souvlakies* which they insisted foreigners would demand. A few of the villagers put chairs and tables in front of their homes and served simple meals.

Charlie House died in 1961. Having retired from running the Farm School, he and Anne had returned to help out for a year. Joice went out to the Farm School to meet Bruce Lansdale, the new director, and helped Anne to write a biography of Charlie before she and her sister-in-law, Ruth, returned to America. It seemed somehow to complete a pattern; Joice had already written *A Life for the Balkans*, the biography of Charlie's remarkable father.

The deaths of Sydney Loch and Charlie House marked the end of an era of dedicated men who had worked without thought of material reward. They were replaced by career administrators in organisations like UNRRA and a host of foreign charities delivering aid with varying degrees of success.

Joice was still typing up Sydney's book on Athos. With her little Australian flag on the desk in front of her, she worked hard. Sydney's typescript had stopped at Chapter Six. It was not always easy to decipher Sydney's notes, written in pocket-books or old diaries that he had carried with him in a rucksack on his walks around the Holy Mountain. She found letters bearing the crest of the double-headed eagle of the Byzantine Empire, written to Sydney by librarians in the great monasteries and showing traces of candle wax.

She felt close to Sydney as she read and re-read his notes. His book was divided into chapters by topic, describing the history of each monastery and his conversations with the monks. Unlike many of the other authors who visited Athos, Sydney had described the natural beauty of the unpolluted Athos peninsula. Groves of trees sheltered flocks of nightingale and crested hoopoes. He described his beloved Athos as an unspoiled paradise unsullied by pesticides, where time stood still.

Joice sorted through the piles of photographs Sydney had taken and chose the best to use as illustrations. At times she could have wept as she heard that well-remembered voice speaking to her from his notes. From time to time friends from Athos came to the tower to help sort out some problem, as did Sydney's old friend Bishop Timothy Kallistos Ware, who was writing a history of the Orthodox Church. Although he held an ecclesiastical appointment at Oxford, he still retained his parish church on Patmos; Joice and Sydney had often visited him on that most beautiful and unspoiled of Greek islands, staying in the village of Hora. Father Meletios, though frail, was back at Vatopedi. He too came to visit Joice and helped her decipher some of Sydney's more complex notebooks.

Joice was determined Sydney's book would feature the people of Athos and the wit, kindness, and generosity of the black-bearded monks who had become his friends. Although she was a far more lively and amusing writer than Sydney and had done a great deal of work on his manuscript, she had no wish to be seen as the author of this book. Nevertheless, her poetic instinct and reaction to the beauty of the natural world is reflected in descriptions of the snow-covered peak of the Holy Mountain, with its dark pine forests running down to the wine-dark waters of the Aegean. The book describes the wild flowers that grew along the paths, the clear mountain springs and the flocks of nightingales and wood pigeons that inhabited the forests, as well as the shy hares, the dappled roebuck and the tiny flower-filled shrines at each crossing. Joice wrote the blurb for the book, describing Sydney as 'a man who met hermits on their own ground and realised the spiritual urge and powers of self-discipline which drove them to solitude and windswept cliffs. Seldom has a layman been greeted with such affection in monastery or hut'.

Joice was also helped by another close friend, an Englishman named Gerald Palmer, who was a member of the House of Commons at Westminster and had inherited a vast biscuit empire. Like Joice and Sydney, Gerald had been a close friend of Sir Clifford and Lady Norton when they were in the British Embassy in Athens. They had brought him to Athos, which Gerald (like so many others) found a place of spiritual refuge and rebirth. From then on he came each summer to stay in a monastery and always spent a few days with the Lochs. The experience of staying at Athos had such an effect on Gerald Palmer that he converted to Greek Orthodoxy.[6]

Gerald made several photographs to complete those taken by Sydney and took back the finished manuscript to London with him. They decided the title should be *Athos: the Holy Mountain*. Finishing it was Joice's tribute to her husband: as such, she insisted to the publishers that she did not want her name on the cover, even though she had contributed major work in compiling and editing it.

The book, published by Lutterworth Press in 1957, was well reviewed and aroused a great deal of interest among those who loved Greece and its people. Later writers on Athos have acknowledged their debt to Sydney Loch, who provided such a useful reference source. Sydney's book was unique in that he had lived in the shadow of the Holy Mountain for years, and wrote about the people who lived there and their way of life as well as the architecture and priceless artefacts in the monasteries.

Among Sydney's notes, a story related to him by one of the monks at the monastery of Dionysiou fired Joice's imagination. A monk swimming in the sea below the monastery was pursued and half-swallowed by a huge shark. His fellow monks, on the cliffs high above, gestured to the poor man to extend his arms and make the sign of the cross, hoping the shark would find it too difficult to swallow him completely and he might be saved from a grisly death. But the shark did not let go of the swimmer, who screamed in agony in the bloodstained sea. Once more the monks raised their hands above their heads, signifying the poor man should do likewise, let himself be swallowed and so end his suffering. And so the monk disappeared inside the shark.

Day after day the huge shark returned to the waters below the monastery of Dionysiou, seeking fresh prey. The monks devised a plan whereby they hoped to catch the shark and so be able to bury their brother in sanctified ground. They let down a baby goat on a rope to lure the predator, succeeded in catching and killing it, then buried the shark in the monastery churchyard with the monk inside it.

Besides working on Sydney's book, Joice had been considering her planned collection of village tales which the artist Panos Ghika had agreed to illustrate. She was now thinking of making this a book for children, and had already created the character of Christophilos ('Niko'), a small boy living in the village with his mother, baby sister and his aged *yar-yar* or grandmother. His father had died and they were very poor. Christophilos was in fact a composite of Nikos Mitropoulou, Fani's son, and some of his friends. Fani's son Nikos owned two pets, a goat and a donkey. To earn money he would sometimes spend the night on the slopes of Mount Athos guarding sheep belonging to village families to prevent the wolves devouring them. Christophilos seemed to Joice an ideal character to feature in stories about the monks, the villagers and their daily life, so different from that of English or Australian children.

If she used the tale of the monk and the shark for one of her stories, the baby goat could become Christophilos' pet . . . so she reworked the tale. The little boy, who travels about on his donkey, herds the family's goats and has a pet baby goat he loves. One day he takes the goats to graze on the slopes of Mount Athos; looking down, he watches a monk dive into the clear green water and sees a huge shark swimming towards him. Other monks appear—they have come to tell the boy he should not herd his goats on the Holy Mountain. Both Nikos and the monks know there is only one way to save their brother: to throw down Nikos' beloved pet goat to divert the shark.

Joice's story deals with the little boy's sacrifice of his baby goat and his subsequent grief. The monks reward him with money which he gives to his mother. Nikos is now a local hero and gains the right to graze his goats on Athos—but his life has been touched forever by the death of his pet goat.

So Joice's most popular book, *Tales of Christophilos*, slowly took shape. Her loneliness was assuaged as she worked to recreate the unique world of a Greek refugee village seen through the eyes of Christophilos, the boy on the donkey. From her notes and memories she wove tales about the villagers, their superstitions, their feuds, the big turquoise eyes they hung outside their whitewashed houses to ward off evil . . . Easter celebrations with scarlet-painted eggs and candlelight processions; bearded monks arriving in the village from snow-capped Athos to buy milk and *feta*, their black robes flapping around their heels.

Panos Ghika kept his promise. The next time he came to Ouranoupolis on holiday he made some delightful black-and-white illustrations that helped to bring the village to life.

Fani featured in the stories as Nikos' wise and loving mother. *Tales of Christophilos* achieved its popularity because it recreated the tears and laughter of simple people. Although it appeared as a children's book, *Tales of Christophilos* has the ageless appeal of folklore. Joice did not 'write down' to a younger audience; her narrative is strong and direct. As often happens with a book ostensibly published for young readers, it found an older audience as well. A British publisher turned it down but remembering the success of *The Fourteen Thumbs of St Peter*, Joice sent the manuscript to America and received a generous advance from the prestigious Boston publisher Houghton Mifflin, who thought it would be a great success.

When the book appeared reviews praised Joice's skill in bringing to life a typical Greek village, her fluency of language and her characterisation. Then came the most exciting letter of all. She had been awarded the Spring Honor Book Award of the *New York Herald Tribune*. Advance sales were so good it seemed certain it would be a bestseller.

It was typical of Joice that she should put the needs of the village first. From her first royalty cheque she bought six fat-tailed sheep from the island of Chios. 'They look as though they are wearing two tiny pairs of black boots,' she wrote. All of them were in lamb. She kept two of the sheep herself, named them Ella and Stella, took them for walks on the beach and even let them swim below the tower. She also bought a ram named Caspar to help the breeding program. The ram lived in a pen below the tower and became a hand-fed pet. Joice wrote: 'He was very naughty and kept jumping the fence, although it was made higher as he got older.' Villagers were often amused to see Joice chasing the ram down the main street, offering tid-bits to lure him back to his pen.

In those days there were no grants to authors to give them time to write books, but Greece was still very cheap compared to Britain and Australia; Joice managed to exist frugally on journalism and from the proceeds of a small bequest. Always the needs of the village came first. Her main worry was the number of village children who still died of typhoid and blackwater fever because the village wells were close to the stables and often became polluted by manure after a storm.[7]

She persuaded the Society of Friends to put up half the cost of a pipe to bring pure fresh water down from the hills, and paid the other half herself from her American royalties. The project was complex and extremely expensive, requiring an engineer to come to the village to supervise its construction.

When it was completed there was only one outlet at the entrance to the village: they now had to find a way of piping the pure water to a number of outlets in the village centre. Joice had never thought much about money for herself. Why should she need it now? Cheerfully she handed over more money from her royalty cheques to the Mayor to extend the water supply to include a standpipe and seven communal taps in the main street. In time, the lives of countless children were saved.

The Oxford Committee for Famine Relief sent observers to Ouranoupolis. After inspecting the supply of piped water, they agreed to do the same for two more Greek villages. The observers were also interested in the milk-producing sheep from Chios; subsequently Oxfam imported Chios sheep for three other isolated Greek villages.[8] Joice also asked Quaker volunteers working on Chios to send her thirty-five more female lambs and three more rams, which she gave to families who were keen to make cheese.

Joice gained an assistant and loyal friend in Swiss-born Martha Handschin, who came to the village to see Joice's work in action. Martha had worked at the Pestalozzi Children's Village in Switzerland and for the Society of Friends Relief to Northern Greece. Martha, tall and fair-haired, spoke English, French and German. She had a dry sense of humour and was as determined, compassionate and strong-minded as Joice. During the coldest months of the year Joice rented the old stone house in the village which had once belonged to the monks of Vatopedi (the house she and Sydney had stayed in after the earthquake at Ierissos) and lived there with Martha, or else they went to the apartment kept for her at the American Farm School.

Martha helped Joice to compile a book on the properties of natural dyes made from local plants and roots, which was published by an American foundation in Turkey. Fani was now the manager of Pirgos Rugs as well as Joice's housekeeper. With Pirgos Rugs re-established on a firm commercial footing, Joice donated her looms to the village and handed over the business side for administration by Queen Fredericka's Fund.

Her dedication to helping Greek people was once again recognised by the Greek Government; the King of the Hellenes awarded Joice a third medal, acknowledging her efforts on behalf of the former refugee villages and at the American Farm School.

In winter Joice took up her old job of teaching rug weaving and 'natural' dyeing techniques to the girls at the Quaker-run school on the periphery of the Farm School campus. She also gave them lessons in domestic management and courses in reading. As Director of the Girls' School, she worked hard to improve the role of women in Greek village society, to ensure that those who needed it most could gain paid employment and greater self-esteem. She also aimed to raise the school's educational standards. Most parents did not want their girls to become too educated, fearing they would not find husbands. Joice did her best to break down their prejudices.

At Ouranoupolis she wanted to widen educational opportunities for the local children and provide them with the chance of higher education, which was also financed with some of her royalties.

Again Christophilos was Joice's second collection of tales. She related the story of her pet owl, more escapades of the boy on the donkey, his friends and other characters in 'the village at the end of the world'. Once again she wrote about the midwife who acted as marriage broker, gossiping *yar-yars* and village girls without dowries forced to marry men they did not love. For some years *Blackwoods Magazine* published her articles about the villagers under the title 'Modern Athonians', and her travel book, *The Hopping Ha-penny*, was published in London and New York.[9]

Given more time, doubtless Joice would have written more books about the village or even a second novel. But so often, just as she settled down at the typewriter there would come a knock on the door and a request to visit a sick child or a woman in labour who was having difficulty 'making the baby come'. Joice would get up, muttering crossly, but she would always go. Her compassion was boundless, her talent for diagnosing and curing sick people and sick animals remarkable, and the sense of satisfaction she derived from this was only equalled by the pleasure of writing.

In September 1962 Pani Joice Loch was invited to Poland as the guest of the Polish Society of Writers. She flew to Poland via Switzerland and was joined there by Joyce Slater, Estelle's daughter, whom she had asked to accompany her. Joyce had been named for her mother's closest friend, but was given the conventional spelling of the name.

Melchior Wankowicz, the Lochs' author friend from their days in Warsaw, showed the two women around the rebuilt city, now under Communist rule. By now Melchior had a shock of white hair. He was well-known all over Poland from his television appearances, and crowds swarmed around the three of them wherever they went. Joice recognised many buildings from her previous visit in the 1920s. They had been flattened by German bombs but were now rebuilt or restored. She was able to meet many of the Poles she and Sydney had helped to escape from Rumania.

When they went into the countryside, Joice noticed that horse-drawn *furmankas* were still in use. She was disturbed to find that rural poverty was worse in Poland than in Greece. She offered to donate a dozen of her favourite fat-tailed Chios sheep to Poland, to provide good milk and wool; import permits were arranged through the Polish Ministry of Agriculture and in time, the sheep duly arrived.[10] When Joice and Estelle's daughter returned to the tower by the sea at Ouranoupolis, they brought with them cuttings from the rose garden at Chopin's birthplace in Poland.

They found the postman had delivered a copy of a book called *Wild Flower Hunter*, written by H. J. (Helen Josephine) Samuel with the help of Joice's cousin Maie Ryan, now the wife of Sir Richard Casey. This was a biography of Aunt Ellis Rowan, something which Joice had always intended to write but had never had the time. She read the book and told Joyce Slater she found it 'superficial and written in a stilted way'. 'Aunt Ellis wanted *me* to write her biography. I would have made it far more entertaining,' she declared wistfully.[11]

In 1963 Mount Athos was preparing to celebrate its thousandth anniversary as a monastic centre. For this important event, with visitors arriving from all over the world, the Greek Government widened the road from Thessaloniki to Arnea and announced they would seal the road as far as Ouranoupolis. Easy access by a sealed road changed life in the village for ever. Most significantly, a Government doctor was now able to drive out and conduct regular clinics, which removed the burden of medical responsibility from Joice's shoulders.

The sealed road, the rise of tourism, better educational facilities and profitable olive crops meant that village girls and women were able to find alternative forms of paid work. Rug weaving was no longer the vital occupation it had been. Married women began to rent out rooms for additional income. Monks and foreign tourists from all over the world came to Athos, drawn by its unpolluted beauty and spiritual atmosphere. The free hospitality of the monks continued, but visitors' permits were now limited in numbers and duration and had to be obtained in advance from special offices in Thessaloniki or Athens.

British, French and German hitchhikers discovered that Halkidiki was cheaper than Spain, Italy or France. Cars with foreign number plates arrived in large numbers in July and August. Germans bought land outside the village and built holiday villas. To Joice's relief, the mass tourist industry considered Ouranoupolis too far from an airport to be a serious commercial proposition. Life for the villagers was improving; at last the refugee village was beginning to attain a degree of prosperity.

30 THE END OF THE ROAD

In her widowhood Joice missed Sydney continually. As well as their love, their shared aims and values had kept their marriage strong to the end.

Joice's bequests from her mother and Aunt Ethel made it possible for her to see more of the world and to assuage her sense of loneliness after Sydney's death. In a poem titled *Earth Song*, Joice described her love of travel. It was 'her vagrant heart' that had led her into becoming an aid worker and provided the basis for so much of her writing—

My vagrant heart will journey still,
My old bones lagging far behind,
While I essay yet one more hill,
Some hidden treasure-trove to find.[1]

Wherever she went she was asked to give talks on her books and about Pirgos Rugs, and she received warm hospitality from friends and admirers in Europe, Australia and America. In Kenya and Rhodesia she was an honoured guest of the Polish people she had helped escape from Rumania and the Nazi death camps. She visited Egypt and took an extended boat trip on the Blue Nile.

In the past she and Sydney had enjoyed sailing by *kaïke* to the neighbouring island of Thassos, where wild thyme perfumed the air and an ancient Greek amphitheatre overlooked the turquoise sea. Now she would often visit an equally beautiful and unspoiled island further afield which had strong connections with Mount Athos.

On the craggy island of Patmos with its fortress monastery of St John standing guard above the villages far below, she visited Sydney's friend Bishop Timothy Kallistos Ware. During her stay she was shown illuminated manuscripts, gold and silver treasures and embroidered robes that rivalled those of Athos by the monks of St John. She loved taking long walks with views of some of the most magnificent scenery in Greece.

The monks of Patmos, like those of Athos, refused to allow their beautiful island to be spoiled by mass tourism. Sugar-cube houses, painted dazzling white, overlooked a bay that varied from deep blue to turquoise. The hillside town of Hora had narrow twisting streets and forty ancient churches and monasteries. Joice stayed in a walled nunnery whose Mother Superior always made her welcome. She read as widely as ever and remained passionate about art in all its forms, especially the early Christian art of Byzantium. She was planning an enlarged and updated version of her book *Prosforion: Rugs and Plant Dyes* with the assistance of Martha Handschin. This would be a much larger edition for an international readership, with photographs showing the many colours each part of a plant could produce, using different mordants and different periods of immersion in the dye vats.

At the end of 1964, accompanied by Martha and an American friend, Mrs Henry Reed, Joice went by ship to Australia. They took with them twenty Pirgos rugs ranging from some of the first ever produced, using natural, cream and brown wool, to later examples using the varied colours produced by their intricate dyeing process.

An article in Joice's old paper, the Melbourne *Herald*, published on 11 December, was headed 'Rugs that Saved a Greek Village' and was based on a rare interview with Joice, who guarded her privacy. The article related how she lived in a thirteenth-century Byzantine tower and acted as 'mother' and 'doctor' to the villagers of Pirgos. She was reported as saying: 'I've been patching up the villagers and monks ever since my husband and I went to live there. At one time I was the only person in the village who recognised smallpox, as I had dealt with it when I worked in Poland.'[2] Both the *Herald* and the Adelaide *Advertiser* of January 12, 1965 explained how Pirgos Rugs, founded by the heroic Mrs Loch, helped to save a Greek village from starvation, not once but twice.

Pirgos rugs went on display in David Jones' department store in Adelaide and in the David Jones Gallery in Sydney. They were not for sale, but Joice announced that she would donate nine rugs to the people of Australia as a gesture of Greek-Australian friendship.

The exhibition at the David Jones Gallery in Sydney aroused great interest.[3] Interviewed by the *Sydney Morning Herald*, Joice emphasised the importance of hand-woven rugs as an art form and explained that her designs were based on Byzantine art. She said, 'The presentation of ancient designs by means of rugs is my way of showing history through art.'[4]

Inspired by her travels, Joice was now working on new rug designs, including some based on prehistoric motifs she had seen in the caves of Lascaux in France and at Altimira in northern Spain. She was also planning a large illustrated book to be titled *Art In History*, with chapters on Aboriginal art, cave art from France and Spain, early Christian and Byzantine art, Crusader art and Sassanid, Scythian and African carvings. The book's most important chapter, on Byzantine symbols in carvings, metalwork and jewellery would be based on years of painstaking research in monasteries and ancient churches undertaken by herself, Sydney and one of her oldest friends in Greece, the distinguished archaeologist Dr Philip Sherrard, author of a number of books on ancient Greece and Byzantium. She had commissioned Paul Mylonas, a well-known Greek photographer of artworks, to take colour and black-and-white illustrations and was negotiating a contract with a Greek publisher.

The Melbourne exhibition of Pirgos Rugs was held in the South Yarra Galleries. Melbourne was a city with happy memories for Joice, the city where she had studied and worked and where she and Sydney had met and married. The fashionable South Yarra Galleries was run by dealer-collector Violet Dulieu, who held exhibitions of talented young Australian artists such as Charles Blackman, James Gleeson, Justin O'Brien, John Percival and Geoffrey Smart.[5] From time to time she mounted international prestige exhibitions of works which, like Pirgos Rugs, were not for sale.

Before she left Australia, Joice donated (according to Martha Handschin) nine fine examples of all periods of Pirgos Rugs to 'the people of Australia', intending them to be placed in the projected Australian National Gallery in Canberra and other museums.[6] When she returned to her tower she found a letter from Cabinet Minister Malcolm Fraser thanking her for her extremely generous gift. But a deplorable set of circumstances ensued. These nine extremely valuable and irreplaceable hand-woven rugs (today worth some $100,000 to Greek collectors) were loaned to several Australian embassies overseas until in 1980 they passed into the care of Artbank,[7] a Government-funded body. Art-bank found seven of the rugs were missing and then proceeded to loan two more to the Australian Embassy in Athens. Some of the public servants had become so fond of what they considered 'their' rugs that at the end of their period of service they took them home with them—and Art-bank seems to have failed to take measures to recover them. Today, only one Pirgos rug designed by Joice NanKivell Loch remains in Artbank.[8] Subsequently five more rugs (four woven from un-dyed wool) were discovered safely stored by the Australia Council. A NanKivell relative confirms that these were an earlier gift.

The saddest part of this sorry business is that these stolen rugs are irreplaceable. Within two decades the village women and girls at the Farm School had ceased weaving. Today Pirgos rugs, always viewed as collectibles with their authentic Byzantine designs and strict use of natural dyes, have become rare *objets d'art* and soared in price. Those that remain, providing they are in good condition, are greatly sought after in Greece.[9]

In her seventies, Joice's intelligence and determination were undiminished. She was consulted by those interested in the history of Thessaloniki from the days when St Paul preached there. Kyria Loch, the lady of the tower, had a rich store of knowledge garnered over the years about Thessaloniki's role as the second city of the Byzantine empire, its invasions by the Romans, Saracens, Normans and Turks. She was able to talk to visitors about the folklore and costumes of villages throughout Halkidiki and as far north as the Bulgarian border, areas where she and Sydney had travelled extensively on aid missions during the Civil War.

Unfortunately she was having difficulty persuading Moxlo, her Greek publisher, to commit sufficient funds for her lavishly illustrated book *Art In History* and thought she might have to seek an American copublisher. Meanwhile she concentrated her energy on writing an outline and the Australian chapters of her memoirs, which had been commissioned by John Murray in London. She had already typed out copious notes for the rest of her autobiography when, without warning, tragedy struck.

One crisp autumn morning, as she stood on the balcony of the old stone house in the village talking to Fani, Martha and some weavers Joice took a step backwards against the rail. The worm-eaten wood collapsed at her touch and she fell off the balcony, head-first onto the paving stones two metres below. Fani and Martha, distraught, ran down the stairs. Joice lay very still: although she continued breathing she was in a deep coma.[10]

The nearest hospital was in Thessaloniki, two hours away over a bumpy road. She was taken there by car. When she was X-rayed the doctors found she had a badly fractured skull, had broken her right arm and wrist and slightly damaged her left hand. They feared she had suffered brain damage resulting in loss of her power of speech. She lay inert for weeks, hovering between life and death. There was great sorrow and consternation over Kyria Loch's accident and prayers were offered in the village and in some of the monasteries of Athos.

Joice's strength of character and determination ensured a partial recovery, although it was slow. After many months, with the aid of physiotherapists and other specialists she was able to walk and talk again. Her right arm and hand were in plaster for eighteen months and she could no longer type. So, painfully at first, she had to learn to write with her left hand. The worst outcome of her accident was that she suffered severe memory loss. In letters to Simon Young, her editor at John Murrays, and to Philip Sherrard, to whom she sent a draft of the first chapters of her memoirs, she indicated her despair '. . . with my poor bust brain I am not able to finish it,' she told her editor.[11] And in a postscript to a letter to Philip Sherrard she said she thought the memoirs were truly 'bad', and she would not be at all cross should he simply 'throw the manuscript into the fire'.[12]

Rather than burn the pages, her good friend Dr Sherrard volunteered to come and stay in Ouranoupolis with his daughter to help Joice complete her memoirs. With a huge amount of help from Dr Sherrard and from a paid typist, Rita Langford, she managed to finish *A Fringe of Blue*, which was published by John Murray in 1968. In a postcard to Simon Young dated April 1969 (in which Joice refers to herself as 'an Australian bush woman') she praises Philip Sherrard for his kindness in helping her and adds that some of the Greek parts of the book are based on articles she published years before in *Blackwood's Magazine*.

The fracture of her skull badly affected Joice's cognitive skills and her powers of concentration as well as her memory. It was a cruel trick for fate to play on an elderly woman who passionately loved words and was renowned as a brilliant and amusing raconteur. Her recovery was long and slow and she never completely regained her old fluency of ideas or her former encyclopaedic memory.[13]

A Fringe of Blue, named for those blue ribbons the Polish general had commented on long ago, although lively and vivid at times, contains dates and incidents which are sometimes at variance with her previous books and her correspondence. Details of her engagement to Sydney and the route followed in Operation Pied Piper, for example, differ from earlier accounts. Philip Sherrard and Martha Handschin had been able to help with the Greek chapters, but neither of them knew much about distant events and places in Poland and Rumania.

And Joice faced another problem. She had always made believe she was four years younger than Sydney, while in reality she was two years older. According to the mores of the time, to be older than a prospective husband was not a good portent for marriage; hoping to appease his family, she had lopped several years from her age. To do this had been easy for Joice, since all her life she looked considerably younger than she really was. But when she came to write her memoirs, dates and ages quoted in her Queensland and Victorian childhood had to be altered to make them agree with her revised 'new' age. *A Fringe of Blue* opens with Joice's birth given as 1893, six years later than the date shown on her birth certificate.

Joice was, incidentally, not the only writer of her day to have made herself younger. Katharine Susannah Prichard, who also married a younger man—Hugo Throssell who, like Sydney Loch, was a hero of Gallipoli—cheerfully divested herself of a handful of years. Both she and Joice faced the prejudiced notion that women who were presumed to be past childbearing age should not marry someone younger than themselves. The artist Margaret Preston also lowered her age by six years when she married a younger husband.

To help illustrate *A Fringe of Blue*, photographs of those medals which the Andartes had not stolen were taken at the request of John Murray. But at the last moment Joice refused to allow these to be used. Modest as ever about her achievements, she told Simon Young that she feared photographs of her medals could make her appear 'boastful'. Joice was eighty-one by the time *A Fringe of Blue* finally appeared. It was a triumph of will that she managed to complete her memoirs at all after such a severe accident. She dedicated *A Fringe of Blue* to Estelle Slater, whose death in Australia had saddened her. Her memoirs portray the extraordinary life of a strong-minded, compassionate, quick-witted bushwoman whose struggles for refugees and orphans benefited thousands of people in Poland and Greece. The book ends with the arrival of the sealed road to Athos, which she describes as 'unmistakably the start of another era'.

The publishers John Murray were aware of Joice Loch's significance as an Australian author whose books had been published and acclaimed in London as well as in America. Joice started writing in the same era as Katharine Susannah Prichard and Miles Franklin, a period when women found it extremely hard to get their work into print. Accordingly, Murray's decided to donate the typescript of *A Fringe of Blue* to Canberra's National Library.[14] Joice had already expressed to them the hope that her manuscripts would be archived in a museum in Canberra.

The End of the Road

In the last years of her life, such was Joice's fame that a never-ending cavalcade of visitors from Greece and overseas came to visit 'the lady in the tower'.

Kyria Loch's knowledge of local lore was consulted by a Swedish diving expedition which arrived in Ouranoupolis hoping to find ancient Persian galleys from Xerxes' fleet. They believed the galleys had sunk near the Xerxes Canal, which had once emerged near the Tripiti Rock. Joice advised the divers to examine the walls of the sunken city (then thought to be the ruins of Philip of Macedon's Dion, although later experts decided this lay seventeen kilometres south of Katerini; it is more likely to be the ruins of Thisson or Klinai which were on Athos in the pre-Christian era).[15] The walls began some hundreds of metres in front of the tower and were supposed to extend as far as the Drinia Islands.

The diving party discovered foundations of ancient stone fortifications, homes with fireplaces and broad roads showing the marks of chariot wheels. Joice believed the walls they described were similar to those she had seen on the nearby Greek island of Thassos as well as those which, prior to the earthquake, had surrounded the village of Ierissos. The team found her local knowledge was profound and her advice invaluable.

Joice was delighted to learn from the monks that their numbers at Mount Athos had begun to rise again: about thirty new monks were taking up residence each year. There seemed to be no danger that the monasteries might be turned into hotels and the Holy Mountain overrun by tourists, as she had once feared. Most villagers wanted nothing to do with high-rise buildings or huge luxury resorts like those that had started to line and litter the shores of the neighbouring peninsulas of Kassandra and Sithonia.

The majority of tourists to Ouranoupolis came by car from Germany or Scandinavia, and as their numbers increased, two large hotels were built overlooking the beach, but a good distance from the village. To their surprise, village men found that their wives, working as waitresses or maids in these hotels, were often earning more than they did. The arrival of the tourists also meant that the beach in front of the village was cleaned up to allow them to swim and enjoy the sun. Long-limbed Scandinavian blondes sun-baking there drove the local men wild with desire. And the sight of bikini-clad German girls shopping in the village or eating and drinking in the many open-air restaurants and cafes set the old *yar-yars*, still clad from head to toe in black, chattering and grimacing with rage. They remembered the famine years of bitter bread and weed soup.

The village at the end of the world had changed. Food was plentiful, brought by the truckload from Thessaloniki. Few people still made weed soup. Village bread no longer tasted bitter because acorns had been added to it. The sardine catch was plentiful. The olive trees on the rich farmland the villagers had taken by force from the monks of Chilandari bore rich crops of olives. Village women marinated them in a blend of garlic, black pepper, lemon juice and oil, and sold them to local cafes and restaurants.

By common consent no one talked about the great hunger during the Civil War or the atrocities committed by the Andartes. Some villagers whom past poverty had forced to emigrate to Australia and America returned and invested in land along the seashore.

Villagers could now plan for their children to go to high school or even gain tertiary education. And a Government-funded doctor held clinics in the village, in the old stone house where Joice had fallen from the balcony. The Government had at long last confirmed that when Joice died the tower of Prosforion would become a museum of Byzantine art. All the things Kyria Loch had dreamed about and worked so hard to achieve had slowly come true.

In the tower by the sea, Joice's much-loved Angora cats, descendants of Sylvia and Mustapha, purred in her lap as she wrote letters or talked to her many visitors. Slowly her powers of concentration and speech improved. From childhood Joice had possessed the writer's skill of making readers and listeners laugh, gasp or cry at her stories and she was still an excellent if sometimes rambling teller of tales.

She had always been independent and hated enforced inactivity: now that she could no longer stand or walk without her stick she had difficulty caring for herself and relied on the devotion of Fani and Martha. In the 1970s Fani, encouraged by Joice, had started painting icons of extraordinary quality which she either sold to visitors or gave as presents to some of the many monks who came to visit 'the Lady in the Tower'.

Joice enjoyed watching Fani paint. She would spend hours sitting contentedly in the sun with a cat on her lap. Old friends like Gerald Palmer, Philip Sherrard, Lord and Lady Eccles and Joyce Slater came to stay in the tower during the summer months. Bruce Lansdale and his wife Elizabeth (Tad) came often to talk over the old days and new developments at the girls' school. 'Joice was a presence,' Bruce

Lansdale observed. 'She had great wisdom and was always a delightful person to be with.'[16] Fani said simply: 'She was so warm and kind.'

When Joice was ninety-three Oxford's Cygnet Press published a hardback collection of some of her poems printed on fine handmade paper. The collection included the poem 'Exultation'. A two-page Foreword by Gerald Palmer described Joice as 'a bush girl' with a talent for journalism which had taken her from Australia to London. He listed her four great gifts: 'a keen understanding of and compassion for people and animals; a practical ability to treat sickness in either; a strong poetic instinct, and an unrivalled sense of humour, which enlivened her own and other people's lives.'[17] Joice was delighted with the book.

In her final days Fani and Martha cared for Joice devotedly. Fani moved her bed to sleep beside Joice, who gradually grew weaker. She remained convinced that the human spirit is not conquered by death and that somewhere, somehow, she would be reunited with her beloved Sydney.

In the harsh winter of 1982, Joice NanKivell Loch, who had just turned ninety-five, died as she had lived through peace and war, with stoic fortitude. Her death certificate indicates the cause of death as 'brain haemorrhage'.

The villagers of Ouranoupolis could hardly believe that the great Kyria Loch, the heroic woman who had saved them from famine, disease and penury and whose healing presence in the tower's medical centre had been part of their lives, was dead. To them, 'The Lady in the Tower' had seemed immortal. Women dressed in black, whose babies Joice had delivered or saved from illness, wept openly in the streets, telling each other how lucky they had been to have Kyria Loch in their village. Out of respect the shops, the *kafenion* and the cafes took down their bright awnings and closed for three days and nights. Men and women held all-night vigils beside her open coffin.

Joice's funeral was attended by everyone in the village, hundreds of monks from Athos, as well as men and women who arrived by donkey or on foot from Ierissos, where she had saved so many lives. These local mourners were joined by a contingent from the Farm School, and as Chrysanthe Litsas, Bruce and Elizabeth Lansdale, Vouli Prousali and many other friends drove from Thessaloniki to the village, Chrysanthe regaled them with 'Joicean' anecdotes from the past. The Governor of Macedonia attended, as did the British, American and Australian consuls. Martha and Fani bustled about feeding everyone in Joice's white-walled sitting room overlooking the sea, just as they had done when she was alive.

There had been a move to bury Joice at the Farm School beside Sydney, but the village council objected, saying that she was 'their' Kyria Loch and she must be buried in Ouranoupolis. Bishop Timothy Kallistos Ware lived in Oxford, but by chance (or Providence) he happened to be staying in one of the monasteries of Athos. As someone who knew Joice and her books well, he was the ideal person to give the main funeral oration. He spoke first in Greek and then in English; as a historian of the Orthodox Church, he was able to say with certainty that Joice NanKivell Loch was the only foreigner ever accorded the honour of receiving the full Orthodox liturgy. Belonging to no fixed denomination, Kyria Loch had truly been 'a woman of God' who had done more for her fellow human beings than any other woman he could think of; her many medals were an acknowledgement of this fact. The Bishop praised Joice for her dedication to writing and for the forbearance which meant that several books remained unwritten for lack of time, owing to her many acts of kindness to others and her work in establishing Pirgos Rugs, which had helped to save a village under threat from starvation and disease.

He related incidents from Joice's extraordinary life, starting with her birth in a cyclone in tropical Australia, a childhood spent in rural poverty, and her fierce dedication to helping those less fortunate than herself. Kyria Loch had saved thousands of Polish women and orphans, had raised money for medicines and vaccinations or bought them herself, and donated the royalties from her American bestseller to bring a supply of clean drinking water to Ouranoupolis. He outlined her years of devoted but unpaid service to sick children and women in labour. 'Kyria Loch had no children but the children of an entire village were to become hers,' he said. By now all the women and children in the church were weeping.

The Bishop talked of Joice's conviction that kindness to others is more important than creeds or dogmas, her intensely Australian belief in 'giving everyone a fair go', and in the rights of the disadvantaged and dispossessed. He quoted her dictum that education had the power to change lives and talked of the many scholarships she had donated to village children. Her dedication and compassion had improved life for thousands in Poland and Greece. Ouranoupolis had indeed been privileged to have Joice NanKivell Loch as a resident.

The Bishop ended by saying that Joice would be remembered as 'one of the most significant women of the twentieth century'.

After him John Marangos, a Farm School graduate and now the President (Mayor) of Ouranoupolis spoke, revealing that, as a child from a poor home, his fees at the American Farm School had been paid by the Lochs. Like all the Lochs' benefactions, they had insisted that this should not be publicised. Marangos described Joice Loch as 'the saviour of the village in time of need, a quiet benefactor with a dream for what could be achieved by a village of Greek refugees from Asia Minor and Turkey'. He talked of the hardships of the early days, how Kyria Loch's vision of a village with piped water and good educational opportunities had finally been realised after decades of struggle and setbacks. And he drew attention to the Greek, British, Polish and Rumanian medals she had received for humanitarian relief work.

The final oration was given by Bruce Lansdale in his role as Director of the American Farm School. In a voice charged with emotion he described Joice's wide range of talents and her many and varied careers—'journalist, author, humanitarian aid worker, teacher'—and the 'thousand and one quiet ways in which she helped those less fortunate than herself'. She had been 'the village's healer. She treated all those who consulted her without thought of personal gain and treated them in body, mind and spirit. She had no children but became mother to hundreds'.

The funeral procession to the high ground of the cemetery was a traditional Orthodox one, led by the priests from Ouranoupolis, Ierissos and Athos. Over one hundred monks and abbots in their traditional gold and scarlet ceremonial robes carried huge candles and chanted Orthodox liturgies. Joice's coffin had been draped with the Australian and Greek flags. It was borne aloft on the shoulders of men who had been boys when she first arrived in the refugee settlement. Behind them followed a procession of weeping women in black, carrying lighted candles, among whom were Fani Mitropoulou and Martha Handschin. Joice was buried in the highest part of the cemetery in a plot with a view over the blue Aegean.

One of her obituaries in a Quaker magazine *The Wayfarer* praised Joice Loch for 'putting her concern for others before her own comfort, for dedicating her life to the stricken and broken peoples of the world' and for 'carrying out her own credo of providing unstinting kindness to those less fortunate than herself'. She was described as 'unpaid medical advisor, arbitrator and teacher' to the people of Ouranoupolis.

Fani, Martha and the Lansdales knew Joice wanted to be buried beside Sydney, so his coffin was returned from the Farm School by boat and buried beside that of his wife. For the couple who had saved Ouranoupolis, the villagers made a special exception. Their bodies were to be allowed to remain undisturbed beneath their granite slab, close to the Greek village to whose survival they devoted the major part of their lives.

To perpetuate her memory, friends and admirers raised the money for Joice's own poem 'Exultation' to be engraved on her tombstone, a fitting epitaph for a heroic and multi-talented woman.[18]

> *Why should you cry? Do you think I lie*
> *Quietly, silently under the sky?*
> *Why should you weep? Do you think I sleep?*
> *Instead I dance where the wild waves sweep.*
> *You think me dead but I have fled,*
> *While stars were glittering overhead.*

THE ELEVEN MEDALS OF JOICE LOCH

All medals awarded to Joice and Sydney Loch between 1924–1939 were melted down for their metal value by Communist Andartes who pillaged her Greek home in 1944. After World War 2 she received a replica of her British MBE. The gold medals awarded by the Kings of Rumania and Serbia and by President Pilsudski of Poland (by then replaced by Communist dictators) were lost forever. Joice was buried with two of her Greek medals, the rest are held in the tower of Prosforion and will eventually be displayed in a special Joice Loch Memorial Room in the Byzantine Museum in Ouranoupolis.

Poland: Gold Cross of Merit awarded 1922 by President Pilsudski for helping homeless refugees in eastern Poland.

Serbia: Order of St Sava awarded by the King of Serbia, 1924, for work on mosquito eradication programmes against malaria.

Greece: Order of the Phoenix (2) for *'outstanding Greeks and foreigners'* is a gold- rimmed white enamel cross with gold phoenix superimposed. In 1926 Joice was the first foreign woman to be honoured with the Order.

Greece: Orders of the Redeemer (2) Established for *'exceptional services by Greeks or foreigners to the Greek nation'*. The first Order was for running her free medical clinics and the second and higher grade Order for establishing Pirgos Rugs. Both were awarded prior to World War 2. Greece: Gold Medal, National Academy of the Arts awarded 1930s for establishing Pirgos Rugs, which she designed using motifs from Byzantine art.

Rumania: Order of Elizabeth presented by King Carol II of Rumania, Bucharest, 1941, for the care of Polish refugees in Rumania.

Britain: Medal of the Order of the British Empire (MBE) (a silver star on a wine coloured ribbon bordered in white) awarded 1933 for medical rescue work following the earthquake which destroyed Ierissos.

Poland: Gold Cross of Virtue (established 1792) awarded at a ceremony in Jerusalem in 1945 by the exiled Free Polish Government for saving over 1,000 Polish women and children from the Nazis.

Greece: Orders of Beneficence (2) established 1948 for *'Greek or foreign'* women providing outstanding service to Greece'. Enamelled medal pendant from gold crown, inscribed in Greek *'For Helping Others'*. Her first Order of Beneficence (1950) was awarded for re-opening Pirgos Rugs: her second (highest grade of the Order) was for funding a supply of unpolluted water to Ouranoupolis.

EPILOGUE
RECENT DEVELOPMENTS IN THE STORY OF THE LOCHS

Blue Ribbons, Bitter Bread elicited hundreds of letters from readers. One sent a family tree showing that NanKivells lived near Truro in Cornwall in the seventeenth century: another sent plans of George Nankivell's Gippsland farm, even then in an area of high danger from bushfires as the book reveals.

Intrigued by Joice's statement that Sydney had written the 'best book on Gallipoli' I discovered a first edition of *The Straits Impregnable*, which revealed how the horrors of trench warfare changed Sydney from a soldier into a dedicated humanitarian. Sydney's fascinating book with its detailed account of lack of ammunition and the deadly epidemic of dysentery which killed almost as many Anzacs as enemy fire, were deliberately hidden from the public by strict military censorship of letters home, truth being 'the first casualty of war'. Melbourne publisher Harry Champion, fearing that censors Censor would ban Sydney's book, published it as a best-selling novel in July 1916. The book's success went to Champion's head and he rashly added a note to the second edition *This book written in Australia, Egypt and Gallipoli, is true.* As a result, when the second edition appeared in bookshops in November 1916, the Military Censor for Victoria banned it claiming it was true so infringed the War Precautions Act of 1914 and it had to be withdrawn from sale. The Lochs' London publishers, John Murray, were not subject to the same fierce censorship and Sydney's book, the first to reveal the awful conditions for Anzacs at Gallipoli, had considerable success in England.

My husband and I enjoyed Sydney's anti-war book and wanted it republished and HarperCollins of Sydney brought out annotated version of Sydney's account, prefaced by a my brief biography of Sydney. In 2007, supported by Dame Elizabeth Murdoch, Sydney's experiences at Gallipoli were published in Australia under the title *To Hell and Back, the Banned Account of Gallipoli, with an introduction by Susanna and Jake de Vries*. Isis Publishing of Oxford brought out a large print edition of *To Hell and Back* which won praise from British critics with royalties were donated to World Vision to build wells in Third World villages, an aim dear to the Lochs.

Only after *Blue Ribbons* came out did I learn Sydney and Joice were introduced by Melbourne publisher, Harry Champion and Sydney Loch proposed to Joice Nankivell a combined farewell-and-birthday

EPILOGUE

party, given by the Champions just before Sydney was to sail to England. The Lochs' quiet wedding took place at Melbourne's Scots Church but Joice's father refused to attend, convinced would be a disaster. He was wrong. It was a strong and happy union that saved or altered for the better numerous lives in Poland, Greece and the Haifa refugee camp they ran in World War 2.

Years later Sydney Loch's goddaughter and namesake, Sydney White, (née Iaraclis) wrote to tell me how her father was employed to make the furniture for the Lochs' tower home in Ouranoupolis. She had been christened Sydney in honour of her English godfather. Sydney White (who married an Englishman) described how in her childhood, *'My godfather was my saviour. After World War Two I was skeletally thin from malaria when in April 1945 he returned to Ouranoupolis from the war, picked me up, hugged me and said, 'Little Sydney, I love you very much. I'll send you to Thessaloniki and pay for you to go to school there'.*

Joice Loch took the young Sydney Iaraclis to buy suitable clothes for her boarding school. Sydney Loch paid the expensive fees to the Thessaloniki convent for his goddaughter, who as a village girl would have received little schooling in the then remote village of Ouranoupolis. She told me, *'Only many years later did I learn that, as money was short, my godfather had sold his most valuable possession—his Army jeep—so I could fly to London and study nursing there. He advised me to obtain as many diplomas as possible. I followed his advice and obtained nursing qualifications in Midwifery, Orthopaedics and Microbiology. My great regret is that my godfather didn't live long enough to see the result of his generosity, affection and devotion to me.'* The training that her kind-hearted godfather paid for ensured his god-daughter in the course of a forty year career nursed and helped save countless English and Greek lives in various hospitals.

Sydney White was in Ouranoupolis in July 2006, when several rooms, honouring the work of the Lochs were opened to the public in their former tower home by the sea. A Pirgos rug Joice had designed was presented by Mr Paul Tighe, Australian Ambassador to Greece to add to a display of rugs which Joice designed for village women to weave so destitute Greek refugees from Turkish ethnic cleansing could feed their families. Invited to appear on the Australian ABC television programme, *Foreign Correspondent,* Sydney's goddaughter brought tears to the eyes of many television viewers when she told the world *'Without the devotion and generosity of the Lochs, the refugee village of Ouranoupolis would not have survived'.* For my part I am happy to have had the chance of telling the public about the lives of two such wonderful Australians.

A room in the Loch Memorial Museum situated in the former tower home of the Lochs at Ouranoupolis.

Bronzes of Sydney and Joice Loch, displayed in the Loch Museum, Ouranoupolis, which honours their humanitarian work in the Greek refugee village they saved from starvation.

PHOTOGRAPHS COURTESY SYDNEY WHITE

BIBLIOGRAPHY

Abbot, G.F., *Greece and the Allies*, John Murray, London, 1922.

Adelaide, Debra, *Bibliography of Australian Women's Writing*, D.W. Thorpe, Melbourne, 1991.

Asquith, Michael, *Famine: Quaker Work in Russia*, Oxford University Press, London, 1943.

Athanasios, D. Kominos [ed.], *Patmos, Treasures of the Monastery of St John*, Athens, 1988.

Coogan, Tim. P., *Michael Collins*, Hutchinson, London, 1990.

Davies, Professor Norman, *Europe, A History*, Pimlico Press, London, 1997.

Evans, Helen C., *The Glory of Byzantium*. Metropolitan Museum, New York, 1997.

Figes, Orlando, *A People's Tragedy: the Russian Revolution, 1891-1924*, Pimlico Press, London, 1997.

Foster, R.F., *The Oxford Illustrated History of Ireland*, Oxford University Press, New York, 1989.

Greenwood, John Ormerod, *Quaker Encounters: Work of the Friends War Victims Relief Committee*, Vols 1 and 3, William Sessions, York, 1975.

Housepian Dobkin, Professor Marjorie, *Smyrna, 1922, The Destruction of a City*, Faber and Faber, London, 1972 and Kent State University Press, Ohio, 1988.

Hohenzollern, Prince Paul, *The Life of King Carol of Rumania*, Methuen, London, 1979.

Kerr, Professor Joan (ed.), *Heritage: the National* [Australian] *Women's Art Book*, Craftsman House, Sydney, 1997.

Kazhdan, Alexander *et al*, *The Oxford Dictionary of Byzantium*, 3 vols, Oxford University Press, Oxford, 1991.

Langmore, Diane, *Glittering Surfaces: The Life of Maie Casey*, Allen & Unwin, Sydney, 1997.

Loch, Joice NanKivell and Loch, Sydney, *Ireland in Travail*, John Murray, London, 1922.

Loch, Joice NanKivell and Loch, Sydney, *The River of a Hundred Ways: Life in the war-devastated areas of eastern Poland*, George Allen & Unwin, 1924.

Loch, Joice NanKivell, *A Life for the Balkans*, Fleming, Harvill, New York, 1939.

Loch, Joice NanKivell, *Prosforion--Rugs and Dyes*, American Board of Missions, Publications Department, Istanbul, 1964.

Loch, Joice NanKivell, *The Hopping Ha-penny*, J. Methuen & Son, London, and E.P. Dutton, New York, 1956. [American edition now rare: not in Library of Congress catalogue].

Loch, Joice Mary NanKivell, *The Fourteen Thumbs of St Peter*, John Murray, London, 1927 and E.P. Morrow, New York, 1927.

Loch, Joice NanKivell, *A Fringe of Blue: an Autobiography*, John Murray, London and E.P. Morrow, New York, 1968.

Loch, Joice NanKivell, *Collected Poems*, Cygnet Press, Oxford, 1980.

Loch, Sydney, *Athos, the Holy Mountain*, Lutterworth Press, London, 1957.

Lowden, John, *Early Christian and Byzantine Art*, Phaidon, Oxford, 1997.

Manning, Olivia [Smith], *The Balkan Trilogy--Part 1, The Great Fortune, Part 2, The Spoiled City*, Random House, London, 1960 and 1962.

Marder, Brenda, *Stewards of the Land: The American Farm School and Modern Greece*, Columbia University Press, New York, 1979.

Polish Cultural Foundation, *The Crime of Katyn*, Polish Free Press, London, 1948.

McCulloch, Alan and Susan, *Encyclopaedia of Australian Art*, Allen and Unwin, Sydney, 1994.

McRedmond, Louis, *Modern Irish Lives: a Dictionary of 20th Century Irish Biography*, Gill and Macmillan, Dublin, 1996.

Mohr, Anton, *The Oil War*, E.P. Morrow, New York, 1925.

Morrison, George, *The Irish Civil War*, Gill & Macmillan, Dublin, 1981.

Muir, Marcie, *Australian Children's Books*, Vol 1, Andre Deutsch, London, 1970.

NanKivell, Joice, [illus. Edith Alsop], *The Cobweb Ladder*, Lothian Books, Melbourne, Simpkin, London, 1916.

NanKivell, Joice M., *The Solitary Pedestrian*, Australian Authors' Agency, Melbourne, 1918.

NanKivell, Joice, *Tales of Christophilos*, Houghton Mifflin, Boston and Riverside Press, Cambridge, Mass, 1957.

NanKivell, Joice, *Again Christophilos*, Houghton Mifflin, Boston and Riverside Press, Cambridge, Mass., 1959.

Norwich, John Julius, *A Short History of Byzantium*, Faber & Faber, London, 1961.

O'Balance, Edgar, *The Greek Civil War*, Faber & Faber, London, 1966.

Ostrogorsky, D., *History of the Byzantine State*, Oxford University Press, Oxford, 1956.

Pesman, Ros, *Duty Free: Australian Women Abroad*, Oxford University Press, Melbourne, 1966. [The only Australian book to mention the achievements and medals of Joice Loch along with those of other Australian women abroad.]

Provatakis, Theocharis, *Mount Athos*, Rekos, Thessaloniki, [n.d.].

Poynter, Professor J.R., *Doubts and Certainties: The Life of Dr Alexander Leeper*, Melbourne University Press, Melbourne, 1993.

Prichard, Katharine Susannah, *The Real Russia*, Modern Publishers, Sydney, 1934.

Patriarchs of the Holy Community of Mount Athos *et al*, *Treasures of Mount Athos: Illustrated catalogue of the 1997 exhibition held in Thessaloniki in 1997*, Byzantine Museums and Ministry of Culture, 1997.

Sherrard, Dr Philip, *Athos, the Holy Mountain*, Overlook Press, New York, 1985. [Dr Sherrard, the distinguished archaeologist and historian helped Loch finish her autobiography after her accident and was granted permission to use several photos by Sydney Loch in this book.]

Sherrard, Dr Philip. *The Greek East and the Latin West*, Oxford University Press, 1959.

Watt, Richard M., *Bitter Glory: Poland and its fate, 1918-1939*, Simon and Schuster, New York, 1979.

Ware, Timothy, Kallistos, *The Orthodox Church*, University Press, Baltimore, Maryland, 1963, London, 1964. [Bishop Ware officiated at Joice Loch's funeral and nominated her as the only non-Orthodox person honoured by receiving the full Orthodox liturgy.]

Wilson, Roger C., *Quaker Relief: an account of the relief work of the Society of Friends, 1940-1948*, Allen and Unwin, London, 1952.

Woodhouse, C.M., *The Story of Modern Greece*, Faber & Faber, London, 1968.

Zweig, Ferdynand, *Poland between two wars, a study of social and economic change*, London, Secker and Warburg, 1944.

ENDNOTES

Chapter 1—CHILD OF THE CYCLONE
1. According to Joice NanKivell Loch's *A Fringe of Blue: an Autobiography*, John Murray, London, 1968, the NanKivell land was near Truro in Cornwall. The family was large, split between England, France, Australia and New Zealand. One of her ancestors had been Mayor of Truro while other NanKivells had been pirates and buccaneers. The spelling of the family name varies. A cousin, Rex Nan Kivell, is famous for donating his valuable collection to the Australian people and it is shared by the National Library of Australia and the National Gallery in Canberra.
2. Joice inherited this silver teapot, which I was shown when I visited Ouranoupolis.
3. Joice relates the story of her maternal grandmother's divorce and remarriage in *A Fringe of Blue, op cit*, p 5. George NanKivell referred to Emily Lawson as 'flighty and a bad influence on the children' and refused to let Edith contact her. The scandal of her parents' divorce and its sad consequences may explain why Edith refused to divorce George NanKivell.
4. Loch, Joice NanKivell, *A Fringe of Blue: an Autobiography, op cit*.
5. An account of the firm of Fanning NanKivell & Sons appears in *ADB*, Vol 4, pp 152-153 in the entries for William Fanning (1816-1887) and his son, Edward Fanning (1848-1917). Fanning NanKivell was registered in Britain and in Melbourne and their ships and warehouses were heavily mortgaged in the early 1880s to invest in Queensland sugar. In 1882, Thomas NanKivell and Edward Fanning invested jointly in grazing land near Tambo. See Record of Crown Lands offered for Sale at Public Auction, 1882, Department of Lands, New South Wales. Joice's father, George NanKivell, managed the firm's Tambo property before going north to manage Farnham for Fanning NanKivell.
6. The birth certificates of Joice Mary NanKivell and her younger brother, Charles Gordon Lincoln NanKivell, are held in the State Archives of Queensland.
7. *ADB*, Vol 4, entry under Fanning, Edward, cites Gairloch (4,600 acres) and Macknade (6,856 acres). Gairloch employed 90 Kanakas, 25 Malay field workers, 20 Chinese cooks and mill workers and 10 European overseers. Farnham, with 5,000 acres was larger than Gairloch and doubtless had a similar number of imported workers. According to the *ADB*, Hamleigh, the company's fourth plantation had been established by a British cane planter with substantial plantations in Java and Fanning NanKivell bought a half-share in what became their fourth Herbert River property.
8. Loch, Joice NanKivell, *A Fringe of Blue: an Autobiography, op cit*, p 9.
9. Neame family diary, John Oxley Library, State Library of Queensland.
10. Nankivell, Joice M., *The Solitary Pedestrian*, Australian Author's Agency, Melbourne, 1918.
11. See *Australian Encyclopedia*, Angus & Robertson, 1925 pp 651-655; Graves, Adrian Arthur, *Cane and Labour, The Political Economy of the Queensland sugar industry 1862-1906*, Edinburgh University Press, 1993; Hokanson, Stig R., Arrival, acceptance and abolition, indentured labour in the Queensland sugar industry 1863-1916, Griffith University, Brisbane, 1887.

Chapter 2—PARROT PIE AND PIGWEED SALAD
1. Neame family diary, John Oxley Library, State Library of Queensland, Brisbane, gives the full story of the non-payment of Fanning NanKivell's mortgages to the Neame brothers and their settlement with Fanning NanKivell. Thomas NanKivell escaped bankruptcy by donating assets to his wife. Edward Fanning managed to reorganise his finances and continued to deal in shipping cargoes, according to his entry in *ADB*, Vol 4.
2. Loch, Joice NanKivell, *A Fringe of Blue: An Autobiography*, John Murray, London, 1968, pp 44-48.
3. See NanKivell, Joice M., *The Solitary Pedestrian*, Australian Author's Agency, Melbourne, 1918, for many of her Queensland stories including the death of her Aborignal playmate, Tinker.

ENDNOTES

4   The land once occupied by Farnham is situated between Ingham and the smaller town of Halifax. Today a sewage treatment plant operates on part of the plantation; another section is known as 'the old Mills Farm'. Nothing remains of Farnham homestead. Information provided by Councillor Vi Groundwater.
5   Decades later, travelling by train in Britain, Joice met a NanKivell cousin who had grown up on a sugar plantation in the West Indies. He was the offspring of an inter-racial marriage. She records their encounter in *A Fringe of Blue: an Auto-biography, op cit*.
6   According to the City of Prahran Rate Book for 1888 (Prahran Library, Melbourne), Thomas Nankivell had by now moved to a smaller but still substantial house at 57 Toorak Road, listed as having 10 rooms. In 1891 the house was re-numbered 431 Toorak Road, located close to the junction of Kensington and Toorak Roads, near Como House. It was subsequently demolished and the land subdivided. It is now the site of luxury apartments.

Chapter 3—RURAL POVERTY AT BOOLARA
1   Loch, Joice NanKivell, *A Fringe of Blue: an Autobiography*, John Murray, London, 1968, p 9.
2   *Ibid*, p 13.
3   *Ibid*, p 20.
4   *Ibid*, p 26.
5   NanKivell, Joice M., *The Solitary Pedestrian*, Australian Author's Agency, Melbourne, 1918, pp 51-54.
6   The story of the rabbit dinner given to the guests is related by Joice in *The Solitary Pedestrian, op cit*.
7   World War 1 ensured that Maie Ryan (later Lady Casey) never had her planned coming-out ball. Instead she did voluntary war work and, chaperoned by her ambitious mother, attended the few debutante balls that did take place in London during the war. Maie did not make her 'glittering' marriage to Richard Casey, diplomat, administrator and eventually Governor-General of Australia until she was in her early thirties, by which time Joice was married and working in Poland.

Chapter 4—THE WILD COLONIAL GIRL
1   Loch, Joice NanKivell, *A Fringe of Blue: an Autobiography*, John Murray, London, 1968, pp 37-38.
2   The school may have been the predecessor of Firbank, the well-known Melbourne girls' school which several younger members of the NanKivell family attended.
3   NanKivell, Joice M., *The Solitary Pedestrian*, Australian Author's Agency, Melbourne, 1918, pp 80-81.
4   The story of Joice's suitor, Percy B, is related in an amusing way in Loch, Joice NanKivell, *A Fringe of Blue: an Autobiography*, op cit, pp 49-51

Chapter 5—'THE COBWEB LADDER'
1   For descriptions of Geoff NanKivell's time in Queensland, see Loch, Joice NanKivell, *A Fringe of Blue: an Autobiography*, John Murray, London, 1968, and NanKivell, Joice M., The Solitary Pedestrian, Australian Author's Agency, Melbourne, 1918.
2   Details of life at Drouin are from Loch, Joice NanKivell, *A Fringe of Blue: an Autobiography, op cit*.
3   Ibid, p 52.
4   Nankivell, Joice, M., *The Cobweb Ladder, op cit*, contains fourteen illustrations by Edith Alsop—a Melbourne artist who worked on an important series of murals in Melbourne's Homeopathic Hospital, and exhibited in Sydney and Melbourne with Jessie Trail, another talented artist. For entries on Joice NanKivell Loch, see Muir, Marcie, *Australian Children's Books*, Vol 1, Andre Deutsch, London, 1970 p 293, and Adelaide, Debra, *Bibliography of Australian Women's Writing*, D.W. Thorpe, Melbourne, 1991.
5   Due to a wartime paper shortage, *The Cobweb Ladder*, was printed for Lothian Book Publishing Co. of Melbourne in England in 1916. A British edition was published in 1916 by Simpkin, London. This large format handsomely produced children's book has become rare, valuable and highly sought after. The author catalogued a copy in 1980 when she was

in charge of the Rare Book Department of Lawson's Auctioneers, Sydney and its sale aroused a great deal of interest.
6 Grenbry Outhwaite's subsidy towards the colour printing in *Elves and Fairies* is referred to in Anita Calloway's notes on Ida Rentoul Outhwaite in *Heritage: The National Women's Art Book*, Craftsman House, Sydney, 1995, p 422. Edith Alsop's disappointment that *The Cobweb Ladder* (illustrated in black and white) was severely damaged by the addition of colour plates in *Elves and Fairies* comes from Calloway's notes on Alsop in the same book, p 304. Calloway describes Alsop's illustrations as 'seven very beautiful pictures [which] by rights should have led to a brilliant career for their artist'. (Muir lists 17 plates; possibly there were different editions for Britain and America and for Australia.) After this setback Alsop did not continue as a book illustrator but taught wood engraving and exhibited. Joice NanKivell would not write another children's book for forty years.

Chapter 6—A HERO OF GALLIPOLI

1 Loch, Joice NanKivell, *A Fringe of Blue: an Autobiography*, John Murray, London, 1968, p 54.
2 Dr Leeper's employment of Joice NanKivell during his time as Warden of Trinity College is mentioned in his biography, *Doubts and Certainties: The Life of Dr Alexander Leeper* by Professor J.R.Poynter, Melbourne University Press, Melbourne, 1997, p 484 and in Loch, Joice NanKivell, *A Fringe of Blue, op cit*, p 53.
3 NanKivell, Joice M., *The Solitary Pedestrian*, Australian Author's Agency, Melbourne, 1918, is one important source of information about Joice's childhood in Queensland and Victoria. Her poem about the lambs was included in a collection of her poems published by the Cygnet Press, Oxford, 1980.
4 Review dated 1918 of *The Solitary Pedestrian*, op cit, in the State Library of Victoria. Kenyon Historical Press Cuttings File, 1908-1942. In Reel 3, Vols 4-10 Joice is described as a clever writer and an excellent horsewoman.
5 Sydney's full name was Frederick Sydney Loch. His father's name appears on the marriage certificate as Frederick Pharye Loch, gentleman. Marriage Certificate dated 22 February, 1919, held by the Registry of Births, Marriages and Deaths, Melbourne.
6 Descriptions of Sydney Loch provided by former staff of the American Farm School, Thessaloniki, and by Martha Handschin.
7 Joice was always extremely reticent about her feelings. In her memoirs she devotes two lines to her meeting with Sydney and her marriage, and she never spoke about their relationship. The cover blurb of *A Fringe of Blue* implies that the Lochs married in Britain but Joice wrote nothing about the ceremony. Only after fruitless searches through the British National Records Office and the Scottish Registrar-General's Office did I discover they had married in Melbourne. All her wedding photos and medals were destroyed by guerillas who vandalised her Greek home in 1943.
8 From Joice's account of her voyage in *A Fringe of Blue, op cit*, it does appear that the newly married couple travelled separately to Britain.
9 Langmore, Diane, *Glittering Surfaces: The Life of Maie Casey*, Allen & Unwin, Sydney, 1997, pp 27-28. Maie Ryan (later Lady Casey) carefully weeded out of her collected correspondence any letters from people she believed had no social significance. Joice's memoirs mention childhood visits to Maie Ryan, but Maie's memoirs ignore Joice, the poor relation. Diane Langmore, current editor of the *Australian Dictionary of Biography* has confirmed in writing to me that, due to Joice Loch's honours and achievements, she would be included in a proposed volume of 'missing persons' of the ADB.
10 The Lochs' London apartment 'near Hyde Park' is referred to at the opening of *Ireland in Travail*, John Murray, London, 1924.
11 The Australian writer Katharine Susannah Prichard, a contemporary of Joice Loch, described how difficult she found it to obtain work in Fleet Street, where there were very few women journalists at this period.
12 Thanks to Virginia Murray, director of John Murray publishers, for information. In a letter to the author, 19.11.98., she states that two of Murray's directors, Sir John Murray and Lord Gorrel, were likely to have provided the Lochs with letters of introduction to Yates and others of the Irish literati.

Endnotes

Chapter 7—IRELAND
1. Groups fighting for an Irish Republic included the Irish Nationalists; the Fenians; the Irish Volunteers; the Patriots; Sinn Fein; and Michael Collins' Irish Republican Army, which he had formed out of members of the Irish Republican Brotherhood and his own friends. The term IRA did not come into wide use until years later. In *Ireland in Travail*, the Lochs tend to lump all Republican movements together as Sinn Fein or the Republican Army.
2. I have cited additional facts the Lochs may not have known from Ranelagh, John, *Ireland: An Illustrated History*, Oxford University Press, New York, 1981, pp 227-257; Foster, R.F., *The Oxford Illustrated History of Ireland*, Oxford University Press, New York, 1989, pp 237-250; and Coogan, T.P., *Michael Collins*, Hutchinson, London, 1990.
3. Cited in Joice Loch's chapters in *Ireland in Travail*, John Murray, London, 1922. The Contents page states which author wrote which chapter.
4. The Lochs were careful not to name Major X. He might have been Captain Hardy, one of the few British agents to survive Bloody Sunday; like Major X, he was sent to Belfast on undercover work.
5. Coogan, T.P., *Michael Collins, op cit*.
6. Loch, Joice NanKivell and Loch, Sydney, *Ireland in Travail*, op cit, p 68.
7. Loch, Joice NanKivell, *A Fringe of Blue: an Autobiography*, John Murray, London, 1968, p 66.
8. The Lochs gave no street address for Mrs Slaney's house in Ireland in Travail, possibly fearing IRA retaliation. Forty years later, when writing *A Fringe of Blue: an Autobiography*, Joice gave the address as Ely Place, but carefully omitted a street number.
9. George Russell (1867-1935), who befriended the Lochs and wrote under the pseudonym Æ (short for the Greek *Aeon*) was an unforgettable character, larger than life. He was an author, playwright, poet of fantasy and editor of agricultural and political journals. His most famous work was the play *Deirdre*, staged at the Abbey Theatre. His home in Dublin was a meeting place for intellectual discussion of art, literature, the theatre, economics and politics. He was a member of Sinn Fein and like Michael Collins and many of the writers in the circle to which he introduced the Lochs, favoured the Anglo-Irish Treaty as a stepping-stone to a republic.

Chapter 8—IRELAND'S BITTER WAR OF INDEPENDENCE
1. The names Slaney and O'Grady are false; the Lochs used them in their book *Ireland in Travail* to protect the individuals concerned. In her memoirs *A Fringe of Blue: an Autobiography*, John Murray, London, 1968, written decades later, Joice gives Mr O'Grady's role to a man by the name of O'Connor, probably his real name. But Mrs Slaney's real name is not revealed; Joice referring to her as 'our grim landlady, who had the worst characteristics of the worst of the Irish'.
2. Loch, Joice NanKivell and Loch, Sydney, *Ireland in Travail*, John Murray, London, 1922 describes the Lochs' version of the events of 'Bloody Sunday'.
3. *Ibid*, p 142.
4. *Ibid*, p 144.
5. *Ibid*, p 157.
6. McRedmond, Louis, *Modern Irish Lives: A Dictionary of 20th Century Irish Biography*, Gill & Macmillan, Dublin, 1996. Biographical details of Desmond and Mabel FitzGerald, pp 102-103.
7. Darrell Figgis was later captured, sentenced and jailed. Eventually he committed suicide. Today he is better known under his pseudonym 'Michael Ireland' and for a book published in 1927 under his own name, *Recollections of the Irish War*.

Chapter 9—'IRELAND IN TRAVAIL'—THE FINAL CHAPTERS
1. This conversation appears in the Loch's book *Ireland in Travail*, John Murray, London, 1922, and in a greatly abbreviated form in *A Fringe of Blue: an Autobiography*, John Murray, London, 1968.
2. Loch, Joice NanKivell, *A Fringe of Blue: an Autobiography, op cit*, pp 64-66.

3   Ranelagh, John, *Ireland: An Illustrated History*, Oxford University Press, New York, 1981, p 241.
4   *Ibid*, pp 266-267.
5   Loch, Sydney and Loch, Joice, *Ireland in Travail, op cit.*
6   Ring, Jim, *Erskine Childers*, John Murray, London, 1996.
7   Desmond Fitzgerald became an excellent Irish Foreign Minister and Senator as well as an important literary figure.
8   Joice Loch's account of the Dail meeting from *Ireland in Travail, op cit.*
9   In 1938, when the Irish adopted a new constitution, Professor Douglas Hyde (1860-1945) became the first President of Eire. Different sources quote the price on Michael Collins' head as varying between ;bp4,000—;bp10,000. However, Collins' biographer Tim Pat Coogan states that officially no reward was ever offered by the British for the capture of Michael Collins, alive or dead. Perhaps the Lochs heard rumours of an official reward from Major X.
10 Loch, Joice NanKivell and Sydney, *Ireland in Travail, op cit.*
11 Loch, Joice NanKivell and Sydney *Ireland in Travail, op cit.* and Morrison, George, *The Irish Civil War*, Gill and Macmillan, Dublin, 1982, p 1.
12 Loch, Joice NanKivell, *A Fringe of Blue: an Autobiography, op cit*, p 67.

Chapter 10—OFF ON A MISSION

1   Morrison, George, *The Irish Civil War*, Gill & Macmillan, Dublin, 1981, pp 2-3.
2   Loch, Joice and Loch, Sydney, *Ireland in Travail*, John Murray, London, 1922, pp 295-296.
3   *Ibid*, p 297.
4   The most fully documented account of Michael Collins' death comes from Coogan, T.P., *Michael Collins: a Biography*, Hutchinson, London, 1990.
5   Endpapers for *Ireland in Travail* carried advertisements for John Murray's current publications about Ireland and its history, including books by Lady Gregory (one of the founders of Dublin's famous Abbey Theatre) and by the poet W.B. Yeats.
6   These remarks do not apply to present day Quakers. Since the 1920s the Quaker Movement has adapted to the times without compromising important matters of conscience; they remain non-dogmatic and devoted to humanitarian aims. There are no longer strict codes of dress and deportment as there were when the Lochs went to work with the Quakers in Poland.
7   At the time of writing, the Pripet Marshes are part of Bielo-Russia and the Ukraine; most of the area remains poverty-stricken due to racial tensions. This highly fertile land has served as a battleground between Poland, the Ukraine and Russia for centuries.
8   Greenwood, John Ormerod, *Quaker Encounters: Friends War Victims Relief Committee 1914-23*, Vol 1, William Sessions, York, 1975, p 235, cites the names of the dead volunteers. Joice mentions 'three dead Quaker relief workers'.
9   Davies, Professor Norman, *Europe, A History*, Pimlico, London, 1997, pp 934-936. In the opinion of many historians, the battle of Zamosc saved Europe from becoming Communist. 20,000 Polish *uhlans* or cavalry defeated General Budenny's cavalry and led to a treaty between Poland and Russia.

Chapter 11—A PALACE IN WARSAW

1   Greenwood, John Ormerod, *Quaker Encounters, Friends War Victims Relief Committee 1914-23*, Vol 1, William Sessions, York, 1975, pp 234-235 gives details. The Menshikovs had been Treasurers to the Tsar for generations, and as such, immensely wealthy.
2   Descriptions of life with the Quakers in Poland are provided in Joice Loch's autobiography, *A Fringe of Blue*, John Murray, London, 1968 and by her colleague Francesca Wilson, In the Margins of Chaos, George Allen & Unwin, London, n.d.
3   Loch, Joice M. NanKivell and Loch, Sydney, *The River of a Hundred Ways: Life in the war-devastated areas of eastern Poland*, George Allen & Unwin, London, 1924.
4   Slightly different versions of this story appear in *The River of a Hundred Ways, Life in the war-devastated areas of eastern Poland, op cit*, and in A Fringe of Blue, op cit.

Endnotes

5. *The River of a Hundred Ways: Life in war-devastated areas of eastern Poland, op cit*, pp 234-239 quotes this number of horses hired from the Polish Army and states that the following year Sydney bought 1,000 horses from them. The Lochs may not have known this but some of the horses Friends War Relief purchased from the Polish Government had been confiscated from Ukrainian farmers by the Polish Army before the Polish-Russian war.
6. Loch, Joice NanKivell, *A Fringe of Blue: an Autobiography, op cit*, pp 84-85.
7. Loch, Joice M. NanKivell and Loch, Sydney, *The River of a Hundred Ways, Life in the war-devastated areas of eastern Poland, op cit*.
8. *Ibid:* description of the forest of Selecz.

Chapter 12—WOLVES IN THE BLIZZARD

1. Volhynia is now part of Western Ukraine. :
2. Incidents in this chapter are from Loch, Joice, *A Fringe of Blue an Autobiography*, John Murray, London, 1968 and Loch, Joice NanKivell and Loch, Sydney, *The River of a Hundred Ways: Life in war-devastated eastern Poland*, George Allen and Unwin, London, 1924.

Chapter 13—THE FOURTEEN THUMBS OF ST PETER

1. See Loch, Joice NanKivell and Loch, Sydney, *The River of a Hundred Ways: Life in war-devastated eastern Poland*, George Allen and Unwin, London, 1924.
2. Details about Prince Alexander Makinsky from Loch, Joice NanKivell, *A Fringe of Blue: an Autobiography*, John Murray, London, 1968 and *The River of a Thousand Ways: Life in war-devastated eastern Poland, op cit*.
3. See Loch, Joice NanKivell, *A Fringe of Blue: an Autobiography, op cit*. and Loch, Joice Mary NanKivell, *The Fourteen Thumbs of St Peter*, John Murray, London 1927; E.P. Morrow, New York, 1927.
4. *Ibid.*
5. NanKivell, Joice Mary, *The Fourteen Thumbs of St Peter, op cit*.
6. Loch, Joice NanKivell, *A Fringe of Blue; an Autobiography, op cit*, p 87.
7. *Ibid*, page 86.
8. See Figes, Orlando, *A People's Tragedy: The Russian Revolution, 1891-1924*, Pimlico, London, 1997, which cites comparable accounts of Moscow under the rule of Lenin, written by Jewish-born Emma Goldman. Like Joice Loch, Goldman also describes middle-class girls prostituting themselves for the price of a meal and aristocrats without ration books selling their possessions in the streets of Moscow to buy food.
9. See Loch, Joice NanKivell, *A Fringe of Blue: an Autobiography, op cit*, and NanKivell, Joice Mary, The Fourteen Thumbs of St Peter, op cit.
10. Loch, Joice NanKivell. *A Fringe of Blue: an Autobiography, op cit*, p 89. This story is related in more detail in *The Fourteen Thumbs of St Peter, op cit*.
11. Joice Loch described how the steel works at Stalinsk used slave labour to build their foundations. Not all visitors were so perceptive. In *The Real Russia*, Sydney, 1934, Katherine Susannah Pritchard, who stayed at Stalinsk for a month as the 'guest' of Stalin's government, described how 'The wonders of the world have nothing on Stalinsk—[compared to] the Pyramids, the Great Wall of China, Borobudur. This city ... can stand with any of them'.
12. Wilson, Francesca, *In the Margins of Chaos*. Section titled *Famine Relief in Russia*, published c. 1930, draws similar conclusions to those of Joice Loch. Possibly Francesca Wilson read *The Fourteen Thumbs of St Peter* before writing her account of famine relief in Russia. Greenwood, John, *Quaker Encounters: Friends and Relief*, Volume 1, William Sessions, York, England, 1975, pp 229-249, gives a detailed account of the work of the Quakers at the Buzuluk Mission, on the Volga River.
13. See also Wilson, Francesca, *In the Margins of Chaos*, John Murray, London, 1948, published years after Joice had published her novel set in Russia, for parallels between their accounts.
14. Figes, Orlando, *A People's Tragedy: The Russian Revolution 1891-1924* gives accounts of cannibalism in Samara when families ate the flesh of dead children so the rest might survive. Figes' account includes photographs from Russian archives of partly-eaten children and thousands of corpses awaiting burial.

15 Hurley, Beulah, *International Bulletin*, Friends War Relief. London, May 1922, p 5, cites that between Christmas Day 1921 and 20 January 1922, 2,200 peasants had died in Buzuluk alone while some 250,000 had died in the Samara district. For additional details of the Buzuluk Mission see also *Famine: Quaker Work in Russia* by Michael Asquith, Oxford University Press, 1943.
16 NanKivell, Joice Mary, *The Fourteen Thumbs of St Peter, op cit.*
17 An editor of an atheist paper which is clearly modelled on Bez Boznic is the villain in Joice's novel *The Fourteen Thumbs of St Peter, op cit.* This exhibition, with its aims of shaking the Orthodox religious faith of the peasants, features in the plot of *The Fourteen Thumbs of St Peter, op cit.*

Chapter 14—RIBBONS OF BLUE THAT BIND FOREVER

1 This blank-verse poem titled *Lake Narozc*, and another, *The Eve of St John*, were included in Joice Loch's *Collected Poems*, Cygnet Press, Oxford, in 1980. Friends and admirers who subscribed for its publication included Gerald Palmer, Lord and Lady Eccles, Lord Moran and members of the Churchill family.
2 For this reason Joice named her memoirs *A Fringe of Blue*.
3 See Greenwood, John Ormerod, *Quaker Encounters, Friends and Relief Work*, Vol 3, William Sessions, York, 1975.
4 *Ibid* for accounts of the work of Dr Hilda Clark and Carl Heath.
5 See Professor Marjorie Housepian, *Smyrna: the destruction of a city*, Kent State University Press, Ohio, 1988. The author's father, a young naval lieutenant, was aboard a British warship of the Dardanelles fleet anchored off Smyrna (Izmir). His captain had orders from the British Admiralty that their ship could rescue only British nationals, not Greeks or Armenians as this could upset delicate peace negotiations with Kemal Ataturk. A British search party took a tender ashore looking for British residents and brought back British citizens and several Greek women who claimed their British passports had been burned when their homes were destroyed. The crew spent two days and nights watching Smyrna burn, horrified by the screams coming across the water. Some naval captains issued orders to turn up the ships' radios and gramophones to drown out the cries from the dockside. Housepian cites negotiations with Ataturk over potential oil concessions in Turkish Mesopotamia as the real reason for non-intervention by the Allies and claims Ataturk spread false propaganda that Greek and Armenian residents of Smyrna had set fire to the city and killed Turks before leaving. This sparked anti-Greek riots throughout Asia Minor.

Chapter 15—GREECE—THE DREAM AND THE REALITY

1 The name 'Macedonia' as used by Joice refers to a large area between the Bulgarian border and the Gulf of Salonika, originally occupied by the Romans, then part of the Byzantine Empire and a source of contention for centuries. At the end of the First World War, Macedonia was divided between Greece and the newly-formed Kingdom of the Serbs, Croats and Slovenes, later known as Yugoslavia.
2 Loch, Joice N., *A Fringe of Blue: an Autobiography*, John Murray, London, 1968.
3 65,000 refugees from Smyrna arrived in Thessaloniki during the year 1922, cited in Marder, Brenda, *Stewards of the Land: The American Farm School and Modern Greece*, Columbia University Press, New York, 1979, p 118. The total of refugees who left Turkey for Greece after the Smyrna massacre is estimated as 1,250 Greeks and 100,000 Armenians by Professor Margery Housepian Dobkin in *Smyrna, 1922, the destruction of a city*, Kent State University Press, Ohio, 1988, pp 218-9. Under the Treaty of Lausanne they were exchanged for 350,00 Moslem Turks living and working in Greece. Housepian's figures confirm Joice Loch's account of the huge proportion of widows and orphans, most Greek men of fighting age having been killed by the Turks or taken into slave labour.
4 Joice wrote Dr John House's biography, *A Life for the Balkans*, published in London in 1939, which recounts the adventures of Dr House running missions in the Balkans and in Zaghra,Turkey. Joice also wrote an unpublished ms about Dr and Mrs House, *Two Remarkable People*, which is in the American Farm School archives.

Endnotes

5   Joice's account of the Farm School campus in 1923 is taken from *A Fringe of Blue: an Autobiography*, John Murray, London, 1968, pp 102-110 and from Marder, Brenda, *Stewards of the Land: The American Farm School and Modern Greece*, Columbia University Press, New York, 1979.

Chapter 16—'THE ART OF BEING KIND'
1   Joice began writing her autobiography, *A Fringe of Blue*, after she had suffered a serious fall from a balcony. Her memory was affected and she had problems spelling names accurately. She misspelled the name Bertholf as 'Berthoff'. Archivist and historian Brenda Marder, who taught at the Farm School in the 1960s and has access to their archives, cites the name as Bertholf in her authorised history of the Farm School. I have therefore adopted Marder's spelling.
2   Marder, Brenda, *Stewards of the Land: The American Farm School and Modern Greece*, Columbia University Press, New York, 1979, and in a telephone conversation with the author in July 1999.
3   Under Article 4 of the Treaty of Lausanne, July 1923, all Greek males forcibly detained in Turkey as slave labour were to be sent to mainland Greece immediately. The Turks broke the terms of the Treaty and did not release survivors for another year, by which time most were suffering from disease and malnutrition and unable to support their families. No compensation was ever paid to Greeks who lost homes and livelihoods.
4   Marder, Brenda. *Stewards of the Land: The American Farm School and Modern Greece, op cit.*
5   *Ibid.*
6   Loch, Joice NanKivell, *A Fringe of Blue: an Autobiography*, John Murrray, London, 1968, p 105.
7   *Ibid*, p 112.
8   *Ibid*, p 109.

Chapter 17—IN THE SHADOW OF THE HOLY MOUNTAIN
1   Women are still banned from entering Athos by land or sea. Tour boats depart from Ouranoupolis in summer with women on board but have to keep a distance of 500 metres from the peninsula. Only ten male foreigners are allowed to enter Athos and stay overnight at any one time. Food and a bed are provided. The monasteries are now connected by dirt roads. Standards of accomodation vary from monastery to monastery. Full details are given in *The Lonely Planet Guide to Greece*. Permits and a letter of recommendation from the visitor's consulate is needed plus a valid passport; it is vital to book well in advance.
2   The *pirgos* or watch tower in which the Lochs lived was known as the tower of Prosforion and today is a museum of Byzantine art. A feasibility study for a Joice Loch Memorial Room has been carried out by the Directorate, but at the time of writing no date for its opening has been announced.
3   Byzantium was the Christian empire founded by the Emperor Constantine in the fourth century. Its capital, Greek-speaking Byzantium, was also known as Constantinopolis, (the city of Constantine). Following the Turkish conquest of the city it became known as Istanbul.
4   At this period Athos was in decline, although Sydney's book does not stress this point. Historian John Julius Norwich visited Athos in the 1960s, three decades after the Lochs arrived there. He speculated that the dilapidated, almost empty monasteries would one day be converted to luxury hotels. The 1960s and 1970s saw many hippies arrive in search of cheap accommodation and food: some of them succumbed to the beauty and magic of the Athos peninsula and became monks, arresting the decline. Numbers have risen during the 1980s and 1990s. At the time of writing, the Greek Government and UNESCO have donated $19 million per year for the preservation of the monasteries and their treasures, to be administered by the Directorate of Byzantine Antiquities.

Chapter 18—WILD HERBS AND BITTER BREAD
1   Loch, Joice NanKivell, *A Fringe of Blue: an Autobiography*. John Murray, London, 1968.

2 Loch, Joice NanKivell, *Prosforion–Rugs and Dyes*. American Board of Missions Publications Department, Istanbul, 1964. Joice gives 1926 as the date she and Sydney moved into the tower and explains how the Mayor of Pirgos petitioned the Governor of Macedonia to change the name of the village.
3 Loch, Sydney. *Athos, the Holy Mountain*, Lutterworth Press, London, 1957, p 13.
4 Fani Mitropoulu, Joice's former housekeeper to Susanna de Vries, 1996. Fani came to Ouranoupolis in 1923 from the Princes' Islands where her parents had a successful farm.

Chapter 19—THE TOWER BY THE AEGEAN SEA
1 The wooden table and chairs that Joice commissioned from the village carpenter were still stored in the tower of Prosforion in 1996 when the author visited it.
2 Joice Loch to John Murray, London July 1924.
3 Letters to John Murray, London from 27 September, 1925 chart the progress of the *The Fourteen Thumbs of St Peter*.
4 Joice Loch to Dr Philip Sherrard, month not given, 1968, refers to his daughter seeing the ghost of the murdered monk in the tower.
5 Thanks to John Murray Publishers, London. Photocopies of Joice's letters are now in the National Library of Australia, Canberra.
6 Joice used the stories of the Rug Miser and the rich rats and the feuding midwives in *Tales of Christophilos*, Houghton Mifflin, Boston and Riverside Press, Cambridge, Mass, 1957.

Chapter 20—RUG WEAVING SAVES A VILLAGE
1 Pirgos Rugs are no longer woven. As a result they have become highly prized by Greek collectors. A large Pirgos Rug in the Vatopedi Tree of Life or the leaping dolphin pattern, designed by Joice, is now worth between $20-$40,000 depending on size and condition. The loss of eight of the nine valuable rugs donated to 'the people of Australia' by Joice Loch has meant that, although the National Library of Australia in Canberra would like to archive Joice's personal papers and photographs, in 1996 the Director of Byzantine Antiquities in Thessaloniki told the author: 'If Australian curators couldn't keep the Pirgos rugs safely, why *should* we donate Kyria Loch's papers to an Australikan institution?'
2 In 1964 Joice published an account of the plant dyes used by Pirgos Rugs and gave a listing of her designs. (Loch, Joice NanKivell, *Prosforion Rugs and Dyes*. American Board of Missions Publications Department, Istanbul, 1964, footnote 7). The book was dedicated to Martha Handschin, who had helped to research and formulate new dyes from local plants.
3 Interview with Joice Loch, Melbourne *Herald*, Friday, 11 December, 1969.

Chapter 21—EARTHQUAKE
1 Loch, Joice NanKivell, *A Fringe of Blue: an Autobiography*, John Murray, London, 1968, pp 143-148 relates the story of the earthquake at Ierissos as does an article by Joice NanKivell in the Melbourne *Herald* dated 12 November, 1932. Her previous article, *The Ruin of Corinth*, appeared in the Melbourne *Herald* 3 July 1928.
2 *Ibid.*
3 *Ibid.*
4 *Prosforion Rugs and Dyes*, American Board of Missions Publication Department, 1964, Istanbul, explains the story of the decline of Pirgos Rugs when the Germans invaded Greece in World War 2. In 1952, at the invitation of King George of Greece, Joice re-started Pirgos Rugs using her Byzantine-inspired designs and gradually introduced new ones, based on cave paintings at Lascaux in France, Altamira in Spain, and motifs found in tombs at Pazyryk in Siberia.

Chapter 22—THE RAPE OF POLAND
1 Loch, Joice NanKivell. *A Fringe of Blue: an Autobiography*, John Murray, London, 1968, p 167.
.2 *Ibid.*
3 *Ibid.*
4 Nearly 200,000 Polish refugees, male and female, were interned in Rumania and Hungary after the invasion of Poland, according to a footnote in Greenwood, John, *Quaker Relief*,

ENDNOTES

Vol l, Ebor Press, York, p 313. *Encyclopaedia Britannica*, Vol 18, 1959, p 150 cites 120,000 Polish men assembled in France under General Sikorski as part of the Free Polish Army by the spring of 1940.
5   From *King Carol II of Rumania*, by Prince Paul of Hohenzollern, Methuen, London, 1988.
6   Cited by Francesca Wilson, who ran a Quaker-funded aid centre for Polish refugees in Budapest.
7   Francesca Wilson made her initial inspection tour of Polish refugees interned in Hungary and Rumania in October 1938. Wilson, Francesca, *In the Margins of Chaos*, John Murray, London, 1948, p 238.
8   Davies, Professor Norman, *Europe: A History*, Pimlico, 1997, pp 1004-5. See also *The Crime of Katyn: Facts and Documents*, Polish Cultural Foundation, London, 1948.
9   *Encyclopaedia Britannica*, 1959, Vol 18, p 150 cites General Sikorski as Acting President of Poland as well as Commander in Chief of the Free Polish Army at Angers.
10 Loch, Joice NanKivell. *A Fringe of Blue: an Autobiography*, John Murray, London, 1968.
11 'I'm hungry, hungry, hungry! Give me money.'
12 Greenwood, John, *Quaker Encounters*, Vol 1, *op cit*, states that Dermod O'Donnell handed over command of the Bucharest Mission to Sydney Loch.
13 Polish-born Martin Pilch bought a blackmarket visa in Bucharest in order to escape to France and join the Free Polish Army. He told the author that queues for Ministry-approved visas so long with the process deliberately delayed that buying a blackmarket visa was the quickest way to escape to France or Britain.
14 The first part of Olivia Manning's *The Balkan Trilogy* is set in Bucharest at the outbreak of World War 2. Manning's novel, largely based on events in her own life, agrees with various incidents described by Joice Loch in *A Fringe of Blue, op cit*. Part One of Manning's wartime trilogy, was televised in 1996 by the BBC as 'Fortunes of War'.
15 Loch, Joice NanKivell. *A Fringe of Blue: an Autobiography, op cit*, p 168.
16 *Ibid*, pp 168-169.

Chapter 23—A MEDAL FROM KING CAROL
1   Details about King Carol and his mistress Magda Lupescu are cited in the biography, *King Carol II*, by King Carol's grandson from his first marriage, Prince Henry of Hohenzollern, published by Methuen, London, 1988.
2   Loch, Joice NanKivell, *A Fringe of Blue: an Autobiography*, John Murray, London, 1968, p 176.
3   Cited in Wilson, Francesa, *In the Margins of Chaos: Recollections of relief work in and between three wars*, John Murray, London, 1948, p 238.

Chapter 24—ESCAPE FROM THE IRON GUARD
1   A figure of 9,000 Polish refugees in Hungary just before the Germans took over is cited by John Greenwood in *Quaker Encounters*, Ebor Press, York, 1975, Vol l, p 314 and by Francesca Wilson: *In the Margins of Chaos*, John Murray, London, 1948.
2   Loch, Joice NanKivell, *A Fringe of Blue: an Autobiography*, John Murray, London, 1968, pp 173-4.
3   *Ibid*, pp 173-4.
4   Bessarabia had at one time been part of Russia. In 1939 Russia and Germany signed a pact to carve up Poland between them on the understanding that Germany would help Russia regain territories she considered hers but which had been taken from her under the Treaty of Versailles. By 1941 Russia had switched her alliance to Britain and under that agreement had to release all Polish prisoners in Russia.
5   *Ibid*, pp 172-3.
6   *Ibid*.
7   Greenwood, John, *Quaker Encounters*, Vol 1, Friends and Relief, William Sessions, York, 1976, p 314.

Chapter 25—OPERATION PIED PIPER
1   The plot to assassinate Magda Lupescu is cited in *King Carol II*, by Prince Paul of Hohenzollern, Methuen, London, 1998.

2. The 1959 edition of the *Encyclopedia Brittanica*—see entry under Rumania, pp 644-645, details massacres by the Iron Guard.
3. Loch, Joice NanKivell, *A Fringe of Blue: an Autobiography*, John Murrray, London, 1968.
4. Joice's account in *A Fringe of Blue, op cit*, omits the name of the British Naval cruiser that carried members of Operation Pied Piper from Cyprus to Haifa.

Chapter 26—THE CAMP OF A THOUSAND ORPHANS
1. The figure of 12,000 Poles under the care of the Lochs in Palestine is cited in Loch, Joice NanKivell, *A Fringe of Blue: an Autobiography*, John Murray, London, 1968 and confirmed by John Greenwood in *Quaker Encounters*, William Sessions, York, Vol 1, p 310.
2. See Professor Norman Davies, *Europe: a History*, Pimlico, London, 1997. On 5 March, 1940, Stalin signed an order authorizing the shooting of between 15,000-26,000 prisoners of war, who had been captured in Poland in September 1939 and held in three camps near Smolensk named Kozielsk, Oshtakovo and Starobielsk. Most were reserve officers, all educated men, who represented a threat to Communism. The shootings took several months and finished on 6 June, 1940. Stalin would later suggest to the British that the Polish officers had fled to Manchuria or been shot by the Germans. Mrs Krystina Ivell was taken to Siberia and on release managed to make her way with her mother to Palestine. Krystina was convinced that her father had been shot by the Russians but distressed she could not obtain proof. Only in 1992 did Boris Yeltsin finally admit responsibility (Document by President Yeltsin, published in *Gazeta wyborcza (Warsaw)* no 243 (1016), 15 October 1992).
3. *Ibid*.
4. Davies, Professor Norman, *Europe: a History*, Pimlico, London 1997, pp 1004-5.
5. Loch, Joice NanKivell, *A Fringe of Blue: an Autobiography, op cit*, chapter headed 'Poland on the Move'.
6. *Ibid*, p 199.
7. Wilson, Roger C., *Quaker Relief: an account of the relief work of the Society of Friends, 1940-1948*, Allen and Unwin, London, p 185. Roger Wilson was full of praise for the Lochs. He resigned from the BBC to head what would be known as the Friends War Relief Service Committee and had extensive dealings with Sydney and Joice Loch.
8. Loch, Joice NanKivell, *A Fringe of Blue: an Autobiography, op cit*, p 209. The figure of 12,000 Poles under the care of the Lochs in Palestine is cited here and confirmed in Greenwood, John, *Quaker Encounters, op cit*.

Chapter 27—RETURN TO GREECE: CIVIL WAR
1. O'Balance, Major Edgar, *The Greek Civil War*, Faber and Faber, London, 1966.
2. *Ibid*.
3. *Ibid*.
4. *Ibid*.
5. Among Joice's possessions Jake de Vries photographed in the tower was a brass plate engraved with the legend 'Loch Hall'.
6. Wilson, Roger C., *Quaker Relief: an account of the relief work of the Society of Friends*, Allen and Unwin, London, 1952, pp 187-8. Wilson, as Head of Friends Relief Committee in London visited the Lochs in Greece and praises them for their dedication and imaginative relief schemes. Joice did not record all their schemes to help the villagers. A full record of these is in Sydney Loch's unpublished typescript *Record of work carried out by Joice Loch and himself*, held by the library of the Friends House in London.
7. Loch, Joice NanKivell, *A Fringe of Blue: an Autobiography*, John Murray, London, pp 213-227, documents Joice's return to Ouranoupolis and the death of Madame Sophia and her son.
8. *Ibid*. Changing the names, Joice would retell the story of Aspasia and the Andartes in *Tales of Christophilos*, Houghton Mifflin, Boston and Riverside Press, Cambridge, Mass, 1957.

Chapter 28—'KYRIA LOCH'—THE LADY IN THE TOWER
1. From information kindly supplied by Martha Handschin.

Endnotes

2 Loch, Joice NanKivell *Prosforion-Uranopolis Rugs and Dyes*, American Board of Missions, Ankara, 1964, p 12.
3 Interview with Martha Handshin and Fani Mitroupolou, Ouranoupolis, 1997.
4 Joice Loch in the postcript to Sydney Loch's book *Athos, the Holy Mountain*, Lutterworth Press, London, 1957.
5 Loch, Joice NanKivell. *A Fringe of Blue: An Autobiography*, John Murray, London, 1968, p 241.
6 Information about Sir Clifford and Lady Norton and Gerald Palmer from the Rt Hon Michael Alison, Sir Clifford's godson.
7 Loch, Joice NanKivell, *A Fringe of Blue, op cit*, p 238.
8 *Ibid*.
9 *The Hopping Ha-penny, An Autobiography*, Methuen, London and E.P. Dutton, New York. *Again Christophilos*, Houghton Mifflin, New York and the Riverside Press, Cambridge, Mass, 1959. Details supplied by Martha Handschin from Joice Loch's papers. Not recorded in U.S. Library of Congress Catalogue.
10 Joyce Welsh to Susanna de Vries, Melbourne, 1998.
11 *Ibid*.

Chapter 29—THE END OF THE ROAD
1 Joice wrote Earth Song to be printed in full at the end of *A Fringe of Blue: an Autobiography*, John Murray, London, 1968.
2 Clippings from Adelaide *Advertiser*, January 12, 1965 and Melbourne *Herald*, December 11, 1964 supplied by Martha Handschin.
3 '*Australian dreams—designs by the Aegean*', *Sydney Morning Herald*, month unknown, 1965.
4 *Ibid*.
5 McCulloch, Alan, *The Encyclopedia of Australian Art*, revised and updated by Susan McCulloch, Allen and Unwin, Sydney, 1994, p 832.
6 Joice Loch to Simon Young, London, October 5, 1967.
7 Martha Handschin to Joyce Welsh, 1999. Letter in Joice Loch papers in the tower of Prosforion.
8 Nine Pirgos rugs were donated by Joice to Australia's new National Gallery. Eight of these rugs went missing. Their loss reflects poorly on Australian curatorial abilities and makes the Greeks loath to hand over Joice's papers and one remaining large blue dolphin rug. Because she died intestate, Joice Loch's papers and personal possessions have remained locked in the tower of Prosforion, several hours away from the Directorate of Byzantine Antiquities in Thessaloniki. Short of staff, they were unable to grant access to other British and Australian authors who wanted to see them.
9 As a Commonwealth Valuer of art, the author made inquires about values of Pirgos Rugs in Greece in 1998-1999.
10 The balcony has subsequently been replaced.
11 Letters to Simon Young (editor, John Murray) November 1967 refer to Dr Philip Sherrard's help with the final draft of *A Fringe of Blue*. Joice feared that she could not complete the autobiography to her satisfaction, due to her accident.
12 Joice Loch to Simon Young, John Murray, London, 1 November, 1968.
13 In 1999 Belinda Marder, archivist of the American Farm School, told the author that before Joice fell from the balcony and suffered severe memory loss, she possessed an encyclopaedic knowledge of the customs, roads and villages of Halkidiki and other areas of northern Greece.
14 Joice Loch's typed manuscript of *A Fringe of Blue* is archived in the Manuscripts Collection, National Library of Australia (NLA MS 2812), which also contains the bulk of the Rex Nan Kivell collection of early Australian material, as well as the research notes for this book.
15 Provatakis, Theocharis, *Mount Athos*, Rekos, Thessaloniki [n.d.], c1990.
16 Bruce Lansdale to the author. Telephone interview, July 1999.
17 Loch, Joice NanKivell, *Collected Poems*, Cygnet Press, Oxford, 1980.
18 *Ibid*.

Lightning Source UK Ltd.
Milton Keynes UK
UKHW02f1149031018
329934UK00012B/1028/P